Summer Jobs
USA
1995

44th Edition

**Distributed in the U.K. and Europe
by Vacation Work
9 Park End Street, Oxford OX1 1HJ, England**

Peterson's
Princeton, New Jersey

ISSN 1064-6701
ISBN 1-56079-397-X

Printed in the United States of America

10 9 8 7 6 5 4 3 2 1

Contents

How to Use This Book

What are you going to do to make this summer special? You already have a good start. *Summer Jobs USA 1995* is an indispensable catalog of interesting and enriching summer work experiences for students, teachers, or anyone looking for summer employment. You'll find detailed, up-to-date information on nearly 20,000 positions offered across the country—from counselors, instructors, and lifeguards to theater stagehands, wilderness guides, and office clerical workers. The list is long, and many of these jobs require little or no previous experience.

Search by Your Interests

There are many different ways you can use *Summer Jobs USA 1995* to find the right work opportunity:

- If your primary consideration is the geographic location of a job (if, for instance, you'd like to spend the summer working near your hometown or in a particular area of the country), you can turn directly to the **State-By-State Listings,** where employers are listed alphabetically by state.

- New to this edition of the guide is a section of **Canadian Listings** featuring summer employment opportunities in Canada. The section, which begins on page 277, profiles over thirty employers offering hundreds of summer jobs to young adults.

- If you're interested in working at a U.S. national park, turn to the special section beginning on page 21 that tells you all about job opportunities for U.S. citizens at National Park Service sites in regions throughout the country.

Another way you can put *Summer Jobs USA 1995* to work for you is by looking for jobs according to the services they provide. The opportunities featured in this book are divided into 10 main areas, which are listed in the **Category Index** at the back of the book (beginning on page 292). If you know, for instance, that you want to work at a summer camp that specializes in programs for persons with physical disabilities, turn to the **Category Index** for a listing of all such camps that are featured in the book. Use the following list of categories as your guide:

- Camps—academic, horsemanship, outdoor adventure and travel, performing and fine arts, religious, special needs, sports, general activities, and special focus camps serving those with developmental disabilities, learning disabilities, physical disabilities, and visual impairments
- Conference Centers
- Conservation and Environmental Programs
- Expeditions, Guide Trips, and Tours
- Ranches
- Resorts
- State and National Parks
- Theaters/Summer Theaters
- Theme and Amusement Parks/Attractions
- Volunteer Programs

Of course, if you already know the name of the employer you want to contact, you can simply turn to the **Employer Index** for a page reference to the description of that employer's job opportunities.

If you're interested in knowing what kinds of jobs are most readily available, turn to the **Job Titles Index.** It lists the most frequently cited job titles in the book and the facilities that offer them.

Read the Employer Profiles

Once you have found an employer that interests you, you can read about the opportunities they provide. The **General Information** section of each profile provides details about the location, size, focus, and special features of the facility. You can check the **Profile of Summer Employees** to get an idea of who your coworkers might be. **Employment Information** includes descriptions of available jobs as well as important details about when positions are available, salaries, and special requirements. Any **Benefits** of the workplace, such as gratuities, laundry facilities, health insurance, or the possibility of college credit, are also noted. The **Contact** paragraph provides you with information on how the employer wants you to apply for a position and the application deadline. Finally, most of the employers have chosen to write an additional narrative description of the kinds of employees they are looking for; you can get a good feel for many of the facilities in these **From the Employer** statements.

International applicants for any of the positions found in this guide should pay special attention to valuable information found in both the **Employment Information** and **Contact** sections. If international students are encouraged to apply for available positions, a sentence stating such will appear at the end of the **Employment Information** section. The **Contact** section may list any special application procedures required of international applicants, such as referral through an agency designed to handle these applications. Additional information at the end of a profile may also describe restrictions or requirements for international applications.

The data in this book were collected in the spring and summer of 1994 from employers anxious to fill staff vacancies with high-quality, motivated workers. A representative of each employer completed a questionnaire to describe the job opportunities to be offered in the summer of 1995. Although Peterson's does not assume responsibility for the hiring policies or actions of these employers, we believe that the information listed is accurate and up-to-date.

Learn How to Apply

Summer Jobs USA 1995 features four essays that will provide additional help in your search for a summer job. If you are just learning how to apply for a summer job, be sure to read "Looking for a Summer Job?" beginning on page 8. International job hunters are strongly urged to read "International Applications for Summer Employment and Training" beginning on page 14. "Working for the National Park Service" gives you all the information you'll need if you're a U.S. citizen considering a summer job at a U.S. National Park Service site; this article, which begins on page 21, tells you about the positions offered, job requirements, participating sites, and application contacts. "Do You Want to Work Temporarily in Canada . . ."—new to this year's guide— tells you the steps you need to take before you begin a summer job in Canada;

the article, which begins on page 35, outlines procedures you and your Canadian employer must follow for you to receive employment authorization.

Remember, all the employers listed in this book are actively looking for your help—they are waiting for your application! We hope that this book will help make your summer a fun, interesting—and profitable—experience.

Abbreviation Chart

The following are abbreviations commonly used in the book.

ACA	American Camping Association
ALS	Advanced Life Saving
ARC	American Red Cross
BUNAC	British University North American Club
CAA	Camp Archery Association
CHA	Camp Horsemanship Association
CIT	Counselor-in-training
CPR	Cardiopulmonary Resuscitation
EMR	Educationally Mentally Retarded
EMT	Emergency Medical Technician
EOE	Equal Opportunity Employer
HSA	Horsemanship Safety Association
ICCP	International Camp Counselors Program
IDC	Instructor Development Center
LD	Learning Disabled
LPN	Licensed Practical Nurse
NAUI	National Association of Underwater Instructors
NRA	National Rifle Association
PADI	Professional Association of Diving Instructors
RN	Registered Nurse
SASE	Self-addressed, stamped envelope
SCI	Small Craft Instructor
SLS	Senior Life Saving
WSI	Water Safety Instructor

Looking for a Summer Job?

As an older teenager or young adult concerned about your present and future, working at a job—for pay or not—is an important, if not mandatory, summer undertaking. If you've never done it, looking for a job may seem intimidating—but it's not. Hundreds of thousands of young people *do* find interesting and rewarding jobs every summer.

Many young adults turn to summer employment not only to pay for college expenses but also to earn spending money or even to help out their families. Competition for these jobs can be stiff, but keep in mind that summer employment can provide the background you'll need to compete aggressively both with other college-bound students when applying to schools *and* with other job seekers when looking for a full-time job. Guidance counselors, admissions officers, and corporate human-resource managers look for college and job applications that display outside activities, work experiences, and additional credentials. A good summer job record is a plus that colleges and employers now routinely expect to see.

"Strong academics are not enough any more," says a college admissions officer at a small university in Georgia. "We're looking very hard at what else students are doing, how they use their time, what other skills they are acquiring. Even the less competitive colleges are becoming much more demanding in evaluating prospective students." If you don't need to earn money, working as a volunteer will also give you a competitive edge.

Get Started Now

Landing the summer job that will add to the bottom line in your bank book and bolster your resume is harder than it used to be. "The summer job market has dried up a lot. There are fewer jobs listed than ever," says a high school guidance counselor in New Jersey. And the competition can be tough, you can overcome these obstacles. To increase your chance for success, you must be willing to work at mounting an organized, targeted job search; the sooner you get started, the better!

"The key is to start early," emphasizes the personnel director of a large state park that employs many young people each summer. "You can't wait until May and then see what's around, because there truly won't be anything left. I see this over and over. We have all of our hiring done, and then we get call after call and letter after letter from panicked, although qualified, students who are just applying much too late." A job seeker fortunate enough to get his or her application in early and who is hired also has the opportunity to ensure a somewhat securer summer job situation throughout the

---

Shirley J. Longshore is a writer, editor, and communications consultant. Her articles about business, work, and education have appeared in national publications.

rest of high school or college; those who prove themselves valuable will likely have first crack at getting the job back the following summer. To help you with your search, this book lists nearly 500 U.S. and Canadian employers who are looking for qualified, hard-working people to fill specific openings on their staffs.

Prepare Your Resume and Cover Letter

Your resume should be limited to one page and must communicate your strong points by detailing relevant experience and describing your background. It should present you in a way that will interest an employer enough to arrange an interview.

"I had a student this year who said he didn't have to be convinced that a summer job was important, but he didn't have a clue how to begin looking for one," says a guidance counselor at a large public high school in Florida. "High school students look at me like I'm from outer space when I tell them that, first, they should write a resume. They say things like: 'What would I put on it? I have no real skills; I've never done much of anything. A resume is for older people looking for real jobs.' But when we look at the clubs they have participated in, after-school activities, volunteer work, and baby-sitting jobs, we can often work up quite a list together. It gives young people an idea of what they have to offer an employer."

Everyone has the makings of a resume in their background—even those just starting out. You simply have to look at your past thoroughly. Don't overlook any activities that could enhance your credentials. Don't forget the computer knowledge you gained in school. Do you teach Sunday school? Have you worked in your town's recreation program? Do you assist in a shelter for the homeless or collect newspapers for recycling? All of these activities require skills that can be translated into proven experience for an employer. At the very least, participating in these kinds of activities will show that you are focused, well-rounded, community-minded, responsible, and trustworthy.

A resume should also list people who will give you good recommendations. (Before listing anyone as a reference, check to make sure he or she is willing to be listed.) To prepare a reference list, create a separate page with your name, address, and phone number followed by the names, addresses, and phone numbers of 2–4 people who will verify your skills and testify to the qualities that will convince the employer to hire you.

You may want to tailor your resume to appeal to a particular employer—using a computer makes this easy. Perhaps you are intrigued by a counselor's job at an academic-oriented camp. The resume for that position should contain an item that mentions that you put the skill you show in math to good use tutoring a third-grader after school. Phrase the item: "Demonstrated maturity and responsibility tutoring third-grade student in math in after-school sessions." With this entry on your resume, you are showcasing both a skill at an academic subject and experience working with a younger person. If you're using a computer, this item can easily be deleted from the resume you'll send in application to a job that doesn't involve academics or supervising children.

Your resume should also include items mentioning any athletics training you have had, such as swimming lessons, ballet classes, and team memberships. These activities demand those qualities employers look for—self-discipline, high energy, dedication, and desire for self-improvement.

A college student from Massachusetts didn't think his experience as head cook for the school's international club's dinners was very important. "I just did it for fun," the student admitted. "But then I saw an opening for an assistant chef at a lodge for the summer between my junior and senior years, and I realized I could parlay that experience into a job. It worked."

The best resume is one that is straightforward and clearly presented. If you're composing one for the first time, you should take advantage of the knowledge of older siblings or friends—talk with them and ask to see their resume. Remember, it must state relevant information about you and your skills.

This is where a strong cover letter comes into play. A cover letter serves as your introduction to a potential employer and, hopefully, will interest him or her enough to want to read your resume. A cover letter should draw the reader's attention to those experiences that best relate to the qualifications required for a particular job. For example, if a camp is looking for counselors to lead activities, your letter should mention your involvement in school plays (an item on your resume) and suggest that this experience would enable you to confidently instruct campers in drama or in a stage production. Although a cover letter should be brief and to the point, it doesn't hurt to help the resume reader along by flagging pertinent information. Sell yourself!

My Resume Is Ready—Now What?

After you've identified your skills and written your resume, you need to consider what you want to get out of your summer job. Ask yourself: What do I enjoy doing? What am I really good at? What would I like to learn more about? What work experience would enhance my chances at future opportunities? Do I love to be outdoors in the summer, or do I really prefer the air-conditioned comfort of an office? Is this the time to go far away from home, or would I rather stay close by? Do I need to make money? Keep in mind that some jobs may be too costly for you. If you need to earn money to cover college expenses, for instance, you may not want your pay to be eaten away by transportation and room-and-board costs.

After answering the questions above, turn to the **Category Index** to zero in on the kinds of opportunities that make sense for you. The listings in *Summer Jobs USA 1995* go beyond what you'll find in your local community through the usual pavement-pounding, want-ad-answering, asking-around methods. The jobs in this guide are located all over North America. Some may be in your geographic area, and others may be hundreds or thousands of miles away. Included are camps, resorts, summer theaters, conservation and environmental programs, lodges, ranches, conference and training centers, national parks, and amusement and theme parks that normally hire many young people for each busy summer season. The possibilities are endless, so you don't have to worry about ending up in a job in which you have little interest.

Keep in mind that many summer employers provide on-site training in the particular skills needed for their jobs, so don't be discouraged if your skills don't match exactly. These people are generally looking for qualities other than direct experience—motivation, interest, and the desire to learn. When you read about a position, *read between the lines* to see what kind of employee is really being sought.

Winning Interviews

Once you have contacted the employers you'd like to work for, think about how you'll present yourself at interviews. An interview may take place over the phone or in a face-to-face meeting. In either case, it's an opportunity for you and the employer to get a better sense of each other.

Remember, an interview goes both ways. It is also an opportunity for you to ask any questions and to decide whether you really want the job. You may want to ask about the specific duties, hours, pay, what benefits are provided (such as room and board), and when hiring decisions will be made. Always write a brief, sincere thank-you note to follow up an interview, even if it was very short or conducted by telephone.

It's important to dress appropriately for an in-person interview. Bring with you any credentials that are required (i.e., working papers, birth certificate, school records, or Social Security card). If you don't have a Social Security card, you can—and should—get one right away. You can start the process by calling 800-772-1213, the nationwide toll-free number for Social Security information.

Finding a good summer job opportunity is not an impossible task. There *are* jobs out there. You have a good shot at landing one if you prepare your resume, start going after the jobs you know about early, and present yourself both on paper and in person in the best possible light.

Sample Resume

ANNE MEREDITH

421 South Street
Apartment 2C
City Line, NJ 07685
821-663-4121

218 Tower Hall
State University
Brighton, PA 62451
580-341-6840

EDUCATION:
State University, Brighton, PA
Expected date of graduation, 1997
Major: Biology   GPA: 3.4   Degree track: B.S.

HONORS:
Dean's List, first semester, State University
Science Scholar Award, City Line High School, 1993
State Merit Scholarship Winner

EXPERIENCE:
Head Lifeguard/Swimming Coach
River Edge Athletic Club, Edgeton, NJ
Summer 1993 and 1994
   Responsibilities included scheduling and
   overseeing the summer staff of ten lifeguards
   and serving as one of two coaches for the
   club's competitive children's swim team (35
   members). I also gave private swimming
   lessons to club members.

Lifeguard
YWCA, City Line, NJ; Winter 1992–93

Swimming Instructor/Lifeguard
River Edge Athletic Club; Summer 1992 and 1991

Assistant Swimming Instructor (3- to 5-year-olds)
YWCA, City Line, NJ; Summer 1990

Day Camp Helper (9- and 10-year-olds)
YWCA, City Line, NJ; Summer 1989

ACTIVITIES:
Swim Team, Junior Varsity, State University,
   1993–94
Glee Club, State University, 1993–94
Swim Team, YWCA, City Line, NJ, 1991–93
   Captain, 1991–92
Junior, Senior Chorus, City Line High School, 1990–93
Youth Group, St. John's Church, 1990–93
   President, 1993
Springvale Nursing Home, volunteer visitor, 1992–93

SKILLS:
Red Cross Certification, Lifesaving
Fluency in Spanish
Teaching experience with children and adults
Computer skills: MS-DOS, WordPerfect

Sample Cover Letter

ANNE MEREDITH

421 South Street
Apartment 2C
City Line, NJ 07685
821-663-4121

218 Tower Hall
State University
Brighton, PA 62451
580-341-6840

January 4, 1995

Name of person in charge, title
Name of camp or resort
Street address
Town, state, zip code

Dear Mr. or Ms. (last name):

I saw the listing describing your summer program in Summer Jobs USA 1995. It states that you hire a Waterfront Director, a summer position for which I would like to apply.

As you will see from the attached resume, I am very qualified for such a position. I taught swimming, was a lifeguard, coached a swim team, and swam on my high school team for four years. I have been named to the Junior Varsity Swim Team at State University in both my freshman and sophomore years.

I am experienced at supervising and teaching both adults and children in swimming and waterfront safety. I enjoy working with people and sharing my expertise with them. Your summer program sounds like one in which my skills would be fully utilized.

I would appreciate the opportunity to explore this position with you further. I would be happy to talk with you by telephone or to arrange a personal interview during my winter break, which is until the end of this month.

Thank you for your consideration. I look forward to hearing from you soon. You can reach me at my home number in City Line until January 28th.

Sincerely,

Anne Meredith

International Applications for Summer Employment and Training

by Robert M. Sprinkle

In an effort to provide the most accurate guidance possible for students from outside the United States, Peterson's has asked each employer listed in *Summer Jobs USA 1995* if applications will be accepted from international students who want to come to the United States for the summer. Peterson's has also asked if the employer is willing to undertake the necessary steps—either directly with the U.S. Immigration and Naturalization Service (INS) or through an educational exchange organization—to make it possible for the student to secure a proper U.S. visa that will allow legal employment while in the United States. International applicants should read each profile carefully for this information before applying.

Major changes were made in U.S. immigration laws and related regulations in 1986, 1990, and 1993. These changes established significant penalties for employers who hire foreign nationals illegally and increased the complexity of the U.S. visa system. If an employer in the United States offers you a job, make certain that both you *and* the employer know and follow the requirements of U.S. law *before* you leave home.

Passports

In order to secure a U.S. visa that permits summer employment/training, you must have a valid passport from your own country. Your passport must be valid for six months beyond the date on which you expect to leave the United States. A number of countries have special "passport validity" agreements with the United States under which a passport is considered to be valid for six months beyond the expiration date stated in the passport. In order to avoid last-minute problems, you should contact U.S. consular officials as early as possible to determine the exact requirement for your country.

Visas

Unlike many countries, the United States does not control the activities of noncitizens by the use of work permits, residence permits, police registration, or other documents. Instead, what an individual may or may not do while in the United States

Robert M. Sprinkle is the Executive Director, Association for International Practical Training, Inc., and has written numerous articles on international practical training, overseas employment, and student travel.

depends entirely on the specific type of visa granted. As a result, the United States has the world's most complex visa system—there are currently forty-five different kinds of nonimmigrant visas!

As a general rule, there are only four U.S. visas that are likely to be suitable for students coming to the United States for summer employment or training:

H-2B "TEMPORARY WORKER"

The procedures for this visa require a two-step process to be followed by the employer. First, a "temporary labor" certification must be secured through the state employment service of the area where the individual will work. Following rules established by the U.S. Department of Labor, the employer must submit evidence to demonstrate that: (a) a real job exists (i.e., not a job made up to suit the background of the foreign national); (b) substantial efforts have been made to fill the job with a U.S. citizen; (c) no qualified U.S. citizens can be found for the job; and (d) the job to be filled is of a one-time, seasonal, peak-load, or intermittent nature. Once the "labor certification" has been granted, the employer must then file an application with the U.S. Immigration and Naturalization Service District Office covering the area where the person will work. The total number of H-2B visas is limited to 66,000 per year.

H-3 "TRAINEE"

This visa does not require a "labor certification." The employer must submit the H-3 application to the Immigration Service District Office covering the area where the person will work. The application must include a detailed training plan to show what the trainee will do in the United States, including how much time will be spent in "classroom and other instruction" and how much time will be devoted to "on-the-job" work. The application must also provide information on the position or duties outside the United States for which the individual is being trained and show why the individual cannot receive suitable or similar training in his or her own country.

Q "INTERNATIONAL CULTURAL EXCHANGE VISITOR"

The 1990 Immigration Act added the new "Q" visa, which some employers may wish to use. This visa allows the employer to apply to INS for permission to hire a person from another country who is over 18 years of age for a period of not more than fifteen months to undertake prearranged employment or training *and* to share or demonstrate his or her own culture with Americans. A frequently cited example of a major future "Q" employer is the EPCOT Center at Walt Disney World in Florida. Another example would be a museum or a department of a museum devoted to the art and culture of the student's home country.

The "cultural component" must be an integral part of the employment or training offered. The employer must demonstrate that the individual to be hired is fully able to communicate with Americans about his or her culture as well as being fully qualified for the work aspects of the position. Substantial documentation is required as part of the employer's application.

J-1 "EXCHANGE VISITOR"

> **Special Note:** Unlike all other U.S. visa categories administered by the Immigration Service, the U.S. Information Agency (USIA) has primary responsibility for the regulations governing the use of the J-1 "Exchange Visitor" visa. Revised and substantially expanded regulations for use of the J-1 visa were published in March 1993. However, as of the publication date of *Summer Jobs USA 1995,* a number of issues concerning the implementation and interpretation of the new regulations have not been resolved. Further, all current sponsoring organizations that use the J-1 visa for their participants must complete a "redesignation" process that will extend into 1995. While the information contained in this article is accurate as of the publication date, you should seek updated and current information from U.S. consular officials overseas and/or from individual J-1 sponsoring organizations.

The J-1 visa may be used only by individuals who are participants in educational programs that have been specifically approved by the U.S. Information Agency. There are eleven different J-1 categories, each with its own specific rules and regulations. Approved "Exchange Visitor Programs" are granted only to U.S. sponsoring organizations such as government agencies, schools, hospitals, and private educational exchange organizations. Each sponsor is granted a specific "program description"—a short statement that specifically mentions those activities permitted for participants in the sponsor's specific program.

Of the eleven J-1 categories, only the "trainee" category is suitable for international students coming to the United States for paid practical training. At present, the number of sponsors having J-1 programs that permit practical training employment is extremely limited. The International Association of Students in Economics and Business Management (AIESEC) and the International Association for the Exchange of Students for Technical Experience (IAESTE) Trainee Program are the two principal trainee exchange organizations for students. The maximum length of practical training time permitted any one person (regardless of the number of sponsors or employers) is eighteen months.

A small number of sponsoring organizations have been granted J-1 authorizations for "summer travel/work" programs. These programs permit students to work at any job they may find. However, the J-1 authorizations are not for practical training or for summer camp positions. There are important restrictions: (a) the work experience must occur during the "summer" (November–February for students from the Southern hemisphere) with no extensions permitted, and (b) changes to either another J-1 sponsor or to some other type of visa are not permitted.

A third type of J-1 authorization covers placement in summer camps for camp-counselor experience. Participants must be at least 18 years old. Such placements are limited to a maximum of four months and must be for genuine camp counseling/ teaching assignments. Placements in office, kitchen, or custodial jobs are not permitted. The same individual may not participate in a camp-counselor exchange more than two times.

In some cases, an individual coming to the United States on the J-1 visa may be subject to the "two-year foreign residence requirement" as the result of a "skills list" that the person's home country has asked USIA to establish for its citizens. If the person's field is included on the "skills list" for his/her country, it will generally be necessary for the individual to return to his/her country for a minimum of two years before coming back to the United States on most of the nonimmigrant visas or as a "permanent resident." Most European countries do not have skills lists, but many other countries do, and, if return to the United States within a two-year period is of concern, specific information should be sought from U.S. consular officials.

J-1 Program Sponsors

Trainee Exchange Programs:

AIESEC/US
135 West 60th Street
20th Floor
New York, New York 10020
212-757-3774
Fax: 212-757-4062

AMERICAN-SCANDINAVIAN FOUNDATION
725 Park Avenue
New York, New York 10021
212-879-9779
Fax: 212-249-3444

ASSOCIATION FOR INTERNATIONAL PRACTICAL TRAINING
IAESTE Trainee Program
10400 Little Patuxent Parkway, Suite 250
Columbia, Maryland 21044-3510
410-997-2200
Fax: 410-992-3924

CDS INTERNATIONAL
330 Seventh Avenue
New York, New York 10001
212-760-1400
Fax: 212-268-1288

COUNCIL OF INTERNATIONAL PROGRAMS
1420 K Street, NW, Suite 800
Washington, D.C. 20005
202-842-8424
Fax: 202-842-8627

COUNCIL ON INTERNATIONAL EDUCATIONAL EXCHANGE
205 East 42nd Street
New York, New York 10017
212-661-1414
Fax: 212-972-3231

INTEREXCHANGE
161 Sixth Avenue, Suite 902
New York, New York 10013
212-924-0446
Fax: 212-924-0575

MINNESOTA AGRICULTURAL STUDENT TRAINEE PROGRAM
199 Coffey Hall
University of Minnesota
1420 Eckles Avenue
St. Paul, Minnesota 55108
612-624-3740
Fax: 612-625-7031

OHIO INTERNATIONAL AGRICULTURAL INTERN PROGRAM
113 Agricultural Administration Building
The Ohio State University
2120 Fyffe Road
Columbus, Ohio 43210-1099
614-292-7720
Fax: 614-292-1757

SISTER CITIES INTERNATIONAL
120 South Payne Street
Alexandria, Virginia 22314
703-836-3535
Fax: 703-836-4815

Summer Travel/Work Programs:

COUNCIL ON INTERNATIONAL EDUCATIONAL EXCHANGE
205 East 42nd Street
New York, New York 10017
212-661-1414
Fax: 212-972-3231

INTEREXCHANGE
161 Sixth Avenue, Suite 902
New York, New York 10013
212-924-0446
Fax: 212-924-0575

YMCA INTERNATIONAL PROGRAM SERVICES
71 West 23rd Street
New York, New York 10010
212-727-8800
Fax: 212-727-8814

Camp Counselor Programs and Clearinghouses:

BUNAC (BUNACAMP/ WORK AMERICA/ WORK CANADA)
16 Bowling Green Lane
London EC1R 0BD
England
071-251-3472

CAMP AMERICA
37A Queen's Gate
London SW7 5HR
England
071-581-7373

CAMP COUNSELORS USA
420 Florence Street
Palo Alto, California 94301
415-617-8390
800-999-CAMP
Fax: 415-321-3261

INTEREXCHANGE
161 Sixth Avenue, Suite 902
New York, New York 10013
212-924-0446
Fax: 212-924-0575

YMCA INTERNATIONAL PROGRAM SERVICES
71 West 23rd Street
New York, New York 10010
212-727-8800
Fax: 212-727-8814

If an employer's applications for an H-2B, H-3, or Q visa are successful, the District Office of the Immigration and Naturalization Service will advise the U.S. Embassy in the student's country. The student can then secure the visa and travel to the United States. In the case of the J-1 visa, the sponsoring organization that has agreed to include the student issues a U.S. government document called an IAP-66 (a "Certificate of Eligibility"). The IAP-66 is sent to the student to use to apply for the J-1 visa in his or her country.

Upon entering the United States, the admitting Immigration Inspector issues a Form I-94 (Arrival/Departure Record), on which is noted the specific visa granted and the date when the "Permit-to-Stay" expires. Admission to the United States in the H-2B, H-3, or trainee category of the J-1 visa with such status being noted on the Form I-94 is the only documentation needed for the student to proceed to the work-place and take up the assignment.

Employment Eligibility Verification

The 1986 law requires all U.S. employers to examine documentation proving that persons hired are either citizens of the United States or noncitizens legally authorized for employment during their stay in the United States.

Essentially, the law requires that within three business days after a person is hired, the employer must *physically examine* documentation that (a) establishes proof of the new employee's identity and (b) establishes that the person is either a U.S. citizen or is a noncitizen who has the legal right to be employed in the United States. The law and the related regulations, administered by INS, require that a record of the verification process be maintained in the employer's files for a period of three years after the date of hiring. For this purpose, the INS has developed the I-9 Form.

Virtually all kinds of employment are covered, from a full-time job with a large employer such as IBM to mowing grass on a regular basis for your next door neighbor. Certainly, all of the jobs listed in *Summer Jobs USA 1995* will require you and your employer to complete the I-9 form. The I-9 form is in two parts. You must fill out the top half. You then present the form, together with your documentation, to your employer, who will complete the bottom half of the form.

Income Tax

As a general rule, individuals coming to the United States on any of the visas discussed in this article will be subject to U.S. income tax (and possibly state and local income tax) on the money they earn while in the country. If you leave the country before the end of the current calendar year, you will need to secure a "Certificate of Compliance" (often called a "sailing permit") from the Internal Revenue Service (IRS). You will need to provide documentation that all applicable tax has been paid—income tax will usually be withheld from your pay by the U.S. employer. Between January 1 and April 15 of the year following your employment, you will have to submit an income tax "return" (a form 1040NR) to the IRS. If you have remained in the country from one year to the next, you will also be required to submit a Form 8843 to verify your nonresident status. Tax regulations and procedures are not simple, and you should seek help from your employer and/or your sponsoring organization if you are participating in a J-1 program. You may also wish to secure a copy of IRS Publication 519—"U.S. Tax Guide for Aliens"—which is available free of charge from the Internal Revenue Service.

Social Security Number

In most cases, you will find it necessary to secure a Social Security number, which is widely used in the United States as a basic identification number—it is used in most automated payroll systems, in university enrollment systems, and for transactions such as opening a bank account.

Individuals entering the United States on the J-1 visa will usually be exempt from the U.S. Social Security Tax, but those entering on other visas (F-1, M-1, H-2B, H-3, and Q) can expect to have the tax withheld from their pay.

While it is possible to apply for a Social Security number at an American Embassy or Consulate General, it is often four to six months before the individual receives the number. Since Social Security regulations require an in-person application, it is usually better to take care of this matter after arrival in the United States. Normally, numbers are issued within four to six weeks after the application has been submitted to a local Social Security office.

It will be important for you to provide full documentation that clearly shows that you have a visa that permits employment. The Social Security official to whom you submit your application will want to see your passport, your I-94 form, visa documents (such as the triplicate copy of the IAP-66), and any documents related to your work placement. If you do not present the proper documentation, a Social Security card marked "Not Valid for Employment" will be issued.

Full-Time Students at U.S. Schools

Individuals enrolled at U.S. colleges and universities for full-time academic study are usually admitted on the basis of the F-1 (student), M-1 (student), or student category of the J-1 visa. In each case, internship employment may be possible before graduation, after graduation, or both. When such employment may take place, the length of time allowed and what the employment is called (practical training, curricular practical training, academic training) depend on the specific visa and circumstances of the individual student. Whether before or after graduation and whether on the F-1, M-1, or student category of the J-1 visa, the student remains under the legal sponsorship of the U.S. college or university concerned. Thus, assistance with proper arrangements for periods of employment must be sought from the international student adviser at the student's school.

In Conclusion

Most countries of the world have very strict regulations regarding employment for noncitizens in order to protect job opportunities for their own citizens. The United States is no different from other countries, especially in periods of high unemployment. What is different, however, is the U.S. system of visas and the rules and regulations that apply to each type (and subtype) of visa. The process of securing a proper visa takes a good deal of time (sometimes as long as four to six months) and can often be frustrating. Thus, it is wise to contact prospective employers as early as possible so that the employer has sufficient time to undertake the paperwork involved. If you have applied to or have been accepted by an organization such as AIESEC or IAESTE, make that fact known to the employer as each sponsoring organization has its own internal procedures that must be followed. With careful advance preparation, the complexities of the U.S. visa system can be handled.

Working for the National Park Service

Since its inception in 1916, the National Park Service has been dedicated to the preservation and management of this country's outstanding natural, historical, and recreational areas. Today the National Park Service encompasses more than 350 sites across the United States and in Guam, Puerto Rico, and the Virgin Islands. There are parks of great natural beauty and grandeur, such as the Grand Canyon and Yellowstone; parks that preserve the nation's cultural and historical treasures, such as Mesa Verde, the Statue of Liberty, and Gettysburg Battlefield; and parks of significant recreational value along seashores, lakeshores, and riverways that provide opportunities for outdoor activities and relaxation, such as Assateague Island and Lake Mead. The National Park Service is a bureau of the U.S. Department of the Interior; it should not be confused with the Forest Service of the U.S. Department of Agriculture.

Each year millions of people from the United States and abroad visit these national park areas. To protect park resources and to serve the public, the National Park Service employs a permanent work force and an essential seasonal work force. Besides working in the parks, these employees may also work in the National Park Service headquarters in Washington, D.C., at any of ten regional offices located around the country, or at two special planning and production centers—the Denver Service Center and Harpers Ferry Center. "Seasonals" are hired every year to help permanent staffs at most of these locations, especially during peak visitation seasons. The variety of positions may surprise you. Campground rangers, fee collectors, tour guides, naturalists, landscape architects, firefighters, laborers, law enforcement rangers, lifeguards, clerk-typists, carpenters, historians—persons are hired for these seasonal jobs and for many more. Whatever the job, seasonal employees have the opportunity to learn more about the National Park Service and its mission as well as the opportunity for permanent employment.

Seasonal jobs are difficult to get. Positions are open to U.S. citizens only, and the number of applicants far outnumbers the positions available every year, particularly at larger, well-known parks. Some positions are filled by experienced seasonal employees who have worked previously for the National Park Service, and Office of Personnel Management regulations require that veterans of the U.S. Armed Forces may be given preference among applicants. In the summer season, when most seasonal employees are hired, employment opportunities are extremely competitive. Only those applicants who meet the qualification requirements and conditions of employment described here will receive consideration for seasonal positions. *Competition is usually less keen at smaller, lesser-known parks* and for seasonal jobs in the winter season.

About Seasonal Jobs

Entry-level grades for National Park Service seasonal positions range from GS-2 to GS-4. GS levels indicate the rate of pay for most federal government positions. The

---

Reprinted by permission of the National Park Service, U.S. Department of the Interior.

higher the GS number, the higher the hourly wage. Check with any federal agency or with the Office of Personnel Management for current salary information for these grades. Prevailing local wages (WG) govern maintenance positions, such as seasonal laborer and skilled trades and crafts positions. WG levels indicate the rate of pay for such positions. The higher the WG number, the higher the hourly wage. GS levels and WG levels are not equivalent. WG wages are paid on an hourly basis according to prevailing wage rates.

The standard work week is 40 hours. Overtime may be required; additional compensation is provided for extra hours worked. Most seasonal positions require irregular hours of work, including weekends, holidays, and evenings. Most seasonal park rangers and maintenance personnel are required to wear the official Park Service uniform; specific requirements and ordering information are contained in the employment package forwarded to successful applicants. A uniform allowance authorization, which partially covers expenses, is issued before entry on duty.

Applicants should address specific questions about housing, area living conditions, and similar matters to the park or office where employment is desired. Seasonal employee housing may or may not be available. Because many positions require strenuous activity, a medical examination may be required at the applicant's expense before appointment.

General Information on Applying

Additional information and applications are available at the Park Service's ten regional offices or at each park office. Regional offices are listed at the end of this article with addresses and telephone numbers. If your present address is not your permanent address, list both on your application and indicate when you will be at each. It is important that you show a telephone number where you can be reached.

While most seasonal positions are available in the summer season, a few are filled during the winter at some parks, including positions at the Everglades, Death Valley, Joshua Tree, and the Virgin Islands. For information on application and filing procedures for winter employment, contact the regional office in the geographic area in which you want to work.

Seasonal Positions

PARK RANGER

Grades: GS-2, GS-3, GS-4

Duties

Vary greatly from position to position and may include:
- providing visitor services, such as interpreting a park's natural, historic, or archeological features through talks, guided walks, and demonstrations or working at an information desk
- planning and implementing resource management programs, including fire control
- performing search-and-rescue activities
- law enforcement and providing for the public's safety
- fee collection

- radio dispatching
- firefighting
- lifeguarding
- conservation and restoration activities

Most of these positions are filled in the summer season. In the National Capital Region (Washington, D.C., area), jobs involving visitor information services usually begin before June 1. Most history-related jobs are in the Mid-Atlantic, Southeast, and National Capital regions. Most archeology-related jobs are in the Western and Southwest regions.

Qualifications

All applicants must be U.S. citizens.

GS-2: six months of experience of a general nature in park operations or in related fields, a high school diploma, or a high school equivalency certificate.

GS-3: one year of general experience in park operations and one season (at least 90 days) as a seasonal Park Ranger, GS-2, or at least 90 days of equivalent specialized experience gained in similar work experience; successful completion of one academic year (45 quarter hours) of college may be substituted for experience requirements if the course work included 9 quarter hours of field-oriented natural science, social science, history, archeology, police science, park and recreation management, community outdoor recreation, dramatic arts, or other disciplines related to park management.

GS-4: eighteen months of general experience in park operations or in related fields and six months of specialized experience or one season (at least ninety days) as a seasonal Park Ranger, GS-3; successful completion of two academic years (90 quarter hours) of college may be substituted for experience requirements if the course work included 16 quarter hours of field-oriented natural science, social science, history, archeology, police science, park and recreation management, community outdoor recreation, dramatic arts, or other disciplines related to park management.

Additional requirements:
- must be 18 years of age or 16 if high school graduate (positions involving law enforcement or public safety duties generally are restricted to persons at least 21 years old)
- must be in excellent physical condition
- may be required to have a valid driver's license
- should have vision correctable to 20/30 (Snellen) in each eye (if your vision is less than 20/30 in one eye, you can be considered if the other eye tests 20/20 with or without glasses)
- some severe physical disabilities may disqualify an applicant if the condition would interfere with the performance of the job

How to Apply

Contact any National Park Service regional or park office for a seasonal job application—Form 10-139 (*not* Form SF-171). To apply for a summer seasonal position, submit a completed application between September 1 and (postmarked by) January 15 to Seasonal Employment Unit, National Park Service, P.O. Box 37127, Room 2225, Washington, D.C. 20013-7127. It is essential that applicants for these positions indicate (1) earliest reporting date and latest departure date, (2) types of positions for which application is being made, (3) two parks where consideration is desired, (4) lowest grade or salary that will be accepted, and (5) any particular specialization, such as law enforcement or interpretation.

RECREATION AID/ASSISTANT (LIFEGUARD)
Grades: GS-3 through GS-6

Duties
- guards and manages beach and swimming areas
- performs lifesaving and rescue work as needed (rivers, lakes, and oceans)

Positions are available at national recreation areas, seashores, and lakeshores, including Assateague Island, Cape Cod, Cape Hatteras, Chickasaw, Coulee Dam, Delaware Water Gap, Fire Island, Gateway, Golden Gate, Gulf Islands, Lake Mead, Padre Island, Pictured Rocks, Point Reyes, and Sleeping Bear Dunes.

Qualifications
All applicants must be U.S. citizens.

GS-3: one year of general experience that has provided a familiarity with the routines and procedures followed in one or more of the various types of work situations; such situations should have involved simple clerical, supply, or other work that has enabled the applicant to demonstrate alertness, reliability, and an ability to deal with others.

GS-4: must meet requirements for GS-3 level and demonstrate possession of one year of appropriate recreation experience.

GS-5 and GS-6: for each grade above the GS-4 level, in addition to the general requirement for GS-3 level, one year of appropriate recreational experience is required; one year of that experience must have been at a level of difficulty and responsibility comparable to that of the next lower grade level in the Federal Service; for all grade levels, the applicant's record must show that his or her experience has provided the ability to perform work at the level of the position to be filled.

Additional requirements:
- must be at least 18 years old and hold a current American Red Cross Certificate in Standard First Aid, a current Red Cross Life Saver's Certificate, or a Water Safety Instructor's Certificate
- some seasonal park rangers perform lifesaving and rescue work in their overall duties; in these cases, applicants must meet the lifesaving and rescue qualifications required for seasonal lifeguard applicants
- passing a performance test may be required

How to Apply
Contact any National Park Service regional office between September 1 and January 15 for forms and instructions.

ARCHITECTURE AND LANDSCAPE ARCHITECTURE TECHNICIAN
Grades: GS-4, GS-5

Duties
- produces drawings of structures of historical, architectural, landscape, engineering, industrial, and maritime significance

Positions occur in various areas of the United States.

Qualifications
All applicants must be U.S. citizens.

GS-4: must have completed at least two years in an accredited program that includes at least 18 semester hours in architecture/landscape architecture.

GS-5: successful completion of a full five-year course of study at a college or university, leading to a bachelor's degree, with major study in architecture/landscape architecture.

How to Apply

Contact Summer Program Administrator, HABS/HAER Division, National Park Service, P.O. Box 37127, Washington, D.C. 20013-7127. Applicants must submit a personal qualifications statement (SF-171), a letter of recommendation from a faculty member or employer familiar with the applicant's work, and a sample indicating drafting ability (copies of sketches, lettering, and precision drafting).

ARCHITECT/LANDSCAPE ARCHITECT

Grades: GS-5 and above

Duties

- produces drawings of structures of historical, architectural, landscape, engineering, industrial, and maritime significance
- provides assistance to technicians preparing field notes and developing and editing measured drawings

Positions occur in various areas of the United States.

Qualifications

All applicants must be U.S. citizens.

GS-5 and above: must, as a minimum, have a B.A. or B.S. degree in architecture or landscape architecture, with at least one course in architectural or landscape history.

GS-7 and above: should currently be working toward a master's or doctoral degree in a subject matter area listed above.

How to Apply

See application procedures listed under job description for Architecture and Landscape Architecture Technician.

HISTORIAN

Grades: GS-5, GS-7, and above

Duties

- conducts research using primary and secondary sources to produce inventories
- reports on specific sites, structures, or technical processes

Positions occur in various areas of the United States.

Qualifications

All applicants must be U.S. citizens.

A graduate degree in architectural history, history of technology, American civilization, historic preservation, or a related field is preferred; a B.A. is required.

How to Apply

Applicants should contact Summer Program Administrator, HABS/HAER Division, National Park Service, P.O. Box 37127, Washington, D.C. 20013-7127. Applicants must submit a personal qualifications statement (SF-171), a letter of recommendation from a faculty member or employer familiar with the applicant's work, and a paper demonstrating primary research in architectural history, landscape architectural history, or history of technology or a paper focusing on an aspect of the built environment.

CLERICAL POSITIONS
Grades: GS-1, GS-2, GS-3, GS-4

Duties
- performs duties of receptionist, administrative clerk, and clerk-typist as well as data entry

Jobs are limited; most are at National Park Service Headquarters in Washington, D.C. A few are in parks or in regional and field offices.

Qualifications

All applicants must be U.S. citizens.

GS-1: no education or experience required.

GS-2: high-school graduate or three months of experience.

GS-3: one year of college or six months of experience.

GS-4: two years of college or one year of experience.

Additional requirements:
- for typing positions, applicants must be able to type 40 words per minute

How to Apply

Applicants should submit a completed application Form SF-171 directly to the Headquarters office or the regional or park office where work is desired. Applications are accepted in accordance with the filing dates specified in the Office of Personnel Management's *Summer Job Announcement Number 414*. There is no written test for summer clerical jobs.

LABORER
Grades: WG-2, WG-3

Duties
- performs unskilled outdoor work on trails and for forestry programs, other park maintenance activities, and similar work in which physical labor must be performed

Most positions occur in the summer season. Wages are paid on an hourly basis according to prevailing wage rates.

Qualifications

All applicants must be U.S. citizens.

WG-2 and WG-3: excellent physical condition and ability to perform the job's duties.

How to Apply

Contact the regional office in the geographic area in which you want to work for application forms and procedures.

SKILLED TRADES AND CRAFTS
Grades: WG-4 and above

Duties
- performs work of skilled and semiskilled trade positions, such as carpenter, mechanic, axeman, sawyer (woodworker), trail maintenance worker, motor vehicle operator, and others

Wages are paid on an hourly basis according to local prevailing wage rates.

Qualifications
All applicants must be U.S. citizens.
WG-4 and above: helper- or journeyman-level proficiency is usually required.

How to Apply
Contact sites in the area in which work is desired for application forms and procedures.

Other Employment Opportunities

Hotels, lodges, restaurants, stores, transportation services, marinas, and many other visitor facilities in National Park System areas are operated by private companies and individuals called park concessioners, who recruit and hire their own employees. These are not Federal Government positions. Concessioners usually pay the minimum wage set by the state in which their operation is located. Although some pay a small bonus at the end of the season, they do not pay or make arrangements for travel to and from the parks. Contact the National Park Service regional office covering the location in which you'd like to work or the park itself for names and addresses of concessioners. Write to the concessioner for applications and information about concession jobs, salaries, and working and living conditions.

National Parks Service Regional Offices and Sites

ALASKA REGION
Includes Alaska.

Alagnak Wild River
Alaska Public Lands Information Center (Anchorage)
Alaska Public Lands Information Center (Fairbanks)
Alaska Regional Office
Anchorage Interagency Visitor Center
Aniakchak National Monument
Aniakchak National Preserve
Bering Land Bridge National Preserve
Cape Krusenstern National Monument
Denali National Park
Denali National Preserve
Fairbanks Interagency Visitor Center
Gates of the Arctic National Park
Gates of the Arctic National Preserve

Glacier Bay National Park
Glacier Bay National Preserve
Katmai National Park
Katmai National Preserve
Kenai Fjords National Park
Klondike Gold Rush National Historical Park
Kobuk Valley National Park
Lake Clark National Park
Lake Clark National Preserve
Noatak National Preserve
Northwest Alaska Areas
Sitka National Historical Park
Wrangell–St. Elias National Park
Wrangell–St. Elias National Preserve
Yukon–Charley Rivers National Preserve

For information on seasonal employment opportunities in this region, contact: National Park Service, 2525 Gambell Street, Anchorage, Alaska 99503; telephone: 907-257-2574.

PACIFIC NORTHWEST REGION
Includes Idaho, Oregon, and Washington.

City of Rocks National Reserve
Coulee Dam National Recreation Area
Crater Lake National Park
Craters of the Moon National Monument
Ebey's Landing National Historical Reserve
Fire Management Office
Fort Clatsop National Memorial
Fort Vancouver National Historic Site
Hagerman Fossil Beds National Monument
John Day Fossil Beds National Monument
Klondike Gold Rush National Historical
    Park–Seattle Unit

Lake Chelan National Recreation Area
McLoughlin House National Historic Site
Mount Rainier National Park
Nez Perce National Historical Park
North Cascades National Park
Olympic National Park
Oregon Caves National Monument
Oregon National Historic Trail
Pacific Northwest Regional Office
Ross Lake National Recreation Area
San Juan Island National Historical Park
Whitman Mission National Historic Site

For information about seasonal employment opportunities in this region, contact: National Park Service, 83 South King Street, Suite 212, Seattle, Washington 98104; telephone: 206-553-4409.

WESTERN REGION
Includes Arizona, California, Guam, Hawaii, and Nevada.

American Memorial Park
Cabrillo National Monument
Casa Grande National Monument
Channel Islands National Park
Chiricahua National Monument
Coronado National Memorial
Death Valley National Monument
Devils Postpile National Monument
Eugene O'Neill National Historic Site
Fort Bowie National Historic Site
Fort Point National Historic Site
Golden Gate National Recreation Area
Grand Canyon National Park
Great Basin National Park
Haleakala National Park
Hawaii Volcanoes National Park
Hohokam Pima National Monument
Horace M. Albright Training Center
John Muir National Historic Site
Joshua Tree National Monument
Kalaupapa National Historical Park
Kaloko-Honokohau National Historical Park
Kings Canyon National Park
Lake Mead National Recreation Area
Lassen Volcanic National Park
Lava Beds National Monument
Montezuma Castle National Monument
Muir Woods National Monument
National Park of Samoa

Organ Pipe Cactus National Monument
Pacific Area Office
Petrified Forest National Park
Pinnacles National Monument
Point Reyes National Seashore
Pu'uhonua o Honaunau National Historical
    Park
Puukohola Heiau National Historic Site
Redwood National Park
Saguaro National Monument
San Francisco Maritime National Historical
    Park
Santa Monica Mountains National Recreation
    Area
Sequoia and Kings Canyon National Parks
Sequoia National Park
Southern Arizona Group
Tonto National Monument
Tumacacori National Monument
Tuzigoot National Monument
USS Arizona Memorial
Walnut Canyon National Monument
War in the Pacific National Historical Park
Western Architecture and Conservation
    Center
Western Regional Office
Whiskeytown Unit
Yosemite National Park

For information about seasonal employment opportunities in this region, contact: National Park Service, 600 Harrison Street, Suite 600, San Francisco, California 94107; telephone: 415-744-3888.

ROCKY MOUNTAIN REGION

Includes Colorado, Montana, North Dakota, South Dakota, Wyoming, and Utah.

Arches National Park
Badlands National Park
Bent's Old Fort National Historic Site
Big Hole National Battlefield
Bighorn Canyon National Recreation Area
Black Canyon of the Gunnison National
 Monument
Bryce Canyon National Park
Canyonlands National Park
Capitol Reef National Park
Cedar Breaks National Monument
Colorado National Monument
Curecanti National Recreation Area
Denver Service Center
Devils Tower National Monument
Dinosaur National Monument
Florissant Fossil Beds National Monument
Fort Laramie National Historic Site
Fort Union Trading Post National Historic
 Site
Fossil Butte National Monument
Glacier National Park
Glen Canyon National Recreation Area
Golden Spike National Historic Site
Grand Teton National Park
Grant-Kohrs Ranch National Historic Site

Great Sand Dunes National Monument
Greater Yellowstone Coordinating
 Commission
Hovenweep National Monument
International Peace Garden
Jewel Cave National Monument
John D. Rockefeller Junior Memorial
 Parkway
Knife River Indian Village National Historic
 Site
Little Bighorn Battlefield National
 Monument
Mesa Verde National Park
Mormon Pioneer National Historic Trail
Mount Rushmore National Memorial
Natural Bridges National Monument
Pipe Spring National Monument
Rainbow Bridge National Monument
Rocky Mountain National Park
Rocky Mountain Regional Office
Theodore Roosevelt National Parks
Timpanogos Cave National Monument
Wind Cave National Park
Yellowstone National Park
Yucca House National Monument
Zion National Park

For information about seasonal employment opportunities in this region, contact: National Park Service, P.O. Box 25287, Denver, Colorado 80225; telephone: 303-969-2777.

SOUTHWEST REGION

Includes Arkansas, Louisiana, New Mexico, Oklahoma, and Texas.

Alibates Flint Quarries National Monument
Amistad National Recreation Area
Arkansas Post National Memorial
Aztec Ruins National Monument
Bandelier National Monument
Big Bend National Park
Big Thicket Land Acquisition Office
Big Thicket National Preserve
Buffalo National River
Buffalo National River Land Acquisition
 Office
Canyon de Chelly National Monument
Capulin Volcano National Monument
Carlsbad Caverns National Park

Chaco Culture National Historical Park
Chamizal National Memorial
Chickasaw National Recreation Area
El Malpais National Monument
El Morro National Monument
Fort Davis National Historic Site
Fort Smith National Historic Site
Fort Union National Monument
Gila Cliff Dwellings National Monument
Guadalupe Mountains National Park
Hot Springs National Park
Hubbell Trading Post National Historic Site
Jean Lafitte National Historical Park and
 Preserve

Lake Meredith National Recreation Area
Lyndon B. Johnson National Historical Park
Masau Trail
Natchez National Historical Park
Navajo National Monument
Padre Island National Seashore
Palo Alto Battlefield National Historic Site
Pea Ridge National Military Park
Pecos National Historical Park
Petroglyph National Monument
Poverty Point National Monument
Rio Grande Wild and Scenic River
Salinas Pueblo Missions National Monument

San Antonio Missions National Historical
   Park
Santa Fe National Historic Trail
Southwest Cultural Resources Center
Southwest Regional Office
Spanish Colonial Research Center
Sunset Crater Volcano National Monument
White Sands National Monument
Wupatki National Monument
Wupatki/Sunset Crater/Walnut Canyon
   National Monument
Zuni-Cibola National Historical Park

For information about seasonal employment opportunities in this region, contact:
National Park Service, P.O. Box 728, Santa Fe, New Mexico 87501; telephone: 505-988-6076.

MIDWEST REGION
Includes Illinois, Indiana, Iowa, Kansas, Michigan, Minnesota, Missouri, Nebraska, Ohio, and Wisconsin.

Agate Fossil Beds National Monument
Apostle Islands National Lakeshore
Brown *v.* Board of Education National
   Historic Site
Chicago Cultural Center
Chicago Portage National Historic Site
Chimney Rock National Historic Site
Cuyahoga Valley National Recreation Area
David Berger National Memorial
Dayton Aviation Heritage National Historical
   Park
Effigy Mounds National Monument
Father Marquette National Memorial
Fort Larned National Historic Site
Fort Scott National Historic Site
Gateway Park
George Rogers Clark National Historical
   Park
George Washington Carver National
   Monument
Grand Portage National Monument
Harry S. Truman National Historic Site
Herbert Hoover National Historic Site
Homestead National Monument of America
Hopewell Culture National Historical Park
Ice Age National Scenic Trail
Ice Age National Scientific Reserve
Illinois and Michigan Canal

Indiana Dunes National Lakeshore
Isle Royale National Park
James A. Garfield National Historic Site
Jefferson National Expansion Memorial
   National Historic Site
Keweenaw National Historical Park
Lewis and Clark National Historic Trail
Lincoln Boyhood National Memorial
Lincoln Home National Historic Site
Lower St. Croix National Scenic Riverway
Midwest Archeological Center
Midwest Regional Office
Mississippi National River and Recreation
   Area
Mississippi River Corridor Heritage
   Commission
Missouri National Recreation River
Niobrara/Missouri National Riverways
North Country National Scenic Trail
Ozark National Scenic Riverways
Perry's Victory and International Peace
   Memorial
Pictured Rocks National Lakeshore
Pipestone National Monument
Saint Croix National Scenic Riverway
Scotts Bluff National Monument
Sleeping Bear Dunes National Lakeshore
Ulysses S. Grant National Historic Site

Voyageurs National Park
Warren G. Harding Memorial

William Howard Taft National Historic Site
Wilson's Creek National Battlefield

For information about seasonal employment opportunities in this region, contact: National Park Service, 1709 Jackson Street, Omaha, Nebraska 68102; telephone: 402-221-3456.

SOUTHEAST REGION

Includes Alabama, Florida, Georgia, Kentucky, Mississippi, North Carolina, Puerto Rico, South Carolina, Tennessee, and the Virgin Islands.

Abraham Lincoln Birthplace National Historic Site
Andersonville National Historic Site
Andrew Johnson National Historic Site
Big Cypress Land Acquisition Office
Big Cypress National Preserve
Big South Fork National River and Recreation Area
Biscayne National Park
Blue Ridge Parkway
Brices Cross Roads National Battlefield Site
Buck Island Reef National Monument
Canaveral National Seashore
Cape Hatteras National Seashore
Cape Lookout National Seashore
Carl Sandburg Home National Historic Site
Castillo de San Marcos National Monument
Charles Pinckney National Historic Site
Chattahoochee River National Recreation Area
Chickamauga and Chattanooga National Military Park
Christiansted National Historic Site
Congaree Swamp National Monument
Cowpens National Battlefield
Cumberland Gap National Historical Park
Cumberland Island National Seashore
De Soto National Memorial
Everglades National Park
Federal Law Enforcement Training Center
Fort Caroline National Memorial
Fort Donelson National Battlefield
Fort Donelson National Cemetery
Fort Frederica National Monument
Fort Jefferson National Monument
Fort Matanzas National Monument
Fort Pulaski National Monument
Fort Raleigh National Historic Site
Fort Sumter National Monument

Great Onyx Job Corps Civilian Construction Center
Great Smoky Mountains National Park
Guilford Courthouse National Military Park
Gulf Islands National Seashore
Horseshoe Bend National Military Park
Jimmy Carter National Historic Site
Kennesaw Mountain National Battlefield Park
Kings Mountain National Military Park
Mammoth Cave National Park
Martin Luther King Jr. National Historic Site
Moores Creek National Battlefield
Natchez Trace National Scenic Trail
Natchez Trace Parkway
Ninety Six National Historic Site
Obed Wild and Scenic River
Ocmulgee National Monument
Oconaluftee Job Corps Civilian Construction Center
Overmountain Victory National Historic Trail
Russell Cave National Monument
Salt River Bay National Historical Park and Ecological Preserve
San Juan National Historic Site
Shiloh National Cemetery
Shiloh National Military Park
Southeast Archeological Center
Southeast Regional Office
Stones River National Battlefield
Stones River National Cemetery
Timucuan Ecological and Historic Preserve
Tupelo National Battlefield
Tuskegee Institute National Historic Site
Vicksburg National Cemetery
Vicksburg National Military Park
Virgin Islands National Park
Wright Brothers National Memorial

For information about seasonal employment opportunities in this region, contact: National Park Service, Richard B. Russell Federal Building, 75 Spring Street, SW, Atlanta, Georgia 30303; telephone: 404-331-5711.

MID-ATLANTIC REGION

Includes Delaware, Pennsylvania, and most areas of Maryland, Virginia, and West Virginia.

Allegheny Portage Railroad National Historic Site
American Industrial Heritage Project
Appalachian National Scenic Trail
Appomattox Court House National Historical Park
Assateague Island National Seashore
Benjamin Franklin National Memorial
Bluestone National Scenic River
Booker T. Washington National Monument
Colonial National Historical Park
Delaware and Lehigh Commission
Delaware National Scenic River
Delaware Water Gap National Recreation Area
Edgar Allan Poe National Historic Site
Eisenhower National Historic Site
Fort McHenry National Monument and Historic Shrine
Fort Necessity National Battlefield
Fredericksburg and Spotsylvania National Military Park
Fredericksburg National Cemetery
Friendship Hill National Historic Site
Gauley River National Recreation Area
George Washington Birthplace National Monument

Gettysburg National Cemetery
Gettysburg National Military Park
Gloria Dei (Old Swedes) Church National Historic Site
Green Springs National Historic Landmark District
Hampton National Historic Site
Hopewell Furnace National Historic Site
Independence National Historical Park
Jamestown National Historic Site
Johnstown Flood National Memorial
Maggie L. Walker National Historic Site
Mid-Atlantic Regional Office
New River Gorge Land Resources Office
New River Gorge National River
Petersburg National Battlefield
Pinelands National Reserve
Poplar Grove National Cemetery
Richmond National Battlefield Park
Shenandoah National Park
Steamtown National Historic Site
Thaddeus Kosciuszko National Memorial
Thomas Stone National Historic Site
Upper Delaware Scenic and Recreation River
Valley Forge National Historical Park
Yorktown National Cemetery

For information about seasonal employment opportunities in this region, contact: National Park Service, 143 South Third Street, Philadelphia, Pennsylvania 19106; telephone: 215-597-4971.

NATIONAL CAPITAL REGION

Includes Washington, D.C., and nearby areas in Maryland, Virginia, and West Virginia.

Antietam National Battlefield
Antietam National Cemetery
Arlington House (The Robert E. Lee Memorial)
Baltimore-Washington Parkway
Battleground National Cemetery
C & O Canal National Historic Park
Carter Barron Amphitheater
Catoctin Mountain Park
Chesapeake and Ohio Canal National Historical Park

Clara Barton National Historic Site
Claude Moore Colonial Farm
Constitution Gardens
Ford's Theatre National Historic Site
Fort Dupont Activity Center
Fort Washington Park
Frederick Douglass Home
George Washington Memorial Parkway
Glen Echo Park
Great Falls Park
Greenbelt Park

Harpers Ferry Center
Harpers Ferry Job Corps Civilian
Construction Center
Harpers Ferry National Historical Park
John F. Kennedy Center
Kennilworth Aquatic Gardens
Lyndon B. Johnson Memorial Grove-on-the-
Potomac
Lincoln Memorial
Manassas National Battlefield Park
Monocacy National Battlefield
Museum and Archives Regional Storage
Facility
National Capital Parks (Central)
National Capital Parks (East)
National Capital Regional Office
National Mall

Old Post Office Observation Tower
Oxon Hill Farm
Pennsylvania Avenue National Historic
Site
Piscataway Park
Potomac Heritage National Scenic Trail
Prince William Forest Park
Rock Creek Park
Sewall-Belmont House National Historic
Site
Stephen T. Mather Training Center
Thomas Jefferson Memorial
United States Park Police
Washington Monument
White House
Williamsport Presidential Training Center
Wolf Trap Farm Park

For information about seasonal employment opportunities in this region, contact: National Park Service, 1100 Ohio Drive, SW, Washington, D.C. 20242; telephone: 202-619-7256.

NORTH ATLANTIC REGION

Includes Connecticut, Maine, Massachusetts, New Hampshire, New Jersey, New York, Rhode Island, and Vermont.

Acadia National Park
Adams National Historic Site
Blackstone River Valley
Boston African-American National Historic
Site
Boston National Historical Park
Cape Cod National Seashore
Castle Clinton National Monument
Eastern Field Archeology Center
Edison National Historic Site
Eleanor Roosevelt National Historic Site
Ellis Island
Federal Hall National Memorial
Fire Island National Seashore
Fort Stanwix National Monument
Frederick Law Olmsted National Historic
Site
Gateway Job Corps Civilian Construction
Center
Gateway National Recreation Area
General Grant National Memorial

Hamilton Grange National Memorial
Home of Franklin D. Roosevelt National
Historic Site
John Fitzgerald Kennedy National Historic
Site
Longfellow National Historic Site
Lowell National Historical Park
Manhattan Sites
Martin Van Buren National Historic Site
Minute Man National Historical Park
Morristown National Historical Park
North Atlantic Historic Preservation Center
North Atlantic Regional Office
Roger Williams National Memorial
Roosevelt Campobello International Park
Roosevelt-Vanderbilt Headquarters
Sagamore Hill National Historic Site
Saint Croix Island International Historic Site
Saint Paul's Church National Historic Site
Saint-Gaudens National Historic Site
Salem Maritime National Historic Site

Saratoga National Historical Park
Saugus Iron Works National Historic Site
Springfield Armory National Historic Site
Statue of Liberty National Monument
Theodore Roosevelt Birthplace National
   Historic Site
Theodore Roosevelt Inaugural National
   Historic Site
Touro Synagogue National Historic Site
Vanderbilt Mansion National Historic Site
Weir Farm National Historic Site
Women's Rights National Historical Park

For information about seasonal employment opportunities in this region, contact:
National Park Service, 15 State Street, Boston, Massachusetts 02109; telephone: 617-223-5101.

Do You Want to Work Temporarily in Canada . . .

What You Need to Know

If you wish to work temporarily in Canada, you will likely require an **employment authorization.** An employment authorization is issued by an immigration officer after a Canada Employment Centre (CEC) approves your job offer.

This article outlines what you and your employer must do *before* you arrive in Canada. For additional advice, contact the Canadian Embassy, High Commission, or Consulate General near you.

Additional procedures may be required if you wish to work in Quebec. For further information, contact the Canadian Embassy abroad or a Canada Immigration Centre in Canada.

What Your Employer Must Do

Your employer must give details of your job offer to a Canada Employment Centre (CEC). An employment counsellor will check to determine if your offer of employment meets the prevailing wages and working conditions for the occupation concerned. A check will also be made to see if the job cannot be filled by a suitably qualified and available Canadian or permanent resident. If these conditions are met, the CEC will approve your job offer. They will then issue a confirmation of offer of employment and send this to the Canadian Embassy, High Commission, or Consulate in your country.

The employer will be provided with a copy of the confirmation of offer of employment, to be forwarded to you. Your employer is responsible for arranging your worker's compensation and medical coverage when you arrive in Canada.

Some jobs may be exempt from CEC approval, and either the CEC or a visa office at a Canadian embassy or consulate can advise you on this.

What You Must Do

The Canadian visa office near you will contact you upon receipt of your confirmation of offer of employment. You may be asked to go to an interview or to send some information by mail. You may also be asked to have a medical checkup, which you will have to pay for yourself. If you qualify and have all the necessary documents, you will receive an employment authorization and will possibly have a separate visitor visa placed in your passport.

Produced by Public Affairs Employment and Immigration Canada. Reproduced with the permission of Citizenship and Immigration Canada and Supply and Services Canada, 1994. To obtain more copies, contact: Public Enquiries Centre, Ottawa–Hull, Canada K1A 0J9; 819-994-6313; fax: 819-994-0116.

The employment authorization will state that you can work at a specific job for a specific period of time for a specific employer. You will need to produce the authorization when you arrive in Canada, as well as your passport, visa (if issued), and airline tickets.

There is a processing fee when you submit an application for an employment authorization. There are no refunds if your application is refused. Please request the Public Enquiries Centre's brochure on immigration fees or ask an immigration officer for fee information.

Different procedures exist for citizens or permanent residents of the United States. You should seek clarification from the nearest Canadian embassy or consulate; general procedures are stated later in this article.

An employment authorization will not be issued to you to come to Canada to look for work. *It is valid only for the specific job, the specific amount of time, and the employer stated on the form.*

When You Arrive in Canada

When you arrive at the port of entry to Canada, show your confirmation of offer of employment, your employment authorization, and other papers to an immigration officer. You will be given forms to fill out so that you can get a Social Insurance Number (SIN). These forms and proper identification, such as a birth certificate, should be taken to a counsellor at a CEC, who can help you if you have trouble filling them out. When you receive your SIN card, you will have to give your number to your employer.

Your employment authorization is not a contract. Your job can be ended by you or your employer at any time. However, if your duties change or the job is to be extended, you must contact a Canada Immigration Centre right away, before the expiry date of your current authorization.

Some Workers Can Apply at a Port of Entry

Most foreign workers must apply for employment authorization outside of Canada, but if you are a resident of the United States, Greenland, or St. Pierre and Miquelon, you can apply for an employment authorization when you arrive at a port of entry to Canada. To apply this way, you must produce your confirmation of offer of employment and other papers when you arrive at the port of entry. Remember that you must find out what papers you will need *before* arriving in Canada. Check with the Canadian Embassy, High Commission, or Consulate General.

Remember

- There is a nonrefundable fee to process a request for an employment authorization.
- Most foreign workers must get their employment authorizations before arriving in Canada. Visitors *cannot* obtain employment authorization while in Canada.
- You must follow the terms of your employment authorization while in Canada. If you do not, you may be asked to leave the country.

- CEC staff in Canada and visa officers in your home country cannot help you find a job.
- If you want to work temporarily or if you have further questions about working in Canada, contact the nearest Canadian Embassy, High Commission, or Consulate.
- Canada's Immigration Legislation and Regulations are under review at this time. Please check with your Canada Immigration Centre or a Canadian diplomatic mission abroad to ensure you have the most up-to-date information.

State-by-State Listings

ALABAMA

CAMP SCOUTSHIRE WOODS
6051 Scoutshire Camp Road
Citronelle, Alabama 36522
General Information Traditional Girl Scout residential camp. Established in 1945. Owned by Girl Scouts of the Deep South Council. Affiliated with American Camping Association. 120-acre facility located 30 miles north of Mobile. Features: horseback riding trails; spring-fed lake for swimming, canoeing, and sailing; 8 cabins with room for 10; 14 tents with room for 4; sports field.
Profile of Summer Employees Total number: 25; average age: 21; 100% female, 10% minorities, 95% college students, 80% local residents, 15% teachers. Nonsmokers preferred.
Employment Information Openings are from June 15 to July 31. Jobs available: 2 *horseback directors* (1 assistant) with CHA certification; 10 *unit leaders and unit counselors;* 1 *craft director;* 1 *business manager;* 1 *assistant camp director;* 1 *health supervisor/nurse;* 4 *waterfront directors* (3 assistants).
Benefits On-site room and board at no charge, laundry facilities, health insurance.
Contact Betty Kincaid, Director of Properties and Camping, Camp Scoutshire Woods, Department SJ, 3483 Springhill Avenue, Mobile, Alabama 36608; 205-344-3330, Fax 205-344-4181. Application deadline: June 15.

From the Employer *We offer a six-day precamp training session for first aid and CPR.*

CAMP SKYLINE
Mentone, Alabama 35984
General Information Residential camp located on top of Lookout Mountain serving 260 girls. Established in 1947. Owned by Cash Summer Camps. Affiliated with American Camping Association, Christian Camping International. 80-acre facility located 45 miles southwest of Chattanooga, Tennessee. Features: 1 Western and 2 English riding rings; river with slide, rope swing, and "blob;" private freshwater lake and swimming pool; Riverside historical hotel for teenagers; beach volleyball court; outdoor basketball court; 4 tennis courts; softball fields; ropes course; climbing tower; open-air gymnasium; fine arts building; lodge.
Profile of Summer Employees Total number: 100; average age: 19; 5% male, 95% female, 10% high school students, 90% college students, 2% international, 5% local residents. Nonsmokers only.
Employment Information Openings are from June 1 to August 10. Jobs available: 2 *sports instructors* (archery, tennis, swimming, diving, horseback riding, and gymnastics)*; lifeguards* with WSI certification; *fine and performing arts instructors* (music, dance, arts and crafts, and drama)*; riflery instructors; cheerleading/flag twirling/baton twirling instructors; computer instructors; ropes-course instructors; nature specialists; canoeing/sailing instructors; Christian leadership instructors.* All positions offered at $800–$1000 per season.

Benefits On-site room and board at no charge.
Contact Susan Hooks, Director, Camp Skyline, Department SJ, P.O. Box 287, Mentone, Alabama 35984; 205-634-4001, Fax 205-634-4601.

ALASKA

ALASKAN WILDERNESS OUTFITTING COMPANY, INC.
P.O. Box 1516
Cordova, Alaska 99574
General Information Organization operating fishing lodges and floatplane tours of Alaska. Established in 1984. Owned by Pat Magie and Tom and Katie Prijatel. Affiliated with Alaska Visitors' Association. Located 150 miles southeast of Anchorage. Features: wilderness; wildlife; beautiful scenery; lodges on salt water, mountain lakes, and rivers.
Profile of Summer Employees Total number: 15; average age: 22; 75% male, 25% female, 75% college students. Nonsmokers preferred.
Employment Information Openings are from May 1 to October 15. Jobs available: 8 *experienced fishing guides* at $1200–$1600 per month; 4 *camp cooks* at $1200–$1600 per month; 2 *general laborers* at $800–$1200 per month; 2 *assistant cooks* at $800–$1200 per month.
Benefits On-site room and board at no charge, laundry facilities.
Contact Pat Magie, President, Alaskan Wilderness Outfitting Company, Inc., P.O. Box 1516, Cordova, Alaska 99574; 907-424-5552. Application deadline: April 15.

AMERICA & PACIFIC TOURS, INC. (A&P)
West Fifth Avenue and K Street, Suite 434
Anchorage, Alaska 99510
General Information Japanese land operator for Japanese tourists providing planned, individualized, and special guided trips of Alaska. Established in 1972. Owned by Keizo Sugimoto. Affiliated with Alaska Visitors' Association, Anchorage Convention and Visitors' Bureau, Alaska Sportfishing Association. Features: endless hours of daylight; beautiful scenery and wildlife; King and Silver Salmon fishing; coastal trail; hiking trails.
Profile of Summer Employees Total number: 15; average age: 23; 50% male, 50% female, 50% minorities.
Employment Information Openings are from May 20 to September 15. Spring break, Christmas break positions also offered. Jobs available: 8 *tour guides* with current driver's license and fluency in Japanese at $1300 per month. International students encouraged to apply.
Benefits On-site room and board at $150 per month, travel reimbursement.
Contact Keizo Sugimoto, President, America & Pacific Tours, Inc. (A&P), P.O. Box 10-1068, Anchorage, Alaska 99510; 907-272-9401, Fax 907-272-0251. Application deadline: April 30.

CAMP TOGOWOODS
HC 30, Box 5400
Wasilla, Alaska 99654

General Information Residential program of traditional camping activities for girls ages 7–15. Established in 1958. Owned by Girl Scouts Susitna Council. Affiliated with American Camping Association. 250-acre facility located 58 miles north of Anchorage. Features: freshwater lake frontage; 20 hours of daylight; location 3 hours from Mt. McKinley (tallest peak in North America); wood-fired lakeside sauna; platform tents; rustic log lodges.

Profile of Summer Employees Total number: 21; average age: 22; 100% female, 5% minorities, 95% college students, 10% local residents. Nonsmokers preferred.

Employment Information Openings are from June 3 to August 9. Jobs available: 10 *counselors* at $1800 per season; 1 *waterfront director* with lifeguard certification at $2000 per season; 2 *certified lifeguards* at $1800 per season; 2 *cooks* at $1800 per season; 1 *food service manager* at $2200 per season; 1 *assistant director* at $2500 per season; 1 *nurse* with RN license at $2500 per season; 1 *business manager* at $1800 per season.

Benefits Preemployment training, on-site room and board at no charge, health insurance.

Contact Jane Straight, Camp Director, Girl Scouts Susitna Council, Camp Togowoods, 3911 Turnagain Street, Anchorage, Alaska 99517; 907-248-2250, Fax 907-243-4819. Application deadline: February 15.

From the Employer *Togowoods employees develop teaching and counseling skills during an intensive six-day training period where they meet fellow staff members from across the country. Counselors work in pairs with groups of 8–10 campers. All staff members have a one-week midseason break so that they can travel in Alaska.*

RAINBOW KING LODGE
P.O. Box 106
Iliamna, Alaska 99606

General Information Luxury sportfishing lodge offering weekly guest packages for the upper-income market. Established in 1971. Owned by Tom Robinson. Affiliated with Aircraft Owners and Pilots Association, International Game Fish Association, Alaska Professional Sportfishing Association. 4-acre facility located 190 miles southwest of Anchorage. Features: remote Alaskan surroundings and scenic beauty; world-class fishing; 4 private aircraft fly-outs for crew; mountain-bike trails; rustic lodge setting; wildlife, including bear, moose, and caribou.

Profile of Summer Employees Total number: 36; average age: 25; 65% male, 35% female, 80% college students, 5% retirees, 5% local residents.

Employment Information Openings are from June 1 to October 1. Jobs available: 14 *fishing guides* with first aid/CPR certification and fly-fishing and boating experience at $1050–$1850 per month; 10 *lodge workers, experienced preferred,* at $1050–$1700 per month; 4 *maintenance personnel, experience preferred,* at $1050–$1850 per month.

Benefits On-site room and board at no charge, laundry facilities.

Contact Randy Toppen, Manager, Rainbow King Lodge, 333 South State Street, Suite 126,

Lake Oswego, Oregon 97034; 800-458-6539, Fax 503-635-3079. Application deadline: April 1.

From the Employer *Rainbow King Lodge offers the opportunity to visit some of the most pristine wilderness areas in North America. The clientele that visit Rainbow King Lodge each year are often prominent and influential in their respective professions. Professional networking opportunities are excellent. Working for Rainbow King Lodge may be the only chance many people will ever get to experience the wilderness that the Alaskan Peninsula offers.*

ARIZONA

GRAND CANYON NATIONAL PARK LODGES
P.O. Box 699
Grand Canyon, Arizona 86023
General Information National park concessioner providing all hotel, restaurant, retail, and transportation services on the south rim of the Grand Canyon. Established in 1901. Owned by AMFAC Resorts, Inc. Located 80 miles north of Flagstaff. Features: location within Grand Canyon National Park, south rim; hotels; restaurants; retail shops.
Profile of Summer Employees Total number: 1,100; 30% minorities, 20% college students, 20% retirees, 30% local residents.
Employment Information Openings are from February 15 to January 3. Year-round positions also offered. Jobs available: *guest room attendant; kitchen/utility personnel; retail clerk; cashier; busperson; hosts/hostesses; cooks; cooks' helpers.* All positions offered at $4.25–$5.65 per hour.
Benefits College credit, on-site room and board at $16 per week, laundry facilities, health insurance, food in employee cafeterias at cost.
Contact Personnel Department, Grand Canyon National Park Lodges, Department SJ, P.O. Box 699, Grand Canyon, Arizona 86023; 602-638-2343.

ONSHORE OFFSHORE EXPLORATIONS
P.O. Box 3032
Flagstaff, Arizona 86003
General Information Camp serving 250 people through a program of outdoor exploration and cross-cultural exchange. Established in 1988. Owned by Ted Dennard and Karen McCarthy. Affiliated with Association for Experimental Education, Independent Educational Consultants Association. Features: deep river canyons; high desert plateaus; Alpine mountains; rich Native-American culture; meaningful cultural exchange.
Profile of Summer Employees 50% male, 50% female, 10% minorities, 5% high school students, 10% college students, 10% international, 15% local residents. Nonsmokers preferred.
Employment Information Openings are from May 1 to August 1. Spring break, year-round positions also offered. Jobs available: *instructor* at $200 per week; *provisioner* at $200 per week; *intern* (volunteer).
Benefits On-site room and board at no charge.
Contact Ted Dennard, Co-Director, Onshore Offshore Explorations, Department SJ, P.O. Box 3032, Flagstaff, Arizona 86003; 800-947-4673. Application deadline: April 1.

ORME SUMMER CAMP
HC 63, Box 3040
Mayer, Arizona 86333-9799
General Information Residential coed camp serving up to 200 campers with a large variety of indoor and outdoor activities. Established in 1929. Owned by The Orme School. Affiliated with American Camping Association, Western Association of Independent Camps. 40,000-acre facility located 60 miles north of Phoenix. Features: location on the 40,000-acre Orme Ranch; fully equipped gymnasium; 4 fields; 1 regulation, lighted rodeo arena; Olympic-size pool; 20,000 volume library.
Profile of Summer Employees Total number: 35; 50% male, 50% female, 2% minorities, 80% college students, 1% retirees, 18% international, 10% local residents, 15% teachers. Nonsmokers preferred.
Employment Information Openings are from June 25 to August 14. Jobs available: *outdoor adventure/survival instructor* with Outward Bound or NOLS graduate or equivalent at $1000–$1300 per season; *senior counselors* at $750–$1100 per season; *arts and crafts director* with teaching experience at $900–$1100 per season. International students encouraged to apply.
Benefits Preemployment training, on-site room and board at no charge, laundry facilities, travel reimbursement.
Contact Benjamin W. Powers, Director, Orme Summer Camp, Department SJ, The Orme Summer Camp, Mayer, Arizona 86333; 602-632-7601, Fax 602-632-7605. Application deadline: April 17.

From the Employer *Our camp features horsemanship, rodeo sports, outdoor adventure, mountain biking, field and gym sports, arts and crafts, southwest travel, and optional academics at the Orme School campus. Free CPR certification is provided for all staff, as well as a free Camp Horsemanship Association certification at basic level (allow five days before precamp).*

ARKANSAS

NOARK GIRL SCOUT CAMP
Route 3, Box 22
Huntsville, Arkansas 72740
General Information Residential camp serving approximately 600 girls ages 7–17 over a seven-week period. Established in 1967. Owned by Noark Girl Scout Council. 1,039-acre facility located 40 miles east of Fayetteville. Features: location in Ozark Mountains; primitive outdoor living; tennis/sports complex; 25-acre multipurpose meadow; outdoor amphitheater; craft houses.
Profile of Summer Employees Total number: 25; average age: 20; 5% male, 95% female, 95% college students, 75% local residents, 5% teachers.
Employment Information Openings are from June 11 to August 6. Jobs available: 6 *unit leaders* (minimum age 21) with maturity and recreation/physical education degree (preferred) at $110–$200 per week; 12 *unit counselors* (minimum age 18) at $90–$150 per week; 1

waterfront director (minimum age 21) with WSI and lifeguard certification, ability to teach children, supervise instructors, keep records, and organize large groups at $110–$200 per week; 1 *health supervisor* (minimum age 21) with RN, LPN, or paramedic license at $150–$250 per week; 2 *swimming instructors* with WSI certification ($10–$50 weekly bonus added to salary); *business manager* (minimum age 21) with experience in business methods, record keeping, buying, and inventory control at $110–$200 per week.

Benefits Formal ongoing training, on-site room and board at no charge, laundry facilities, health insurance.

Contact Camp Director, Noark Girl Scout Camp, Department SJ, P.O. Box 6353, Springdale, Arkansas 72766; 501-750-2442, Fax 501-750-4699. Application deadline: April 15.

YORKTOWN BAY
361 Camp Yorktown Lane
Mountain Pine, Arkansas 71956

General Information Residential camp serving 100–120 young people with disabilities per week. Established in 1965. Owned by Arkansas-Louisiana Conferences of Seventh-day Adventists. Affiliated with American Camping Association, Christian Horsemanship Association. 60-acre facility located 15 miles northwest of Hot Springs. Features: extensive freshwater lake; riding trails; waterskiing slalom course; aquatics program, including canoeing, swimming, sailing, and waterskiing.

Profile of Summer Employees Total number: 35; average age: 21; 50% male, 50% female, 10% minorities, 20% high school students, 70% college students. Nonsmokers only.

Employment Information Openings are from June 1 to August 15. Jobs available: *horseback-riding instructors* with CHA certification; *counselors/activities specialists; waterfront personnel* with WSI, CPR, and lifeguard certification.

Benefits On-site room and board at no charge, laundry facilities.

Contact Joe Watts, Director, Yorktown Bay, P.O. Box 31000, Shreveport, Louisiana 71130; 318-631-6240, Fax 318-631-6277. Application deadline: February 1.

CALIFORNIA

AMERICAN ADVENTURES
6762A Centinela Avenue
Culver City, California 90230

General Information Camping tours for international clientele across North America, including New England, the southwestern United States, western Canada, and Alaska. Established in 1981. Owned by AmeriCan Adventures. Affiliated with Federation of International Youth Travel Organizations, Travel Industry Association of America, Alliance of Canadian Travel Associations. Features: custom-made tents and camping equipment; fleet of customized 15-passenger vans; bases in Los Angeles, New York, and Vancouver, British Columbia.

Profile of Summer Employees Total number: 75; average age: 26; 50% male, 50% female, 10% minorities, 85% college students, 5% international, 5% local residents. Nonsmokers preferred.

Employment Information Openings are from May 1 to October 31. Jobs available: 75 *tour drivers/leaders* with strong leadership and driving skills and knowledge of history/

culture and current events of North America (foreign language and first aid skills helpful) at $210–$330 per week.

Benefits   Preemployment training, on-site room and board at no charge, travel reimbursement, end-of-season bonus.

Contact   Tara Warren, Operations Manager, AmeriCan Adventures, 6762 A Centinela Avenue, Culver City, California 90230; 310-390-7495, Fax 310-390-1446.

From the Employer   *We provide a two- to three-week preseason training program. Drivers/ leaders are welcome to participate in a variety of activities such as horseback riding and white-water rafting on a complimentary basis.*

BOULDER LODGE
June Lake, California 93529

General Information   Motel with fishing and family resort in the summer; ski resort in the winter. Established in 1956. Owned by Boulder Lodge, Inc. Affiliated with American Automobile Association. 5-acre facility located 120 miles south of Carson City, Nevada. Features: 5 wooded acres of lake frontage; indoor heated pools and sauna; tennis court; private fishing pier; proximity to east gate of Yosemite Park; proximity to Mammouth Mountain and Devil's Postpile National Monument.

Profile of Summer Employees   Total number: 15; average age: 30; 60% male, 40% female. Nonsmokers preferred.

Employment Information   Openings are from June 1 to October 30. Year-round positions also offered. Jobs available: 2 *front desk persons* (minimum age 20) with references; 6 *cleaning persons* (minimum age 20) with references; 1 *maintenance person* (minimum age 20); *swimming instructors* with WSI certification and references. All positions offered at $5 per hour.

Benefits   Laundry facilities, bonus paid for every hour worked by a full-term employee, bonus available for outstanding performance through Labor Day, room at $20 per week with kitchen facilities for staff members to cook their own food.

Contact   Mrs. D. Oldfield, Boulder Lodge, Department SJ, Box 68, June Lake, California 93529; 619-648-7533, Fax 619-648-7330. Application deadline: May 1 (November 1 for winter season; preference given to early applicants).

From the Employer   *Working at Boulder Lodge gives employees an opportunity to enjoy mountain living in a beautiful recreational area.*

CAMP JCA SHOLOM
34342 Mulholland Highway
Malibu, California 90265

General Information   Residential Jewish camp offering a warm, supportive atmosphere for campers ages 7–17. Established in 1951. Owned by Jewish Community Centers Association. Affiliated with American Camping Association, United Way. 135-acre facility located 25 miles north of Los Angeles. Features: new Olympic-size swimming pool; expanded ropes course; location in beautiful Malibu Mountains; proximity to Pacific Ocean (5 miles); 15 miles of hiking trails.

Profile of Summer Employees   Total number: 75; average age: 20; 50% male, 50% female, 10% minorities, 20% high school students, 78% college students, 10% international, 70% local residents. Nonsmokers preferred.

Employment Information   Openings are from June 24 to August 22. Winter break positions also offered. Jobs available: 40 *counselors* with high school senior status; 8 *swimming* *and water safety instructors* with CPR, ALS, and WSI certification; 1 *ropes-course leader* with ability to lead groups through high and low elements; 1 *song leader* with ability to lead camp-wide singing of American and Hebrew folk songs, highly spirited nature, and guitar-playing skills; 1 *Jewish education instructor* with knowledge of Jewish traditions, culture, history, and entertainment, as well as the ability to develop and lead camp-wide programs, including all-day Shabbat programs; 3 *unit heads* with college degree, three years of camping experience, and good Jewish program skills (graduate training or social work experience helpful); 2 *teen travel leaders* (minimum age 21) with college degree, knowledge of outdoors (experience with children essential), and current first aid and CPR certification; 1 *experienced registered nurse* with ability to run the infirmary, supervise nurse's aide, and interact well with parents; 1 *bus driver* with current Class II California driver's license and a clean driving record (knowledge of mountain driving extremely helpful). All positions offered at $1000–$3000 per season.

Benefits On-site room and board at no charge, laundry facilities.

Contact Bill Kaplan, Program Director, Camp JCA Sholom, Department SJ, 5870 West Olympic Boulevard, Los Angeles, California 90036; 213-857-0036, Fax 213-937-9426. Application deadline: March 31.

CAMP LA JOLLA-SANTA BARBARA
6585 El Colegio Road
Goleta, California 93117

General Information Coeducational weight-loss/fitness camp for ages 8 and older serving separate age groups in sports, nutrition, and behavior modification. Established in 1979. Owned by Nancy Lenhart. Affiliated with American Camping Association. Features: gymnasium and university facilities; new suite-style residences with private baths and lounges; exclusive indoor/outdoor dining; volleyball and tennis courts; university-size swimming pool, indoor pool, and jacuzzi; aerobics and weight room; gorgeous hiking and biking trails; 1¼ miles from beach.

Profile of Summer Employees Total number: 35; average age: 22; 20% male, 80% female, 25% minorities, 5% high school students, 95% college students, 30% local residents, 20% teachers. Nonsmokers preferred.

Employment Information Openings are from June 12 to August 20. Jobs available: 10 *exercise specialists* with WSI and lifeguard certification at $600–$1600 per season; 15 *counselors* at $600–$1600 per season; 3 *nutritionists* at $600–$1600 per season; 3 *behavior modification specialists* at $600–$1600 per season; 2 *nurses* with RN, EMT, or LVN license at $1800–$2600 per season; *aerobics instructors* at $600–$1600 per season; *tennis instructors* at $600–$1600 per season.

Benefits College credit, preemployment training, on-site room and board at no charge, laundry facilities, health insurance, all field trips, special outings, and cultural events paid for by camp.

Contact Nancy Lenhart, Director, Camp La Jolla-Santa Barbara, 1150 Pine Street, Coronado, California 92118; 800-825-8746, Fax 619-435-8188. Application deadline: April 15.

From the Employer *All staff members attend a seven-day training session prior to campers' arrival. The director, Nancy Lenhart, is a certified camping director with extensive weight-management counseling experience.*

CAMP MARIASTELLA
P.O. Box 99
Wrightwood, California 92397
General Information Residential camp for girls ages 6–15 with six 1-week sessions. Established in 1946. Owned by Sisters of Social Service. Affiliated with American Camping Association, Religiously Affiliated Camps, Big Pines Camp Association. 220-acre facility located 80 miles northeast of Los Angeles. Features: swimming pool; lodge with rock fireplace; local national park camping areas; local ski and recreation area; 220 acres of beautiful forest populated with pine trees; Pacific Crest Trail running through a canyon on camp property; excellent hiking opportunities.
Profile of Summer Employees Total number: 55; average age: 24; 5% male, 95% female, 65% minorities, 15% high school students, 74% college students, 1% retirees, 5% international, 20% local residents, 5% teachers. Nonsmokers preferred.
Employment Information Openings are from June 1 to August 21. Year-round positions also offered. Jobs available: 3 *swimming instructors* with WSI certification (preference given to those who speak English and Spanish) at $700–$1500 per season; 1 *arts and crafts instructor* with preference given to those who are bilingual (English-Spanish) at $800–$1100 per season; 1 *nature specialist* with preference given to those who are bilingual (English-Spanish) at $800–$1100 per season; 1 *program director* with preference given to those who are bilingual (English-Spanish) at $1500–$1700 per season; 1 *office coordinator* with preference given to those who are bilingual (English-Spanish) at $8–$10 per hour; 5 *unit coordinators* with preference given to those who are bilingual (English-Spanish) at $800–$1100 per season; 30 *general counselors* with preference given to those who are bilingual (English-Spanish) at $500–$800 per season; 1 *driver* with valid California Class B driver's license and a clean driving record at $600–$1000 per season; 6 *experienced kitchen helpers* with food-handling cards. International students encouraged to apply.
Benefits College credit, on-site room and board at no charge, laundry facilities, health insurance, tuition reimbursement, vegetarian menu available, religious sensitivity.
Contact Sr. Una Feeney, SSS, Director, Camp Mariastella, Department SJ, 1120 Westchester Place, Los Angeles, California 90019; 213-733-1208. Application deadline: May 1.

From the Employer *Camp Mariastella offers staff training during which employees are oriented in all phases of the camp experience, including cultural sensitivity, teaching, conflict resolution, and certification in CPR and first aid. We offer a counselor-in-training program for girls ages 15–17. Working in our camp is an excellent way to fulfill service hours.*

CAMP MOUNTAIN MEADOWS
Sequoia National Forest
California
General Information Residential Girl Scout camp serving 75–100 campers weekly with high adventure activities, including backpacking, mountain biking, and horseback riding. Established in 1954. Owned by Girl Scouts Joshua Tree Council. Affiliated with American Camping Association. 15-acre facility located 60 miles north of Bakersfield. Features: location in the southern Sierra Nevadas (Greenhorn Mountain); small, friendly camp; primitive sites (sleeping under the stars); permits to use miles of U.S. Forest Service hiking and riding trails.
Profile of Summer Employees Total number: 30; average age: 21; 2% male, 98% female, 20% minorities, 10% high school students, 75% college students, 5% retirees, 7% international, 25% local residents, 10% teachers. Nonsmokers preferred.

Employment Information Openings are from June 20 to August 20. Jobs available: 3 *unit leaders* (minimum age 21) at $1400 per season; 10 *assistant unit leaders* (minimum age 18) at $1200 per season; 3 *specialists* with backpacking, counselor-in-training, mountain-biking, and rock-climbing experience at $1500 per season; 1 *nurse* with RN, LPN, or EMT license at $2100 per season; 1 *maintenance person* at $5600 per season.

Benefits College credit, preemployment training, on-site room and board at no charge.

Contact Outdoor Program Manager, Camp Mountain Meadows, P.O. Box 2164, Bakersfield, California 93303; 805-327-1409, Fax 805-327-3837. Application deadline: May 15.

From the Employer *At a weeklong precamp training session, staff members are trained on safety issues, diversity awareness, group interaction, success counseling, and the camp program. Staff members develop positive leadership and communication skills while sharing ideas and experiences with new friends from across the country.*

CAMP SCHERMAN
Mountain Center, California 92561

General Information Residential Girl Scout camp serving over 2,000 girls per season. Established in 1968. Owned by Girl Scout Council of Orange County. Affiliated with Girl Scouts of the United States of America, American Camping Association. 700-acre facility located 50 miles west of Palm Springs. Features: high desert chaparral; 2 lakes; pool; miles of trails; modern cabins and facilities.

Profile of Summer Employees Total number: 90; average age: 21; 5% male, 95% female, 10% minorities, 90% college students, 5% international, 5% local residents. Nonsmokers preferred.

Employment Information Openings are from June 9 to August 25. Jobs available: 30 *unit staff members* at $1792 per season; 10 *staff supervisors* at $2048 per season; 1 *counselor-in-training director* at $2112 per season; 1 *counselor-in-training assistant director* at $1856 per season; 1 *boating director* with lifeguard training, first aid, and CPR certification at $2176 per season; 1 *waterfront director* with lifeguard training, first aid, and CPR certification at $2176 per season; 5 *waterfront staff members* with lifeguard training, first aid, and CPR certification at $1920 per season; 5 *boating staff members* with lifeguard training, first aid, and CPR certification at $1920 per season; 5 *program assistants* with skills in nature, arts and crafts, archery, and rock climbing at $1792 per season; 5 *experienced riding assistants* at $1792 per season; 4 *program directors* with skills and experience in nature, arts and crafts, archery, or rock climbing at $2048 per season; 2 *awareness aide staff members* with experience working with disabled campers at $1792 per season; 5 *kitchen staff members* at $2227 per season; 2 *pack-out cooks* at $2227–$2406 per season. International students encouraged to apply.

Benefits Preemployment training, on-site room and board at no charge.

Contact Patty Thomas, Director of Outreach/Camp Director, Camp Scherman, Department SJ, P.O. Box 3739, Costa Mesa, California 92628-3739; 714-979-7900. Application deadline: May 1.

From the Employer *Camp Scherman employees experience diverse and unique opportunities all summer long. There is an informative and interesting seven-day training session that focuses on communication, leadership skills, and innovative programs. There is no typical day; each day is filled with new activities, adventures, and challenges. Staff members experience a hardworking and fun-filled summer.*

EMANDAL–A FARM ON A RIVER
16500 Hearst Road
Willits, California 95490

General Information   Coeducational residential camp for 50 youngsters ages 7–15 for the first half of the summer and a family vacation farm for 45–55 people of all ages for the second half. Established in 1908. Owned by Clive and Tamara Adams. Affiliated with American Camping Association, Western Association of Independent Camps. 1,000-acre facility located 140 miles north of San Francisco. Features: location adjacent to a river and national forest; organic farm and garden; proximity to town (16 miles); spring water; nonsmoking environment.

Profile of Summer Employees   Total number: 20; average age: 25; 50% male, 50% female, 1% minorities, 15% high school students, 50% college students, 1% retirees, 10% international, 20% local residents. Nonsmokers only.

Employment Information   Openings are from April 1 to November 30. Jobs available: 15 *camp counselors* (six-week position) at $890 per season; 8 *family camp workers* (six-week position) at $170 per week; 2 *gardeners* (entire summer) at $170 per week; 1 *pickle maker* (August–October) at $170 per week; 2 *farm workers* (until Thanksgiving) at $170 per week; *gardener's apprentice* (volunteer from April–November).

Benefits   College credit, preemployment training, on-site room and board at no charge, laundry facilities, health insurance.

Contact   Tamara Adams, Director, Emandal–A Farm on a River, Department SJ, 16500 Hearst Road, Willits, California 95490; 707-459-5439, Fax 707-459-1808. Application deadline: April 15.

From the Employer   *We are a family of different people from different places, coming together for a short time to share our thoughts, dreams, and ways of life to help each other understand why we are the way we are.*

FOUNDATION FOR THE JUNIOR BLIND
5300 Angeles Vista Boulevard
Los Angeles, California 90043

General Information   Residential camp serving blind and visually impaired children and their families. Established in 1955. Owned by Foundation for the Junior Blind. Affiliated with American Camping Association. 50-acre facility located 10 miles north of Malibu. Features: near Malibu and the Santa Monica mountains; horse program; great swimming pool; outstanding and caring staff; beach trips every session.

Profile of Summer Employees   Total number: 60; average age: 20; 50% male, 50% female, 25% minorities, 90% college students, 8% international, 25% local residents. Nonsmokers preferred.

Employment Information   Openings are from June 11 to August 23. Spring break, winter break, Christmas break, year-round positions also offered. Jobs available: 15 *girls' counselors* at $1100 per season; *swimming instructors* with WSI, first aid, and CPR certification at $1100–$1500 per season; *experienced horse instructors* with first aid and CPR certification at $1100–$1500 per season; *experienced arts and crafts instructor* at $1100 per season; *experienced drama instructor* at $1100 per season; *music staff* with ability to play guitar and lead songs at $1100 per season; 15 *boys' counselors* at $1100 per season. International students encouraged to apply.

Benefits   College credit, preemployment training, formal ongoing training, on-site room and board at no charge, laundry facilities, health insurance, honorarium/stipend of over $1000, leadership experience.

Contact   Noel Torres, Director of Recreation, Foundation for the Junior Blind, Department SJ, 5300 Angeles Vista Boulevard, Los Angeles, California 90043; 800-352-2290, Fax 213-296-0424. Application deadline: April 1.

HUNEWILL GUEST RANCH
Twin Lakes Road
Bridgeport, California 93517
General Information   Guest ranch accommodating 45–55 guests weekly. Established in 1930. Owned by Hunewill family. Operated by Hunewill Land and Livestock. Affiliated with Dude Ranchers' Association. 4,800-acre facility located 120 miles south of Reno, Nevada. Features: lush meadows; working cattle ranch; view of Sierra Nevada Mountains; individual cottages; Victorian ranch house with kitchen and dining room; 100 horses for riding.
Profile of Summer Employees   Total number: 19; average age: 21; 25% male, 75% female, 5% high school students, 85% college students, 10% local residents. Nonsmokers preferred.
Employment Information   Openings are from May 15 to October 3. Jobs available: 4 *experienced waiters/waitresses* at $185–$200 per week; 3 *cabin staff* with ability to work quickly at $175 per week; 1 *experienced maintenance person* with carpentry, plumbing, and electrical experience at $190 per week; 1 *cook* with previous cooking experience or cooking school certificate at $1400–$1700 per month; 1 *experienced breakfast/pastry chef* with experience baking for groups at $1200 per month; 3 *wranglers* with extensive horse experience and good people skills at $800–$900 per month.
Benefits   On-site room and board at $158 per month, laundry facilities, free horseback riding during time off, tips that range from $30–$90 weekly.
Contact   Betsy Hunewill Elliott, Assistant Manager, Hunewill Guest Ranch, Department SJ, 101 Hunewill Lane, Wellington, Nevada 89444; 702-465-2238. Application deadline: January 15.

From the Employer   *Hunewill Guest Ranch employees have great fun, develop lasting friendships with the other employees, and often develop contacts with our clientele that help them find jobs in their chosen field of study. Because the ranch is located in a prime vacation area, free time can be spent riding horseback, hiking, fishing, biking, and in other related activities.*

JAMESON RANCH CAMP
Glennville, California 93226
General Information   Private residential camp involving children in a mountain ranch life-style. Established in 1934. Owned by Ross and Debby Jameson. Affiliated with American Camping Association, Western Association of Independent Camps. 520-acre facility located 40 miles east of Bakersfield. Features: elevation of 4,600 feet; property bordered on two sides by Sequoia National Forest; status as self-sufficient ranch; lake for boating and fishing; farm animals; noncompetitive environment; nestled in rolling hills and oaks with majestic pines.
Profile of Summer Employees   Total number: 25; average age: 21; 50% male, 50% female, 20% minorities, 90% college students, 5% retirees, 10% international, 5% local residents, 5% teachers. Nonsmokers only.
Employment Information   Openings are from June 18 to September 3. Jobs available: 2 *swimming instructors* with WSI certification at $2000 per season; 4 *lifeguards* with ALS certification at $2000 per season; 1 *rock-climbing instructor* at $2000 per season; 2 *horse instructors* at $2000 per season; 2 *crafts instructors* at $2000 per season; 1 *mountain-biking*

instructor at $2000 per season; 1 *drama instructor* at $2000 per season; 1 *horse-vaulting instructor* at $2000 per season; 1 *archery instructor* at $2000 per season; 1 *riflery instructor* at $2000 per season; 2 *kitchen persons* at $2000 per season; 1 *head cook* at $3000 per season; 1 *photography instructor* at $2000 per season. International students encouraged to apply.

Benefits   College credit, preemployment training, formal ongoing training, on-site room and board at no charge, laundry facilities, workmen's compensation insurance.

Contact   Mr. Ross Jameson, Owner/Director, Jameson Ranch Camp, Department SJ, P.O. Box 459, Glennville, California 93226; 805-536-8888. Application deadline: May 30.

From the Employer   *We have a one-week precamp orientation where employees are trained in group interaction, program area set-up activities, and overall counselor preparation. The staff-camper ratio is 1:5.*

LOS ANGELES DESIGNERS' THEATRE
Box 1883
Studio City, California 91614-0883
General Information   Summer theater that produces stage productions and teaches theatrical producing, including the legal aspects of production. Established in 1970. Owned by Los Angeles Designers' Theatre. Affiliated with United States Institute for Theatre Technology. Features: over 100 lighting instruments and a computerized dimmer board; 16 channels of sound in theater; proximity to CBS studio center, Warner Bros. studios, Universal Studios, Disney studios, ABC, and NBC studios; proximity to CBS Columbia Square and dozens of recording studios; contact with hundreds of agents, managers, and directors; proximity to USC, UCLA, Loyola, Pepperdine, CalTech, Cal Arts, and other universities and colleges, as well as over 100 theaters.

Profile of Summer Employees   Total number: 72; average age: 30; 50% male, 50% female, 20% minorities, 15% high school students, 30% college students, 2% retirees, 35% local residents, 20% teachers. Nonsmokers preferred.

Employment Information   Openings are from January 1 to December 31. Year-round positions also offered. Jobs available: 1 *director; actors and actresses; singers and dancers;* 1 *set designer;* 1 *lighting designer;* 1 *property designer;* 1 *sound designer;* 1 *costume designer;* 1 *program/graphics designer;* 4 *crew members;* 2 *cutters/drapers (first hands);* 2 *electricians;* 3 *carpenters;* 1 *musical director;* 1 *choreographer;* 1 *box office/house manager.*

Benefits   College credit, preemployment training, formal ongoing training, tuition reimbursement, plenty of networking opportunities in the entertainment capital of the world.

Contact   Richard Niederberg, Artistic Director, Los Angeles Designers' Theatre, P.O. Box 1883, Department P, Studio City, California 91614-0883; 213-650-9600.

From the Employer   *This theater is not affiliated with any educational or governmental organization. It is a professional nonprofit theater in its 25th season. An excellent program on producing as a profession is a mainstay, as is our legal aspects of producing TV, film, music, and dance program. Compensation is negotiable on a per show basis, as is job availability. Applicants may send whatever items best demonstrate their artistry, but submissions are nonreturnable.*

SANTA CATALINA SCHOOL SUMMER CAMP
1500 Mark Thomas Drive
Monterey, California 93940
General Information   Residential and day camp for girls ages 8–14 with an emphasis on performing and fine arts and athletics. Established in 1953. Owned by Santa Catalina School.

Affiliated with American Camping Association, Western Association of Independent Camps, National Association of Independent Schools. 35-acre facility located 75 miles south of San Jose. Features: location on Monterey Bay near Carmel; beautiful campus with gardens and Spanish architecture; gymnasium (built 1990); 500-seat theater; dormitories (single and double rooms); 6 tennis courts.

Profile of Summer Employees Total number: 40; average age: 35; 20% male, 80% female, 5% minorities, 40% college students, 5% retirees, 5% international, 60% local residents. Nonsmokers preferred.

Employment Information Openings are from June 14 to July 24. Jobs available: 10 *counselors* with one year of college completed at $750–$1000 per season; 5 *experienced head counselors* with three years of college completed at $850–$1100 per season.

Benefits Preemployment training, on-site room and board at no charge, laundry facilities.

Contact Mrs. Katie M. Aimé, Director of Summer Programs, Santa Catalina School Summer Camp, 1500 Mark Thomas Drive, Monterey, California 93940; 408-655-9386, Fax 408-649-3056. Application deadline: April 1.

From the Employer *The camp offers a great opportunity to gain experience working with children in a beautiful setting. Precamp training includes a workshop on communicating with children and first aid and CPR classes.*

SKY MOUNTAIN CHRISTIAN CAMP
P.O. Box 179
Emigrant Gap, California 95715

General Information Camp conference center serving nondenominational church groups. Established in 1976. Affiliated with American Camping Association, Christian Camping International. 40-acre facility located 65 miles east of Sacramento. Features: location on the shore of Lake Valley Reservoir in Tahoe National Forest; ski resorts only 20 minutes away; proximity to Lake Tahoe (40 miles); elevation of 6,000 feet; new gymnasium; newly remodeled cabins with full bathrooms.

Profile of Summer Employees Total number: 15; average age: 20; 50% male, 50% female, 10% high school students, 90% college students, 20% local residents. Nonsmokers only.

Employment Information Openings are from June 15 to August 25. Jobs available: 3 *experienced kitchen assistants* (minimum age 18) at $125–$175 per week; 4 *dishwashers* (minimum age 18) at $125–$150 per week; 4 *laborers* (minimum age 18) at $125–$150 per week; 2 *lifeguards* (minimum age 18) with senior lifeguard certification at $125–$150 per week; 1 *waterfront coordinator* (minimum age 21) with senior lifeguard certification at $150–$175 per week.

Benefits Preemployment training, on-site room and board at no charge, laundry facilities.

Contact Dezra Saunders, Camp Coordinator, Sky Mountain Christian Camp, P.O. Box 179, Emigrant Gap, California 95715; 916-389-2118. Application deadline: April 30.

SUPERCAMP
California

General Information Residential program for teens that includes life skills and academic courses designed to build self-confidence and lifelong learning skills. Established in 1981. Owned by Bobbi DePorter. Affiliated with American Camping Association, Oceanside Chamber of Commerce, Society of Accelerated Learning and Teaching. Features: dormitory rooms; dining hall; swimming pool; ropes course; 6 different sites; location on college campuses.

Profile of Summer Employees   Total number: 200; average age: 22; 50% male, 50% female, 80% college students. Nonsmokers only.

Employment Information   Openings are from June 20 to August 20. Jobs available: 20 *experienced instructors* with college degree at $750–$2250 per season; 20 *directors* with presentation skills and college degree at $1500–$4500 per season; 10 *counselors* with college degree at $1000–$3000 per season; 3 *nurses* with RN license at $1000–$3000 per season; 76 *team leaders* (peer counselors, ages 18–25) with high school diploma at $500–$1000 per season; 1 *office manager* with high school diploma at $1000–$2000 per season; 3 *paramedics* at $700–$2100 per season.

Benefits   Preemployment training, on-site room and board at no charge, laundry facilities, internships, experience working with teens in an educational and self-esteem building program, excellent experience for education and psychology majors.

Contact   Shelby Reeder, Human Resources Coordinator, SuperCamp, Department SJ, 1725 South Hill Street, Oceanside, California 92054; 800-527-5321, Fax 619-722-3507. Application deadline: May 1.

From the Employer   *SuperCamp employees develop outstanding communications and leadership skills through an extensive five-day training program in which they can meet exciting new people from across the country. Staff members support teens through powerful, life-changing experiences and become familiar with new accelerated-learning techniques. Sessions are held on beautiful college campuses in six locations across the country, including Texas, Illinois, and Massachusetts.*

YMCA CAMP OAKES
P.O. Box 452
Big Bear City, California 92314

General Information   Residential summer camp serving children from around the world in a traditional camp program. Established in 1905. Owned by YMCA of Greater Long Beach. Affiliated with American Camping Association. 230-acre facility located 110 miles east of Long Beach. Features: fully equipped observatory; elevation of 7,300 feet in the San Bernardino Mountains; sailing and waterskiing on Big Bear Lake; extensive equestrian program; canoeing and kayaking on on-site lake; academic program including computer science and ESL.

Profile of Summer Employees   Total number: 60; average age: 23; 50% male, 50% female, 10% minorities, 5% high school students, 95% college students, 10% international, 80% local residents. Nonsmokers preferred.

Employment Information   Openings are from June 18 to September 4. Jobs available: 3 *program directors* (minimum age 21) with three years of experience at $230–$280 per week; 1 *aquatic director* (minimum age 21) with WSI and first aid/CPR certification at $225–$255 per week; 4 *certified lifeguards* (minimum age 18) at $150–$200 per week; 8 *cabin counselors* (minimum age 18) with one year of college completed at $140–$190 per week; 8 *junior counselors* (minimum age 18) at $110–$150 per week; 7 *program specialists* (minimum age 18) with experience in riflery, crafts, wrangling, nature, archery, ropes-challenge course, or astronomy at $140–$190 per week; 1 *health-care coordinator* (minimum age 21) with RN or EMT training at $175–$250 per week; 4 *experienced cooks* (minimum age 18) at $120–$225 per week. International students encouraged to apply.

Benefits   Preemployment training, on-site room and board at no charge, laundry facilities.

Contact   Michael McGinnis, Program Director, YMCA Camp Oakes, Department SJ, P.O. Box 90995, Long Beach, California 90809-0995; 310-496-2756, Fax 310-425-1169. Application deadline: May 31 (outside California, call 800-642-2014).

COLORADO

ASPEN LODGE AT ESTES PARK
6120 Highway 7
Estes Park, Colorado 80517
General Information Ranch resort catering to families, conferences, and special functions. Established in 1940. Owned by Tom and Jill Hall. Affiliated with Colorado Dude and Guest Ranch Association, American Automobile Association, Mobil Travel Guide. 82-acre facility located 65 miles northwest of Denver. Features: location bordering Rocky Mountain National Park; full recreation and sports facilities.
Profile of Summer Employees Total number: 35; average age: 20; 50% male, 50% female. Nonsmokers only.
Employment Information Openings are from May 1 to October 1. Year-round positions also offered. Jobs available: 5 *sports center attendants* at $4.25 per hour; 3 *children's counselors* at $4.25 per hour; 10 *waitstaff members* at $3 per hour; 2 *housekeepers* at $4.25 per hour; 8 *wranglers* with extensive horse experience at $4.25 per hour; 1 *bartender* at $3 per hour; 6 *groundskeepers* at $4.25 per hour; 2 *conference attendants* at $4.25 per hour.
Benefits On-site room and board at $175 per month, laundry facilities, $.75 per hour bonus at the end of the season.
Contact Personnel Manager, Aspen Lodge at Estes Park, Department SJ, 6120 Highway 7, Estes Park, Colorado 80517; 303-586-8133, Fax 303-586-8133 Ext. 410. Application deadline: April 15 (applications accepted year-round).

BAR LAZY J GUEST RANCH
447 County Road 3, Box N
Parshall, Colorado 80468
General Information Guest ranch with capacity for 40 people. Established in 1912. Owned by Lawrence and Barbara Harmon. Affiliated with Colorado Dude and Guest Ranch Association, Dude Ranchers' Association, Granby Chamber of Commerce. 70-acre facility located 105 miles northwest of Denver. Features: horseback riding; Colorado River fishing; gold medal water (⅔ miles privately owned); trout pond (stocked yearly, no license needed); swimming pool and jacuzzi; jeep rides; evening activities, including square dances, staff shows, campfires, and a local rodeo.
Profile of Summer Employees Total number: 18; average age: 21; 50% male, 50% female, 82% college students, 18% retirees. Nonsmokers only.
Employment Information Openings are from May 1 to September 30. Jobs available: 1 *experienced head wrangler* at $800 per month; 5 *experienced wranglers* at $450 per month; 2 *counselors* with experience working with children at $400 per month; 2 *waitresses/waiters* at $400 per month; 2 *housekeepers* at $400 per month; 1 *kitchen helper* at $400 per month; 1 *assistant cook* at $500 per month.
Benefits Formal ongoing training, on-site room and board at no charge, laundry facilities.
Contact Larry Harmon, Owner, Bar Lazy J Guest Ranch, Box N, Parshall, Colorado 80468; 303-725-3437. Application deadline: May 1.

CENTRAL CITY OPERA
Denver, Colorado

General Information Opera house that produces three mainstage performances per summer between late June and early August. Established in 1932. Owned by Central City Opera House Association. Affiliated with Opera America. Located 40 miles west of Denver. Features: opera house; location within a historic landmark city.

Profile of Summer Employees Total number: 17; average age: 23; 50% male, 50% female, 20% minorities, 85% college students, 7% retirees, 40% local residents.

Employment Information Openings are from June 1 to August 15. Jobs available: 1 *house manager* at $200–$300 per week; 1 *assistant house manager* at $180–$200 per week; 2 *office assistants* at $170–$180 per week; 2 *music librarians* at $170–$180 per week; 2 *production assistants* at $170–$180 per week; 2 *public relations assistants* at $170–$180 per week; 2 *gift shop managers* at $170–$180 per week; 2 *costume shop assistants* at $170–$180 per week; 2 *gardeners* at $170–$180 per week.

Benefits On-site room and board at no charge, laundry facilities, travel reimbursement.

Contact Curt Hancock, Festival Administrator, Central City Opera, Department SJ, 621 17th Street, Suite 1601, Denver, Colorado 80293; 303-292-6500. Application deadline: April 1.

CHEROKEE PARK RANCH
P.O. Box 97
Livermore, Colorado 80536

General Information Summer guest ranch providing fun outdoor activities for the entire family and specializing in Western hospitality. Established in 1880. Owned by William and Elizabeth Elfland. Affiliated with Colorado Dude and Guest Ranch Association, Dude Ranchers' Association, Colorado Hotel and Lodging Association. 200-acre facility located 90 miles northwest of Denver. Features: heated outdoor swimming pool and hot tub; recreation hall with Ping-Pong and pool tables; adjacent to a national forest; main lodge with 5 guest cabins and 7 staff cabins; outdoor volleyball, basketball, and horseshoes.

Profile of Summer Employees Total number: 17; average age: 20; 42% male, 58% female, 11% minorities, 90% college students, 12% local residents. Nonsmokers preferred.

Employment Information Openings are from May 16 to September 30. Jobs available: 5 *wranglers* with CPR certification (preferred) at $350 per month; 2 *children's counselors* with CPR/first aid and lifesaving certification at $350 per month; 5 *housekeepers/waitresses/waiters* at $350 per month; 1 *cook* at $550 per month; 1 *assistant cook/secretary* at $350–$450 per month.

Benefits On-site room and board at no charge, laundry facilities.

Contact Director, Cherokee Park Ranch, Department SJ, P.O. Box 97, Livermore, Colorado 80536; 303-493-6522. Application deadline: April 15.

From the Employer *Staff members at Cherokee Park Ranch enjoy the opportunity to serve others in a beautiful Rocky Mountain environment. Interacting with new people helps to develop critical interpersonal and communication skills. Guests and staff come from across the country. Staff members build lasting relationships that provide many opportunities for future growth.*

COFFEE BAR CAFE
167 East Elkhorn Avenue, P.O. Box 2210
Estes Park, Colorado 80517

General Information Family restaurant seating 58 persons and serving breakfast, lunch, and dinner. Established in 1940. Owned by Robert Akins. Affiliated with National Restaurant Association, Colorado Restaurant Association, Estes Park Chamber of Commerce. Located 75 miles northwest of Denver. Features: proximity to Rocky Mountain National Park (3 miles); spectacular mountain scenery; proximity to Boulder's shopping and entertainment (35 miles); opportunities to meet guests and other students from throughout the United States and Europe; proximity to outdoor activities (such as hiking, biking, horseback riding, fishing, and swimming).

Profile of Summer Employees Total number: 16; average age: 19; 40% male, 60% female, 10% minorities, 80% college students, 10% local residents. Nonsmokers preferred.

Employment Information Openings are from May 1 to October 15. Year-round positions also offered. Jobs available: 5 *experienced servers* at $2.25 per hour; 2 *hosts* at $5–$6 per hour; 4 *dishwashers* at $5.50–$6 per hour; 3 *experienced line cooks* at $6–$7.50 per hour; 2 *kitchen assistants* at $5.50–$6 per hour.

Benefits College credit, meal furnished with work shift, eligibility for end-of-season bonus.

Contact Robert Akins, Owner, Coffee Bar Cafe, Department SJ, P.O. Box 2210, Estes Park, Colorado 80517; 303-586-3589. Application deadline: April 1.

COLORADO MOUNTAIN RANCH
P.O. Box 711
Boulder, Colorado 80306

General Information Residential and day camps each serving approximately 90 campers, boys and girls ages 6–16. Established in 1927. Owned by Walker family. Affiliated with American Camping Association, National Wildlife Federation. 200-acre facility located 10 miles west of Boulder. Features: location surrounded by Roosevelt National Forest with access to Indian Peaks Wilderness and Rocky Mountain National Park; heated swimming pool and large lake for sailing and canoeing; elevation of 8,500 feet in the Colorado Rockies; 6 vans and 2 buses for trips; challenge ropes course; lodge, cabins, old-style miner's tent, and tipi village.

Profile of Summer Employees Total number: 65; average age: 22; 40% male, 60% female, 5% minorities, 90% college students, 5% international. Nonsmokers only.

Employment Information Openings are from June 5 to August 20. Jobs available: 4 *swimming instructors,* with one required to have WSI certification and three required to have LGI certification at $900–$975 per season; 8 *wranglers* at $900–$975 per season; 1 *archery instructor* at $900–$975 per season; 1 *riflery instructor* at $900–$975 per season; 1 *arts and crafts instructor* at $900–$975 per season; 3 *gymnastics instructors* at $900–$975 per season; 1 *head cook/kitchen manager* at $1500 per season; 7 *kitchen workers* at $975 per season; 3 *maintenance persons* at $975 per season; 3 *bus drivers* at $1075 per season; 8 *cabin counselors* at $975 per season; 10 *day-camp counselors* at $975 per season; 1 *drama instructor* at $975 per season; 1 *Indian lore instructor* at $975 per season; 2 *office staff members* at $975 per season; 2 *backpacking instructors* at $975 per season; 2 *ropes-course instructors* at $975 per season; 2 *sailing/outcamp/canoeing instructors* at $975 per season; 1 *nanny* at $975 per season; 2 *outcamp/hiking instructors* at $975 per season.

Benefits Preemployment training, on-site room and board at no charge, workmen's compensation insurance, laundry service.

Contact The Walkers, Directors, Colorado Mountain Ranch, Department SJ, P.O. Box 711, Boulder, Colorado 80306; 303-442-4557. Application deadline: May 1.

COLVIG SILVER CAMPS
9665 Florida Road
Durango, Colorado 81301

General Information   Outdoor adventure camp located in beautiful natural surroundings. Established in 1970. Owned by Craig Colvig Trust. Affiliated with American Camping Association. 600-acre facility located 200 miles north of Albuquerque. Features: located in the mountains and bordered by a national forest; ropes course; 3 lakes; archaeological area; 14,000-foot peaks.

Profile of Summer Employees   Total number: 45; average age: 25; 50% male, 50% female, 90% college students, 5% local residents. Nonsmokers preferred.

Employment Information   Openings are from June 5 to August 20. Jobs available: *counselors* at $650 per season; *assistant counselors* at $600 per season; *nurse* at $800 per season; *wrangler* at $800 per season. All applicants must have first aid and CPR certification.

Benefits   College credit, preemployment training, on-site room and board at no charge, laundry facilities, health insurance.

Contact   Jim Colvig, Director, Colvig Silver Camps, 9665 Florida Road, Durango, Colorado 81301; 303-247-2564, Fax 303-247-2547. Application deadline: March 30.

COULTER LAKE GUEST RANCH
P.O. Box 906
Rifle, Colorado 81650

General Information   Dude and guest ranch serving 25–30 people in a rustic Rocky Mountain setting. Established in 1939. Owned by Sue and Norm Benzinger. Affiliated with Colorado Dude and Guest Ranch Association, Dude Ranchers' Association, Rifle Chamber of Commerce, Colorado Visitors Bureau, Colorado Outfitters Association. 23-acre facility located 185 miles west of Denver. Features: 11½-acre lake with fishing; 8 cabins with lodge; miles of trails for 28–30 hours of horseback riding weekly with little duplication; whitewater rafting nearby.

Profile of Summer Employees   Total number: 9; average age: 22; 40% male, 60% female, 90% college students, 1% local residents. Nonsmokers only.

Employment Information   Openings are from May 15 to October 1. Christmas break positions also offered. Jobs available: *maintenance staff* with experience with horses (salary depends on experience) at $95 per week; *wrangler/trail guide* with experience with horses and fencing (salary depends on experience) at $95 per week; *inside staff* (housekeepers, servers, bussers, cleaners, dishwashers, and others) at $90 per week.

Benefits   On-site room and board at no charge, use of recreational facilities on days off, tip pool distributed weekly.

Contact   Sue or Norm Benzinger, Owners, Coulter Lake Guest Ranch, Department SJ, P.O. Box 906, Rifle, Colorado 81650; 303-625-1473. Application deadline: March 31.

CROSS BAR X YOUTH RANCH
2111 County Road 222
Durango, Colorado 81301

General Information   Bible-centered camp serving 20 low-income youths. Established in 1977. Owned by Cross Bar X Youth Ranch, Inc. Affiliated with Christian Camping International. 35-acre facility located 12 miles east of Durango. Features: a lake for swimming and fishing; proximity to Rocky Mountains; obstacle course; trails for horseback riding and mountain biking.

Profile of Summer Employees Total number: 9; average age: 22; 50% male, 50% female, 100% college students. Nonsmokers only.

Employment Information Openings are from June 1 to August 15. Jobs available: 8 *counselors;* 1 *cook; activities coordinator* with experience in backpacking, mountain biking, and leadership. All positions offered at $50 per week.

Benefits College credit, preemployment training, on-site room and board at no charge, laundry facilities.

Contact Nick Brothers, Director, Cross Bar X Youth Ranch, Department SJ, 2111 County Road 222, Durango, Colorado 81301; 303-259-2716. Application deadline: May 1.

From the Employer *Cross Bar X staff benefit from a 1½-week training program where they learn to help children work through problems and difficult situations in an atmosphere of encouragement and fun. Staff develop strong communication skills by leading games, Bible lessons, counseling sessions with campers, and activities.*

CURECANTI NATIONAL RECREATION AREA
102 Elk Creek
Gunnison, Colorado 81230

General Information National recreation area with a focus on natural and cultural history interpretation serving 1.1 million visitors per year. Established in 1965. Owned by United States Department of the Interior, National Park Service. 40,000-acre facility located 15 miles west of Gunnison. Features: location on Blue Mesa Lake (Colorado's largest body of water—20 miles long with 96 miles of shoreline); full-service marinas for boating/fishing; visitor center and ranger stations providing area information and sales items (mostly books); both developed and remote camping sites; beautiful expanse of high desert sage country surrounded by snow-capped mountains and many other geological features.

Profile of Summer Employees Total number: 14; average age: 23; 50% male, 50% female, 2% minorities, 50% college students, 25% retirees, 2% local residents.

Employment Information Openings are from May to September. Year-round positions also offered. Jobs available: *environmental education interns; interpretation interns.* All applicants must have education or life science background. All positions offered at $35 per week.

Benefits College credit, formal ongoing training, on-site room and board at no charge, laundry facilities, $7 per day stipend to offset food costs, workmen's compensation insurance.

Contact Mitzi Frank, Supervisory Park Ranger, Curecanti National Recreation Area, Department SJ, 102 Elk Creek, Gunnison, Colorado 81230; 303-641-2337, Fax 303-641-3127. Application deadline: January 15.

DON K RANCH
2677 South Siloam Road
Pueblo, Colorado 81005

General Information Dude ranch serving up to 55 guests weekly in a Western atmosphere. Established in 1947. Owned by Smith family. Affiliated with Colorado Dude and Guest Ranch Association, Dude Ranchers' Association. 1,360-acre facility located 60 miles southwest of Colorado Springs. Features: ranch surrounded by 250,000 acres of the San Isabel National Forest; tennis court; hot tub and large heated swimming pool with diving board and slide; beautiful hiking trails; white-water rafting; brunch rides; gourmet meals and evening activities; setting in the hills; complete horseback riding program for guests with their own horse for the week and trail rides.

Profile of Summer Employees Total number: 22; average age: 22; 40% male, 60% female, 90% college students, 5% international. Nonsmokers preferred.

Employment Information Openings are from May 15 to September 30. Jobs available: 6 *experienced wranglers* with extensive riding experience and knowledge of horses at $350 per month; 3 *children's counselors* with riding experience, ability to plan activities, lifesaving certification, and ability to work well with children at $350 per month; 3 *waitstaff members* at $350 per month; *dishwashing person* at $350 per month; 1 *cook* at $800 per month; 1 *assistant cook* with baking skills at $450 per month; 3 *cabin housekeepers* at $350 per month; 1 *outdoor maintenance person* at $350 per month; 1 *experienced nanny* with ability to care for owner's children and perform light housekeeping at $350 per month; 1 *office/store person* with ability to answer telephone, check in guests, assemble mailings, perform as store clerk, and stock and clean store at $350 per month.

Benefits On-site room and board at no charge, laundry facilities, tips, use of facilities on days off, opportunity to meet interesting people from around the world.

Contact Darlene, Mark, or Mary Smith, Don K Ranch, Department SJ, 2677 South Siloam Road, Pueblo, Colorado 81005; 719-784-6600. Application deadline: April 1.

DROWSY WATER RANCH
P.O. Box 147 J
Granby, Colorado 80446

General Information Mountain dude ranch serving 60 guests weekly. Established in 1929. Owned by Ken and Randy Sue Fosha. Affiliated with Colorado Dude and Guest Ranch Association, Dude Ranchers' Association, Colorado Hotel and Motel Association. 600-acre facility located 110 miles west of Denver. Features: swimming pool; location in Colorado mountains; beautiful scenery; spa; miles of hiking/riding trails; proximity to Rocky Mountain National Park; creek running through the ranch.

Profile of Summer Employees Total number: 26; average age: 21; 48% male, 52% female, 15% high school students, 75% college students, 5% local residents. Nonsmokers only.

Employment Information Openings are from May 15 to September 19. Jobs available: 7 *experienced horse wranglers/guides* with first aid certification at $1200 per month; 3 *maintenance staff members* at $1200 per month; 3 *assistant cooks, experience preferred,* at $1200 per month; 1 *experienced head chef* at $1500 per month; 2 *dishwashers* at $1200 per month; 2 *experienced counselors* with first aid certification at $1200 per month; 6 *housekeeping staff members/wait persons* at $1200 per month; 1 *experienced office person* at $1200 per month.

Benefits College credit, on-site room and board at no charge, laundry facilities, tips, use of all facilities, horseback riding.

Contact Randy Sue Fosha, Owner, Drowsy Water Ranch, P.O. Box 147 J, Granby, Colorado 80446; 303-725-3456.

From the Employer *This is a great opportunity to meet and entertain guests from all parts of the world. Working for Drowsy Water Ranch provides our employees with good training in serving and interacting with a broad cross-section of people.*

ELK MOUNTAIN RANCH
Buena Vista, Colorado 81211

General Information Guest ranch serving 35 guests on a weekly basis, lasting from June through the end of September. Established in 1981. Owned by C. LaRue and Susan Boyd.

Operated by Thomas K. and Sue L. Murphy, Ranch Managers. Affiliated with Colorado Dude and Guest Ranch Association, Dude Ranchers' Association, Colorado Hotel and Motel Association. 5-acre facility located 120 miles southwest of Denver. Features: exceptional wilderness setting; elevation of 9,600 feet; small size; true mountain getaway surrounded by the San Isabel National Forest; exceptional terrain and panoramic vistas, white-water rafting, trips to Aspen, trapshooting, hayrides, and square dances.

Profile of Summer Employees Total number: 13; average age: 21; 50% male, 50% female, 100% college students. Nonsmokers only.

Employment Information Openings are from May 15 to October 1. Jobs available: 1 *cook* with high-quality service and love of great food at $575 per month; 6 *wranglers* with experience riding and/or instructing horsemanship and basic knowledge of horses (care, feeding, and grooming) at $425 per month; 1 *experienced children's counselor* at $400 per month; 5 *waitstaff/housekeeping personnel/dishwashers* with service- and quality-oriented personality at $400 per month; 1 *assistant cook* at $400 per month; 1 *general maintenance person* with knowledge of minor repairs, groundskeeping, and vehicle maintenance at $425 per month.

Benefits College credit, on-site room and board at no charge, laundry facilities, days off, tips that average $750 per person per month of employment.

Contact Sue Murphy, Manager, Elk Mountain Ranch, Department SJ, P.O. Box 910, Buena Vista, Colorado 81211; 719-539-4430. Application deadline: April 15.

From the Employer *Elk Mountain Ranch is a small, family-oriented guest ranch whose staff members give extremely personalized service. The ranch is secluded with a fantastic view of the Collegiate Range, and its staff of approximately 13 become family.*

FLYING G RANCH, TOMAHAWK RANCH
400 South Broadway
Denver, Colorado 80209

General Information Residential camps serving approximately 1,500 girls ages 6–17 throughout the summer. Established in 1945. Owned by Girl Scouts–Mile-Hi Council. Affiliated with American Camping Association, Camp Horsemanship Association. 320-acre facility located 65 miles southwest of Denver. Features: proximity to Pike National Forest; hiking and backpacking in the Colorado Rocky Mountains; ropes adventure course; small working farm; rock climbing; horseback riding.

Profile of Summer Employees Total number: 60; average age: 20; 1% male, 99% female, 5% minorities, 1% high school students, 90% college students, 1% retirees, 1% international, 75% local residents.

Employment Information Openings are from June 12 to August 17. Jobs available: 2 *experienced assistant camp directors/program directors* at $150–$250 per week; 2 *health supervisors* with RN or LPN license at $250–$290 per week; 11 *troop leaders* with supervisory skills and experience working with children at $130–$175 per week; 27 *assistant troop leaders* with experience working with children at $95–$130 per week; 1 *horseback riding director* with ability to teach, train, and supervise campers and staff in horsemanship at $135–$180 per week; 6 *horseback riding counselors* with training in Western riding at $95–$130 per week; 2 *arts and crafts specialists* with ability to teach craft activities to a variety of age levels at $95–$155 per week; 2 *nature specialists* at $95–$155 per week; 1 *sports/archery instructor* at $95–$155 per week; 1 *experienced farm specialist* with ability to care for small farm animals and teach programs at $95–$155 per week; 1 *experienced rock-climbing/ropes-course instructor* with training in different levels of rock climbing at $95–$155 per week; 1 *arts/drama specialist* with ability to teach music, dance, puppetry, or theater to groups of children at $95–$155 per week; 2 *campcraft specialists* with knowledge of hiking, backpacking, compass use, and cooking at $95–$155 per week.

Benefits Preemployment training, on-site room and board at no charge, laundry facilities, health insurance, time off during camp.

Contact Debora A. Speicher, Camp Administrator, Flying G Ranch, Tomahawk Ranch, Department SJ, 400 South Broadway, Denver, Colorado 80209; 303-778-8774, Fax 303-733-6345. Application deadline: May 1.

From the Employer *Working at Flying G Ranch or Tomahawk Ranch gives employees the opportunity to live and play in the Rocky Mountains and make lasting friendships with staff members from all over the United States and the world.*

GENEVA GLEN CAMP
Indian Hills, Colorado 80454

General Information Residential coed camp offering two-week sessions for 220 children ages 6–16. Established in 1922. Operated by Ken and Nancy Atkinson. 500-acre facility located 20 miles west of Denver. Features: 400-foot zip line ropes course; extensive riding trails; barn; swimming pool; archery and riflery ranges; theme programming.

Profile of Summer Employees Total number: 98; average age: 22; 45% male, 55% female, 20% minorities, 30% high school students, 65% college students, 10% retirees, 5% international, 60% local residents, 20% teachers. Nonsmokers preferred.

Employment Information Openings are from June 15 to August 15. Jobs available: *nurse* with Colorado registration or reciprocity at $2500–$2800 per season; *cook* at $1250–$1500 per season; *maintenance crew* at $450 per season; *nurse's aide* with LPN, nursing student, or advanced first aid, EMT, or equivalent certification at $1500; *counselors* with first aid, CPR, and horseback-riding experience (preferred) at $700–$900 per season; *swimming instructors* with WSI, LGT, CPR, and first aid certification at $800–$900 per season.

Benefits Formal ongoing training, on-site room and board at no charge, travel reimbursement, health insurance.

Contact Ken and Nancy Atkinson, Directors, Geneva Glen Camp, Department SJ, P.O. Box 248, Indian Hills, Colorado 80454; 303-697-4621, Fax 303-697-9429. Application deadline: April 25.

HARMEL'S RANCH RESORT
6748 County Road 742
Almont, Colorado 81210

General Information Family-oriented guest ranch with 38 lodging units, stables, dining room, lounge, heated pool, and general store. Established in 1959. Owned by Bill and Jody Roberts. Affiliated with Colorado Dude and Guest Ranch Association. 300-acre facility located 150 miles west of Colorado Springs. Features: horseback riding; heated swimming pool; river rafting; mountain biking; 2 trout streams on premises; nearby rock climbing.

Profile of Summer Employees Total number: 50; average age: 21; 50% male, 50% female, 5% high school students, 75% college students, 20% local residents. Nonsmokers preferred.

Employment Information Openings are from May 15 to September 30. Jobs available: 7 *wranglers* with first aid and CPR certification at $475 per month; 15 *housekeepers/ waitpersons* at $400 per month; 2 *children's program personnel* with elementary education degree (preferred) at $400 per month; 3 *store and office personnel* at $400 per month; 3 *ranch hands* at $400 per month; 3 *kitchen workers* at $400 per month.

Benefits College credit, on-site room and board at no charge, laundry facilities, free use of ranch amenities, uniforms (shirts), end-of-season tip pool.

Contact Brad Milner, Manager, Harmel's Ranch Resort, P.O. Box 944, Gunnison, Colorado 81230; 303-641-1740. Application deadline: March 1.

From the Employer *Harmel's five-day, 45- to 50-hour work week allows ample opportunity to enjoy the beautiful surroundings and to take advantage of many activities, including horseback riding, rafting, mountain biking, swimming, hiking, rock climbing, and camping.*

HOLIDAY INN RESORT AND CONFERENCE CENTER OF ESTES PARK
101 South St. Vrain, P.O. Box 1468
Estes Park, Colorado 80517

General Information Resort offering guests 155 rooms in an exceptional setting. Established in 1968. Owned by Forever Living Resorts. 2-acre facility located 65 miles northwest of Denver. Features: new conference center; surrounding high mountain valley at an elevation of 7,500 feet; downtown shopping within 1 mile; proximity to Rocky Mountain National Park; game and fitness rooms with an indoor pool and hot tub; restaurant, lounge, and banquet facilities.

Profile of Summer Employees Total number: 40; average age: 23; 50% male, 50% female, 90% college students, 10% international.

Employment Information Openings are from May 10 to October 15. Year-round positions also offered. Jobs available: 4 *buspersons;* 10 *waitstaff* at $2.50 per hour; 4 *hosts* at $5 per hour; 4 *cooks* at $5.50 per hour; 4 *kitchen help* (pantry, dishwashing) at $5 per hour; 2 *housepeople* with ability to perform custodial duties, luggage handling, and conference set-ups at $5 per hour; 15 *room attendants* (housekeeping) at $5 per hour; 4 *front-desk personnel* at $5 per hour; 20 *banquet staff members* at $2.50 per hour. International students encouraged to apply.

Benefits College credit, formal ongoing training, on-site room and board at $21 per week, 70 percent off all meals in the restaurant, limited summer housing.

Contact Paula Dunfee, Human Resource Director, Holiday Inn Resort and Conference Center of Estes Park, Department SJ, P.O. Box 1468, Estes Park, Colorado 80517; 303-586-2332, Fax 303-586-2332 Ext. 299. Application deadline: April 1.

From the Employer *Holiday Inn employees have the opportunity to achieve high self-esteem while interacting with persons of all ages. Cross-training in the hospitality industry is highlighted, thus providing job diversity. Outdoor enthusiasts have unlimited resources while forming lifelong friendships.*

THE HOME RANCH
54880 Routt County Road 129
Clark, Colorado 80428

General Information Ranch resort accommodating 42 guests per week. Established in 1978. Owned by L. Kendrick Jones. Operated by Jodee S. Richison. Affiliated with Relais et Chateaux, Mobil Travel Guide, Colorado Dude and Guest Ranch Association. 1,500-acre facility located 172 miles west of Denver. Features: Rocky Mountain setting; wilderness hiking trails; horseback-riding trails; fly fishing in the Elk River.

Profile of Summer Employees Total number: 34; average age: 30; 50% male, 50% female, 5% minorities, 5% high school students, 50% college students, 5% retirees, 5% international, 30% local residents. Nonsmokers preferred.

Employment Information Openings are from June 1 to October 15. Winter break, Christmas break positions also offered. Jobs available: 3 *children's counselors* with first aid certification; 2 *kitchen helpers;* 6 *waiters/waitresses;* 6 *housekeepers;* 4 *maintenance personnel;* 2 *hiking guides* with first aid certification; 6 *wranglers* with first aid certification; 2 *dishwashers;* 3 *cooks.* All positions offered at $800 per month.

Benefits   On-site room and board at no charge, laundry facilities, limited use of facility, bonus.

Contact   Will W. Hardly, Manager, The Home Ranch, Department SJ, Box 822, Clark, Colorado 80428; 303-879-1780, Fax 303-879-1795. Application deadline: May 30.

From the Employer   *At the Home Ranch you make great contacts with the guests and meet super staff members.*

LONGACRE EXPEDITIONS
Taylor Park, Colorado

General Information   Adventure travel program emphasizing group living skills and physical challenges. Established in 1981. Owned by Longacre Expeditions. 60-acre facility located 30 miles east of Crested Butte.

Profile of Summer Employees   Total number: 20; average age: 25; 50% male, 50% female, 10% minorities, 40% college students, 30% local residents. Nonsmokers only.

Employment Information   Openings are from June 14 to July 31. Jobs available: 8 *assistant trip leaders* (minimum age 21) at $150–$175 per week; 1 *mountaineering instructor* (minimum age 21) at $300–$400 per week; 1 *rock-climbing instructor* (minimum age 21) at $300–$400 per week; 3 *support and logistics staff members* (minimum age 21) at $150–$175 per week.

Benefits   Preemployment training, on-site room and board at no charge, Pro-Deal package.

Contact   Roger Smith, Longacre Expeditions, RD 3, Box 106, Newport, Pennsylvania 17074; 717-567-6790.

From the Employer   *There is an eight-day precamp staff training period emphasizing hard and soft skills. Individual advancement is expected of returning staff. First-time staff usually join as assistant trip leaders and support personnel. In the following season, most graduate to trip leader. Continued advancement leads to positions as base camp manager or course director. We offer advanced and leadership training programs. Activities include backpacking, mountaineering, rock climbing, mountain biking, and wilderness first aid.*

NORTH FORK GUEST RANCH
55395 Highway 285, P.O. Box B
Shawnee, Colorado 80475

General Information   Ranch providing an all-inclusive package (meals, activities, and lodging) for 40–45 guests per week. Established in 1985. Owned by Dean May. Affiliated with Colorado Dude and Guest Ranch Association, Dude Ranchers' Association. 520-acre facility located 50 miles southwest of Denver. Features: outdoor heated swimming pool; indoor hot tub; river and pond fishing; beautiful surroundings for hikes; overnight pack trips, lunch rides, and cookouts.

Profile of Summer Employees   Total number: 20; average age: 20; 40% male, 60% female, 90% college students, 10% local residents. Nonsmokers only.

Employment Information   Openings are from April 1 to November 1. Jobs available: 2 *cooks* at $400–$500 per month; 5 *waitresses/waiters and cabin staff members* at $300–$400 per month; 7 *experienced wranglers* with CPR and first aid training at $400–$500 per month; 3 *kids' counselors* with WSI certification (preferred), CPR and first aid training (preferred), and lifeguard certification at $300–$400 per month; 3 *maintenance persons* at $300–$400 per month.

Benefits College credit, on-site room and board at no charge, one 24-hour period off per week, tip pool, ability to take part in all activities offered.

Contact Dean and Karen May, Owners/Managers, North Fork Guest Ranch, Department SJ, P.O. Box B, Shawnee, Colorado 80475; 800-843-7895, Fax 303-674-1432.

From the Employer *North Fork Ranch is a guest ranch that focuses on the family. Staff members gain a unique experience in helping to provide the best vacation families can have. We offer a beautiful setting for young people from all over the country to meet and work for the summer.*

PEACEFUL VALLEY LODGE AND RANCH RESORT
Box 2811, Star Route
Lyons, Colorado 80540

General Information Dude ranch serving 80–130 people in weeklong programs. Established in 1953. Owned by Mabel Boehm. Affiliated with Colorado Dude and Guest Ranch Association, Dude Ranchers' Association, American Automobile Association. 320-acre facility located 60 miles northwest of Denver. Features: swimming pool; tennis court; location bordered by National Forest; surrounded by magnificent scenery; fishing pond and stream; playground; horseback riding in the Rocky Mountains.

Profile of Summer Employees Total number: 55; average age: 21; 50% male, 50% female. Nonsmokers preferred.

Employment Information Openings are from May 1 to October 31. Year-round positions also offered. Jobs available: 8 *waiters/waitresses* at $600–$800 per month; 3 *dishwashers* at $600–$800 per month; 4 *assistant cooks* at $600–$800 per month; 12 *wranglers* with first aid certification at $700–$900 per month; 4 *counselors* with first aid and water safety certification at $700–$900 per month; 7 *housekeepers* at $600–$800 per month; 2 *drivers/ mechanical personnel* (minimum age 21) with a copy of driver's license and record at $700 per month; 2 *gardeners/grounds crew* at $700 per month; 4 *skilled maintenance staff members* with mechanical aptitude at $700 per month; 1 *office person* with typing ability at $725 per month. International students encouraged to apply.

Benefits On-site room and board at no charge, laundry facilities, use of facilities during time off, opportunities for staff to use their talents (church choir, evening programs, talent show, and melodrama).

Contact Personnel Director, Peaceful Valley Lodge and Ranch Resort, Department SJ, Star Route Box 2811, Lyons, Colorado 80540; 303-747-2881, Fax 303-747-2167. Application deadline: March 1.

From the Employer *Our staff members have the opportunity to work hard while growing on a personal level, meeting unique people among the guests and staff, and learning the art of genuine hospitality. Depending on your effort, a summer at Peaceful Valley Lodge can be an experience you will always treasure.*

POULTER COLORADO CAMPS
P.O. Box 772947-P
Steamboat Springs, Colorado 80477

General Information Residential camp serving 80 campers ages 7–18 per session with strong group dynamics and outdoor education emphasis with frequent wilderness excursions. Established in 1957. Owned by The Whiteman School, Inc. Affiliated with American

Camping Association. 180-acre facility located 150 miles northwest of Denver. Features: well-equipped gymnasium with climbing wall; athletics field; outdoor sand volleyball court; riding trails through the woods; spacious dormitory cabins; easy access to private hot springs.

Profile of Summer Employees Total number: 35; average age: 21; 43% male, 57% female, 10% minorities, 14% high school students, 71% college students, 5% international, 15% teachers. Nonsmokers only.

Employment Information Openings are from June 3 to August 20. Jobs available: 1 *nurse* with RN license at $1500 per season; 3 *experienced cooks* at $1000–$2000 per season; 3 *wranglers* with strong horsemanship and teaching skills at $1000–$1500 per season; 1 *experienced program coordinator* with strong organizational and leadership skills (camp experience preferred) at $1000–$1500 per season; 4 *experienced wilderness instructors* (minimum age 21) with technical skills and teaching experience at $1100–$2000 per season; 1 *arts and crafts counselor* with strong arts/crafts skills and teaching experience at $900–$1000 per season; 10 *experienced senior counselors* with lifeguard training and first aid certification (preferred) and experience working with youth at $900–$1000 per season; 4 *assistant counselors* at $700 per season. International students encouraged to apply.

Benefits Preemployment training, on-site room and board at no charge, local discounts.

Contact Jay B. Poulter, Director, Poulter Colorado Camps, P.O. Box 772947-P, Steamboat Springs, Colorado 80477; 303-879-4816, Fax 303-879-1307. Application deadline: April 1.

From the Employer *Our weeklong orientation, which prepares staff for the demands of being strong, sensitive counselors, includes wilderness skills, first aid, programming, and dealing with camper concerns. Our small camper groups with at least 2 counselors make this a very personalized experience with great flexibility for developing an individualized program. Group wilderness outings are emphasized.*

ROCKY MOUNTAIN PARK COMPANY (THE TRAIL RIDGE STORE)
Rocky Mountain National Park
Estes Park, Colorado 80517

General Information Facility providing high-quality gifts and food service to national park visitors. Only visitor services operation inside Rocky Mountain National Park. Established in 1937. Owned by Forever Resorts. Affiliated with Tourist Industry Retail Merchants' Association, Indian Arts and Crafts Association, National Parks Conference of Concessioners. 1-acre facility located 22 miles west of Estes Park. Features: 71 peaks over 12,000 feet high; site in area above timberline in Alpine tundra; 355 miles of incredible hiking trails; location at 12,000-foot elevation (spectacular views).

Profile of Summer Employees Total number: 55; average age: 23; 33% male, 67% female, 4% minorities, 75% college students, 25% retirees, 5% international, 2% local residents. Nonsmokers preferred.

Employment Information Openings are from May 31 to October 15. Jobs available: 20 *gift shop sales clerks* with outgoing and energetic personality at $195–$202 per week; 14 *snack bar assistants* with outgoing and energetic personality at $195–$202 per week; 4 *stockroom assistants* with ability to perform heavy lifting at $195–$202 per week; 4 *parking attendants* with outgoing and patient personality at $195–$202 per week; 3 *experienced sales supervisors* at $260–$270 per week; 2 *experienced food supervisors* at $260–$270 per week; 3 *experienced merchandising assistants* with three months of merchandising experience or six credit hours in color and design at $198–$215 per week. International students encouraged to apply.

Benefits College credit, preemployment training, on-site room and board at $60 per week, transportation to and from work each day, subsidized activities program, personalized employee meal program.

Contact William K. Almond, General Manager, Rocky Mountain Park Company (The Trail Ridge Store), Department SJ, P.O. Box 2680, Estes Park, Colorado 80517; 303-586-9319, Fax 303-586-2332. Application deadline: May 29.

From the Employer *A summer with the Rocky Mountain Park Company is fast-paced and intense. We work in a spectacular location, high above timberline, with ready access to pristine wilderness and a full range of urban activities in Boulder and Denver. We employ students and retirees from all over the world, encouraging development of lifelong friendships.*

ROCKY MOUNTAIN VILLAGE–HOME OF THE EASTER SEAL HANDICAMP
2644 County Road 306, Empire Junction
Empire, Colorado 80438

General Information Residential camp serving physically and developmentally disabled children and adults. Established in 1951. Owned by Colorado Easter Seal Society. Affiliated with American Camping Association. 95-acre facility located 40 miles west of Denver. Features: located in front range of the Rocky Mountains with Continental Divide visible from site; large trout ponds; mountain trails for biking and hiking; tennis court; computers; central location between Denver, Vail, and Winter Park.

Profile of Summer Employees Total number: 45; average age: 21; 45% male, 55% female, 20% high school students, 75% college students, 5% local residents. Nonsmokers preferred.

Employment Information Openings are from May 20 to August 31. Jobs available: 1 *program director* at $1600 per season; 1 *assistant cook* at $2000–$2100 per season; 1 *head nurse* with RN license (from Colorado or state with Colorado reciprocity) at $3000–$4500 per season; 1 *trip specialist* (minimum age 21) with outdoor camping experience at $1200–$1500 per season; 1 *arts and crafts instructor* (minimum age 21) at $1200–$1400 per season; 1 *computer specialist* (minimum age 21) at $1200–$1400 per season; 1 *animal specialist* (minimum age 21) at $1200–$1400 per season; 1 *pool specialist* (minimum age 21) with WSI/lifesaving certification at $1200–$1400 per season; 1 *athletics specialist* (minimum age 18) at $1200–$1400 per season; 8 *girls' counselors* (minimum age 18) at $1000–$1200 per season; 8 *boys' counselors* (minimum age 18) at $1000–$1200 per season; 4 *girls' counselors-in-training* (ages 16–18) at $650–$750 per season; 4 *boys' counselors-in-training* (ages 16–18) at $650–$750 per season; 3 *maintenance helpers* (minimum age 16) at $1000–$1200 per season; 3 *kitchen helpers* (minimum age 16) at $1000–$1200 per season; 1 *secretary* (minimum age 16) at $1000–$1200 per season.

Benefits College credit, preemployment training, on-site room and board at no charge, laundry facilities, chance to gain experience working with people who have various types of disabilities.

Contact Mellodee Lowther, Director, Rocky Mountain Village–Home of the Easter Seal

Handicamp, Department SJ, P.O. Box 115, Empire, Colorado 80438; 303-892-6063. Application deadline: March 15.

From the Employer *At Rocky Mountain Village, staff members are introduced to a variety of disabilities. Staff learn about what kinds of things people with head injury, muscular dystrophy, cerebral palsy, and Down's Syndrome must face every day. Special sessions such as "Talking with Technology" offer nonverbal children the opportunity to learn to use augmentative communication boards. If you are looking for an experience that will broaden your knowledge and perspective, Rocky Mountain Village provides a wonderful opportunity found nowhere else in the United States.*

SANBORN WESTERN CAMPS
Florissant, Colorado 80816

General Information Boys' and girls' camps serving ages 7–17 in two- to five-week sessions. Established in 1949. Owned by Sanborn Western Camps. Affiliated with American Camping Association. 6,000-acre facility located 35 miles west of Colorado Springs. Features: 6,000 acres of private land; outstanding program variety; mountain climbing/backpacking; Western horsemanship; natural sciences programs; water sports.

Profile of Summer Employees Total number: 120; average age: 23; 50% male, 50% female, 20% minorities, 10% high school students, 90% college students, 5% international. Nonsmokers preferred.

Employment Information Openings are from June 9 to August 25. Year-round positions also offered. Jobs available: 8 *riding instructors* at $900 per season; 8 *canoeing instructors* at $900 per season; 8 *rock-climbing instructors* at $900 per season; 20 *backpacking instructors* at $900 per season; 10 *ecology instructors* at $900 per season; 8 *tennis instructors* at $900 per season; 4 *drama instructors* at $900 per season; 4 *geology instructors* at $900 per season; 8 *swimming instructors* at $900 per season; 8 *arts and crafts instructors* at $900 per season; 8 *campcraft instructors* at $900 per season; 8 *rafting instructors* at $900 per season; 8 *sports instructors* at $900 per season; 8 *caving instructors* at $900 per season; 10 *mountaineering instructors* at $900 per season; *cooks* at $1800–$2000 per season; *nurses* at $2200–$2500 per season; *interpreters* at $900 per season. International students encouraged to apply.

Benefits College credit, preemployment training, on-site room and board at no charge, laundry facilities, health insurance.

Contact Rick Sanborn, Director, Sanborn Western Camps, Department SJ, Sanborn Western Camps, Florissant, Colorado 80816; 719-748-3341, Fax 719-748-3259. Application deadline: May 10.

From the Employer *Sanborn camps provide challenging leadership and teaching experiences in a variety of noncompetitive outdoor programs. Backpacking, horseback riding, and many other camping adventures are ideal for developing lasting friendships and a new understanding of ourselves and our world. Applicants must have a strong interest in working with children and the outdoors.*

SKY HIGH RANCH
30924 North Highway 67
Woodland Park, Colorado 80863

General Information Residential camp for girls in grades 2–12. Weekly capacity is 130 campers. Established in 1951. Owned by Girl Scouts–Wagon Wheel Council. Affiliated with American Camping Association. 880-acre facility located 25 miles west of Colorado Springs.

Features: beautiful Colorado mountain location at 8,200 feet bordering national forest land; 2 ponds; equestrian center.

Profile of Summer Employees Total number: 34; average age: 22; 5% male, 95% female, 11% minorities, 60% college students, 50% local residents, 10% teachers. Nonsmokers preferred.

Employment Information Openings are from June 3 to July 29. Jobs available: 1 *camp director* (minimum age 25) with two years of administrative experience at $300–$350 per week; 1 *assistant camp director* at $220–$270 per week; 1 *program specialist* at $105–$150 per week; 1 *health supervisor* with RN or MD license at $200–$250 per week; 6 *unit leaders* at $130–$150 per week; 14 *unit counselors* at $95–$110 per week; 1 *head cook/food supervisor* at $200–$250 per week; 1 *assistant cook* at $110–$175 per week; 2 *kitchen assistants* at $95–$125 per week; 1 *riding director* with CHA certification (preferred) at $140–$160 per week; 2 *riding assistants* at $105–$125 per week; 1 *waterfront director* with lifeguard and CPR certification at $140–$160 per week; 1 *waterfront assistant* with lifeguard and CPR certification at $105–$125 per week; *CIT director* at $130–$150 per week.

Benefits College credit, preemployment training, on-site room and board at no charge, laundry facilities, health insurance.

Contact Wynne Whyman, Director, Program and Property, Sky High Ranch, Department SJ, 3535 Parkmoor Village Drive, Colorado Springs, Colorado 80917-5298; 719-597-8603, Fax 719-597-8606. Application deadline: May 15.

TUMBLING RIVER RANCH
P.O. Box 30
Grant, Colorado 80448

General Information Guest ranch serving families. Established in 1940. Owned by Jim and Mary Dale Gordon. Affiliated with Colorado Dude and Guest Ranch Association, Dude Ranchers' Association. 200-acre facility located 62 miles southwest of Denver. Features: log cabins (all rooms have fireplaces); two lovely rock lodges.

Profile of Summer Employees Total number: 30; average age: 20; 50% male, 50% female. Nonsmokers preferred.

Employment Information Openings are from May 15 to October 1. Winter break positions also offered. Jobs available: *waitresses/waiters; cabin staff; cooks; assistant cooks; secretary; children's counselors* with first aid certification; *drivers; mechanics; wranglers* with first aid certification; *general maintenance personnel; groundskeepers.*

Benefits College credit, formal ongoing training, on-site room and board at no charge, laundry facilities, end-of-summer bonus.

Contact Mary Dale Gordon, Owner, Tumbling River Ranch, P.O. Box 30, Grant, Colorado 80448; 303-838-5981. Application deadline: April 1.

VAIL ASSOCIATES, INC.
P.O. Box 7
Vail, Colorado 81658

General Information Owners and operators of Vail, Beaver Creek, and Arrowhead ski resorts. Established in 1962. Owned by Gillett Holdings, Inc. Affiliated with Colorado Ski Country USA. Located 100 miles west of Denver. Features: location in the heart of the Rocky Mountains; year-round recreation facilities; family-oriented resort area.

Profile of Summer Employees Total number: 300; average age: 30; 50% male, 50% female.

Employment Information Openings are from May 31 to September 1. Winter break,

Christmas break, year-round positions also offered. Jobs available: *hospitality positions* at $6–$7.25 per hour; *food service personnel* at $6 per hour; *golf course staff* at $6 per hour; *grounds/maintenance persons* at $6 per hour; *childcare staff* at $6 per hour; *day camp attendants* at $6 per hour; *lift-operations personnel* at $6.50 per hour; *wranglers* at $6 per hour.

Benefits   Formal ongoing training, on-site room and board at $300 per month, laundry facilities, health insurance, free season ski pass (winter employees), employee day care.

Contact   Personnel Office, Vail Associates, Inc., P.O. Box 7, Vail, Colorado 81658; 303-479-3060.

VILLAGE AT BRECKENRIDGE RESORT
655 Park Street, P.O. Box 8329
Breckenridge, Colorado 80424

General Information   Resort hosting individuals, families, groups, and conventions in 7 hotel/lodge buildings with 305 rooms. Established in 1988. Owned by Mr. Ron Tuchschmidt. Affiliated with Colorado Restaurant Association, Breckenridge Resort Chamber, Summit County Resort Chamber. 20-acre facility located 80 miles west of Denver. Features: location at the base of mountains in a town listed on the National Register of Historic Places; health-club facilities with hot tub and pools; hiking and biking trails; pond for fishing and paddle boating; mall and plaza for convenient shopping; location close to chair lifts, Alpine Slide, a human maze, horseback riding, and white-water rafting.

Profile of Summer Employees   Total number: 200; average age: 25; 50% male, 50% female, 10% minorities, 40% college students, 5% international, 45% local residents. Nonsmokers preferred.

Employment Information   Openings are from May 30 to September 30. Spring break, winter break, Christmas break, year-round positions also offered. Jobs available: *front-desk clerks* with congenial personality at $6–$7 per hour; *reservationists* with excellent phone and computer skills at $6–$6.25 per hour; *PBX operators* with excellent phone skills at $6 per hour; *experienced cooks (all types)* at $7–$10 per hour; *reliable kitchen stewards* at $6.25 per hour; *waitstaff* with pleasant, service-oriented attitude at $2.13 per hour; *buspersons* with pleasant, service-oriented attitude at $4.50–$6.50 per hour; *experienced cashiers/hosts/hostesses* with pleasant and detail-oriented personality at $5.50–$6 per hour; *housekeepers* with friendly, thorough, and efficient work habits at $6–$12 per hour; *laundry personnel* at $6–$6.50 per hour; *grounds staff* at $6–$6.50 per hour; *health-club attendants* with friendly personality at $5.50–$6 per hour. International students encouraged to apply.

Benefits   On-site room and board at $495 per month, free employee meal per shift worked, uniforms (if required), 10 percent employee discount in our restaurants.

Contact   Keith Schmotzer, Human Resource Director, Village at Breckenridge Resort, Department SJ, P.O. Box 8329, Breckenridge, Colorado 80424; 303-453-2000, Fax 303-453-1878.

From the Employer   *At the Village at Breckenridge Resort, we have a great staff and great opportunities for career growth.*

WILDERNESS TRAILS RANCH
23486 County Road 501
Bayfield, Colorado 81122

General Information   American-plan ranch accommodating 50 guests weekly. Established in 1950. Owned by Gene and Jan Roberts. Affiliated with Mobil Travel Guide, American

Automobile Association, Colorado Dude and Guest Ranch Association. 160-acre facility located 230 miles north of Albuquerque, New Mexico. Features: spectacular scenery; 72-foot heated pool and hot tub; clean air; secluded wilderness location; variety of horse trails.

Profile of Summer Employees Total number: 30; average age: 21; 50% male, 50% female, 87% college students, 7% international, 7% local residents. Nonsmokers only.

Employment Information Openings are from May 1 to October 1. Jobs available: 10 *experienced wranglers* with first aid certification; 8 *cabin/kitchen staff members;* 3 *children's counselors* with first aid certification; 2 *office/clerical persons* with clerical and computer experience; 1 *grounds/maintenance person* with electrical and woodworking experience; 1 *kitchen aide* with organizational skills and cooking experience. All positions offered at $765–$1200 per month.

Benefits College credit, preemployment training, on-site room and board at no charge, laundry facilities, use of recreational/ranch facilities.

Contact Jan Roberts, Owner, Wilderness Trails Ranch, 776 County Road 300, Durango, Colorado 81301; 303-247-0722, Fax 303-247-1006. Application deadline: April 1.

From the Employer *We require our staff to be at the ranch ten days prior to opening for a special orientation and training session. Living quarters are dormitory-style. We hire a few staff members to stay though the first week of October. All staff members are invited to participate in ranch activities, including riding, waterskiing, and meals. There is a weekly staff show.*

WILDLIFE CAMPS
Estes Park, Colorado 80517

General Information Coeducational residential camp offering environmental education programs for youngsters ages 9–17. Established in 1971. Owned by National Wildlife Federation. Affiliated with American Camping Association. Situated on 1,000 acres. Features: comfortable cabins; view of the Rocky Mountains; miles of hiking trails; rock-climbing and rapelling wall; volleyball and recreation field; waterfront location.

Profile of Summer Employees Total number: 45; average age: 23; 60% male, 40% female, 1% minorities, 95% college students, 1% international, 3% local residents. Nonsmokers preferred.

Employment Information Openings are from June 1 to August 25. Jobs available: 30 *counselors/instructors* with outdoor education experience and first aid certification at $1100–$1900 per season; 12 *backpacking leaders* with trip-leading experience and first aid certification at $1400–$1600 per season; 1 *waterfront supervisor* with WSI certification at $1100 per season; 2 *nurses* with RN license at $3500 per season.

Benefits College credit, on-site room and board at no charge, laundry facilities, health insurance.

Contact Susan Johnson, Manager, Youth Programs, Wildlife Camps, 1400 16th Street, NW, Washington, D.C. 20036; 800-245-5484, Fax 703-442-7332. Application deadline: February 15.

From the Employer *These twelve-day sessions offer counselors/instructors an opportunity to educate and inspire children through environmental education. During the five-day staff training, instructors will have time to prepare lessons. Generally, 2 staff members and 14 campers share a cabin.*

YMCA OF THE ROCKIES, CAMP CHIEF OURAY
1101 County Road 53, Box 648
Granby, Colorado 80446
General Information   Residential camp for boys and girls ages 8–15. Established in 1907. Operated by YMCA of the Rockies. Affiliated with American Camping Association, Christian Camping International, Young Men's Christian Association. 4,950-acre facility located 80 miles northwest of Denver. Features: beautiful mountain setting.
Profile of Summer Employees   Total number: 75; average age: 21; 50% male, 50% female, 5% high school students, 95% college students, 1% international. Nonsmokers preferred.
Employment Information   Openings are from May 30 to August 15. Jobs available: 1 *program director* with CPR/first aid certification at $150–$200 per week; 2 *nurses* with RN (preferred, EMT or LPN acceptable) at $250–$450 per week; 1 *maintenance person* (minimum age 21) with a clean driving record and CPR/first aid certification at $100–$130 per week; 3 *leadership training directors* with residential camp experience (preferred) and CPR/first aid certification at $115 per week; 4 *wranglers* with experience teaching camp riding programs (preferred) and CPR/first aid certification at $100–$150 per week; 25 *cabin counselors* with CPR/first aid certification at $90–$105 per week; 1 *travel coordinator* (minimum age 21) with a clean driving record and CPR/first aid certification at $100–$125 per week; 1 *riding director* (minimum age 21) with barn management experience at $125–$175 per week; 1 *ropes/challenge course director* (minimum age 21) with recent experience on ropes elements and ability to earn certification on ropes course at $125–$150 per week.
Benefits   Preemployment training, on-site room and board at no charge, laundry facilities, health insurance, salary increase for returning staff members, bonus for completion of employment agreement.
Contact   Director, YMCA of the Rockies, Camp Chief Ouray, Box 648, Granby, Colorado 80446; 303-887-2152 Ext. 4174. Application deadline: March 1.

YMCA OF THE ROCKIES, ESTES PARK CENTER
Estes Park, Colorado 80511-2550
General Information   Large Christian-oriented family resort and conference center offering a day camp and serving an average of 3,500 family and conference guests daily during the summer months. Established in 1907. Owned by YMCA of the Rockies. Affiliated with YMCA of the Rockies. 750-acre facility located 70 miles west of Denver. Features: location bordered on 3 sides by Rocky Mountain National Park; indoor pool; gymnasium; Nautilus weight room; horseback riding into Rocky Mountain National Park; extensive hiking programs.
Profile of Summer Employees   Total number: 370; average age: 21; 40% male, 60% female, 8% minorities, 60% college students, 30% retirees, 14% international, 2% local residents, 2% teachers. Nonsmokers preferred.
Employment Information   Openings are from April 1 to October 31. Spring break, winter break, Christmas break, year-round positions also offered. Jobs available: 12 *front-desk clerks* with computer and public relations skills at $90 per week; 2 *switchboard operators* with computer and public relations skills at $90 per week; 3 *secretaries/receptionists* with computer and public relations skills at $90 per week; 3 *registered nurses* with current nursing certification at $265 per week; 105 *food-service personnel* at $90 per week; 80 *room service (housekeeping) staff members* at $90 per week; 12 *maintenance workers* with good driving record at $90 per week; 18 *lodge/dormitory attendants and hosts/hostesses* at $90 per week; 10 *craft shop staff members* with artistic talent and/or experience with arts and crafts at $90 per week; 12 *general store salespeople* at $90 per week; 6 *pool guards* with lifeguard certification (Red Cross or YMCA) at $90 per week; 40 *day camp/adventure camp counselors* with training and/or practical experience in education/day camp work at $90 per week; 2

miniature golf and roller-skating rink attendants at $90 per week; *experienced environmental education counselor* with background in environmental sciences at $90–$110 per week. International students encouraged to apply if pursuing YMCA career.

Benefits Preemployment training, on-site room and board at no charge, laundry facilities, bonus and shared gratuity for those who complete their employment satisfactorily.

Contact Human Resources Director, YMCA of the Rockies, Estes Park Center, YMCA of the Rockies, Estes Park Center, Estes Park, Colorado 80511-2550; 303-586-3341 Ext. 1032, Fax 303-586-6078. Application deadline: April 30 for summer employment.

From the Employer *We work hard and play hard in one of the most beautiful mountain areas in the world, where most staff members cultivate the best friendships of their lifetimes. Offering a Christian-oriented environment with a year-round chaplain, we strive to help people develop in mind, body, and spirit.*

YMCA OF THE ROCKIES, SNOW MOUNTAIN RANCH
P.O. Box 169
Winter Park, Colorado 80482

General Information YMCA conference center and family resort accommodating up to 1,700 guests a day. Established in 1969. Operated by YMCA of the Rockies. Affiliated with Colorado Visitors Bureau, American Hotel/Motel Association, Denver Convention and Visitors Bureau. 5,000-acre facility located 70 miles northwest of Denver. Features: location near Winter Park ski resort and Rocky Mountain National Park; planned activities for staff on time off; hiking, horseback riding, and mountain biking available on site; free use of roller-skating rink, indoor pool, and basketball and volleyball courts; Christian activities planned for staff; 70 kilometers of groomed cross-country ski trails.

Profile of Summer Employees Total number: 130; average age: 20; 40% male, 60% female, 10% minorities, 2% high school students, 45% college students, 15% retirees, 25% international, 3% local residents. Nonsmokers preferred.

Employment Information Openings are from May 20 to August 28. Spring break, winter break, Christmas break, year-round positions also offered. Jobs available: 10 *lifeguards* with American Red Cross lifeguard certification at $100 per week; 2 *crafts shop instructors* at $90 per week; 10 *day-camp counselors* at $90 per week; 32 *housekeeping personnel* at $90 per week; 28 *food-service personnel* at $90 per week; 10 *maintenance personnel* at $90 per week; 9 *retail sales personnel* at $90 per week; 12 *front-desk clerks* at $90 per week; 35 *resident-camp counselors* at $95 per week. International students encouraged to apply.

Benefits College credit, formal ongoing training, on-site room and board at no charge, laundry facilities, internships, free use of recreation facilities and discount in gift shop, 40-hour work week (normally) with 2 days off each week.

Contact Julie Orr, Human Resources Director, YMCA of the Rockies, Snow Mountain Ranch, P.O. Box 169, Winter Park, Colorado 80482; 303-887-2152, Fax 303-449-6781.

CONNECTICUT

CAMP AWOSTING
Litchfield Hills
Bantam, Connecticut 06750

General Information Residential camp for 140 boys offering a coeducational program with Camp Chinqueka. Established in 1900. Affiliated with American Camping Association,

Connecticut Camping Association. 125-acre facility located 12 miles south of Torrington. Features: large sports field; 3½-mile lake for extensive aquatic program with over 50 boats; go-cart and minibike tracks; 3 outdoor tennis courts; excellent food service program.

Profile of Summer Employees Total number: 40; average age: 22; 90% male, 10% female, 5% minorities, 90% college students, 10% international. Nonsmokers preferred.

Employment Information Openings are from June 21 to August 21. Jobs available: *waterfront staff; archery staff; riflery staff; fencing staff; woodworking staff; crafts staff; sports staff; music/dance staff; outdoor camping staff; photography staff; journalism staff; computer staff; go-cart/minibike staff; drama staff.* All positions offered at $1000–$1400 per season. International students encouraged to apply.

Benefits College credit, preemployment training, formal ongoing training, on-site room and board, end-of-season bonus, $300 to $600 in parent tips, Red Cross certification.

Contact Buzz Ebner, Director, Camp Awosting, Department SJ, Litchfield Hills, Bantam, Connecticut 06750; 203-567-9678, Fax 203-868-0081. Application deadline: May 15.

CAMP CHINQUEKA
Litchfield Hills
Bantam, Connecticut 06750

General Information Residential camp serving 125 girls and offering a coeducational program with Camp Awosting. Established in 1955. Owned by Ebner Family. Affiliated with American Camping Association, Connecticut Camping Association. 100-acre facility located 10 miles south of Torrington. Features: large sports field; 3 outdoor tennis courts; extensive aquatic program with over 40 boats and canoes; 3 large halls for dancing, fencing, and gymnastics.

Profile of Summer Employees Total number: 35; average age: 21; 10% male, 90% female, 5% minorities, 90% college students, 10% international. Nonsmokers preferred.

Employment Information Openings are from June 21 to August 21. Jobs available: *waterfront staff; archery staff; riflery staff; fencing staff; woodworking staff; crafts staff; sports staff; music and dance staff; outdoor camping staff; photography staff; journalism staff; computer staff; go-carts and minibike staff; drama staff.* All positions offered at $1000–$1400 per season. International students encouraged to apply.

Benefits College credit, preemployment training, formal ongoing training, on-site room and board at no charge, laundry facilities, end-of-season bonus, $300 to $600 in parent tips, Red Cross certification.

Contact Barbara V. Ebner, Director, Camp Chinqueka, Department SJ, Litchfield Hills, Bantam, Connecticut 06750; 203-567-9678.

CAMP HEMLOCKS
P.O. Box 198
Hebron, Connecticut 06248

General Information Residential camp serving 100 physically disabled persons. Established in 1950. Owned by Easter Seal Society of Connecticut. Affiliated with National Easter Seal Society, American Camping Association. 160-acre facility located 30 miles southeast of Hartford. Features: barrier-free design; indoor pool; modern facilities; located in central Connecticut.

Profile of Summer Employees Total number: 60; average age: 19; 33% male, 67% female, 10% high school students, 55% college students, 25% international.

Employment Information Openings are from May 27 to August 14. Year-round positions also offered. Jobs available: *assistant program director* with three years of camp experience at $200 per week; *arts and crafts leader* at $150 per week; *nature/activity leader* at $150 per week; *outdoor living skills instructor* at $150 per week; *physical recreation leader* at $150 per week; *assistant aquatics director* with WSI certification at $160 per week; 6 *cabin leaders* with college junior or senior status at $130 per week; 48 *general counselors* (minimum age 18) at $110–$125 per week; 10 *counselors-in-training* (ages 16–18) at $65 per week.

Benefits Preemployment training, on-site room and board at no charge, laundry facilities.

Contact Mr. Sunny P. Ku, Summer Camp Director, Camp Hemlocks, Department SJ, P.O. Box 198, Hebron, Connecticut 06248; 203-228-9496, Fax 203-228-2091. Application deadline: May 15.

CAMP JEWELL YMCA
Prock Hill Road
Colebrook, Connecticut 06021

General Information Full-featured coeducational residential camp with teen adventure trips and year-round environmental education. Established in 1901. Owned by YMCA of Metro Hartford. Affiliated with American Camping Association. 500-acre facility located 35 miles northwest of Hartford. Features: location in the foothills of the Berkshires; 50-acre private lake; cabins with fireplace and bathroom/shower; 3 ropes courses and new rope swing at waterfront; dynamic new treehouse cabins.

Profile of Summer Employees Total number: 150; average age: 21; 50% male, 50% female, 10% minorities, 15% high school students, 65% college students, 1% retirees, 10% international, 25% local residents. Nonsmokers only.

Employment Information Openings are from June 17 to August 20. Year-round positions also offered. Jobs available: 2 *experienced ropes-course directors* at $1500–$2000 per season; 1 *experienced waterfront director* with lifeguard/WSI certification at $1500–$2000 per season; 15 *teen trip leaders* (minimum age 21) at $1400–$1800 per season; 6 *experienced village directors* at $1500–$2000 per season; 3 *crafts program specialists* at $1500–$2000 per season; 2 *sailing program specialists* at $1400–$1600 per season; 2 *tennis program specialists* at $1350–$1500 per season; 4 *aquatic program specialists* at $1350–$1500 per season; 1 *drama program specialist* at $1350–$1500 per season; 1 *naturalist* at $1500–$1800 per season; *leaders-in-training director* at $1500–$1800 per season.

Benefits Preemployment training, on-site room and board at no charge, laundry facilities, health insurance.

Contact Paul Kamin, Camp Director, Camp Jewell YMCA, Department SJ, Prock Hill Road, Colebrook, Connecticut 06021; 203-379-2782, Fax 203-379-2782. Application deadline: June 1.

From the Employer *Our two-week resident camp provides opportunities for both campers and staff to grow. There are 2 counselors and 8 campers in each of our winterized cabins. We recruit nationally and internationally so that you will work with high-quality, committed peers.*

CAMP WASHINGTON
190 Kenyon Road
Lakeside, Connecticut 06758

General Information Residential coeducational camp serving a diverse population of 125 campers weekly. Established in 1917. Operated by Episcopal Diocese of Connecticut. Affiliated with Connecticut Camping Association, American Camping Association, International

Association for Conference Center Administrators. 300-acre facility located 50 miles west of Hartford. Features: new conference center; winterized heated cabins; rural location; 300 acres of woodlands and trails; Adirondack shelter for backcountry camping; private swimming and canoeing pond.

Profile of Summer Employees   Total number: 50; average age: 21; 50% male, 50% female, 15% minorities, 50% high school students, 50% college students, 20% international, 50% local residents. Nonsmokers preferred.

Employment Information   Openings are from June 15 to August 25. Jobs available: 6 *waterfront staff members* with WSI certification and lifeguard training at $1000–$1500 per season; 16 *general counselors* with experience working with children at $800–$1300 per season; 8 *program coordinators* with ability to teach a specific activity at $1000–$1500 per season; 1 *nurse* with RN license at $1500–$3000 per season; 2 *head counselors* at $1500–$1900 per season. International students encouraged to apply.

Benefits   Preemployment training, formal ongoing training, on-site room and board, laundry facilities, travel reimbursement.

Contact   Elia Vecchitto, Camp Director, Camp Washington, Department SJ, 190 Kenyon Road, Lakeside, Connecticut 06758; 203-567-9623, Fax 203-567-3037. Application deadline: March 1.

From the Employer   *There is a seven-day intensive staff orientation prior to opening, including cultural sensitivity training. All staff members are certified in CPR and standard first aid. We offer a collegial working atmosphere with nonconventional, alternative programming and weekly Eucharists. There are 2 staff members, 1 counselor-in-training, and 14 campers to a cabin. The staff and camper population is very diverse, and there is a high rate of return for both staff and campers.*

CAMP YANKEE TRAILS
Plains Road
Stafford Springs, Connecticut 06076

General Information   Residential camp serving girls ages 6–16 in traditional and specialized one- and two-week programs and weekend programs, accommodating 150 girls in six units of tents or shelters. Established in 1959. Owned by Connecticut Yankee Girl Scout Council, Inc. Affiliated with American Camping Association, Girl Scouts of the United States of America. 362-acre facility located 20 miles east of Hartford. Features: 6-acre lake with swimming and boating facilities; wooded area; hiking trails; variety of ecosystems for study and exploration.

Profile of Summer Employees   Total number: 20; average age: 21; 5% male, 95% female, 10% minorities, 5% high school students, 70% college students, 10% international, 60% local residents. Nonsmokers preferred.

Employment Information   Openings are from June 25 to August 12. Jobs available: 4 *swimming instructors* with basic lifeguard training and small craft instructor, first aid, CPR, and BLS certification at $1400–$1700 per season; 6 *counselors/unit leaders* at $1050–$1300 per season; 2 *activity specialists* at $1300–$1450 per season; 1 *health services supervisor* at $1700–$1800 per season; 1 *assistant camp director* at $3000–$3500 per season; *waterfront director* at $1900–$2200 per season.

Benefits   Preemployment training, on-site room and board at no charge, laundry facilities, health insurance, opportunity to learn management, leadership, teaching, and/or programming skills.

Contact   Alythea McKinney, Program Specialist, Camp Yankee Trails, Department SJ,

Connecticut Yankee Girl Scout Council, 1577 New Britain Avenue, Farmington, Connecticut 06032; 203-677-2667, Fax 203-678-8787. Application deadline: March 31.

From the Employer *Our staff orientation week is filled with opportunities for individual and group development. Sessions on outdoor cooking, safety, communication in a group setting, effective supervision, and recognizing signs of child abuse are included. If you are looking for a camp where other staff members support you and encourage you to share your talents, where you are important in creating a special place in campers' lives, we invite you to find out more about Camp Yankee Trails.*

CHANNEL 3 COUNTRY CAMP
73 Times Farm Road
Andover, Connecticut 06232

General Information Residential camp serving 480 boys and girls each season. Enrollment is open, but preference is given to underprivileged children. Established in 1910. Owned by Almada Lodge Times Farm Camp Corporation Board of Directors. Operated by WFSB-TV 3. Affiliated with American Camping Association. 335-acre facility located 20 miles east of Hartford. Features: stocked trout-fishing stream; Olympic-size swimming pool; new playfield/ground; hardwood forest and trails setting; beach volleyball.

Profile of Summer Employees Total number: 43; average age: 25; 50% male, 50% female, 35% minorities, 75% college students, 15% international, 60% local residents. Nonsmokers preferred.

Employment Information Openings are from June 20 to August 21. Jobs available: 8 *counselors* with two years of organizational camp experience and college junior or senior or status at $1000–$2000 per season; 1 *swimming director* with lifeguard training, WSI, American Red Cross BLS, and CPR certification at $1300–$2300 per season; 1 *creative crafts instructor* with child-handicraft experience and college junior or senior status at $1100–$2100 per season; 1 *environmental education instructor* with interest and experience in nature and college junior or senior status at $1100–$2100 per season; 1 *archery instructor* (minimum age 18) with archery safety course certification at $1100–$2100 per season; 1 *health-care director* (minimum age 21) with American Red Cross first aid, BLS, and CPR certification at $1800–$3000 per season; 2 *swimming instructors* (minimum age 19) with WSI and American Red Cross ALS certification (preferred) at $1100–$2100 per season; 2 *athletics instructors* at $1100–$2100 per season.

Benefits Preemployment training, on-site room and board at no charge, laundry facilities, health insurance, 48-hour period off with entire staff every 2 weeks, unique opportunity to work with underprivileged inner-city youth.

Contact Director, Channel 3 Country Camp, 73 Times Farm Road, Andover, Connecticut 06232; 203-742-CAMP. Application deadline: May 15.

From the Employer *We offer a six-day preseason training session that gives new and returning staff members unique opportunities for networking.*

LAUREL RESIDENT CAMP
175 Clubhouse Road
Lebanon, Connecticut 06247

General Information Residential camp with an informal, educational outdoor program serving 700 girls ages 6–17. Established in 1955. Owned by Connecticut Trails Girl Scout Council. Affiliated with American Camping Association, Camp Horsemanship Association, American Red Cross, National Wildlife Federation. 350-acre facility located 20 miles south of Hartford. Features: large private lake with extensive aquatic programs; horseback riding in 2 lighted rings and trails; live-in cabins and tents; farm animals and garden; high/low ropes course; modern facilities such as program center for gymnastics, cheerleading, and photography. **Profile of Summer Employees** Total number: 60; average age: 20; 5% male, 95% female, 10% minorities, 2% high school students, 50% college students, 10% international, 20% local residents. Nonsmokers preferred.

Employment Information Openings are from June 21 to August 20. Year-round positions also offered. Jobs available: 2 *experienced program directors* at $2200–$2800 per season; 1 *experienced assistant camp director* at $2200–$2800 per season; 1 *business manager* with business training and driver's license at $1200–$1500 per season; 2 *health directors* with nurse, LPN, or EMT license at $2000–$2800 per season; 2 *waterfront directors* (minimum age 21) with lifeguard, CPR, and FA certification at $1500–$1900 per season; 6 *waterfront assistants* with lifeguard, CPR, FA, or WSI certification at $1000–$1300 per season; 8 *unit leaders* with experience supervising children at $1300–$1600 per season; 24 *unit assistants* with experience camping and working with children at $1000–$1200 per season; 1 *experienced food supervisor* at $2500–$2800 per season; 2 *experienced assistant cooks* at $1600–$1900 per season; 4 *kitchen assistants* at $750–$900 per season; 1 *horseback-riding director* with ability to develop and supervise equestrian programs at $1500–$2000 per season; 5 *experienced horseback-riding staff members* at $750–$1600 per season; 1 *experienced arts and crafts director* at $1200–$1600 per season; 1 *experienced ropes-course director* at $1200–$1600 per season; 1 *experienced naturalist* at $1200–$1600 per season; 1 *experienced farm life director* at $1200–$1600 per season; 1 *experienced archery director* at $1200–$1600 per season; 1 *experienced trip leader* at $1200–$1600 per season; 2 *maintenance assistants* with ability to lift and to work outdoors at $800–$1200 per season; 2 *experienced boating instructors* at $1000–$1300 per season.

Benefits College credit, preemployment training, on-site room and board at no charge, laundry facilities, travel reimbursement, health insurance, cultural exchange, recruitment bonus.

Contact Bridget Erin Healy, Outdoor Program/Property Director, Camping Department, Laurel Resident Camp, Department SJ, 20 Washington Avenue, North Haven, Connecticut 06473; 203-239-2922. Application deadline: June 10.

NATIONAL AUDUBON SOCIETY ECOLOGY CAMPS AND WORKSHOPS

613 Riversville Road
Greenwich, Connecticut 06831

General Information Residential camp for adults. Operated by National Audubon Society. 485-acre facility located 40 miles north of New York City. Features: Lake Mead, Indian Spring Pond, and Byram River; over 8 miles of trails through deciduous woods and open meadows.

Profile of Summer Employees 50% male, 50% female, 50% college students, 50% teachers.

Employment Information Openings are from June 15 to August 15. Jobs available: *student assistant* with willingness to wash dishes at $950 per season. International students encouraged to apply.

Benefits College credit, on-site room and board at no charge, laundry facilities.

Contact Ms. Pam Limberger, Program Director, National Audubon Society Ecology Camps and Workshops, 613 Riversville Road, Greenwich, Connecticut 06831; 203-869-5272. Application deadline: March 15.

SJ RANCH, INC.
130 Sandy Beach Road
Ellington, Connecticut 06029

General Information Residential camp offering extensive riding and horse care programs for 40 girls ages 7–15. Established in 1956. Owned by Mary E. Haines. Affiliated with American Camping Association, Camp Horsemanship Association, Connecticut Camping Association. 100-acre facility located 22 miles north of Hartford. Features: 30 horses (camp-owned); tennis court; basketball court; 5-acre lake on property; 3 riding rings; riding trails and cross-country jumps.

Profile of Summer Employees Total number: 10; average age: 20; 10% male, 90% female, 10% high school students, 90% college students, 5% international, 10% local residents. Nonsmokers preferred.

Employment Information Openings are from June 25 to August 25. Jobs available: 4 *riding counselors* with one year of college completed at $800–$1000 per season; *swimming counselor* (minimum age 20) with lifeguard training and BLS/CPR certification at $1000 per season; *crafts, kitchen, general, and sports staff* at $800–$1000 per season.

Benefits College credit, preemployment training, on-site room and board at no charge, opportunity to gain experience and learn to ride.

Contact Pat Haines, Director, SJ Ranch, Inc., 74 Greenwood Street, New Britain, Connecticut 06051; 203-225-9539.

SUNRISE RESORT
Route 151, P.O. Box 415
Moodus, Connecticut 06469

General Information Summer resort catering to families and outing groups. Established in 1917. Owned by Bob Johnson. Affiliated with Middlesex Travel and Tourism Commission, Chamber of Commerce, Economic Development Commission. 140-acre facility located 20 miles southeast of Hartford. Features: 50' x 100' pool; 4 tennis courts; boating on the Salmon River; mountain biking on miles of trails; basketball and volleyball; spa.

Profile of Summer Employees Total number: 150; average age: 21; 40% male, 60% female, 5% minorities, 40% high school students, 40% college students, 5% retirees, 8% international, 75% local residents.

Employment Information Openings are from May 15 to October 15. Jobs available: 4 *lifeguards* with ALS or WSI certification at $2000–$3000 per season; 25 *waiters/waitresses* at $2000–$3500 per season; 15 *housekeeping staff members* at $2000–$3000 per season; 4 *office personnel* with typing ability at $2000–$3500 per season; *tennis instructor* at $2000–$3500 per season.

Benefits College credit, on-site room and board at $40 per week, laundry facilities, use of facilities.

Contact Jim Johnson, Director, Sunrise Resort, Department SJ, P.O. Box 415, Moodus, Connecticut 06469; 203-873-8681. Application deadline: April 1 (deadline for international students is March 1).

From the Employer *At Sunrise, we have workers from all over the country. Those interested in the hospitality industry gain a realistic experience of an independently owned business. Many workers have made lifelong friendships, which go along with hard work.*

WESTPORT COUNTRY PLAYHOUSE
25 Powers Court
Westport, Connecticut 06880
General Information   Professional summer theater producing six plays each year. Established in 1931. Owned by Playhouse Limited Partnership. Operated by Connecticut Theatre Foundation. Affiliated with Actors' Equity Association, Council of Stock Theaters. 3-acre facility located 47 miles north of New York City. Features: historic site; red barn atmosphere; 700-seat theater; near the beach; close to New York City.
Profile of Summer Employees   Total number: 50; average age: 28; 50% male, 50% female, 10% high school students, 40% college students, 50% local residents. Nonsmokers preferred.
Employment Information   Openings are from June 5 to September 10. Jobs available: 8 *technical interns* at $60 per week; 2 *administrative/press interns* at $125 per week; 6 *box office staff members* at $200 per week; 3 *production staff members* at $200–$400 per week.
Benefits   College credit, eligibility for points in the Actors' Equity Association membership candidate program, off-site shared housing at $50 per week.
Contact   Julie Monahan, General Manager, Westport Country Playhouse, Department SJ, P.O. Box 629, Westport, Connecticut 06881; 203-227-5137, Fax 203-221-7482. Application deadline: May 1.

From the Employer   *The history of the Westport Country Playhouse reads like a* Who's Who *of the American theater. This is an opportunity to work with top professionals out of New York and make contacts that can be helpful later on.*

DELAWARE

CHESAPEAKE BAY GIRL SCOUT COUNCIL
501 South College Avenue
Newark, Delaware 19713
General Information   Residential and day camps serving girls ages 6–16 during June, July, and August. Established in 1912. Owned by Chesapeake Bay Girl Scouts, Inc. Affiliated with American Camping Association, Girl Scouts of the United States of America, National Society of Fund Raising Executives. 265-acre facility located 40 miles south of Philadelphia, PA. Features: location on Chesapeake Bay; environmentally pleasant surroundings for nature study (forest, meadows, wetlands, and the beach); sailing, waterskiing, windsurfing, and canoeing; location close to Baltimore, Washington, DC, and Philadelphia; swimming pool.
Profile of Summer Employees   Total number: 40; average age: 20; 5% male, 95% female, 10% minorities, 20% high school students, 60% college students, 20% international, 20% local residents. Nonsmokers preferred.
Employment Information   Openings are from June 19 to August 16. Jobs available: 1 *assistant director* with CPR certification, first aid training, driver's license, and bachelor's degree at $1700–$2000 per season; 1 *program director* with first aid certification and bachelor's degree at $1200–$1400 per season; 1 *leadership development director* with CPR and first aid certification, driver's license, and bachelor's degree at $1200–$1400 per season; 1 *business manager* with driver's license and bachelor's degree at $1300–$1600 per season; 1 *beach/aquatics director* (minimum age 21) with WSI, first aid, CPR, and USCG Boat Pilot or American Red Cross Small Craft Instructor certifications at $1500–$1700 per season; 1 *pool director* (minimum age 21) with Maryland State Pool Operator, WSI, Red Cross

Advanced Lifesaving, first aid, and CPR certifications at $1200–$1400 per season; 1 *aquatics assistant* with certifications in advanced lifesaving or WSI, first aid, CPR, waterskiing, rowing, canoeing, and sailing at $1000–$1200 per season; 4 *experienced unit leaders* (minimum age 21) with training in Girl Scout program or camp counseling at $1200–$1400 per season; 12 *experienced assistant unit leaders* (minimum age 18) with group leader course, CIT, or LIT background at $900–$1100 per season.

Benefits Preemployment training, on-site room and board, laundry facilities, health insurance.

Contact Danette Rahn, Environmental Education Specialist, Chesapeake Bay Girl Scout Council, Department SJ, 501 South College Avenue, Newark, Delaware 19713; 302-456-7150, Fax 302-456-7188. Application deadline: June 1.

FLORIDA

ACTIONQUEST PROGRAMS
P.O. Box 5507
Sarasota, Florida 34277

General Information On-board program serving an average of 300 teenagers in twelve different three-week sessions. Intensive sailing, dive training, and other water sports emphasized. Established in 1970. Owned by James Stoll. Affiliated with American Sailing Association, American Waterskiing Association, United States Windsurfing Association, United States Sailing Association. Features: 50-foot sailing yachts.

Profile of Summer Employees Total number: 25; average age: 28; 60% male, 40% female, 50% college students, 10% international. Nonsmokers only.

Employment Information Openings are from June 15 to August 25. Jobs available: 12 *United States Coast Guard licensed sailing teachers or British Yachtmasters* at $3000 per season; 12 *diving instructors* with PADI instructor-level certification and USCG license at $2200 per season; *U.S. Sailing certified windsurfing instructors* at $1000 per season. International students encouraged to apply.

Benefits On-site room and board at no charge, travel reimbursement, all expenses paid, opportunity to travel in British Virgin Islands.

Contact Mr. James Stoll, Director, Actionquest Programs, Department SJ, P.O. Box 5507, Sarasota, Florida 34277; 813-924-2115, Fax 813-924-6075.

From the Employer *At a three-day preprogram orientation, all employees participate in workshops on safety and accident prevention, cultural sensitivity, and the facilitation of group interaction. College students with over one year of verifiable sea time in sailing yachts over thirty feet may also inquire for open positions. Those without significant experience or instructor certification need not apply.*

CAMP KEYSTONE
19215 Crescent Road
Odessa, Florida 33556

General Information Residential camp serving 150 campers per week. Established in 1945. Owned by Janice and Earl Rodda. Affiliated with American Red Cross, World Wildlife Federation, National Water Ski Association, National Wildlife Association, National Archery

Association. 90-acre facility located 20 miles north of Tampa. Features: large sports area; 30-acre lake for waterskiing and swimming; 6 miles of riding trails; 1 outdoor tennis court; 2 sand volleyball courts; miniature farm for farm and nature studies.

Profile of Summer Employees Total number: 50; average age: 22; 50% male, 50% female, 10% minorities, 10% high school students, 90% college students, 1% international. Nonsmokers only.

Employment Information Openings are from June 5 to August 15. Year-round positions also offered. Jobs available: *swimming instructors/counselors* with WSI and lifeguard certification at $600–$1200 per season; *counselors/activity instructors* (minimum age 18) at $600–$1100 per season; *nurse* with RN or LPN certification at $1500–$2000 per season; *horseback-riding instructor* at $800–$1500 per season; *waterfront director* at $1500–$2000 per season; *waterskiing instructor* at $900–$1500 per season. International students encouraged to apply.

Benefits Preemployment training, on-site room and board at no charge, laundry facilities.

Contact Janice Rodda, Co-Director, Camp Keystone, Department SJ, 19215 Crescent Road, Odessa, Florida 33556; 813-920-2921, Fax 813-920-4922. Application deadline: May 31.

From the Employer *At Camp Keystone, we offer a three-day precamp orientation where all staff members participate in workshops on safety and accident issues, cultural sensitivity, and the facilitation of group interaction. Usually, 2 employees and 8 campers share a cabin.*

CAMP THUNDERBIRD
909 East Welch Road
Apopka, Florida 32712

General Information Residential camp serving 96 developmentally disabled campers by offering a summer of fun mixed with social and independent living skills. Established in 1985. Owned by Florida Foundation for Special Children. Affiliated with American Camping Association, Florida Association for Retarded Citizens. 20-acre facility located 20 miles northwest of Orlando. Features: location on Wekiwa Springs State Park property; Florida pine and oak sandhill; swimming pool and lake; new dorms with ceiling fans/air conditioning; sports court; campfire area and amphitheater.

Profile of Summer Employees Total number: 48; average age: 25; 25% male, 75% female, 17% minorities, 50% college students, 50% international, 35% local residents. Nonsmokers preferred.

Employment Information Openings are from June 18 to August 25. Jobs available: 20 *cottage counselors* with experience working with the mentally retarded at $1100–$1200 per season; 4 *swimming pool staff members* with WSI and lifeguard certification at $1100–$1300 per season; 3 *experienced kitchen staff members*. International students encouraged to apply.

Benefits College credit, preemployment training, on-site room and board at no charge, laundry facilities.

Contact Nancy Johnson, Camp Director, Camp Thunderbird, Department SJ, 909 East Welch Road, Apopka, Florida 32712; 407-889-8088, Fax 407-889-5710. Application deadline: April 15.

From the Employer *Staff members have the opportunity to meet young people hired from seven different countries. All employees receive extensive precamp training, including CPR certification, classes on behavior management techniques for working with the developmentally disabled, and team-building activities. Camp is minutes from Orlando attractions and Florida's beaches. Camp Thunderbird offers an unforgettable summer experience of fun, rewarding work, and learning.*

CAMP UNIVERSE
Lake Miona
Wildwood, Florida 34785

General Information Residential camp for 200 active children. Established in 1958. Owned by Camp Universe, Inc. Situated on 110 acres. Features: horse trails; 3-mile freshwater lake; 20-acre athletic field; Olympic-size swimming pool; circus pavilion, including trapeze, highwire, stilts, and clown school; 4 tennis courts (2 lighted adjoining an 18-hole golf course).

Profile of Summer Employees Total number: 70; average age: 25; 50% male, 50% female, 10% minorities, 4% high school students, 60% college students, 30% international, 10% local residents, 3% teachers. Nonsmokers preferred.

Employment Information Openings are from June 11 to August 20. Jobs available: 60 *skilled counselors* with ability to teach their specialty—soccer, canoeing, arts and crafts, riflery, archery, and more; *camp nurses* with RN license or equivalent; 2 *pianists* with ability to accompany shows, as well as ability to play by ear and transpose; 2 *lead singers* with ability to play guitar well and know camp-type and rock songs by heart. All positions offered at $600–$1800 per season. International students encouraged to apply.

Benefits Formal ongoing training, on-site room and board at no charge, laundry facilities.

Contact Peggy Mermell, Director, Camp Universe, Department SJ, 5875 SW 129 Terrace, Miami, Florida 33156; 305-666-4500. Application deadline: June 1.

From the Employer *Counselors attend a five-day precamp training and orientation program. There are 10 campers and 2 counselors to a cabin, which are air conditioned and have internal plumbing.*

CORKSCREW SWAMP SANCTUARY
375 Sanctuary Road
Naples, Florida 33964

General Information National Audubon Society sanctuary encompassing 10,560 acres of Florida wilderness. Management goals are preservation of natural ecosystem and public education through extensive visitor programs. Established in 1954. Owned by National Audubon Society. 10,560-acre facility located 15 miles northeast of Naples. Features: North America's largest nesting colony of endangered wood storks; 2-mile boardwalk trail for visitors; visitor center with interpretive displays and gift shop; largest remaining stand of ancient subtropical bald cypress forest in the world.

Profile of Summer Employees Total number: 2; average age: 20; 50% male, 50% female, 100% college students. Nonsmokers preferred.

Employment Information Openings are from May 15 to August 15. Year-round positions also offered. Jobs available: 2 *seasonal naturalists* at $100 per week.

Benefits Formal ongoing training, on-site room and board at no charge, laundry facilities, $50 uniform allowance.

Contact Joel Rhymer, Assistant Manager, Corkscrew Swamp Sanctuary, Department SJ, Route 6, Box 1875-A, Naples, Florida 33964; 813-657-3771, Fax 813-657-6869. Application deadline: March 15.

From the Employer *The seasonal naturalist position offers professional training and on-the-job experience in one of the country's most spectacular natural areas. Seasonal naturalists serve as additions to the sanctuary staff, providing visitor services, environmental education and interpretation, and resource management as needed.*

NICK BOLLETTIERI TENNIS CAMP AT BRADENTON, FLORIDA

5500 34th Street West
Bradenton, Florida 34210

General Information   A nine-month residential academy serving 300 students from 32 different countries with a program that emphasizes tennis techniques, physical conditioning, and mental efficiency. Also, weekly and summer camp sessions held year-round and during the summer months, respectively. Established in 1978. Owned by International Management Group. Affiliated with United States Tennis Association, United States Professional Tennis Association, David Leadbetter Golf. 23-acre facility located 5 miles north of Sarasota. Features: 75 tennis courts (all surfaces); 2 swimming pools; fully equipped gymnasium and sports medicine center; large sports fields (multiple sports); large recreation centers; high-tech room.

Profile of Summer Employees   Total number: 100; average age: 25; 80% male, 20% female, 70% minorities, 5% high school students, 95% college students, 35% international, 35% local residents. Nonsmokers only.

Employment Information   Openings are from June 15 to August 15. Year-round positions also offered. Jobs available: 40 *tennis instructors* at $200–$300 per week; 14 *night workers* at $150–$250 per week; 1 *lifeguard* at $150–$200 per week; 4 *bus drivers* at $6–$9 per hour; 25 *tennis coaches* at $200–$300 per week; 5 *administrative/clerical staff members* at $5–$6.50 per hour. International students encouraged to apply.

Benefits   College credit, preemployment training, formal ongoing training, on-site room and board at no charge, laundry facilities, travel reimbursement.

Contact   Tennis Department Coordinator, Nick Bollettieri Tennis Camp at Bradenton, Florida, Department SJ, 5500 34th Street West, Bradenton, Florida 34210; 813-755-1000, Fax 813-798-0198. Application deadline: May 10.

From the Employer   *The Nick Bollettieri Tennis Academy is the largest, most sophisticated tennis teaching operation in the world, with summer camps available for adults and juniors in the United States (10–15 locations) and worldwide (7–10 locations). In addition, we operate a fully accredited tennis college offering a two-year degree. By way of these associations, there are a wide variety of employment, work/play, and internship possibilities available in several different fields and locations for full-time and summer work.*

SABIN-MULLOY-GARRISON TENNIS CAMP

11550 Lastchance Road
Clermont, Florida 34711

General Information   Residential camp for boys and girls who have an interest in competitive tennis. Established in 1961. Owned by Dickey W. Garrison. 5-acre facility located 40 miles west of Orlando. Features: lake for water sports; 4 clay tennis courts and 1 hard surface tennis court; area attractions to visit in Orlando vicinity; tournaments outside camp program.

Profile of Summer Employees   Total number: 4; average age: 20; 50% male, 50% female, 25% minorities, 75% college students, 25% international, 25% local residents. Nonsmokers only.

Employment Information   Openings are from June 20 to August 10. Jobs available: *cook; tennis instructors.* All positions offered at $700–$800 per season. International students encouraged to apply.

Benefits   On-site room and board at no charge.

Contact   Dickey W. Garrison, Owner, Sabin-Mulloy-Garrison Tennis Camp, 11550 Lastchance

Road, Clermont, Florida 34711; 904-394-3543, Fax 904-394-3543. Application deadline: March 31.

From the Employer *Our camp is unique in that it is operated from a home with a maximum of 24 campers. This offers a close family atmosphere where we get to know each camper as an individual.*

SEACAMP, INC.
Big Pine Key, Florida 33043
General Information Nonprofit residential marine science/scuba facility for teenagers with an international staff and clientele. Established in 1966. Owned by Seacamp Association, Inc. Affiliated with American Camping Association, Association of Independent Camps. 10-acre facility located 130 miles southwest of Miami. Features: private deepwater harbor and fleet of program vessels; full lab facilities; 5,000-gallon saltwater filtration system; location bordering on the Coupon Bight Aquatic Preserve; proximity (7 miles) to Looe Key Marine Sanctuary (coral reef tract); access to both the Atlantic Ocean and the Gulf of Mexico.
Profile of Summer Employees Total number: 60; average age: 21; 50% male, 50% female, 10% minorities, 40% college students, 5% retirees, 15% international.
Employment Information Openings are from May 31 to August 26. Jobs available: 20 *cabin counselors* with scuba certification and one year of college completed; 15 *science instructors* with college degree in biology and scuba certification; 6 *scuba instructors* (minimum age 21) with scuba instructor certification (PADI, NAUI, etc.); 1 *arts and crafts director* (minimum age 21); *dining hall manager* with one year of college completed and strong organizational abilities; *administrative positions.*
Benefits College credit, preemployment training, formal ongoing training, on-site room and board at no charge, health insurance, use of staff boats during time off, scuba available during time off, Florida Keys at your door.
Contact Grace Upshaw, Director, Seacamp, Inc., Department SJ, Seacamp Route 3, Box 170, Big Pine Key, Florida 33043; 305-872-2331, Fax 305-872-2555. Application deadline: April 15.

GEORGIA

CAMP BARNEY MEDINTZ
Route 3, Box 3828
Cleveland, Georgia 30528
General Information Residential camp serving 650 campers ages 7–16 during two 4-week sessions. Camp also offers Wonder Weeks, serving second and third graders during two 2-week sessions, and Chalutzim, serving children ages 9–16 with special needs during a four-week session. Established in 1963. Owned by Atlanta Jewish Community Center. Affiliated with Atlanta Jewish Federation/Jewish Community Centers Association, The United Way, American Camping Association. 500-acre facility located 80 miles north of Atlanta. Features: Olympic-size swimming pool; sports fields; tennis complex; 30-horse stable with miles of riding trails; open-air gymnasium with an indoor and outdoor stage; 2 self-contained lakes for canoeing, sailing, windsurfing, and waterskiing; view of Blue Ridge

Mountains; cultural arts facility with theater, dance, photography, videography, arts and crafts, and pottery.

Profile of Summer Employees Total number: 150; average age: 19; 50% male, 50% female, 5% minorities, 28% high school students, 66% college students, 5% international, 65% local residents.

Employment Information Openings are from June 5 to August 15. Jobs available: 40 *counselors* (minimum age 18) at $750–$1500 per season; 10 *waterfront staff members* (minimum age 18) with LGT, WSI, CPR, and first aid certification at $750–$2200 per season; 10 *nature crafts staff members* with CPR and first aid certification at $750 per season; 2 *songleaders* at $1200–$2000 per season; 8 *horseback staff members* at $750–$2000 per season; 2 *theater directors* at $1200–$1800 per season; 10 *special-needs staff members* at $1200–$1800 per season.

Benefits College credit, preemployment training, formal ongoing training, on-site room and board at no charge, laundry facilities.

Contact Mark Balser, Assistant Director, Camp Barney Medintz, Department SJ, 5342 Tilly Mill Road, Atlanta, Georgia 30338; 404-396-3250, Fax 404-698-2055. Application deadline: March 1.

From the Employer *Staff from throughout the United States receive precamp orientation. Camp focuses on outdoor activities and Jewish culture. Staff members must be caring, creative, and talented; have respect for others and the environment; and work well with children.*

CAMP LOW
1912 Rose Dhu Road
Savannah, Georgia 31419

General Information Residential girls' camp serving 96 campers per week. Established in 1957. Operated by Girl Scout Council of Savannah. Affiliated with Girl Scouts of the United States of America, American Camping Association. 300-acre facility located 6 miles north of Savannah. Features: location on an island surrounded by salt marshes; lodge/dining hall; 4 units with platform tents or cabins; unit house; swimming pool; dock for canoeing and crabbing.

Profile of Summer Employees Total number: 20; average age: 22; 5% high school students, 90% college students, 5% international.

Employment Information Openings are from June 16 to August 10. Jobs available: *waterfront director* (minimum age 21) with WSI and lifeguard certification at $185 per week; *unit leaders* at $150–$165 per week; *assistant unit leaders* at $125 per week; *assistant camp director* at $210 per week; *business manager* at $150 per week; *certified lifeguards* at $150 per week.

Benefits College credit, preemployment training, on-site room and board at no charge, laundry facilities, health insurance.

Contact Kathy Kelley, Camp Services Director, Camp Low, Department SJ, P.O. Box 9389, Savannah, Georgia 31412; 912-236-1571, Fax 912-236-5703. Application deadline: May 31.

CAMP WOODMONT FOR BOYS AND GIRLS ON LOOKOUT MOUNTAIN
1339 Yankee Road
Cloudland, Georgia 30731
General Information Residential camp serving up to 80 boys and girls ages 6–14 for one- to two-week sessions. Established in 1981. Owned by Jane and Jim Bennett. Affiliated with American Camping Association. 160-acre facility located 28 miles south of Chattanooga, TN. Features: small family-type camp atmosphere; lake for canoeing and fishing; proximity to Cloudland Canyon State Park and other scenic areas; numerous riding trails for Western trail riding; well-built facilities, roomy cabins, and nice bathrooms.
Profile of Summer Employees Total number: 12; average age: 21; 50% male, 50% female, 100% college students. Nonsmokers only.
Employment Information Openings are from June 15 to August 15. Jobs available: 10 *counselors* with CPR/FA certification at $400–$700 per season. International students encouraged to apply.
Benefits Preemployment training, on-site room and board at no charge.
Contact Jane and Jim Bennett, Camp Directors, Camp Woodmont for Boys and Girls on Lookout Mountain, Department SJ, 2339 Welton Place, Dunwoody, Georgia 30338; 404-457-0862. Application deadline: May 1.

From the Employer *Camp Woodmont counselors have the opportunity of doing a wide range of activities since it is a very small camp. Counselors also have the opportunity to be creative, develop leadership skills, and learn the importance of being versatile while working with boys and girls from diverse backgrounds.*

HAWAII

CAMP MOKULEIA
68-729 Farrington Highway
Waialua, Hawaii 96791
General Information Residential coeducational camp serving 92 campers weekly. Established in 1947. Owned by The Episcopal Church in Hawaii. Affiliated with American Camping Association. 27-acre facility located 37 miles northwest of Honolulu. Features: Hawaii beachfront location; excellent beach and reef for exploration; mountain and beachfront hiking trails nearby; ropes course; basketball court; ocean swimming, snorkeling, and outrigger canoeing.
Profile of Summer Employees Total number: 30; average age: 21; 50% male, 50% female, 35% minorities, 17% high school students, 35% college students, 5% retirees, 3% international, 50% local residents. Nonsmokers preferred.
Employment Information Openings are from June 23 to August 14. Winter break positions also offered. Jobs available: 1 *experienced waterfront director* with WSI, lifeguard, CPR, and AFA certification at $1100 per season; 1 *sports director* with study in physical education or related field and CPR, AFA, and OLS certification at $1100 per season; 1 *arts director* with study in languages, drama, dance, arts and crafts, music, or related fields and CPR and AFA certification at $1100 per season; 14 *counselors* with camping experience and

CPR and AFA certification at $1000 per season; 7 *aides (volunteer)* with CPR and AFA certification. International students encouraged to apply.

Benefits   Formal ongoing training, on-site room and board at no charge, laundry facilities, health insurance, accident insurance, workmen's compensation insurance.

Contact   Verta Betancourt, Summer Camp Director, Camp Mokuleia, Department SJ, 68-729 Farrington Highway, Waialua, Hawaii 96791; 808-637-6241, Fax 808-637-5505. Application deadline: March 1.

From the Employer   *Camp Mokuleia, located on the scenic north shore of Oahu, offers a rewarding and challenging summer to those who qualify to become part of a dynamic staff. A five-day precamp training program prepares you for the great experience and honor of being part of a great team.*

HAWAIIAN VENTURES
Hawaii Preparatory Academy
Kamuela, Hawaii 96743-0428

General Information   Coeducational residential camp for teenagers based on two islands. Established in 1988. Owned by Hawaii Preparatory Academy and Akahi Farm. Operated by Philip Lilienthal. 55-acre facility located 2 miles from Kamuela. Features: accessibility to all beaches and adventure sites; fully equipped gymnasium; modern swimming pool; 3 large sports fields; 4 tennis courts; surrounding acres of ranch land and forest.

Profile of Summer Employees   Total number: 4; average age: 26; 50% male, 50% female. Nonsmokers preferred.

Employment Information   Openings are from July 1 to August 6. Spring break positions also offered. Jobs available: *general counselor* with WSI or lifeguard certification; *experienced general counselor.* All positions offered at $100 per month.

Benefits   On-site room and board, travel reimbursement.

Contact   Philip Lilienthal, Executive Director, Hawaiian Ventures, Department SJ, 1606 Washington Plaza, Reston, Virginia 22090; 703-471-1705, Fax 703-437-8620.

From the Employer   *Hawaiian Ventures is a teen program for people mature enough to handle paradise. Explore semi-active volcanoes, camp in mountain craters, explore the clear ocean by snorkel or scuba, learn to surf, explore the incredibly varied mountains and forests as a Hawaiian, not as a tourist. Learn astronomy on Hawaii's highest mountain with a giant telescope. Go on an ocean kayaking trip and camp on a deserted beach. Bike down from a 10,000-foot mountain at sunrise. Work in two community service projects. Form lasting relationships and guide teens.*

TENNIS: EUROPE—CALIFORNIA/HAWAII AND EUROPE
Hawaii

General Information   Program taking junior tennis players ages 14–18 to various USTA-sanctioned tournaments in California, Hawaii, and Europe. Established in 1973. Owned by Dr. Martin Vinokur. Affiliated with United States Professional Tennis Association, United States Tennis Association. Features: 3–40 tennis courts; clubhouse; restaurant; athletics facilities (features vary with location).

Profile of Summer Employees   Total number: 25; average age: 26; 50% male, 50% female, 33% college students. Nonsmokers preferred.

Employment Information   Openings are from June 22 to August 15. Jobs available: 2 *USA tennis coach-chaperones for California/Hawaii traveling team* (minimum age 21) with previous tennis teaching experience; 22 *tennis coach-chaperones for traveling team in*

Europe (minimum age 21) with previous tennis teaching experience. All positions offered at $350 per season. International students encouraged to apply.

Benefits Preemployment training, on-site room and board at no charge, travel reimbursement, free trip worth about $1200 each week, tennis clothing and equipment at preferred players' prices, access to adult tournaments.

Contact Dr. Martin Vinokur, Director, TENNIS: EUROPE—California/Hawaii and Europe, Department SJ, 146 Cold Spring Road, #13, Stamford, Connecticut 06905; 203-964-1939, Fax 203-967-9499. Application deadline: March 15.

From the Employer *TENNIS: EUROPE provides a very valuable experience for future jobs because of the tremendous amount of responsibilities assumed by employees. Leading a junior tennis team of 14 players for 3½ to 5 weeks allows employees to gain personal growth, self-confidence, and a wide variety of job-related skills from accounting to goodwill ambassador to teaching advanced juniors. TENNIS: EUROPE conducts an extensive pre-trip orientation to prepare employees for every aspect of this challenging position.*

IDAHO

HIDDEN CREEK RANCH
7600 East Blue Lake Road
Harrison, Idaho 83833

General Information Guest ranch conducting six-day programs with daily scheduled activities such as horseback riding, hayrides, barrel racing rodeo, mountain biking, pond fishing, trap shooting, archery, campfires, hiking, pontoon boat tours, and Native American skill work and activities. Established in 1992. Owned by Iris Behr and John Muir. Affiliated with Dude Ranchers' Association, Idaho Guest and Dude Ranch Association, Idaho Outfitters and Guides Association, National Wildlife Federation, American Quarter Horse Association, Arabian Horse Registry of America, American Paint Horse Association, Appaloosa Horse Club, American Morgan Horse Association. 570-acre facility located 40 miles south of Coeur d'Alene. Features: 65 riding horses and 40 mountain bikes; mountain horseback riding trails overlooking the Coeur d'Alene chain of lakes; 3-acre fishing and swimming pond; 2 hot tubs; 7,000-square foot lodge with 6 guest cabins; employee housing with large recreation room and satellite TV system; tipi village and sweat lodge.

Profile of Summer Employees Total number: 18; average age: 24; 50% male, 50% female, 85% college students, 5% local residents. Nonsmokers preferred.

Employment Information Openings are from April 1 to October 31. Jobs available: 1 *cook* with standard first aid/CPR certification at $700–$1000 per month; 1 *assistant cook* with standard first aid/CPR certification at $500–$700 per month; 4 *wranglers* with standard first aid/CPR certification and horse background at $500–$700 per month; 2 *children's counselors/ wranglers* with standard first aid/CPR certification and horse background at $500–$700 per month; 5 *housekeepers/waiters/waitresses* with standard first aid/CPR certification at $400–$500 per month; 2 *maintenance personnel/waiters/waitresses* with standard first aid/CPR certification (some horse experience helpful) at $500–$700 per month; 1 *kitchen assistant* (prep/dishwasher) with standard first aid/CPR certification at $400–$500 per month; 1 *groundskeeper/waiter/waitress* with standard first aid/CPR certification and interest in organic gardening and biological controls at $500–$700 per month.

Benefits College credit, on-site room and board at no charge, laundry facilities, participation with guests in activities and meals, use of guest facilities on days off, share of gratuity pool and bonus at end of employment term.

Contact   Iris Behr, Owner, Hidden Creek Ranch, Department SJ, 7600 East Blue Lake Road, Harrison, Idaho 83833; 208-689-3209, Fax 208-689-9115. Application deadline: April 31.

From the Employer   *At Hidden Creek Ranch our employees have the opportunity to get back to nature. We offer our guests a vacation with a family atmosphere in a true wilderness setting. Whether the employee has dreams of living the "life of a cowboy," practicing organic gardening and environmental stewardship, or learning survival and Native American skills, we all work at Hidden Creek Ranch for a vision to reconnect ourselves and our guests with Mother Earth.*

REDFISH LAKE LODGE
Box 9
Stanley, Idaho 83278
General Information   Family-oriented rustic lodge on a lake in the Sawtooth Mountains. Established in 1929. Affiliated with National Restaurant Association, National Federation of Independent Businesses, Stanley and Sawtooth Chambers of Commerce. 20-acre facility located 160 miles northeast of Boise. Features: location on Redfish Lake; proximity to Sawtooth Mountains for hiking and camping; Salmon River fishing and rafting; white sand beaches.

Profile of Summer Employees   Total number: 50; average age: 21; 50% male, 50% female, 1% minorities, 1% high school students, 98% college students, 1% retirees, 50% local residents.

Employment Information   Openings are from May 1 to October 5. Jobs available: 6 *cooks* with one year of restaurant line experience at $650–$800 per month; 7 *waitresses/waiters* at $570 per month; 4 *buspersons* at $570 per month; 3 *dishwashers* at $570 per month; 8 *housekeepers* at $570 per month; 3 *service station personnel* at $570 per month; 5 *marina personnel* at $570 per month; 1 *bartender* at $570 per month; 4 *store personnel* at $570 per month; 2 *front-desk personnel* at $570 per month; 3 *maintenance personnel* at $570 per month.

Benefits   College credit, on-site room and board at no charge, laundry facilities, cash bonus for work through Labor Day, flexible scheduling, use of boats.

Contact   Jack See, Manager, Redfish Lake Lodge, Department SJ, Box 9, Stanley, Idaho 83278; 208-774-3536. Application deadline: May 15.

ILLINOIS

CAMP CEDAR POINT
Route 1, Box 377
Makanda, Illinois 62958
General Information   Girl Scout residential camp serving 150 girls weekly for both Girl Scouts and nonmembers ages 6–17. Established in 1953. Owned by U.S. Department of Interior: Crab Orchard National Wildlife Refuge. Operated by Shagbark Girl Scout Council. Affiliated with American Camping Association. 250-acre facility located 110 miles south of

St. Louis, Missouri. Features: located in Crab Orchard National Wildlife Refuge; extensive freshwater lake for swimming and boating; rolling hills, woods, and open meadows; 8 living units of platform tents and hogans; 12 miles from a university community.

Profile of Summer Employees Total number: 40; average age: 21; 5% male, 95% female, 10% minorities, 90% college students, 5% international, 40% local residents. Nonsmokers only.

Employment Information Openings are from June 5 to August 6. Jobs available: 1 *experienced program coordinator* at $175–$200 per week; 1 *waterfront director* (minimum age 21) with WSI and lifeguarding certification at $175–$200 per week; 1 *assistant waterfront person* (minimum age 21) with WSI and lifeguarding certification at $160–$175 per week; 5 *waterfront instructors* (minimum age 18) with lifeguarding and WSI certification (preferred) at $140–$150 per week; 1 *sailing instructor* (minimum age 18) with sailing, lifeguarding, and WSI certification (preferred) at $140–$160 per week; 8 *unit leaders/counselors* (minimum age 21), *experience preferred,* at $150–$165 per week; 15 *assistant unit leaders/counselors* (minimum age 18) at $135–$145 per week; 1 *environmentalist* (minimum age 18), *experience preferred,* at $135–$155 per week; 1 *arts/crafts instructor* (minimum age 18), *experience preferred,* at $135–$155 per week; 1 *nurse* with RN license at $175–$200 per week.

Benefits College credit, on-site room and board at no charge, laundry facilities, health insurance, preemployment training including certification in American Red Cross community first aid/CPR and Project Wild instruction.

Contact Janet Ridenour, Camp Director, Shagbark Girl Scout Council, Camp Cedar Point, Department SJ, P.O. Box 549, Herrin, Illinois 62948; 618-942-3164, Fax 618-942-7153. Application deadline: May 1.

From the Employer *Staff members live in platform tents (or hogans) with 4 counselors to a tent. Campers live in tents and hogans nearby. Salaries are negotiable and are based on skills and experience.*

CAMP MEDILL MCCORMICK
Box 1616
Rockford, Illinois 61110

General Information Girl Scout residential camp serving ages 6–17 with six-day general sessions throughout the summer, a ten-day teenage session, and an opportunity to work with grandparents and campers for a special weekend. Established in 1939. Operated by Rock River Valley Council of Girl Scouts, Inc. Affiliated with American Camping Association, Girl Scouts of the United States of America. 400-acre facility located 80 miles west of Chicago. Features: trails in the hills and woods along riverfront; extensive wildlife; swimming pool and shower facility; canoes; teams course; platform tents; lodges.

Profile of Summer Employees Total number: 18; average age: 18.

Employment Information Openings are from June 10 to August 9. Jobs available: 6 *general counselors* at $1300–$1600 per season; 1 *health supervisor* with RN, EMT, or MD license at $1800–$2200 per season; 3 *certified lifeguards* with first aid and CPR certification at $1400–$1700 per season; *assistant cook* at $1200–$1300 per season; *photographer* at $1400–$1600 per season; *naturalist* at $1400–$1600 per season; *arts and crafts instructor* at $1400–$1600 per season.

Benefits On-site room and board at no charge, laundry facilities.

Contact Su Nichols, Camp Director, Camp Medill McCormick, Box 1616, Rockford, Illinois 61110; 815-962-5591, Fax 815-962-5658. Application deadline: April 1.

CAMP TAPAWINGO
Route 5, Box 15
Metamora, Illinois 61548
General Information   Residential camp serving 120 Girl Scouts and non-Girl Scouts per week. Established in 1957. Owned by Kickapoo Council of Girl Scouts. Affiliated with American Camping Association. 640-acre facility located 20 miles east of Peoria. Features: pool; fitness course; teams course; small lake.
Profile of Summer Employees   Total number: 25; average age: 20; 100% female, 1% minorities, 98% college students, 15% local residents. Nonsmokers preferred.
Employment Information   Openings are from June 3 to August 12. Jobs available: 1 *assistant director* (minimum age 21) at $170–$200 per week; 1 *program director* (minimum age 21) at $155–$185 per week; 1 *business manager* (minimum age 21) at $155–$185 per week; 1 *health supervisor* (minimum age 21) with RN, LPN, or EMT license at $170–$200 per week; 1 *waterfront director* (minimum age 21) with WSI certification at $155–$185 per week; 1 *lakefront director* with lifeguard certification and canoeing background at $155–$185 per week; 2 *waterfront assistants* with lifeguard certification at $133–$163 per week; 1 *teams course/campcraft instructor* (minimum age 21) at $155–$185 per week; 1 *experienced riding instructor* (minimum age 21) at $155–$185 per week; 5 *unit leaders* (minimum age 21) at $138–$168 per week; 10 *unit assistants* (minimum age 18) at $128–$158 per week; 2 *swimming instructors* (minimum age 18) with WSI certification at $600 per season. International students encouraged to apply as long as they apply through Camp America.
Benefits   Preemployment training, on-site room and board at no charge, health insurance.
Contact   Beth Stalker, Director of Program and Properties, Camp Tapawingo, Department SJ, 1103 West Lake, Peoria, Illinois 61614; 309-688-8671, Fax 309-688-7358. Application deadline: April 30.

From the Employer   *Camp Tapawingo offers many activities for staff members, such as helping girls develop positive attitudes and values through hiking, sharing, campfires, crafts, and environmental activities. Each unit has platform tents with cots and an all-weather building for shelter and other camp programs.*

CENTER FOR AMERICAN ARCHEOLOGY
P.O. Box 366
Kampsville, Illinois 62053
General Information   Archaeological field school training high school, college, and adult students in archaeological excavation, laboratory analysis, geomorphology, botany, zoology, experimental archaeology, and lithic analysis. Established in 1954. Affiliated with Society for American Archeology, Illinois Archaeological Survey, American Anthropology Association. 40-acre facility located 75 miles northwest of St. Louis, Missouri. Features: ecology hike; quaint village setting; historic building; museum; laboratories.
Profile of Summer Employees   Total number: 10; average age: 25; 50% male, 50% female, 10% minorities, 100% college students.
Employment Information   Openings are from June 1 to August 31. Jobs available: 2 *chaperones/teaching assistants;* 1 *archaeological field supervisor;* 1 *assistant field supervisor;* 2 *undergraduate teaching assistants;* 2 *graduate teaching assistants;* 1 *laboratory technician.* International students encouraged to apply.
Benefits   Preemployment training, on-site room and board, compliments academic career objectives in the sciences, social studies, and education.
Contact   Harry Murphy, Director of Education, Center for American Archeology, Depart-

ment SJ, P.O. Box 366, Kampsville, Illinois 62053; 618-653-4316, Fax 618-653-4232. Application deadline: April 1.

From the Employer *Traditionally the advantage of employment at the Center for American Archaeology is the association and involvement in nationally and internationally recognized research. The experience gained through employment is valuable for meeting future academic and employment career objectives. Students find it stimulating and rewarding to be part of a cadre of researchers.*

PEACOCK CAMP
38685 North Deep Lake Road
Lake Villa, Illinois 60046

General Information Residential camp for 36 children ages 7–17 with physical disabilities, offered every two weeks. Established in 1935. Owned by Peacock Camp. Affiliated with American Camping Association. 22-acre facility located 40 miles north of Chicago. Features: outdoor heated pool with ramp; nature trail with wheelchair fitness course; lake and pontoon boat; arts and crafts cabin; recreation pavilion; lodge.

Profile of Summer Employees Total number: 23; average age: 21; 5% high school students, 70% college students, 5% international, 5% local residents, 15% teachers. Nonsmokers preferred.

Employment Information Openings are from June 10 to August 15. Jobs available: 5 *counselors/aquatics instructors* with lifeguard experience (preferred) at $1425 per season; 1 *counselor/aquatics team leader* with WSI certification and lifeguard training at $1600 per season; 1 *counselor/arts and crafts team leader* at $1600 per season; 5 *counselors/arts and crafts instructors* at $1425 per season; 1 *counselor/recreation team leader* at $1600 per season; 5 *counselors/recreation personnel* at $1425 per season; 1 *head counselor* at $1900 per season; 1 *nurse* with RN license at $3800 per season; 2 *cooks* at $2000 per season; 1 *night attendant* at $2000 per season; 1 *maintenance person* at $1500 per season.

Benefits College credit, preemployment training, on-site room and board at no charge, laundry facilities, free certification in CPR, first aid, and lifeguard training.

Contact Dave and Peggy Bogenschutz, Camp Directors, Peacock Camp, 38685 North Deep Lake Road, Lake Villa, Illinois 60046; 708-356-5201.

SUPERCAMP
Lake Forest Academy
Lake Forest, Illinois 60045

General Information Residential program for teens that includes life skills and academic courses designed to build self-confidence and lifelong skills. Established in 1981. Owned by Bobbi DePorter. Affiliated with American Camping Association, Society of Accelerated Learning and Teaching, Oceanside Chamber of Commerce. Located 45 miles east of Chicago. Features: freshwater lake; wooded area; swimming pool; dormitory rooms; ropes course.

Profile of Summer Employees Total number: 200; average age: 22; 50% male, 50% female, 80% college students. Nonsmokers only.

Employment Information Openings are from June 20 to August 20. Jobs available: 16 *team leaders/peer counselors* at $500–$1000 per season; 7 *logistics leaders/classroom assistants* at $500–$1000 per season; 1 *licensed paramedic* at $700–$2800 per season; 1 *licensed nurse* at $1000–$4000 per season.

Benefits Preemployment training, on-site room and board at no charge, laundry facilities, internships, excellent experience for education and psychology majors.

Contact Shelby Reeder, Human Resources Coordinator, SuperCamp, Department SJ, 1725 South Hill Street, Oceanside, California 92054; 800-527-5321, Fax 619-722-3507. Application deadline: May 1.

From the Employer *SuperCamp employees develop outstanding communications and leadership skills through an extensive five-day training program, where they can meet exciting new people from across the country. Staff members support teens through powerful, life-changing experiences and become familiar with new accelerated-learning techniques. Sessions are held on beautiful college campuses in six locations across the country, including Texas, Illinois, and Massachusetts.*

WHITE PINES RANCH
3581 Pines Road
Oregon, Illinois 61061

General Information Summer camp serving children, weekend retreat serving youth groups, and outdoor education center serving schools. Established in 1964. Owned by Andee Brehm, Gig Bellos, and Sue Andrew. Affiliated with Camp Horsemanship Association. 200-acre facility located 100 miles west of Chicago. Features: true rural Western setting; 200 acres of riding trails and 90 horses; swimming pool.

Profile of Summer Employees Total number: 15; average age: 21; 40% male, 60% female, 8% minorities, 10% high school students, 40% college students, 5% international, 17% local residents, 20% teachers. Nonsmokers preferred.

Employment Information Openings are from April 1 to August 28. Year-round positions also offered. Jobs available: 6 *counselors* at $100–$120 per week; 2 *lifeguards* at $100–$120 per week; 4 *kitchen staff* at $80–$110 per week; 4 *trail guides* at $100–$120 per week.

Benefits Preemployment training, on-site room and board at no charge, laundry facilities, worker's compensation insurance.

Contact Andee Brehm, Director of Summer Camp, White Pines Ranch, Department SJ, 3581 Pines Road, Oregon, Illinois 61061-9225; 815-732-7923. Application deadline: March 1.

INDIANA

CAMP FOR CHILDREN WITH DIABETES AT HAPPY HOLLOW
RR 2, Box 382
Nashville, Indiana 47448

General Information Residential camp serving 110 inner-city diabetic and asthmatic children per week. Established in 1950. Owned by Happy Hollow Camp. Operated by United Way. Affiliated with Happy Hollow Children's Camp, Inc. 776-acre facility located 10 miles east of Columbus. Features: lake for swimming and boating; horseback riding program; athletics fields; hiking trails; farm program; ropes course.

Profile of Summer Employees Total number: 35; average age: 22; 50% male, 50% female, 20% minorities, 10% high school students, 90% college students, 2% international, 20% local residents. Nonsmokers preferred.

Employment Information Openings are from June 1 to August 1.

Benefits On-site room and board at no charge, laundry facilities, health insurance.
Contact Bernie Schrader, Director, Happy Hollow Camp, Camp for Children with Diabetes at Happy Hollow, Department SJ, RR 2, Box 382, Nashville, Indiana 47448; 812-988-4900, Fax 812-988-4900. Application deadline: April 1.

From the Employer *At Happy Hollow, there is a mix of several types of user groups, mature staff, and extensive medical coverage.*

CULVER SUMMER CAMPS
Box 138 CEF
Culver, Indiana 46511
General Information Six-week all-activity program followed by a two-week session of nine specialty camps. Established in 1902. Owned by Culver Educational Foundation. Operated by Culver Educational Foundation. Affiliated with American Camping Association, North Central Association of Colleges and Schools, Independent Schools Association of the Central States. 1,800-acre facility located 35 miles south of South Bend. Features: location on second-largest natural lake in Indiana; 15 outdoor tennis courts; indoor riding and polo arena; fully equipped gymnasium with indoor track and swimming pool; indoor ice arena for skating and hockey; new library and academic buildings.
Profile of Summer Employees Total number: 250; average age: 35; 60% male, 40% female, 5% minorities, 20% college students, 5% retirees, 1% international, 10% local residents, 64% teachers. Nonsmokers preferred.
Employment Information Openings are from June 20 to August 15. Jobs available: 4 *swimming instructors* with lifeguard and WSI certification at $1200–$1400 per season; *tennis instructors* at $1200–$1400 per season; 35 *counselors* with at least one year of college and experience working with children at $1300–$1500 per season; *soccer instructors* at $1200–$1400 per season.
Benefits Preemployment training, on-site room and board at no charge, laundry facilities, free use of golf course, tennis courts, sailboats, and other facilities, tuition reduction for employees' children.
Contact Frederick D. Lane, Director, Culver Summer Camps, Department SJ, Box 138 CEF, Culver, Indiana 46511; 800-221-2020, Fax 219-842-8462. Application deadline: December 15 (most positions are filled by February 15).

From the Employer *At a five-day precamp orientation program, employees participate in workshops on safety, accident prevention, cultural sensitivity, group dynamics, and child psychology. Senior counselors are available to guide and counsel new staff. Culver's military organization provides staff members an opportunity to learn, grow, and work in a structured leadership-oriented environment.*

DUDLEY GALLAHUE VALLEY CAMPS
Morgantown, Indiana
General Information Residential camp serving approximately 128–140 campers weekly and biweekly. Established in 1961. Owned by Hoosier Capital Girl Scouts. 800-acre facility located 45 miles south of Indianapolis. Features: beautiful wooded area; 45-acre man-made lake; location in hills of scenic Brown County.
Profile of Summer Employees Total number: 30; average age: 23; 2% male, 98% female, 5% minorities, 5% high school students, 80% college students, 10% local residents. Nonsmokers preferred.
Employment Information Openings are from June 8 to August 12. Jobs available: 1

experienced director with successful completion of Girl Scout, American Camping Association, or college camp director training course; experience in planning and implementing outdoor living experiences; ability to select, train, and supervise staff; and college degree or equivalent; 1 *experienced assistant director* with successful completion of Girl Scout, American Camping Association, or college camp director training course; experience in planning and implementing outdoor activities in camps; ability to select, train, and supervise staff; and college degree or equivalent; 1 *business manager* with business training (typing, bookkeeping, and office practice), sound judgment in purchasing supplies, and experience coordinating business activities; 1 *health supervisor* with state license or registration as a physician, physician's assistant, RN, LPN, paramedic, camp health director, or EMT; advanced first aid and/or CPR certification; emotional stability to meet emergencies; and knowledge of medicine and pesticide storage and use; 1 *experienced food supervisor* with minimum of two years of training in institutional management specializing in food service; 4 *cooks* with ability to provide records of necessary health exams required by Department of Health; 4 *experienced unit leaders* with first aid and lifesaving training, training in Girl Scout program, and management and organizational skills; 12 *experienced assistant unit leaders* with completion of group leadership, counselor-in-training, or leader-in-training course; *waterfront unit leader, canoe/sailing trip leader, smallcraft instructor* with current American Red Cross WSI, ALS, and CPR training certification; YMCA Aquatic Leader Examiner; or Boy Scouts of America National Aquatic Instructor certification; *waterfront assistant, canoe/sailing assistant* with current basic swimming instructor certification issued by the American Red Cross or equivalent from the YMCA or Boy Scouts of America; *trip unit leader* with leadership, outdoor, and program specialty training and work experience as a teacher or counselor of children; *experienced horseback unit leader* with leadership, outdoor, and program specialty training.

Benefits   College credit, preemployment training, formal ongoing training, on-site room and board at no charge, laundry facilities.

Contact   Bonnie Closey, Outdoor Program Specialist, c/o Hoosier Capital Girl Scout Council, Dudley Gallahue Valley Camps, Department SJ, 615 North Alabama Street, Room 235, Indianapolis, Indiana 46204; 317-634-8393, Fax 317-631-5440. Application deadline: June 1.

From the Employer   *All resident camp staff participate in a one-week precamp training session that usually includes first aid training and racial diversity training. Generally, staff members have a platform tent in the unit area with girls in the remainder of tents. Time off is usually from Sunday to Tuesday every two weeks in addition to some time off during the evenings.*

HOWE MILITARY SCHOOL SUMMER CAMP
P.O. Box P
Howe, Indiana 46746

General Information   Residential camp serving 96 children ages 8–16 for six weeks. Program includes academic classes for high school students in the morning and camp activities the rest of the day. Owned by Howe Military School. 50-acre facility located 45 miles east of South Bend. Features: freshwater lake; high ropes course; gymnasium; tennis court; track.

Profile of Summer Employees   Total number: 25; average age: 25; 80% male, 20% female, 5% minorities, 5% high school students, 60% college students, 10% local residents. Nonsmokers preferred.

Employment Information   Openings are from June 22 to August 7. Jobs available: 6 *cabin counselors* with one year of college completed at $1200 per season; 3 *waterfront staff* *members* with WSI and lifeguard certification at $1000–$1200 per season; 2 *math instructors* with a major in teaching at $1000–$1200 per season; 2 *English instructors* with a major in teaching at $1000–$1200 per season; 1 *licensed nurse* at $1200–$1800 per season; 2 *certified high ropes course instructors* at $1000–$1200 per season; *activities director* at $1000 per season.

Benefits Preemployment training, on-site room and board at no charge, laundry facilities.
Contact David Busch, Camp Director, Howe Military School Summer Camp, Howe Military School, Howe, Indiana 46746; 219-562-2131, Fax 219-562-3678. Application deadline: April 1.

From the Employer *Our precamp orientation covers all areas required by the American Camping Association. Staff members complete first-aid and CPR training and participate in group discussions concerning responsibilities and expectations during camp.*

IOWA

CAMP COURAGEOUS OF IOWA
RR 2, P.O. Box 557
Monticello, Iowa 52310

General Information Year-round residential and respite care facility for children and adults with disabilities. Established in 1972. Owned by Camp Courageous of Iowa. Affiliated with American Camping Association. 40-acre facility located 35 miles east of Cedar Rapids. Features: indoor swimming pool; gymnasium; 100' x 100' lodge with storm shelter; modern winterized camper cabins; high and low ropes course elements; limestone bluffs for rock climbing, rappelling, and caving.

Profile of Summer Employees Total number: 40; average age: 23; 40% male, 60% female, 3% minorities, 75% college students, 1% retirees, 10% international, 5% local residents. Nonsmokers only.

Employment Information Openings are from May 23 to August 19. Year-round positions also offered. Jobs available: 15 *camp counselors* with a sincere desire to work with people with disabilities at $450–$700 per month; 1 *canoeing specialist* with lifeguard training certification at $450–$700 per month; 1 *swimming specialist* with lifeguard training and emergency water-safety certification at $450–$700 per month; 1 *nature specialist* with experience leading nature activities and working with small farm animals at $450–$700 per month; 1 *recreation specialist* with experience with activities for people with disabilities at $450–$700 per month; 1 *fine arts specialist* with experience teaching fine arts (music, dance, and drama) for people with disabilities; 1 *crafts specialist* with experience with projects for people with disabilities at $450–$700 per month. International students encouraged to apply if they have a current J-1 visa and a sponsoring agency.

Benefits College credit, preemployment training, formal ongoing training, on-site room and board at no charge, laundry facilities, health insurance, opportunity to work with a wide variety of people with disabilities.

Contact Jeanne Muellerleile, Camp Director, Camp Courageous of Iowa, Department SJ,

P.O. Box 557, Monticello, Iowa 52310; 319-465-5916, Fax 319-465-5919. Application deadline: May 15.

From the Employer   *During the weeklong orientation, staff members receive CPR and first aid certification at no charge. A physical examination from camp doctors for all employees and medication manager certifications for activity specialists are also available at no charge. Staff members live in separate quarters from campers and rotate cabin duty. Employees work with a variety of campers who have special needs, which makes working at Camp Courageous a tremendous growing experience.*

CAMP HANTESA
RR 1
Boone, Iowa 50036

General Information   Residential and day camp serving boys and girls ages 5–18. Established in 1919. Operated by Camp Fire Boys and Girls. Affiliated with American Camping Association. 144-acre facility located 4 miles south of Boone. Features: swimming pool; river canoeing; nature exploration; sailing; horseback riding; campcraft; trips.

Profile of Summer Employees   Total number: 40; average age: 20; 30% male, 70% female, 1% minorities, 99% college students, 80% local residents. Nonsmokers preferred.

Employment Information   Openings are from June 1 to August 20. Spring break, winter break, Christmas break, year-round positions also offered. Jobs available: 20 *general counselors* with interest in children at $1000 per season; 1 *swimming instructor* with WSI certification at $1000 per season; 1 *swimming guard* with lifeguard training at $1000 per season; 6 *unit directors* with management skills at $1000 per season; 1 *arts and crafts instructor* at $1000 per season; 5 *cooks* at $1000 per season; 3 *riding instructors* with riding skills (English or Western styles) at $1000 per season.

Benefits   College credit, preemployment training, on-site room and board at no charge, laundry facilities, health insurance.

Contact   Suz Welch, Director Camp Hantesa, Camp Hantesa, Department SJ, 1450 Oriole Road, Boone, Iowa 50036; 515-432-1417, Fax 515-432-1294. Application deadline: March 31.

From the Employer   *Although many of our counselors are generalists, we hire a few specialists. We have a minimum three-week training session in which staff members learn many new skills. Staff members live in cabins with campers to establish a group for activities.*

CAMP HITAGA
5551 Hitaga Road
Walker, Iowa 52352

General Information   Residential camp serving boys and girls from kindergarten through twelfth grade. Conference center serving community groups. Established in 1931. Owned by Iowana Council of Camp Fire. Affiliated with Camp Fire Boys and Girls, American Camping Association, United Way. 240-acre facility located 20 miles north of Cedar Rapids. Features: swimming pool; 4 miles of riding trails; river bordering camp for canoeing; extensive hiking and nature trails; rustic-style dining lodge with fireplace; sleeping units with cabins, tents, covered wagons, and treehouses.

Profile of Summer Employees   Total number: 18; average age: 20; 25% male, 75% female, 100% college students, 25% local residents. Nonsmokers preferred.

Employment Information   Openings are from June 10 to August 15. Jobs available: *riding* *and waterfront staff heads* at $1000–$1250 per season; *general counselors* at $750–$1000 per season; *cook* at $1000–$1200 per season; *health aide* at $1000–$1200 per season; *assistant director* at $1200–$1500 per season. International students encouraged to apply.

Benefits On-site room and board at no charge, laundry facilities, health insurance.

Contact Deanna Samuelson, Outdoor Program Director, Camp Hitaga, Department SJ, 534 11th Street, Marion, Iowa 52302; 319-377-8323. Application deadline: April 15.

From the Employer *At a six-day precamp orientation, all employees participate in workshops on team building, risk management, activity procedures, and the facilitation of group interaction. Hitaga's program is very flexible, allowing for staff input and creativity.*

LUTHERAN LAKESIDE CAMP
RR Box 6655
Spirit Lake, Iowa 51360

General Information Residential camp for Christian education. Established in 1960. Owned by Luthern Lakeside Camp Association. Affiliated with Evangelical Lutheran Church of America. 130-acre facility located 140 miles east of Sioux Falls, South Dakota. Features: ½ mile of shoreline; boating activities; challenge course; hiking trails; swimming pool; extensive natural surroundings.

Profile of Summer Employees Total number: 30; average age: 21; 50% male, 50% female, 30% minorities, 5% high school students, 95% college students, 20% international, 50% local residents, 2% teachers. Nonsmokers preferred.

Employment Information Openings are from June 1 to August 24. Jobs available: 2 *maintenance personnel, experience preferred,* at $1325 per season; 14 *counselors, experienced preferred,* at $1325 per season; 1 *lifeguard* with first aid/CPR and lifeguard certification at $1325 per season; 1 *waterfront director, experience preferred,* with first aid/CPR and lifeguard certification at $1400 per season; 1 *canteen staff member* at $1325 per season; 1 *activities director* at $1400 per season; 1 *program director* at $1400 per season. International students encouraged to apply.

Benefits College credit, preemployment training, formal ongoing training, on-site room and board at no charge, laundry facilities.

Contact Daniel Kalh, Executive Director, Lutheran Lakeside Camp, Department SJ, 2491 170th Street; 712-336-2109. Application deadline: June 1.

From the Employer *At a two-week preprogram orientation, employees participate in workshops on safety and accident prevention, cultural awareness, the facilitation of group interaction, first aid/CPR certification, and instruction on teaching youth. Employees can participate in activities such as sailing, boating, waterskiing, archery, and craft making.*

KENTUCKY

CAMP WOODMEN OF THE WORLD
Route 2, Box 44A
Murray, Kentucky 42071

General Information Residential camp serving Woodmen of the World members ages 8–15; also a senior encampment serving adults ages 60 and over with a general camp program that provides transportation Monday and Friday. Established in 1983. Owned by

West Kentucky Woodmen of the World Youth Camp and Resort, Inc. Affiliated with American Camping Association, National Arbor Day Foundation, National Rifle Association. 13.50-acre facility located 4 miles north of Murray. Features: junior-size Olympic swimming pool; 2 tennis courts; low challenge course; high ropes course; basketball courts; 18-hole miniature golf course; NRA-approved rifle and archery ranges.

Profile of Summer Employees   Total number: 24; average age: 20; 50% male, 50% female, 2% minorities, 30% high school students, 70% college students, 2% international, 40% local residents.

Employment Information   Openings are from June 1 to August 8. Jobs available: *experienced (or certified) archery instructor* (minimum age 18)*; experienced arts and crafts instructor* (minimum age 18)*; experienced general counselors* (minimum age 18)*; rifle instructor* (minimum age 18) with experience or NRA certification; *water safety instructor/pool manager* (minimum age 18) with WSI certification. All positions offered at $600–$900 per season.

Benefits   Preemployment training, on-site room and board at no charge, laundry facilities, health insurance, lifeguard certification, Red Cross CPR and first aid certification.

Contact   Colleen Anderson, Camp Director, Camp Woodmen of the World, 401 A Maple Street, Murray, Kentucky 42071; 502-753-4382. Application deadline: May 1.

From the Employer   *There are 2–3 staff members to a cabin with 14–20 campers. Staff training is seven to nine days long to include certifications. In 1994, a family camping program was implemented so that families can share the camping experience.*

LIFE ADVENTURE CAMP
Estill County, Kentucky

General Information   Primitive wilderness camp with weekly programs that serve 32–40 campers, ages 10–18, who have either emotional or behavioral problems or who are in need of enhanced self-esteem, cooperation, and team-building skills. Established in 1976. Operated by Life Adventure Camp, Inc. Affiliated with American Camping Association, United Way. 500-acre facility located 65 miles east of Lexington. Features: 6 caves; 2 creeks; 500 acres of hiking trails; nature trail; group challenge course.

Profile of Summer Employees   Total number: 16; average age: 21; 31% male, 69% female, 6% high school students, 94% college students, 50% local residents. Nonsmokers preferred.

Employment Information   Openings are from May 9 to August 20. Jobs available: 12 *counselors* (beginning May 27) with first aid/CPR certification, one year of college or related work experience, some camping or outdoor experience, ability to live and work comfortably in a primitive outdoor setting, and some experience in a leadership role with children, preferably with children who have emotional and/or behavioral problems at $1000–$1300 per season; 1 *food director* (beginning May 9) with experience with food management and valid driver's license at $900–$1000 per season; 1 *health supervisor* (beginning May 16) with first aid/CPR certification and valid driver's license at $1200–$1400 per season. International students encouraged to apply (an in-person interview is required).

Benefits   College credit, preemployment training, formal ongoing training, on-site room and board, first aid/CPR training, free room (board not included).

Contact   Mike Knight, Program Director, Life Adventure Camp, Department SJ, 1122 Oak Hill Drive, Lexington, Kentucky 40505; 606-252-4733. Application deadline: May 1.

From the Employer   *Life Adventure Camp provides you with unique, valuable training for working with special needs children. In addition, our wilderness setting challenges you in ways that enhance your professional and personal growth.*

LOUISIANA

CAMP FIRE CAMP WI-TA-WENTIN
2126 Oak Park Boulevard
Lake Charles, Louisiana 70601
General Information Three-week day camp and two-week resident camp. Established in 1955. Owned by Camp Fire Council of Sowela. 96-acre facility located 13 miles north of Lake Charles. Features: location on Burnett's Bay; large swimming pool; screened cabins with ceiling fans; large kitchen/dining lodge.
Profile of Summer Employees Total number: 18; average age: 21; 50% male, 50% female, 5% minorities, 20% high school students, 80% college students, 85% local residents, 10% teachers. Nonsmokers preferred.
Employment Information Openings are from March 1 to May 1. Jobs available: *lifeguards* at $600–$675 per season; *general counselors* at $525–$600 per season; *canoe instructor* at $550–$625 per season; *sports director* at $550–$625 per season; *program director* at $550–$625 per season; *water safety instructor* at $700–$850 per season.
Benefits On-site room and board at no charge, laundry facilities.
Contact Betty McManus, Executive Director, Camp Fire Camp Wi-Ta-Wentin, Department SJ, 2126 Oak Park Boulevard, Lake Charles, Louisiana 70601; 318-478-6550. Application deadline: May 1.

From the Employer *All employees gain Red Cross first aid certification.*

MARYDALE RESIDENT CAMP
10317 Marydale Road
St. Francisville, Louisiana 70775
General Information Residential camp serving girls ages 8–18 with a general outdoor program and specialty programs in horseback riding and swimming. Established in 1948. Owned by Audubon Girl Scout Council. Affiliated with Girl Scouts of the United States of America, American Camping Association, Camp Horsemanship Association. 400-acre facility located 35 miles north of Baton Rouge. Features: miles of riding/hiking trails; location 2 hours from New Orleans in the heart of plantation country; Olympic-size pool; lake for canoeing; equestrian unit/barn, bunkhouse, and 2 arenas.
Profile of Summer Employees Total number: 40; average age: 20; 1% male, 99% female, 25% minorities, 5% high school students, 95% college students, 90% local residents. Nonsmokers preferred.
Employment Information Openings are from June 6 to July 23. Jobs available: 5 *unit leaders* (minimum age 21) at $800–$850 per season; 14 *counselors* (minimum age 18) at $100–$110 per week; 4 *waterfront personnel* with American Red Cross certification and WSI certification (possible nine-week contract) at $100–$125 per week; 4 *riding personnel* (minimum age 18) with CHA certification or documented experience (possible nine-week contract) at $100–$125 per week; 2 *licensed RN and EMT staff* (minimum age 21); *program director* with camp experience, preferably in Girl Scout programming, at $1000–$1200 per season; *business manager/assistant director* (minimum age 25) with nine-week contract at $1200–$1400 per season; *naturalist* at $800–$1000 per season.
Benefits College credit, preemployment training, formal ongoing training, on-site room and board at no charge, laundry facilities, health insurance, time to explore own interests.
Contact Gretchen Morgan, Program Director, Marydale Resident Camp, Department SJ,

8417 Kelwood Avenue, Baton Rouge, Louisiana 70806-4884; 800-852-8421, Fax 504-927-8402. Application deadline: May 1.

From the Employer *All staff members attend a six-day training session that includes certification programs in community first aid, Project Wild and Project Learning Tree, as well as workshops on values, self-esteem building, legal issues and liabilities in children's programming, and conflict resolution.*

MAINE

ALFORD LAKE CAMP, INC.
RR 2
Union, Maine 04862

General Information Residential facility offering a multiactivity program for 175 children ages 8–15, extensive trip programs for girls and/or boys on the Appalacian Trail and in Great Britain, and exchange programs in Mexico, Russia, and Japan. Established in 1907. Owned by the McMullan family. Affiliated with American Camping Association, Maine Youth Camping Association, American Camping Foundation Scholarship Program. 416-acre facility located 10 miles east of Camden. Features: clear, protected, 550-acre lake; location 2½ hours from Acadia National Park; proximity to rivers, mountains, forests, and fields; woods, fields, hills, and tree farm; excellent recreational and educational facilities.

Profile of Summer Employees Total number: 90; average age: 21; 2% male, 98% female. Nonsmokers only.

Employment Information Openings are from June 16 to August 16. Jobs available: 2 *swimming instructors* with WSI and American Red Cross lifeguard certification; 2 *sailing instructors* with Red Cross lifeguard training and sailing experience; 1 *nature counselor* with background in nature, environmental studies, and related fields; 1 *tennis counselor* with teaching experience; 1 *certified gymnastics instructor* with teaching experience; 1 *drama instructor* with teaching and production experience; 1 *sailboarding instructor* with sailboarding experience and ALS certification (minimum); 1 *campcraft instructor* with Maine trip-leading certification; 1 *canoeing instructor* with Red Cross canoeing (or equivalent) and ALS certification (minimum); 1 *riding instructor* with British Horse Society or Pony Club certification or equivalent; 1 *office person* with knowledge of computers and attention to detail. All positions offered at $900–$1200 per season. International students encouraged to apply.

Benefits Preemployment training, formal ongoing training, on-site room and board at no charge, laundry service, camp clothing provided on a loan basis.

Contact Sue McMullan, Director, Alford Lake Camp, Inc., Department SJ, 17 Pilot Point Road, Cape Elizabeth, Maine 04107; 207-799-3005, Fax 207-799-5004. Application deadline: May 1.

From the Employer *Alford Lake provides outstanding precamp staff training, including trip leader instruction, first aid, and learning and reacquainting with child development and living issues. Staff members come together to create a climate of respect, trust, and warmth as we contribute to the growth of our entire summer community.*

CAMP ANDROSCOGGIN
Wayne, Maine 04284

General Information Private residential camp serving 200 boys from the United States and abroad. Established in 1907. Owned by Peter Hirsch. Affiliated with American Camping Association, Maine Youth Camping Association. 125-acre facility located 50 miles northwest of Portland. Features: waterfront location with 1,900 feet of shoreline; 4 sports fields; 12 tennis courts; extensive arts and camping programs; ropes course; climbing wall; central location with easy access to coast, mountains, and state parks.

Profile of Summer Employees Total number: 80; average age: 21; 90% male, 10% female, 80% college students, 10% international, 10% local residents. Nonsmokers preferred.

Employment Information Openings are from June 20 to August 20. Jobs available: 10 *swimming instructors* with WSI certification or lifeguard training at $850–$1250 per season; 3 *sailing instructors* at $850–$1250 per season; 3 *canoeing instructors* at $850–$1250 per season; 4 *waterskiing instructors* at $850–$1250 per season; 4 *baseball instructors* at $850–$1250 per season; 4 *basketball instructors* at $850–$1250 per season; 4 *soccer instructors* at $850–$1250 per season; 10 *tennis instructors* at $850–$1250 per season; 2 *lacrosse instructors* at $850–$1250 per season; 1 *drama instructor* at $850–$1250 per season; 1 *woodworking instructor* at $850–$1250 per season; 1 *photography instructor* at $850–$1250 per season; 1 *campcraft instructor* at $850–$1250 per season; 2 *nurses* at $2000–$2500 per season; 1 *archery instructor* at $850–$1250 per season; 1 *riflery instructor* at $850–$1250 per season; 1 *windsurfing instructor* at $850–$1250 per season; 1 *radio broadcasting instructor* at $850–$1250 per season; 1 *bicycling instructor* at $850–$1250 per season; 1 *kayaking instructor* at $850–$1250 per season; 1 *animation/video instructor* at $850–$1250 per season; 1 *trip and ropes-course instructor* at $850–$1250 per season; *ceramics instructor* at $850–$1250 per season; *crafts instructor* at $850–$1250 per season. International students encouraged to apply.

Benefits College credit, preemployment training, on-site room and board at no charge, laundry facilities, travel reimbursement.

Contact Peter Hirsch, Director, Camp Androscoggin, Department SJ, 601 West Street, Harrison, New York 10528; 914-835-5800. Application deadline: May 1.

From the Employer *Our extensive program and facilities, professional staff, and close-knit camp setting offer counselors a unique opportunity to work with children and have a positive impact on their development.*

CAMP ARCADIA
Route 121
Casco, Maine 04015

General Information Residential camp for girls serving 140 campers for part of the season or seven full weeks. Established in 1916. Owned by Anne H. Fritts and Louise L. Henderson. Affiliated with American Camping Association, Audubon Society, Camp Archery Association, Maine Youth Camping Association. 365-acre facility located 35 miles northwest of Portland. Features: extensive freshwater lake frontage on Pleasant Lake with two natural sandy beaches; sunny fields and pine woods; 4 outdoor tennis courts; screened-in summer lodges; proximity to mountains and ocean; riding ring and stables at the edge of a 10-acre field with riding trails.

Profile of Summer Employees Total number: 58; average age: 21; 10% male, 90% female, 5% minorities, 75% college students, 10% international. Nonsmokers preferred.

Employment Information Openings are from June 19 to August 15. Jobs available: 3 *swimming instructors* with WSI and lifeguard training certification at $900 per season; 1

archery instructor at $900–$1100 per season; 3 *canoeing instructors* with lifeguard training certification at $900–$1500 per season; 3 *tennis instructors* with tennis team background at $900–$1500 per season; 1 *music instructor* with piano-playing and camp song leadership ability at $900–$1200 per season; 3 *sailing instructors* with lifeguard training and knowledge of racing at $900–$1300 per season; 2 *weaving instructors* with knowledge of floor, table, and hand looms at $900–$1200 per season; 2 *riding instructors* with English balance seat-riding and stable-management ability at $900–$1400 per season; 2 *arts and crafts instructors* with silk-screening, block-printing, batik, drawing, and painting experience at $900–$1200 per season; 1 *ceramics instructor* with electric kiln and potter's wheel experience at $900–$1200 per season; 2 *drama instructors* with experience in children's drama, directing, lighting, and sets at $900–$1500 per season; 3 *trip instructors* (minimum age 21) with driver's license at $900–$1500 per season; 1 *environmental (nature) instructor* at $900–$1200 per season; 2 *office workers* with 50 wpm typing and knowledge of computers at $900–$1200 per season; 1 *photography instructor* with black-and-white darkroom experience at $900–$1200 per season.

Benefits College credit, formal ongoing training, on-site room and board at no charge, laundry facilities, travel reimbursement, health insurance.

Contact Anne H. Fritts, Director, Camp Arcadia, Department SJ, Pleasantville Road, New Vernon, New Jersey 07976; 201-538-5409. Application deadline: May 1.

CAMP CEDAR
P.O. Box 240
Casco, Maine 04015-0240

General Information Residential private camp for 250 boys offering one 8-week session including athletics and other activities. Established in 1954. Owned by Henry and William Hacker. Affiliated with American Camping Association, New England Camping Association, Maine Youth Camping Association. 80-acre facility located 30 miles north of Portland. Features: beautiful Maine lake; indoor gym; 9 tennis courts; street hockey rink; climbing wall and ropes course; regulation soccer, lacrosse, and baseball fields.

Profile of Summer Employees Total number: 100; average age: 21; 80% male, 20% female, 10% minorities, 5% high school students, 80% college students, 10% international, 5% local residents. Nonsmokers preferred.

Employment Information Openings are from June 20 to August 20. Jobs available: 75 *counselors* with ability to teach an activity; 10 *swimming instructors* with WSI certification; *tennis instructors* with high school or college varsity experience; *experienced rock climbers* with background in technical rock climbing, top roping, and belaying. All positions offered at $900–$1500 per season.

Benefits College credit, preemployment training, formal ongoing training, on-site room and board at no charge, laundry facilities, travel reimbursement, health insurance.

Contact Jeff Hacker, Director, Camp Cedar, Department SJ, 1758 Beacon Street, Brookline, Massachusetts 02146; 617-277-8080, Fax 617-277-6609. There is no deadline, but positions are usually filled by the end of April.

From the Employer *The work at Camp Cedar can be hard, but it is also fun and rewarding. You can help children learn new skills and teach them how to live with one another while learning more about yourself. We provide an excellent orientation and ongoing counselor education as well as super living and activity facilities.*

CAMP KOHUT
Oxford, Maine 04270

General Information Residential camp serving 75 girls and 75 boys with traditional activities in four- or eight-week sessions. Focuses on single-gender classes within one campus facility. Established in 1907. Owned by Lisa Tripler. Affiliated with American Camping Association, Maine Youth Camping Association. 115-acre facility located 50 miles north of Portland. Features: large, beautiful, quiet 1-mile lakefront; wide-open sunny fields and shaded woods; 6 outdoor tennis courts; screened cabins and indoor plumbing; large theater and recreation halls; 2 basketball courts, 2 large sports fields, and 2 baseball diamonds; location 1 hour from ocean and 1 hour from the White Mountains.

Profile of Summer Employees Total number: 50; average age: 21; 50% male, 50% female, 1% minorities, 73% college students, 2% retirees, 25% international, 5% local residents, 25% teachers. Nonsmokers preferred.

Employment Information Openings are from June 1 to August 31. Jobs available: 35 *general staff members* (minimum age 19 or completing first year of college) at $900–$3000 per season. All applicants must have enthusiasm, friendliness, energy, and reliability. International students encouraged to apply.

Benefits College credit, preemployment training, formal ongoing training, on-site room and board at no charge, travel reimbursement, health insurance, tuition reimbursement, laundry service, competitive salaries, good food, regular time off.

Contact Lisa Tripler, Director, Camp Kohut, Department SJ, Two Tall Pine Road, Cape Elizabeth, Maine 04107; 207-767-2406, Fax 207-767-0604. Application deadline: June 1.

From the Employer *We offer a comprehensive range of waterfront and land sports activities and a dynamic arts program in a caring, fun environment. Our girls' and boys' programs are run independently with joint mealtimes and occasional all-camp events. The camper-staff ratio is approximately 3:1. All staff members have a specialty area of instruction or responsibility.*

CAMP LAUREL
Readfield, Maine 04355

General Information Camp welcoming 300 boys and girls ages 7–16 from all over the United States as well as several other countries. Established in 1949. Owned by Ron and Ann Scott. Affiliated with American Camping Association, Maine Youth Camping Association. 150-acre facility located 17 miles west of Augusta. Features: located 1 hour from Maine seacoast; 14 tennis courts; magnificent waterfront; excellent facilities; friendly family atmosphere; outstanding staff.

Profile of Summer Employees Total number: 130; average age: 23; 50% male, 50% female. Nonsmokers preferred.

Employment Information Openings are from June 21 to August 21. Jobs available: *swimming instructors; tennis instructors* with college team-playing experience; *windsurfing/ sailing instructors; waterskiing instructors; field sports instructors* (volleyball, soccer, and softball)*; dramatics instructors; horseback-riding instructor* with English-style riding experience; *arts and crafts instructor; ceramics instructor; gymnastics instructor; archery instructor; piano/music instructor; photography instructor; AM radio personality; nature instructor; nurses.* All positions offered at $1000 per season.

Benefits Preemployment training, formal ongoing training, on-site room and board at no charge, laundry facilities, travel reimbursement, excellent facilities for use during time off (when available), staff lounge and snack bar, fitness facility.

Contact   Ron P. Scott, Camp Director, Camp Laurel, Department SJ, P.O. Box 4378, Boca Raton, Florida 33429; 407-391-1579, Fax 407-391-4692.

CAMP MATOAKA FOR GIRLS
RFD 2
Oakland, Maine 04963

General Information   Residential camp serving 200 girls with a variety of activities. Established in 1951. Owned by Mike, Paula, and Sue Nathanson. Affiliated with American Camping Association, Maine Youth Camping Association, Private Independent Camps. 150-acre facility located 9 miles west of Waterville. Features: 1½ miles of shore frontage with 4 water-ski boats; largest recreation hall in New England; gym and dance complex; island on lake for overnight camping; 5 lighted tennis courts; 25-meter heated swimming pool with 3 water slides.

Profile of Summer Employees   Total number: 120; average age: 23; 20% male, 80% female, 3% minorities, 10% high school students, 45% college students, 2% retirees, 30% international, 10% local residents. Nonsmokers preferred.

Employment Information   Openings are from June 15 to August 17. Jobs available: 6 *swimming instructors* with WSI certification at $1100–$1300 per season; 6 *arts and crafts instructors* with a major in fine arts at $1000–$1200 per season; 2 *sewing instructors* with a major in home economics at $1200 per season; 6 *tennis instructors* with college team experience at $1000–$1400 per season; 3 *gymnastics instructors* with college team experience at $1000–$1200 per season; 6 *ski instructors* with high skill level at $1100–$1500 per season; 3 *drama/music instructors* with a major in theater/drama at $1100–$1300 per season; 4 *experienced trip instructors* at $1200–$1400 per season; 4 *land sports instructors* with a major in physical education or health/recreation at $1000–$1300 per season; 2 *ropes-course instructors* with Project Adventure or Outward Bound certification at $1500 per season; 3 *English equitation instructors* with high skill level and horsemanship certification at $1100–$1300 per season; 6 *small craft instructors* with Red Cross, CPR, and lifeguard certification at $1100–$1300 per season; 1 *pianist/accompanist* with ability to sight read at $1100 per season; 2 *dance instructors* with a major in dance/movement and aerobics instructor experience at $1100–$1200 per season; 2 *photographers* with a major in photography at $1100–$1300 per season; 7 *video/radio personnel* with a major in video/radio/communication at $1150–$1400 per season.

Benefits   College credit, preemployment training, on-site room and board at no charge, laundry facilities, travel reimbursement, camp facilities, including fitness equipment, available during free time.

Contact   Michael Nathanson, Director/Owner, Camp Matoaka for Girls, 8751 Horseshoe Lane, Boca Raton, Florida 33496; 800-MATOAKA, Fax 407-488-6386. Application deadline: May 1.

From the Employer   *We offer a ten-day precamp staff orientation that includes lectures by specialists.*

CAMP O-AT-KA, INC.
Route 114, Box 744
East Sebago, Maine 04029

General Information   Residential camp for boys ages 8–15 with traditional structured program of land and water sports and activities with a Christian background. Established in 1906. Owned by O-AT-KA, Inc. Affiliated with American Camping Association, Maine

Youth Camping Association. 75-acre facility located 30 miles west of Portland. Features: location on ½ mile of Sebago Lake shorefront; fleet of Town Class sailboats for sailing or racing; 6 outdoor tennis courts.

Profile of Summer Employees Total number: 55; average age: 30; 95% male, 5% female, 5% minorities, 36% high school students, 55% college students, 5% retirees, 7% international, 2% local residents. Nonsmokers preferred.

Employment Information Openings are from June 12 to August 13. Jobs available: 3 *swimming instructors* with lifeguard certification at $800–$1600 per season; 2 *unit group leaders* with teaching experience/certification in elementary level at $1700–$2800 per season; 1 *experienced athletics director* at $1400–$2200 per season; 2 *certified riflery/archery instructors* at $1000–$1600 per season; 8 *cabin counselors* (minimum age 18) with one year of college experience at $800–$1700 per season; 1 *experienced arts and crafts/woodworking instructor* at $800–$1600 per season; 1 *program director* with experience in teaching/coaching at $1600–$2500 per season; *waterfront director* with WSI certification at $1600–$2500 per season. International students encouraged to apply.

Benefits Preemployment training, on-site room and board at no charge, recognition awards and salary increases for superior performance in each unit, bonus pay for recruiting campers and other staff, bonus pay for certification in certain skills such as lifeguarding, WSI, and riflery.

Contact Director, Camp O-AT-KA, Inc., 170 Linden Street, Wellesley, Massachusetts 02181; 617-237-7574, Fax 508-533-2544. Application deadline: May 1.

From the Employer *Off-season employment is available to summer employees. Call or send resume.*

CAMP PINECLIFFE
Harrison, Maine 04040

General Information Traditional residential camp offering high-quality instruction at all levels. Established in 1917. Owned by Susan Lifter. Affiliated with American Camping Association, Maine Youth Camping Association. 150-acre facility located 40 miles northwest of Portland. Features: access to the ocean (1 hour) and the White Mountains (under 1 hour); extensive freshwater lake; wooded environment with shaded paths; 6 lighted clay tennis courts for night play; open fields; large buildings for indoor activities in inclement weather.

Profile of Summer Employees Total number: 75; average age: 21; 20% male, 80% female, 10% minorities, 95% college students, 25% international, 15% local residents. Nonsmokers only.

Employment Information Openings are from June 15 to August 20. Jobs available: 5 *swimming instructors* with WSI certification at $800–$1500 per season; 5 *waterskiing instructors* with lifesaving certification at $800–$1500 per season; 3 *boating/sailing instructors* with Red Cross lifesaving certification at $800–$1500 per season; 1 *experienced drama instructor* at $1000 per season; 1 *dance instructor* at $800–$1200 per season; 1 *music instructor* with ability to play piano by ear at $1200–$1500 per season; 2 *arts and crafts instructors* at $800–$1200 per season; 1 *silversmithing instructor* at $1000–$1500 per season; 1 *ceramics instructor* at $800–$1100 per season; 4 *tennis instructors* with high school or college team experience at $1000–$2000 per season; 1 *riding instructor* with Pony Club experience at $800–$1000 per season; 3 *land sports instructors* at $800–$1000 per season; 1 *archery instructor* at $1000–$1200 per season; 1 *gymnastics instructor* at $1000–$1200 per season. International students encouraged to apply (must apply through Camp America).

Benefits College credit, preemployment training, on-site room and board at no charge, laundry facilities, travel reimbursement.

Contact Susan R. Lifter, Director, Camp Pinecliffe, Department SJ, 277 South Cassingham Road, Bexley, Ohio 43209; 614-236-5698, Fax 614-235-CAMP. Application deadline: May 1.

From the Employer *Camp Pinecliffe's staff members attend a six-day precamp orientation where all employees participate in workshops on safety and accident prevention, as well as facilitation of group interaction. Generally, 2 staff members and 8 campers share a cabin. We offer excellent training for students considering teaching for their life work, in addition to good solid practice for teachers who are already committed. We welcome applicants seeking camp experience for all ages. Approximately one-third of our staff comes from places such as England, Australia, and New Zealand.*

CAMP PONDICHERRY
RR 2, Box 588
Bridgton, Maine 04009

General Information Residential camp serving girls ages 7–17. Established in 1970. Owned by Kennebec Girl Scout Council, Inc. Affiliated with Girl Scouts of the United States of America, American Camping Association, Maine Youth Camping Association. 700-acre facility located 40 miles northwest of Portland. Features: located in the foothills of the White Mountains; miles of hiking trails; beautiful lake for swimming and boating; modern dining hall; shaded camp sites and platform tents with wooden roofs; unsurpassed views of woods, lake, and mountains.

Profile of Summer Employees Total number: 40; average age: 22; 1% male, 99% female, 1% high school students, 97% college students, 25% international, 50% local residents. Nonsmokers preferred.

Employment Information Openings are from June 26 to August 20. Jobs available: *health supervisor* with RN, LPN, or EMT licensed at $240 per week; *waterfront director* with certification in first aid, CPR, lifesaving training, and Red Cross WSI at $230 per week; *waterfront assistants* with lifeguard certification at $120 per week; *small craft instructor* with lifeguard training and canoeing instructor certification at $150 per week; *assistant camp director* at $240 per week; *office assistant* at $165 per week; *nature consultant* at $165 per week; *arts and crafts consultant* at $165 per week; *counselor-in-training director* at $165 per week; *unit leader* at $165 per week; *assistant unit leaders* at $110 per week; *Junior Maine Guide leader* at $165 per week; *kitchen helper* at $85 per week; *handy person* at $140 per week; *pack-out person* at $95 per week. International students encouraged to apply through BUNAC or CCUSA only.

Benefits College credit, preemployment training, on-site room and board at no charge, laundry facilities, travel reimbursement, health insurance.

Contact Jean M. Schroeder, Program Manager, Kennebec Girl Scout Council, Inc., Camp Pondicherry, Department SJ, P.O. Box 9421, South Portland, Maine 04116-9421; 207-772-1177, Fax 207-874-2646. No application deadline, but most positions are filled by April 1.

From the Employer *All staff members participate in a five-day precamp training that provides workshops on team building and communication; age characteristics and age-appropriate activities; first aid, emergency procedures, and crisis planning; campcraft skills; contemporary issues; and an overview of the Girl Scout program. Camp Pondicherry has a diverse staff with at least 25 percent international staff members. Most camp staff live in tents with 4–5 staff members per unit. Administrative staff live in an old farmhouse.*

CAMP RUNOIA
RR 1, Box 775, Point Road
Belgrade Lakes, Maine 04918

General Information Residential girls' camp with traditional activities serving 75 campers. Established in 1907. Owned by Philip J. and Elizabeth N. Cobb. Affiliated with American Camping Association, Maine Youth Camping Association. 60-acre facility located 83 miles north of Portland. Features: extensive waterfront area and activities; location in central Maine Lakes area; proximity to Maine coast and mountains; excellent English riding program; canoe and mountain trips.

Profile of Summer Employees Total number: 30; average age: 25; 5% male, 95% female, 10% high school students, 45% college students, 5% retirees, 15% international, 10% local residents, 15% teachers.

Employment Information Openings are from June 15 to August 15. Jobs available: 5 *waterfront-trip instructors* with WSI certification and lifeguard, basic sailing, canoeing, and campcraft skills at $1000–$1500 per season; 1 *arts and crafts instructor* with diverse and creative program ideas and organizational skills at $1000–$1500 per season; 1 *tennis instructor* with ability to develop a program that includes instruction, competition, and fun challenges at $1000–$1500 per season; *riflery instructor* with NRA certification at $1000–$1500 per season; *experienced archery instructor* (certification required) at $1000–$1500 per season; *riding instructor* (English technique) with equestrian background at $1000–$1500 per season; *assistant riding instructor* at $900–$1200 per season. International students encouraged to apply.

Benefits College credit, preemployment training, formal ongoing training, on-site room and board at no charge, laundry facilities.

Contact Ms. Pamela Cobb, Director, Camp Runoia, Department SJ, 56 Jackson Street, Cambridge, Massachusetts 02140; 617-547-4676, Fax 617-547-4676. Application deadline: March 1.

From the Employer *At Camp Runoia, we offer challenging and rewarding opportunities for education majors and teachers who will build lifelong skills, establish friendships, and help others grow. Our camp cultivates diverse use of skills and shared responsibilities. There is a 1:3 staff-camper ratio. Generally, 3 counselors and 8–12 campers share a cabin. We serve high-quality, nutritious food in a beautiful location with a friendly atmosphere.*

CAMP SKYLEMAR
Route 114
Naples, Maine 04055

General Information Sports-oriented seven-week program for boys ages 8–16. Established in 1949. Owned by Lee Horowitz and Herb Blumenfeld. Affiliated with American Camping Association, Maine Youth Camping Association, Private Independent Camps. 200-acre facility located 30 miles east of Portland. Features: excellent facilities including spring-fed lake; lakeside setting near White Mountains in an area with many tourist attractions; golf course on premises; 3 basketball courts (indoor and outdoor); 8 tennis courts; numerous athletics fields.

Profile of Summer Employees Total number: 40; average age: 20; 90% college students, 5% international, 5% local residents. Nonsmokers preferred.

Employment Information Openings are from June 24 to August 17. Winter break positions also offered. Jobs available: 4 *swimming instructors* with WSI certification at $1200–$1500 per season; 15 *experienced general sports counselors* at $1000–$1500 per season; 2 *experienced arts and crafts instructors* at $1000–$1200 per season; 2 *boating and skiing* *instructors* with small craft certification at $1000–$1400 per season; 3 *certified lifeguards* at $1000–$1400 per season; 1 *riflery instructor* with NRA instructor certification at $1000–$1400 per season; 2 *experienced trip counselors* at $1000–$1400 per season.

Benefits   College credit, preemployment training, formal ongoing training, on-site room and board at no charge, laundry facilities, travel reimbursement, use of all facilities, transportation to town every night, great food, excellent salary.

Contact   Lee Horowitz, Director, Camp Skylemar, Department SJ, 7900 Stevenson Road, Baltimore, Maryland 21208; 410-653-2480, Fax 410-653-1271. Application deadline: April 20.

From the Employer   *Camp Skylemar is located in a beautiful area with many camps nearby. Most of our staff return year after year, as do the campers. Typically, 2 staff members and 6 children live in a cabin. Although counselors concentrate on instruction in the area of their expertise, they have the opportunity to assist in other areas of interest is available.*

CAMP TAPAWINGO
Route 93
Sweden, Maine 04040

General Information   Residential private girls' camp offering an eight-week program. Established in 1919. Owned by Jane Lichtman. Affiliated with American Camping Association, Appalachian Mountain Club, Maine Youth Camping Association, United States Lawn Tennis Association. 200-acre facility located 50 miles northwest of Portland. Features: 22 cabins with electricity and running water; 8 tennis courts (6 Har-Tru, 2 all-weather); beautiful setting on crystal-clear lake close to the mountains with swim lanes and boating areas; soccer/field hockey and softball fields; 2 basketball courts; 2 riding rings, extensive trails, and stables.

Profile of Summer Employees   Total number: 60; average age: 25; 10% male, 90% female, 1% minorities, 80% college students, 8% international, 1% local residents, 20% teachers. Nonsmokers only.

Employment Information   Openings are from June 19 to August 19. Jobs available: 2 *art instructors* at $800 per season; 1 *stained glass instructor* at $800 per season; 1 *ceramics instructor* at $800 per season; 2 *experienced gymnastics instructors* at $800 per season; 1 *piano accompanist* with sight-reading and transposing ability at $800 per season; 5 *tennis instructors* at $800 per season; 2 *sailboard/sailing instructors* with lifeguard certification and instructor rating at $800 per season; 2 *canoe instructors* with lifeguard certification and instructor rating at $800 per season; 4 *waterskiing instructors* with lifeguard certification and instructor rating at $800 per season; 8 *swimming instructors* with WSI and lifeguard certification at $800 per season; 2 *nurses* with RN license at $2000 per season; 1 *photography instructor* with knowledge of black-and-white photography and developing at $800 per season; 6 *trip leaders* with lifeguard, first aid, and CPR certification at $800 per season; 2 *dramatics instructors* at $800 per season; 2 *ropes instructors* with first aid, CPR, and instructor certification at $800 per season.

Benefits   College credit, preemployment training, on-site room and board at no charge, laundry facilities, travel reimbursement, use of facilities during free time.

Contact Becky Schumacher, Assistant Director, Camp Tapawingo, Department SJ, P.O. Box 1353, Scarborough, Maine 04070-1353; 207-883-7052.

From the Employer *We are a residential camp with a family atmosphere where over 90 percent of our campers and many of our staff return each summer. High standards and safety are stressed in this traditional camp program. A six-day extensive training program is conducted in preparation for working with the campers. All counselors teach daily in a specific department. One female counselor shares bunk responsibilities with another counselor for 6–8 campers. Counselors have an opportunity to develop leadership, teaching, and group skills in a work setting and to develop long-lasting friendships.*

CAMP WAZIYATAH
RR 2, Box 465
Harrison, Maine 04040

General Information Traditional residential camp serving 220 campers. Established in 1922. Owned by Tom and Nancy Armstrong. Affiliated with American Camping Association, Maine Youth Camping Association. 150-acre facility located 40 miles northwest of Portland. Features: 3½-mile crystal-clear lake; old farm house with arts media theater, dance room, studio, photo lab, and video facilities; 10 tennis courts, 3 basketball courts, volleyball court, 2 soccer fields, baseball and softball fields; riding stables, ring, and trails; rifle range, archery range, fencing court, and indoor/outdoor theater; gymnasium.

Profile of Summer Employees Total number: 100; average age: 23; 55% male, 45% female, 2% minorities, 70% college students, 3% retirees, 45% international, 2% local residents, 10% teachers. Nonsmokers only.

Employment Information Openings are from June 15 to August 23. Jobs available: 6 *swimming instructors* with WSI certification; 2 *sailing instructors* with Red Cross sailing certification; 2 *windsurfing instructors* with Red Cross sailing certification; 4 *waterskiing instructors* with experience as a boat driver; 1 *certified canoe instructor;* 2 *rifle instructors* with NRA certification; 1 *certified archery instructor;* 2 *trip leaders* with CPR, first aid, and lifeguard certification; 2 *experienced baseball/softball instructors;* 3 *experienced arts and crafts instructors;* 2 *experienced theater personnel;* 1 *experienced song leader; tennis instructors; English riding instructors.* All positions offered at $900–$1200 per season.

Benefits Preemployment training, on-site room and board at no charge, laundry facilities, transportation on days off, staff lounge, lobster banquet.

Contact Tom and Nancy Armstrong, Directors, Camp Waziyatah, P.O. Box 86569, Madeira Beach, Florida 33738; 800-732-0223, Fax 813-391-7119. Application deadline: April 15.

From the Employer *At our one-week orientation, all staff members participate in activity workshops on safety and accident prevention. CPR and first aid certification are available. Also, there is a two-day training period under the direction of a professional child consultant. Group interaction is emphasized.*

CAMP WEKEELA
RFD 1, Box 275, Route 219
Canton, Maine 04221

General Information Residential traditional coeducational camp serving 240 campers with an emphasis on sports, water sports, and arts. Established in 1922. Owned by Eric and Lauren Scoblionko. Affiliated with American Camping Association, United States Lawn Tennis Association, Maine Youth Camping Association. 100-acre facility located 10 miles southeast of Lewiston. Features: magnificent property and facilities; lakeside setting at mountain base; proximity to Portland (1 hour) and Boston (3 hours); ocean and mountains nearby.

Profile of Summer Employees   Total number: 110; average age: 21; 50% male, 50% female, 85% college students, 10% international, 5% local residents. Nonsmokers only.

Employment Information   Openings are from June 15 to August 20. Jobs available: *ropes instructors* at $900–$1100 per season; *pioneering staff* at $900–$1100 per season; *tennis staff* at $900–$1500 per season; *gymnastics staff* at $900–$1400 per season; *folksingers* at $900–$1300 per season; *piano/music staff* at $900–$1300 per season; *land sports staff* at $900–$2000 per season; *creative arts staff* at $900–$1300 per season; *woodworking staff* at $1100–$1500 per season; *ceramics staff* at $900–$1100 per season; *theatrical arts staff* at $900–$1500 per season; *radio staff* at $900–$1200 per season; *video/photo staff* at $900–$1200 per season; *waterfront staff* at $900–$1600 per season; *waterskiing staff* at $900–$1500 per season.

Benefits   College credit, preemployment training, on-site room and board at no charge, laundry facilities, travel reimbursement.

Contact   Eric Scoblionko, Director, Camp Wekeela, Department SJ, 2807 C Delmar Drive, Columbus, Ohio 43209; 614-253-3177, Fax 614-253-3661. Application deadline: May 1.

From the Employer   *A strong sense of family and genuine caring pervades every aspect of the program. There are 240 campers to 120 staff members for optimal group interaction. Intercamp competitions, art festivals, trips, and three musicals round out the many options campers have available. Staff members are involved in over 800 activities throughout the summer and enjoy use of all facilities in their free time.*

CAMP WILDWOOD
Swamp Road
Bridgton, Maine 04009

General Information   Traditional boys' sports camp offering special warmth and confidence-building over an eight-week summer experience. Established in 1953. Owned by The Wildwood Corporation. Operated by Mark and Peter Meyer. Affiliated with American Camping Association. 175-acre facility located 35 miles west of Portland. Features: fully equipped gym with 3 full basketball courts; 8 outdoor lighted tennis courts; BMX track; lighted hockey rink; wonderful old lodge built in 1921; beautiful waterfront with skiing, sailing, and windsurfing; groomed baseball, soccer, and lacrosse fields.

Profile of Summer Employees   Total number: 60; average age: 20; 95% male, 5% female, 20% minorities, 90% college students, 10% international, 5% local residents. Nonsmokers preferred.

Employment Information   Openings are from June 20 to August 20. Jobs available: 10 *sports instructors* with college team experience; *certified riflery instructors; waterfront staff* with WSI or lifeguard certification; *archery instructors* with certification (we will provide); *arts and crafts staff* with experience teaching children; *waterski staff* (minimum age 21) with boat-driving experience and patience with beginners; *tripping and canoeing staff; swimming instructors* with WSI certification. All positions offered at $1000–$1500 per season.

Benefits   College credit, preemployment training, on-site room and board at no charge, laundry facilities, health insurance, every other night off beginning at 8:30 p.m., 6 days off, trips with kids every Thursday.

Contact Camp Wildwood, 838 West End Avenue, New York, New York 10025; 212-316-1419. Application deadline: June 1.

From the Employer *There is a one-week long staff orientation before camp starts. Two staff members share a cabin with 6 campers. We have a staff room with a TV and VCR for entertainment on nights off. We try to provide as much fun for the staff as we do for the campers.*

CAMP WINNEBAGO
Route 17
Kents Hill, Maine 22090
General Information Residential camp serving 140 boys for four- and eight-week sessions. Established in 1919. Owned by Philip Lilienthal. Affiliated with American Camping Association, Maine Youth Camping Association, American Independent Camps. 350-acre facility located 17 miles west of Augusta. Features: 7 Har-Tru tennis courts; 2 miles of lake frontage on 1,100-acre Echo Lake; towering pines; cabins surrounded by trees and streams; baseball and soccer fields; hockey rink; beach and regular volleyball; 6 basketball courts.
Profile of Summer Employees Total number: 65; average age: 25; 80% male, 20% female, 10% minorities, 5% high school students, 60% college students, 10% international, 15% local residents. Nonsmokers only.
Employment Information Openings are from June 19 to August 18. Jobs available: 4 *swimming instructors* with WSI or lifeguard certification; 4 *athletics instructors;* 4 *tennis instructors;* 2 *arts and crafts instructors;* 2 *theater instructors;* 2 *experienced photography instructors;* 2 *certified riflery instructors;* 2 *certified archery instructors;* 1 *piano accompanist* with knowledge of show music; 1 *newspaper instructor;* 1 *radio instructor;* 1 *videography instructor;* 3 *camping skills instructors.* All positions offered at $1000–$2000 per season.
Benefits On-site room and board at no charge, laundry facilities, travel reimbursement.
Contact Philip Lilienthal, Director, Camp Winnebago, Department SJ, 1606 Washington Plaza, Reston, Virginia 22090; 703-471-1705, Fax 703-437-8620.

From the Employer *Due to our location, Camp Winnebago is ideally suited for athletic skill development, individual activities, and overnight camping trips. Our full range of activities includes soccer, tennis, canoeing, sailing, waterskiing, archery, riflery, theater, arts and crafts, and much more. Camp Winnebago is a great place to learn new skills and form lasting relationships.*

HIDDEN VALLEY CAMP
Ireland Road
Freedom, Maine 04941
General Information Residential, international, noncompetitive camp offering two 4-week sessions to 220 campers. Established in 1947. Owned by Peter and Meg Kassen. Affiliated with American Camping Association, Maine Youth Camping Association. 200-acre facility located 85 miles east of Portland. Features: farmlike environment; fields and forest; warm atmosphere; location near Atlantic Ocean; llama herd.
Profile of Summer Employees Total number: 90; average age: 24; 40% male, 60% female, 10% minorities, 5% high school students, 40% college students, 3% retirees, 20% international, 10% local residents. Nonsmokers only.
Employment Information Openings are from June 15 to August 20. Jobs available: 3 *swimming instructors* with WSI/lifeguard certification; 3 *experienced ropes instructors;* 3 *experienced dance instructors;* 5 *experienced English riding instructors; soccer instructor;*

stained glass instructor; pottery instructor; experienced animal care person; gymnastics instructor. All positions offered at $800–$1400 per season.

Benefits   College credit, preemployment training, formal ongoing training, on-site room and board at no charge, laundry facilities, internships, vegetarian diet.

Contact   Peter and Meg Kassen, Directors/Owners, Hidden Valley Camp, Department SJ, RR 1, Box 2360, Freedom, Maine 04941; 207-342-5177, Fax 207-342-5685. Application deadline: March 31.

IDLEASE AND SHORELANDS GUEST RESORT
Route 9, P.O. Box 3086
Kennebunk, Maine 04043

General Information   Resort serving visitors to scenic Kennebunkport. Established in 1950. Owned by Sonja Haag-Ducharme. Affiliated with Kennebunk Chamber of Commerce, Maine Innkeepers Association. 4-acre facility located 2 miles west of Kennebunkport. Features: proximity to the beautiful seacoast village of Kennebunkport; great restaurants, art galleries, antique shops, marinas, craft stores, and deep-sea fishing/whale-watching boat trips; many fine sandy beaches located only minutes away; country atmosphere, swimming pool, and outdoor barbeques; bicycle trails; nature preserves; lovely historic homes, including the home of former President George Bush; boat dock and playground.

Profile of Summer Employees   Total number: 3; average age: 22; 20% male, 80% female, 30% high school students, 60% college students, 10% international, 90% local residents. Nonsmokers preferred.

Employment Information   Openings are from June 1 to October 1. Jobs available: 1 *assistant manager* with ability to perform general duties, desk work, scheduling, and supervise hourly help (must be a French-speaking college student or college teacher and be able to work from May to September) at $800–$1000 per month; 4 *housekeeping associates* with ability to stay from June to October (should be college or high school student or teacher) at $150–$200 per week.

Benefits   On-site room and board at no charge, laundry facilities.

Contact   Sonja Haag-Ducharme, Owner, Idlease and Shorelands Guest Resort, Department SJ, P.O. Box 3086, Kennebunk, Maine 04043; 207-985-4460.

From the Employer   *We stress customer service, safety, and cleanliness for all our employees. There is a one-day orientation and weekly staff meetings. Board is free with 2–3 people per room. There is a small sitting room with a refrigerator and two microwaves.*

LONGACRE EXPEDITIONS
Unity, Maine

General Information   Adventure travel program emphasizing group living skills and physical challenges. Established in 1981. Owned by Longacre Expeditions. 60-acre facility located 40 miles west of Bangor.

Profile of Summer Employees   Total number: 30; average age: 25; 50% male, 50% female, 10% minorities, 40% college students, 10% local residents. Nonsmokers only.

Employment Information   Openings are from June 1 to August 15. Jobs available: 16 *assistant trip leaders* (minimum age 21) at $150–$175 per week; 1 *rock-climbing instructor* (minimum age 21) at $360–$450 per week; 4 *support and logistics staff members* (minimum age 21) at $150–$175 per week.

Benefits   Preemployment training, on-site room and board at no charge, Pro-Deal package.

Contact Roger Smith, Longacre Expeditions, RD 3, Box 106, Newport, Pennsylvania 17074; 717-567-6790.

From the Employer *There is an eight-day precamp staff training period emphasizing hard and soft skills. Individual advancement is expected of returning staff. First-time staff usually join us as assistant trip leaders or support personnel. In the following season, most graduate to trip leader. Continued advancement leads to positions as base camp manager or course director. We have intermediate programs, including canoeing, sea kayaking, backpacking, bicycle touring, and rock climbing.*

MAINE TEEN CAMP
RR 1, Box 39
Kezar Falls, Maine 04047

General Information Residential camp for teenagers offering two sessions with 230 campers participating in each session. Established in 1983. Owned by Bob Briskin. Affiliated with American Camping Association, Maine Youth Camping Association. 50-acre facility located 35 miles northwest of Portland. Features: 2 lakes; 5 tennis courts; learning center and theater; modern lodge in a secluded setting; 2 large athletic fields.

Profile of Summer Employees Total number: 70; average age: 25; 47% male, 53% female, 10% minorities, 50% college students, 2% retirees, 30% international, 2% local residents. Nonsmokers preferred.

Employment Information Openings are from June 15 to August 23. Year-round positions also offered. Jobs available: *drum instructor* at $1000 per season; *keyboard instructor* at $1000 per season; *guitar instructor* at $1000 per season; *MIDI instructor* at $1000 per season; *tennis instructor* at $1000 per season; *swimming instructor* at $1000 per season; *jewelry-crafting instructor* at $1000 per season; *dance instructor* at $1000 per season; *theater instructor* at $1000 per season; *sailing/windsurfing instructor* at $1000 per season; *waterskiing instructor* at $1000 per season; *arts instructor* at $1000 per season; *land sports instructor* at $1000 per season; *ropes instructor* at $1000 per season; *waterfront director* at $2500 per season; *trip leaders*. All applicants must have experience and/or certification. International students encouraged to apply.

Benefits College credit, preemployment training, on-site room and board at no charge.

Contact Bob Briskin, Director, Maine Teen Camp, Department SJ, 180 Upper Gulph Road, Radnor, Pennsylvania 19087; 610-527-6759, Fax 610-520-0182. Application deadline: June 10.

From the Employer *All employees arrive at the camp for training at least ten days before the season begins.*

MED-O-LARK
Washington, Maine 04574

General Information Private, residential, and coeducational program specializing in the creative arts, with over 70 activities including sports, waterfront, theater, dance, arts, handicrafts, ropes course, and more. Established in 1972. Owned by Neal Goldberg. Affiliated with American Camping Association, Maine Youth Camping Association. 40-acre facility located 90 miles north of Portland. Features: 4 miles of lake frontage; dance studio; 4 buildings for art studios; 2 sports fields; ropes course (high and low); beautiful comprehensive theater facility.

Profile of Summer Employees Total number: 70; average age: 23; 40% male, 60% female, 50% college students, 20% international. Nonsmokers only.

Employment Information Openings are from June 16 to August 24. Jobs available: 4 *waterfront counselors* with WSI certification at $800–$1000 per season; 2 *registered nurses* at $2000 per season; *dance counselors* at $700–$900 per season; *theater staff* at $700–$900 per season; *art staff* at $700–$900 per season; *sports staff* at $700–$900 per season; *ropes course staff* at $800–$1000 per season.
Benefits Preemployment training, formal ongoing training, on-site room and board at no charge.
Contact Neal Goldberg, Director, Med-O-Lark, 334 Beacon Street, Boston, Massachusetts 02116; 617-267-3483, Fax 617-859-9740. Application deadline: April 1.

OAKLAND HOUSE
Herricks
Sargentville, Maine 04673
General Information Rural low-key family vacation resort accommodating approximately 75 guests. Established in 1889. Owned by Jim Littlefield. Affiliated with Maine Innkeepers Association, State of Maine Publicity Bureau, East Penobscot Bay Resort Association. 100-acre facility located 50 miles south of Bangor. Features: extensive lake and ocean frontage with beaches and rowboats; hiking trails; lawn games; recreation hall; hot-air balloon rides; proximity to Acadia National Park (1 hour).
Profile of Summer Employees Total number: 25; average age: 24; 25% male, 75% female, 5% minorities, 5% high school students, 60% college students, 10% retirees, 5% international, 25% local residents. Nonsmokers preferred.
Employment Information Openings are from June 17 to September 5. Jobs available: 1 *office receptionist* at $209–$249 per week; 3 *housekeepers* at $150–$400 per week; 4 *kitchen staff members* at $209–$249 per week; 2 *maintenance and grounds staff members* at $209–$264 per week; 1 *cabin service staff member* at $150–$300 per week; 5 *waiters/ waitresses* at $150–$400 per week.
Benefits Preemployment training, on-site room and board at $50 per week, laundry facilities, use of recreational facilities in beautiful rural setting, additional merit bonus when employees finish season.
Contact Mr. James Littlefield, Owner, Oakland House, Department SJ, RR 1, Box 400, Brooksville, Maine 04617; 207-359-8521. Application deadline: July 1 (most summer employees are hired by June 1).

QUISISANA RESORT
Center Lovell, Maine 04016
General Information Summer resort for families, couples, and individuals. Established in 1947. Owned by Jane Orans. 55-acre facility located 75 miles west of Portland. Features: 2 sandy beaches on lake; 3 tennis courts; hiking trails.
Profile of Summer Employees Total number: 75; average age: 21; 50% male, 50% female, 90% college students. Nonsmokers preferred.
Employment Information Openings are from June 1 to September 1. Jobs available: *waitstaff; beach staff; office staff; kitchen staff; maintenance persons; chamber staff.*
Benefits On-site room and board at no charge.
Contact Jane Orans, Owner, Quisisana Resort, P.O. Box 142, Larchmont, New York 10538;

914-833-0293. Application deadline: May 15 (applications will be considered only after March 15).

From the Employer *Quisisana offers a full American plan and musical entertainment each evening. We hire both performers and nonperformers to work at Quisisana. All of the dining room waitstaff are performers. Other positions vary, but everyone lives together in a camp-style setting. Many of our staff return year after year for a great summer experience.*

WILD GOOSE . . . FOR BOYS
Great Moose Lake
Harmony, Maine 04942
General Information Private, well-established traditional boys' camp with an international clientele. Serves 68 boys ages 8–14. Established in 1956. Owned by Lorna and William E. Trauth Jr. 1,000-acre facility located 50 miles west of Bangor. Features: location on 8-mile-long lake; first-class facilities and equipment; all major land and water sports; overnight mountain climbing and canoe trips to wilderness areas.
Profile of Summer Employees Total number: 30; average age: 25; 80% male, 20% female, 50% college students. Nonsmokers preferred.
Employment Information Openings are from June 15 to August 16. Jobs available: 10 *counselors* with interest and experience in outdoors and sports; 1 *nurse;* 2 *secretaries/word processors.*
Benefits Preemployment training, on-site room and board at no charge, laundry facilities.
Contact William E. Trauth, Jr., Director, Wild Goose . . . for Boys, Department SJ, 328 Summit Avenue, Leonia, New Jersey 07605; 201-944-6271.

From the Employer *Wild Goose offers an excellent opportunity to work with other professionals at a first-rate facility, teaching motivated youngsters from around the world. Salaries depend on applicant's qualifications.*

WYONEGONIC CAMPS
RR 1, Box 186
Denmark, Maine 04022
General Information Residential girls' camp. Established in 1902. Owned by Carol Sudduth. Affiliated with American Camping Association, Maine Youth Camping Association. 300-acre facility located 40 miles west of Portland. Features: freshwater lake; access to mountains and ocean; rustic setting; pine woods; 6 clay tennis courts; horses, barn, and trails on property.
Profile of Summer Employees Total number: 60; average age: 21; 15% male, 85% female, 5% high school students, 70% college students, 20% international, 5% local residents. Nonsmokers only.
Employment Information Openings are from June 8 to August 28. Christmas break positions also offered. Jobs available: *swimming instructor* with WSI and LGT certification at $800–$1600 per season; *sailing instructor* with LGT certification at $800–$1600 per season; *sailboarding instructor* with LGT certification at $800–$1600 per season; *waterskiing instructor* with LGT certification and boat driving experience at $800–$1600 per season; *tennis instructor* at $800–$1600 per season; *riding instructor* at $800–$1600 per season; *pottery instructor* at $800–$1600 per season; *arts and crafts instructor* at $800–$1600 per season; *canoe trips instructor/trip leader* (minimum age 21) with SFA/LGT certification at $800–$1600 per season; *hiking instructor/trip leader* (minimum age 21) with SFA/LGT certification at $800–$1600 per season; *archery instructor* with Maine State certification at

$800–$1600 per season; *riflery instructor* with NRA certification at $800–$1600 per season; *dramatics instructor* at $800–$1600 per season; *nurses* with RN license at $1800–$2000 per season; *kitchen workers* at $1000–$2000 per season. International students encouraged to apply.

Benefits College credit, preemployment training, formal ongoing training, on-site room and board at no charge, laundry facilities, travel reimbursement, certification training.

Contact Carol S. Sudduth, Director, Wyonegonic Camps, RR 1, Box 186, Denmark, Maine 04022; 207-452-2051, Fax 207-452-2611. Application deadline: May 1.

From the Employer *There is an opportunity for certification clinics before Wyonegonic's five-day preseason orientation. Campers and staff members come from 30 states, with an international clientele of 15 percent and over. The atmosphere is relaxed and noncompetitive. The challenge for staff is to offer high-quality parenting and teaching.*

MARYLAND

BETH TFILOH CAMPS
330 Pleasant Hill Road
Owings Mills, Maryland 21117

General Information Day camp serving 800–900 campers. Established in 1942. Owned by Beth Tfiloh Camps. Affiliated with American Camping Association. 50-acre facility located 15 miles northwest of Baltimore. Features: 8 athletics fields; 2 swimming pools; boating lake; ropes course; private setting; numerous indoor facilities.

Profile of Summer Employees Total number: 280; average age: 31; 40% male, 60% female, 1% minorities, 35% high school students, 40% college students, 1% retirees, 1% international, 99% local residents. Nonsmokers only.

Employment Information Openings are from June 15 to August 15. Jobs available: 10 *swimming instructors* with WSI certification at $1600–$3000 per season; 2 *boating instructors* with ARC canoe instructor and lifeguard certification at $1400–$3000 per season; 2 *experienced certified nature/outdoor education instructors* at $2000–$3000 per season; 2 *experienced ropes-course instructors* at $2000–$3000 per season.

Benefits Professional staff work with colleges that give credit for any employment or training offered.

Contact Personnel, Beth Tfiloh Camps, 3300 Old Court Road, Baltimore, Maryland 21208; 410-653-3322, Fax 410-484-1409. Application deadline: February 1.

CAMPS AIRY AND LOUISE
Maryland .

General Information Residential camps serving boys and girls. Established in 1922. Owned by Aaron and Lilie Straus Foundation. Affiliated with American Camping Association, Maryland Youth Camps. 950-acre facility located 60 miles north of Washington, DC. Features: beautiful open-air theaters; close to the Appalachian Trail and the Blue Ridge Summit; numerous athletics fields; large swimming pools; state-of-the-art health centers.

Profile of Summer Employees Total number: 285; average age: 25; 2% minorities, 95% college students, 3% retirees, 3% international, 10% local residents.

Employment Information Openings are from June 22 to August 21. Jobs available: 30

general counselors; 15 *swimming instructors* with WSI or lifeguard certification; 10 *outdoor living instructors;* 10 *music instructors;* 8 *drama instructors;* 30 *athletics instructors;* 4 *karate instructors;* 2 *riflery instructors* with NRA instructor certification (preferred); 2 *nature instructors;* 6 *arts and crafts instructors;* 3 *ceramics instructors;* 6 *dance instructors;* 4 *archery instructors* with NAA instructor certification (preferred). All positions offered at $700–$1300 per season.

Benefits Preemployment training, on-site room and board at no charge, laundry facilities, travel reimbursement, catered food service, medical staff available at each facility, one 24-hour day off and one night off from 5 p.m. to 7 a.m. per week, 2 staff members per cabin with private counselor rooms.

Contact Ed Cohen, Executive Director, Camps Airy and Louise, Department SJ, 5750 Park Heights Avenue, Baltimore, Maryland 21215; 410-466-9010, Fax 410-466-0560.

ECHO HILL CAMP
13655 Bloomingneck Road
Worton, Maryland 21678

General Information Coeducational residential camp serving 140 campers per session in two-, four-, and eight-week sessions along with a one-week postcamp sail and ski camp and Labor Day weekend family camp. Established in 1944. Owned by Peter P. Rice Jr. Affiliated with American Camping Association. 350-acre facility located 90 miles northeast of Washington, DC. Features: proximity to Chesapeake Bay; 1 mile of sandy beachfront; rustic environment; living quarters on platform tents; extensive waterfront activities; beautiful campus.

Profile of Summer Employees Total number: 45; average age: 20; 55% male, 45% female, 2% minorities, 10% high school students, 70% college students, 10% international, 2% local residents, 10% teachers.

Employment Information Jobs available: *counselors.* International students encouraged to apply.

Benefits Formal ongoing training, on-site room and board at no charge, laundry facilities.

Contact Peter Rice, Director, Echo Hill Camp, Department SJ, Echo Hill Camp, Worton, Maryland 21678; 410-348-5303, Fax 410-348-2010. Application deadline: May 31.

GEORGETOWN PREP SCHOOL SUMMER ENGLISH PROGRAM
10900 Rockville Pike
Rockville, Maryland 20852

General Information Summer English program serving 100 students with diverse international backgrounds. Established in 1989. Owned by Georgetown Prep School. Affiliated with Middle States Association of School and Colleges. 90-acre facility located 8 miles north of Washington, DC. Features: 12 outdoor tennis courts (eight indoor under bubble in winter); indoor swimming pool; 500-seat auditorium; fully equipped double gymnasium; 5 large sports fields and football stadium.

Profile of Summer Employees 60% male, 40% female, 12% minorities, 100% college students, 5% international, 15% local residents. Nonsmokers preferred.

Employment Information Openings are from June 27 to August 5. Jobs available: *teachers* at $1400–$1800 per season. International students encouraged to apply.

Benefits Formal ongoing training, on-site room and board at no charge, laundry facilities.

Contact Ms. Rosita A. Whitman, Director, Georgetown Prep School Summer English

Program, 10900 Rockville Pike, Rockville, Maryland 20852; 301-493-5000, Fax 301-493-5905. Application deadline: April 1.

JOHNS HOPKINS UNIVERSITY-CENTER FOR TALENTED YOUTH
34th and Charles Streets
Baltimore, Maryland 21218
General Information Residential and commuter camps for academically talented youth serving second through sixth graders and seventh graders through 16½-year-olds with concentration on accelerated academic courses and recreational activities. Established in 1980. Features: amenities of a modern university campus.
Profile of Summer Employees Total number: 675; 50% male, 50% female, 10% minorities, 60% college students, 10% local residents. Nonsmokers preferred.
Employment Information Openings are from June 25 to August 7. Jobs available: 6 *site directors;* 6 *academic deans and deans of residential life;* 130 *instructors* at $1500 per season; 130 *teaching/laboratory assistants* at $875 per season; 150 *resident advisers* at $875 per season; 12 *office/general assistants* at $750 per season; 6 *academics counselors.* International students encouraged to apply.
Benefits Preemployment training, on-site room and board at no charge, laundry facilities.
Contact Dr. Luciano Corazza, Director of Academic Programs, Johns Hopkins University-Center for Talented Youth, Department SJ, 3400 North Charles Street, Baltimore, Maryland 21218; 410-516-0337, Fax 410-516-0804. Application deadline: February 1.

WEST RIVER UNITED METHODIST CENTER
Chalk Point Road, P.O. Box 429
Churchton, Maryland 20733
General Information Residential camp on a mile-long waterfront near the Chesapeake Bay. Established in 1951. Owned by Baltimore-Washington Conference of the United Methodist Church. Affiliated with American Camping Association, Christian Camping International, National Camp Leaders/United Methodist. 45-acre facility located 15 miles south of Annapolis. Features: wetlands and shoreline nature study areas; swimming pool and athletics fields; comfortable lodges and retreat center; waterfront activities, including canoeing, rowing, and sailing.
Profile of Summer Employees Total number: 16; average age: 20; 40% male, 60% female, 18% minorities, 12% high school students, 62% college students, 37% local residents. Nonsmokers preferred.
Employment Information Openings are from June 7 to August 22. Year-round positions also offered. Jobs available: 3 *lifeguards* with Red Cross lifeguard training at $175–$200 per week; 1 *head lifeguard* with WSI certification at $200–$250 per week; 1 *sailing instructor* with Red Cross sailing instructor certification at $175–$225 per week; 2 *cooks* at $300–$400 per week; 4 *kitchen aides* at $130–$150 per week; 2 *maintenance personnel* at $130–$150 per week; 2 *program resource persons* with lifesaving training (preferred) at $175–$225 per week; 1 *nurse* at $250–$350 per week.
Benefits On-site room and board at no charge, laundry facilities, health insurance.
Contact Bruce A. VanDervort, Associate Council Director, West River United Methodist

Center, 5124 Greenwich Avenue, Baltimore, Maryland 21229; 410-233-7300, Fax 410-233-7308. Application deadline: January 1.

From the Employer *Our varied camping program includes general activity camps for all age levels, sailing camps, bicycle camps, fishing camps, music and arts camps, camps for senior citizens, and camps for the deaf and hard-of-hearing. Our paid staff works closely with volunteer counselors and program directors.*

YMCA CAMP LETTS
4003 Camp Letts Road, P.O. Box 208
Edgewater, Maryland 21037

General Information Residential camp serving 300 campers during four 2-week sessions. Established in 1906. Owned by YMCA of Metropolitan Washington. Affiliated with American Camping Association, Annapolis Chamber of Commerce, Young Men's Christian Association. 219-acre facility located 25 miles east of Washington, D.C. Features: location on 219-acre peninsula on Rhode River off the Chesapeake Bay; 25-meter freshwater swimming pool; large stables with 28 horses, two riding rings, and miles of wooded trails; land activities area with tennis courts, basketball courts, and large playing fields; well-developed sailing and waterskiing center with Lasers, Optimist, and Flying Scotts; ropes initiative course with high-wire bridge and zip line.

Profile of Summer Employees Total number: 100; average age: 21; 50% male, 50% female, 20% minorities, 10% high school students, 80% college students, 10% international, 5% local residents. Nonsmokers preferred.

Employment Information Openings are from May 1 to September 30. Spring break positions also offered. Jobs available: 5 *crew skippers* (minimum age 21) at $1600–$2100 per season; 30 *counselors* (minimum age 19) with first year of college completed at $1300–$1800 per season; 30 *assistant counselors* (minimum age 18) with high school diploma at $900–$1400 per season; 1 *experienced photographer/editor* with resume at $1300–$1800 per season; 1 *program director* with college upperclassman or graduate status and managerial skills at $1800–$2300 per season; 1 *horsemanship director* with college upperclassman or graduate status and Pony Club background (preferred) at $1800–$2300 per season; 1 *land activities director* with college upperclassman or graduate status, background in physical fitness, and CPR and first aid training at $1800–$2300 per season; 1 *small craft director* with college upperclassman or graduate status, WSI and AWSA certification (preferred), and lifeguarding and CPR certification at $1800–$2300 per season; 1 *sailing director* with lifeguarding and CPR certification and USYRU certification or USCG captain's license (preferred) at $1800–$2300 per season.

Benefits College credit, preemployment training, on-site room and board at no charge.

Contact Patrick Butcher, Executive Director, YMCA Camp Letts, Department SJ, P.O. Box 208, Edgewater, Maryland 21037; 301-261-4286, Fax 301-261-7336.

From the Employer *Precamp training is available in sailing, lifeguarding, first aid, CPR, ropes initiative, and CHA.*

MASSACHUSETTS

BONNIE CASTLE RIDING CAMP
Stoneleigh–Burnham School
Greenfield, Massachusetts 01301
General Information   Residential camp for girls ages 10–15. Established in 1979. Owned by Stoneleigh-Burnham School. Affiliated with New England Association of Schools and Colleges, Independent Schools Association of Massachusetts, National Association of Independent Schools. 100-acre facility located 60 miles north of Hartford, Connecticut. Features: 60 horse stables; 2 indoor riding rings; riding trails; event course; outdoor pool; arts programs, including dance, ceramics, and photography.
Profile of Summer Employees   Total number: 15; average age: 22; 100% female, 10% high school students, 60% college students, 30% local residents. Nonsmokers preferred.
Employment Information   Openings are from July 1 to August 13. Jobs available: 4 *riding instructors* (minimum age 18) at $900–$1200 per season; 1 *arts/photography instructor* (minimum age 18) at $700–$1200 per season; 1 *drama instructor* (minimum age 18) at $700–$1200 per season; 2 *swimming instructors* with WSI certification at $600–$1200 per season.
Benefits   On-site room and board at no charge, laundry facilities.
Contact   Director, Bonnie Castle Riding Camp, Department SJ, Stoneleigh-Burnham School, Greenfield, Massachusetts 01301; 413-774-2711, Fax 413-772-2602. Application deadline: March 30.

CAMP EMERSON
212 Longview Avenue
Hinsdale, Massachusetts 01235
General Information   Residential camp serving 220 boys and girls ages 7–15. Established in 1968. Owned by Marv, Addie, and Sue Lein. Affiliated with American Camping Association, Massachusetts Camping Association, Western Massachusetts Camping Association. 143-acre facility located 150 miles northeast of New York City. Features: new heated pool; freshwater stream-fed lake; proximity to cultural centers of the Berkshires; facilities for all land and water sports, including 6 tennis courts; accessibility to Boston and New York City (approximately 3 hours away); theater, art, and gymnastics centers.
Profile of Summer Employees   Total number: 100; average age: 24; 50% male, 50% female, 70% college students, 30% teachers. Nonsmokers only.
Employment Information   Openings are from June 17 to August 19. Jobs available: *creative arts instructors* with experience in fine arts/drawing and painting, ceramics, sculpting, batik, leather, jewelry, model rocketry, woodworking, photography, yearbook, newspaper/ creative writing, video, and computers at $1100 per season; *performing arts instructors* with experience in dramatics/directing, stagecraft, costuming/sewing, skits and stunts, storytelling, music (all instruments), piano (play by ear and/or play for shows and transpose), dance (jazz/aerobic/ballet/modern), choreography, guitar (play, sing, teach), and puppetry at $1100 per season; *land sports instructors* with experience in archery, basketball, fencing, golf, gymnastics, hockey, judo, karate, soccer, softball, tennis, track, volleyball, fitness, baseball, and lacrosse at $1100 per season; *water sports instructors* with experience in sailing, canoeing, kayaking, water polo, windsurfing, waterskiing, motorboat driving, lifeguarding, competitive swimming (WSI certification), and water aerobics at $1100 per season; *pioneer-*

ing instructor with experience in campcraft, fire building, outdoor cooking, overnight trips, forestry, nature, hiking, fishing, and ropes at $1100 per season; *nurses* with RN license; *administrative program assistant* with word-processing and additional computer skills (such as desktop publishing) at $1100 per season; *key staff* with experience in directing waterfront, aquatics, theater, sports, tennis, art, programming, and wilderness programs; *chefs/cooks.*

Benefits Preemployment training, on-site room and board at no charge, laundry facilities, highly skilled peer group, healthy menu including salad bar and vegetarian fare, staff lounge and after-hours activities.

Contact Sue Lein, Camp Director, Camp Emerson, Department SJ, 78 Deerfield Road, Sharon, Massachusetts 02067; 800-955-CAMP, Fax 617-784-2094. Application deadline: June 1.

From the Employer *At a weeklong orientation, employees are trained on program, philosophy, safety, camper management, supervisory techniques, course planning, and team building. There are 2–3 counselors in a cabin, supervising 6–10 campers. We have a strong elective and creative program where each individual can excel, with opportunities for staff to design and run activities. We are proud of our reputation for providing an environment where staff members and campers can grow.*

CAMP GOOD NEWS
Route 130
Forestdale, Massachusetts 02644

General Information Coeducational residential and day camp serving 220 children ages 6–16. Established in 1935. Owned by Society for Christian Activities. Affiliated with American Camping Association, Pioneers of Camping Club, Cape Cod Canal Region Chamber of Commerce. 214-acre facility located 13 miles east of Hyannis. Features: beautiful wooded area; extensive shorefront on freshwater pond; location 6 miles from ocean on beautiful Cape Cod; sandy beach.

Profile of Summer Employees Total number: 80; average age: 23; 45% male, 55% female, 3% minorities, 1% high school students, 58% college students, 1% retirees, 2% international, 5% local residents. Nonsmokers only.

Employment Information Openings are from June 17 to August 15. Jobs available: 35 *counselors* with college student status at $900–$1100 per season; 10 *kitchen staff members* (minimum age 18) at $800–$1000 per season; 2 *experienced arts and crafts instructors* at $900–$1000 per season; 2 *nurses* at $1000–$1100 per season; 1 *store manager* at $800–$900 per season; *sports experts* with boating certification at $900–$1100 per season.

Benefits Preemployment training, on-site room and board at no charge, laundry facilities, tuition reimbursement.

Contact Faith Willard, Director, Camp Good News, Department SJ, P.O. Box 95, Forestdale, Massachusetts 02644; 508-477-9731, Fax 508-477-8016. Application deadline: May 30.

CAMP PEMBROKE
Pembroke, Massachusetts 02359

General Information Residential Jewish cultural camp serving 275 girls. Established in 1936. Operated by Cohen Foundation. Affiliated with American Camping Association, Massachusetts Camping Association, Association of Independent Camps. 68-acre facility located 30 miles south of Boston. Features: Olympic-size pool; modern plant; proximity to Cape Cod and Boston.

Profile of Summer Employees Total number: 85; average age: 19; 18% high school students, 80% college students, 2% international. Nonsmokers preferred.

Employment Information Openings are from June 25 to August 24. Jobs available: 3 *arts and crafts instructors* at $1350–$1800 per season; 1 *arts and crafts director* at $2000–$2500 per season; 1 *music director* at $2000–$2500 per season; 2 *canoe instructors* at $1350–$2000 per season; 2 *sailing instructors* at $1350–$2000 per season; 3 *swimming instructors* at $1350–$2000 per season; 1 *swimming director* at $2000–$2500 per season; 1 *athletics director* at $2000–$2500 per season; 1 *waterskiing director* at $1500–$1900 per season; 1 *archery instructor* at $1500–$1900 per season.

Benefits College credit, formal ongoing training, on-site room and board at no charge, laundry facilities, gratuities.

Contact Pearl Lourie, Director, Camp Pembroke, Department SJ, 5 Birchmeadow Circle, Framingham, Massachusetts 01701; 508-788-0161, Fax 508-881-1006. Application deadline: April 1.

CAMP ROMACA
Box 402
Hinsdale, Massachusetts 01235

General Information Residential summer girls' camp providing daily instructional clinics, both individually and in small groups. Focus is on land and water sports, creative arts, performing arts, and outdoor living skills. Established in 1930. Owned by Bert Margolis. Affiliated with American Camping Association, Associated Independent Camps, Massachusetts Camping Association. 100-acre facility located 10 miles east of Pittsfield. Features: 9 tennis courts (6 all-weather, 3 clay, 4 lighted); 3 large sports fields, including archery range; fully equipped gymnasium; extensive freshwater lake frontage; large creative arts building; large recreation hall with theater.

Profile of Summer Employees Total number: 50; average age: 20; 10% male, 90% female, 2% minorities, 5% high school students, 85% college students, 8% international, 5% local residents. Nonsmokers only.

Employment Information Openings are from June 20 to August 21. Jobs available: 4 *swimming instructors* with WSI certification at $900–$1200 per season; 5 *tennis instructors* at $900–$1000 per season; 5 *creative/fine arts instructors* with skill in creative area at $900–$1000 per season; 1 *skilled English riding instructor* (minimum age 21) at $1000–$1500 per season; 6 *land sports instructors* with skill in one or more of the following areas: archery, softball, track and field, soccer, basketball, volleyball, golf, and lacrosse at $900–$1000 per season; 1 *performing arts instructor* (music) with high level of skill in playing the piano at $900 per season; 1 *skilled performing arts instructor* (dance) at $900 per season; 3 *performing arts instructors* (drama) with a major in music, drama, or theater arts at $900 per season; 2 *skilled gymnastics instructors* at $900 per season; 4 *skilled sailing/windsurfing instructors* at $900 per season; 2 *skilled boating/canoeing/rafting/kayaking instructors* at $900 per season; 3 *skilled waterskiing instructors* with ability to drive a boat at $900 per season; 1 *photography instructor* with high level of experience with black-and-white/color, dark room, and slides at $900 per season; 2 *nurses* with RN certification at $1000 per season. International students encouraged to apply.

Benefits College credit, formal ongoing training, on-site room and board at no charge, laundry facilities, travel reimbursement, in-bunk bathrooms and showers, 5 days off with use of facility, counselor lounge with VCR for use on days off, nearby bus to towns.

Contact Camp Romaca, Department SJ, 8 Harrowgate Court, Rockville, Maryland 20854; 301-279-2075, Fax 301-279-2178. Application deadline: May 31.

From the Employer *Romaca is an excellent, established, traditional camp where employees make the difference in a child's life. Our orientation has workshops on communication, organizational skills, area techniques, and building self-esteem. We offer staff members opportunities to grow and learn by involvement. Respect of self, other, and the environment are a natural component of our philosophy.*

CAMP WATITOH
Center Lake
Becket, Massachusetts 01223

General Information Residential summer camp serving 200 children with a wide variety of land and water sports activities, including drama, nature, and trips to all Berkshire area attractions. Established in 1937. Owned by Sandy, William, and Suzanne Hoch. Affiliated with American Camping Association, Massachusetts Camping Association, Western Massachusetts Camp Directors' Association. 85-acre facility located 150 miles north of New York City. Features: mountaintop location; attractive lake setting; 2 shops for creative arts.

Profile of Summer Employees Total number: 65; average age: 20; 50% male, 50% female, 85% college students, 10% international. Nonsmokers preferred.

Employment Information Openings are from June 25 to August 22. Jobs available: 6 *swimming instructors* with WSI certification at $1000–$1200 per season; 2 *sailing instructors* at $1000–$1200 per season; 2 *waterskiing instructors* at $1000–$1200 per season; 3 *arts and crafts instructors, experience preferred,* at $1500–$2500 per season; *general sports instructor* at $900–$1600 per season.

Benefits College credit, preemployment training, on-site room and board at no charge, travel reimbursement, health insurance.

Contact William Hoch, Director, Camp Watitoh, 28 Sammis Lane, White Plains, New York 10605; 914-428-1894. Application deadline: June 1.

From the Employer *Watitoh staff members receive the benefits of the "total living experience" of an eight-week residential camp program. This atmosphere provides the opportunity for counselors to make life-lasting friendships while enhancing their own self-confidence and independence.*

COLLEGE LIGHT OPERA COMPANY
Highfield Theatre, P.O. Drawer F
Falmouth, Massachusetts 02541

General Information Residential summer-stock music theater for training undergraduate and graduate students. Established in 1969. Owned by College Light Opera Company Board of Trustees. 6-acre facility located 70 miles south of Boston. Features: full pit orchestra; location on the beach on Cape Cod; status as largest resident theater company in the United States; opportunity to take part in 9 musicals per season.

Profile of Summer Employees Total number: 85; average age: 20; 50% male, 50% female, 5% minorities, 2% high school students, 80% college students, 10% teachers. Nonsmokers preferred.

Employment Information Openings are from June 8 to August 29. Jobs available: 32 *experienced vocalists* (salary is room and board)*; 18 *experienced orchestra staff* at $500 per season; 6 *experienced stage crew* at $500 per season; 5 *experienced costume crew* at $500 per season; 2 *box office treasurers* with outgoing, friendly personality at $900 per season; 1

experienced assistant business manager with word-processing skills at $1000 per season; 1 *experienced publicity director* with word-processing skills at $1000 per season; 1 *experienced choreographer* at $1200 per season; 2 *experienced chorus masters* with piano experience at $900 per season; 2 *experienced piano accompanists* at $800 per season; 1 *experienced costume designer* at $2000 per season; 1 *experienced set designer/technical director* at $2000 per season; 1 *experienced co-op work director* at $2000 per season; 1 *experienced cook* at $2400 per season.

Benefits   College credit, preemployment training, on-site room and board at no charge, accident insurance.

Contact   Ursula P. Haslun, Producer, College Light Opera Company, 162 South Cedar Street, Oberlin, Ohio 44074; 216-774-8485. Application deadline: March 15.

From the Employer   *CLOC welcomes both younger applicants seeking to gain experience in musical theater and the more mature performer, musician, and technician seeking to polish his or her craft by working with a professional staff and participating in nine different productions. We offer excellent training in music theater and theater management in a congenial environment.*

CRANE LAKE CAMP
State Line Road
West Stockbridge, Massachusetts 01266

General Information   Coeducational camp serving children ages 6–15 with traditional sports and a full cultural program. Established in 1922. Owned by Ed and Barbara Ulanoff. Affiliated with American Camping Association. 120-acre facility located 12 miles south of Pittsfield. Features: private spring-fed lake; heated swimming pool; 3 baseball fields; 2 soccer fields; location 3 miles from Tanglewood Music Festival (close to New York City and Boston in the Berkshire Mountains); 10 tennis courts; 4 indoor courts; modern cabins; gymnastics pavilion; 2 arts and crafts studios.

Profile of Summer Employees   Total number: 125; average age: 21; 52% male, 48% female, 75% college students, 15% teachers. Nonsmokers only.

Employment Information   Openings are from June 20 to August 21. Jobs available: 10 *athletics counselors* with a major in physical education or varsity athletics experience at $900–$1200 per season; 6 *waterfront instructors* with small crafts certification and waterskiing, sailing, or canoeing experience at $900–$1200 per season; 4 *experienced gymnastics instructors* at $900–$1200 per season; 2 *arts and crafts instructors* at $900–$1200 per season; *nurse* with RN license at $1600 per season; *nature instructor* at $900–$1200 per season; *horseback-riding instructor* at $900–$1200 per season; *tennis instructor* with college playing experience at $1200–$1500 per season; *pioneering/hiking instructor* at $900–$1200 per season; *painting/sketching instructor* at $900–$1200 per season; *guitar instructor* at $900–$1200 per season; *piano instructor* with ability to play by ear at $900–$1200 per season; *dance staff* at $900–$1200 per season.

Benefits   College credit, preemployment training, formal ongoing training, on-site room and board at no charge, laundry facilities, travel reimbursement, health insurance, car available on days and evenings off, facilities available during time off.

Contact Ed Ulanoff, Director, Crane Lake Camp, Department SJ, 10 West 66th Street, New York, New York 10023; 800-227-2660, Fax 212-742-2960. Application deadline: May 1.

From the Employer *We hold a counselor orientation prior to the arrival of our campers. During this time, our staff cooperates with a visiting child psychologist in role-playing and review of counselor-camper relationships, especially where several cultural backgrounds exist. We invite outside skills and safety personnel to review and train our staff in techniques specific to our various facilities. Specialists in the various disciplines offered at camp provide active-participation sample activities for new staff, while the current staff reviews and guides new employees in camp procedures to improve their confidence and effectiveness. We believe the above combination of skills and awareness training provides a firm foundation for future individual growth in any field of endeavor. Generally, 2 staff members and 6 campers share a cabin.*

ELLIOTT P. JOSLIN CAMP
150 Richardsons Corner Road
Charlton, Massachusetts 01507

General Information Residential boys' camp serving an average of 80 diabetic campers per session for four sessions. Established in 1948. Owned by Joslin Diabetes Center. Affiliated with American Camping Association, American Diabetes Association, International Diabetes Federation. 300-acre facility located 15 miles southwest of Worcester. Features: outdoor pavilion; new outdoor tennis courts with lights; 20-acre private pond; location in secluded area; 3 large sports fields; expansive recreation hall.

Profile of Summer Employees Total number: 54; average age: 20; 75% male, 25% female, 3% minorities, 25% high school students, 65% college students, 8% international, 89% local residents, 10% teachers. Nonsmokers only.

Employment Information Openings are from June 15 to August 21. Winter break positions also offered. Jobs available: 3 *junior counselors* (minimum age 18) at $1100–$1250 per season; 3 *senior counselors* (minimum age 19) at $1300–$2000 per season; 4 *nurses* *(student/graduate/RN)* with certification or enrollment in a nursing program at $1700–$4000 per season; 1 *nutritionist* with certification or enrollment in a nutrition program at $2200–$3000 per season; 1 *experienced head cook* at $2600–$3200 per season; 2 *experienced assistant cooks* at $1600–$2000 per season; 2 *kitchen aides* (minimum age 16) at $1000–$1400 per season; 2 *swimming instructors* with WSI certificate at $2000–$2400 per season; *director of CIT program* at $2600–$3200 per season; *secretary* at $1800–$2800 per season; *accountant/bookkeeper* at $2200–$2800 per season. International students encouraged to apply (must apply through Camp Counselors U.S.A.).

Benefits College credit, preemployment training, formal ongoing training, on-site room and board at no charge, laundry facilities, health insurance, training and treatment for staff members with diabetes, excellent recreation facilities.

Contact Paul Madden, Administrator, Elliott P. Joslin Camp, Department SJ, 1 Joslin Place, Boston, Massachusetts 02215; 617-732-2455, Fax 617-732-2664. Application deadline: June 1.

From the Employer *We offer a 1- to 1½-week preprogram orientation, with additional Red Cross training available throughout the summer. Campers, students, and professionals visit from all over the world to share and learn with us. Our sister camp is nearby, and we offer excellent diabetes training and counseling.*

THE FOLGER HOTEL
89 Easton Street
Nantucket, Massachusetts 02554

General Information   Full-service hotel with sixty rooms and a 100-seat restaurant serving breakfast and dinner. Established in 1900. Owned by Robert B. Bowman. Affiliated with Rotary, Chamber of Commerce, New England Innkeepers Association. 2-acre facility located 48 miles west of Nantucket. Features: flower and water gardens; large porches and verandas; fish ponds; miles of sandy white beaches.

Profile of Summer Employees   Total number: 45; average age: 22; 50% male, 50% female, 10% minorities, 95% college students, 5% international, 5% local residents.

Employment Information   Openings are from May 15 to October 15. Spring break positions also offered. Jobs available: 4 *front desk clerks* at $7.50–$8 per hour; 10 *waitstaff members* at $2.55 per hour; 7 *room attendants* at $6.41 per hour; *kitchen staff* (cooking/pantry) at $275–$475 per week; *restaurant help* (hosts/bartenders) at $6–$7 per hour.

Benefits   On-site room and board at $83 per week.

Contact   Robert B. Bowman, Owner, The Folger Hotel, Department SJ, P.O. Box 628, Nantucket, Massachusetts 02554; 508-228-0313. Application deadline: April 1.

4–H FARLEY OUTDOOR EDUCATION CENTER
615 Route 130
Mashpee, Massachusetts 02649

General Information   Camp emphasizing overnight and day programs for boys and girls ages 7–14. There is limited mainstreaming of special needs children. Established in 1934. Owned by Cape Cod 4-H Camp Corporation. Affiliated with University of Massachusetts Cooperative Extension, United States Department of Agriculture. 32-acre facility located 80 miles south of Boston. Features: freshwater lake (largest on Cape Cod); adjacent woodland areas; located close to ocean; small farm with animals; auditorium/outside amphitheater; nature classroom with native and domestic small animals; biking.

Profile of Summer Employees   Total number: 48; average age: 22; 25% male, 75% female, 10% minorities, 20% high school students, 60% college students, 10% international, 10% local residents. Nonsmokers preferred.

Employment Information   Openings are from July 5 to August 27. Jobs available: 3 *waterfront directors* (minimum age 21) with WSI certification at $200–$230 per week; 8 *lifeguards* with LGT certification or equivalent at $140–$200 per week; 30 *counselors* with specialized program skills and camping experience at $100–$200 per week; 1 *child care coordinator* with background in youth development at $250–$300 per week; 1 *health-care provider* with EMT, RN, or LPN license or special training in first aid at $250–$300 per week; 2 *secretaries* with office skills at $200–$240 per week; 3 *kitchen staff members* at $200–$300 per week; *experienced boat drivers* at $200–$300 per week; *archery instructors* at $200–$230 per week. International students encouraged to apply.

Benefits   Preemployment training, formal ongoing training, on-site room and board at no charge, laundry facilities, health insurance, weekends off.

Contact   Michael Campbell, Executive Director, 4–H Farley Outdoor Education Center, Department SJ, 615 Route 130, Mashpee, Massachusetts 02649; 508-477-0181. Application deadline: April 15 (will accept applications as long as positions are open).

NORTH SHORE MUSIC THEATRE
Dunham Road, P.O. Box 62
Beverly, Massachusetts 01915-0062

General Information Musical theater with an eight-show season of Broadway musicals as well as children's shows, concerts, and special events. Established in 1955. Owned by North Shore Community Arts Foundation, Inc. Affiliated with National Alliance of Musical Theater Producers, Council of Stock Theaters, Actors' Equity Association. Located 25 miles north of Boston. Features: 1,800-seat arena theater; computerized lighting; state-of-the-art sound system; modern production facility; location in the woods on beautifully landscaped grounds; proximity to historic Boston.

Profile of Summer Employees Total number: 50; average age: 21; 40% male, 60% female, 10% minorities, 10% high school students, 90% college students, 75% local residents.

Employment Information Openings are from April 1 to December 23. Jobs available: 20 *technical theater interns, experience preferred,* at $150–$200 per week; 20 *technical theater staff members, experience preferred,* at $200–$400 per week. International students encouraged to apply.

Benefits College credit, preemployment training.

Contact James Alberghini, Production Manager, North Shore Music Theatre, Department SJ, P.O. Box 62, Beverly, Massachusetts 01915-0062; 508-922-8500 Ext. 262, Fax 508-921-0793. Application deadline: April 15.

OFFENSE-DEFENSE TENNIS CAMP
Curry College
Milton, Massachusetts 02186

General Information Tennis camp for boys and girls ages 10–18. Accommodates beginners to tournament players. Established in 1972. Owned by Mike and Judy Meshken. Affiliated with New England Lawn Tennis Association, New England Camping Association, United States Tennis Association. 150-acre facility located 9 miles south of Boston. Features: college dorms; gymnasium; cafeteria; game room; wooded campus; proximity to scenic and historical sites in and near Boston.

Profile of Summer Employees Total number: 70; average age: 23; 60% male, 40% female, 85% college students, 10% local residents. Nonsmokers preferred.

Employment Information Openings are from June 20 to August 20. Jobs available: 16 *general counselors* (ages 19–28) at $880–$1200 per season; 2 *licensed bus drivers* at $1200–$1800 per season; 24 *tennis instructors* with tennis instructor certification or varsity college experience at $800–$1200 per season.

Benefits College credit, preemployment training, formal ongoing training, on-site room and board at no charge, laundry facilities, travel reimbursement, trips to Boston, full day off each week.

Contact Mike Meshken, Director, Offense-Defense Tennis Camp, Department SJ, P.O. Box 295, Trumbull, Connecticut 06611; 800-243-4296. Application deadline: May 1.

From the Employer *Campers and counselors live in college dorms with 2 campers to a room; counselors have private rooms. There are large bathrooms on each floor.*

PIONEER VALLEY COOPERATIVE EXTENSION
335 Russell Street, Suite 1
Hadley, Massachusetts 10035

General Information Residential camp offering programs in many activities, including recreation, crafts, performing arts, water sports, shooting, husbandry, and horseback riding. Established in 1928. Owned by Camp Howe, Inc. Operated by 4-H. Affiliated with American Camping Association, 4-H, University of Massachusetts Cooperative Extension. 52-acre facility located 30 miles north of Springfield. Features: beautiful wooded area; lakefront; surrounded by DAR State Forest; playing fields; secluded glen for ceremonies; hiking and riding trails within camp and state forest.

Profile of Summer Employees Total number: 40; average age: 22; 50% male, 50% female, 10% minorities, 15% high school students, 80% college students, 5% retirees, 15% international, 80% local residents, 10% teachers. Nonsmokers preferred.

Employment Information Openings are from June 1 to August 1. Jobs available: *adventure director* at $1000–$1300 per season; *shooting sports director* at $1000–$1300 per season; *nurse* at $1500–$2000 per season; *swimming instructors/lifeguards* at $800–$1000 per season; *kitchen help/dishwashers* at $500 per season; *general counselors* at $800–$1000 per season; *recreation director* at $1000–$1300 per season; *nature director* at $1000–$1300 per season; *farm animals director* at $1000–$1300 per season; *arts and crafts director* at $1000–$1300 per season; *waterfront director* at $1000–$1300 per season. International students encouraged to apply.

Benefits College credit, preemployment training, formal ongoing training, on-site room and board at no charge, laundry facilities, health insurance.

Contact Philippe E. and Donna Denette, Pioneer Valley Cooperative Extension, Department SJ, 96 Amherst Street, Gramby, Massachusetts 01033; 413-467-7977. Application deadline: February 1.

From the Employer *We provide a two-week staff training period in all areas of camper behavior, safety, and health. Our staff is trained in first aid and CPR. We have a group of handicapped children that staff members learn to integrate into the program. We also have an international staff so employees have the opportunity to learn about other cultures.*

SUMMER THEATER AT MOUNT HOLYOKE COLLEGE
South Hadley, Massachusetts 01075

General Information Professional summer-stock company producing eight mainstage plays and three plays for children in one-week stock. Established in 1970. Owned by Production Arts, Ltd. Affiliated with New England Theater Conference, East Central Theater Conference, Southeast Theater Conference, Theater Communications Group. 20-acre facility located 10 miles north of Springfield. Features: beautiful facility at nation's oldest women's college; proximity to Hartford, Boston, and New York City; access to all gyms, libraries, and pools of Mount Holyoke College.

Profile of Summer Employees Total number: 75; average age: 25; 50% male, 50% female, 5% minorities, 7% high school students, 30% college students, 2% international, 16% local residents.

Employment Information Openings are from May 30 to August 18. Jobs available: 12 *actors* (non-Equity) at $750 per season; 3 *carpenters* at $750 per season; 3 *prop artisans* at $750 per season; 2 *stitchers* at $750 per season; 1 *wardrobe staff member* at $850 per season; 1 *technical director* at $1200 per season; 1 *stage manager* (non-Equity) at $900 per season; 1 *prop master* at $1000 per season; 1 *box office manager* at $750 per season; 1 *house manager* at $750 per season; 1 *business manager* at $900 per season; 1 *publicity assistant* at

$750 per season; 1 *sound designer* at $1000 per season; 1 *costume designer* at $1800 per season; 1 *master electrician* at $1000 per season.

Benefits Formal ongoing training, on-site room and board at no charge, laundry facilities, travel reimbursement, Equity membership candidate points.

Contact Michael Walker, Producing Director, Summer Theater at Mount Holyoke College, Department SJ, South Hadley, Massachusetts 01075; 413-538-2632, Fax 413-538-2512. Application deadline: March 1.

From the Employer *The Summer Theater at Mount Holyoke College allows high school students, college students, and professionals to work side by side while producing eleven shows on two stages in nine weeks. We also provide hands-on experience in all aspects of theater production.*

SUPERCAMP
Westfield, Massachusetts 01086

General Information Residential program for teens designed to build self-confidence and lifelong learning skills through accelerated learning techniques. Established in 1981. Owned by Bobbi DePorter. Affiliated with American Camping Association, Society for Accelerated Learning and Teaching. Closest major city is Hartford, CT. Features: location on beautiful college campus; dormitory rooms; swimming pool; ropes course.

Profile of Summer Employees Total number: 200; average age: 22; 50% male, 50% female, 80% college students, 20% teachers. Nonsmokers only.

Employment Information Openings are from June 20 to August 20. Jobs available: 24 *team leaders* at $500–$1000 per season; 1 *office manager* at $1000–$2000 per season; 1 *licensed paramedic* at $700–$2800 per season; 1 *nurse* at $1000–$4000 per season.

Benefits Preemployment training, on-site room and board at no charge, laundry facilities, internships, experience working with teens in an educational and self-esteem building program, excellent experience for education and psychology majors.

Contact Shelby Reeder, Human Resources Coordinator, SuperCamp, Department SJ, 1725 South Hill Street, Oceanside, California 92054; 800-527-5321, Fax 619-722-3507. Application deadline: May 1.

From the Employer *SuperCamp employees develop outstanding communications and leadership skills through an extensive five-day training program, where they can meet exciting new people from across the country. Staff members support teens through powerful, life-changing experiences and become familiar with new accelerated-learning techniques. Sessions are held on beautiful college campuses in six locations across the country, including Texas, Illinois, and Massachusetts.*

MICHIGAN

AMERICAN YOUTH FOUNDATION–CAMP MINIWANCA
8845 West Garfield
Shelby, Michigan 49455

General Information Camp focusing on developing the leadership capacities of young people by helping them achieve their personal best, lead balanced lives, and serve others. Established in 1924. Owned by American Youth Foundation. Affiliated with American

Camping Association, Association for Experiential Education. 360-acre facility located 70 miles northwest of Grand Rapids. Features: 1 mile of Lake Michigan beach; sand dunes; wooded hills; retreat/conference facility; 2 waterfronts (Lake Michigan and Stony Lake); extensive boating area.

Profile of Summer Employees Total number: 200; average age: 20; 40% male, 60% female, 3% minorities, 10% high school students, 55% college students, 5% retirees, 1% international, 10% local residents. Nonsmokers preferred.

Employment Information Openings are from May 15 to August 31. Year-round positions also offered. Jobs available: 90 *leaders* with college student or teacher status at $115–$220 per week; 26 *central summer staff members* with teacher status at $200–$300 per week; 20 *kitchen personnel* with high school student or retired person status at $90–$105 per week; 10 *camp cleaning personnel* with high school student or retired person status at $90–$105 per week; 16 *building/grounds personnel* with high school student or retired person status at $90–$105 per week; 5 *interns* with junior status in college at $75 per week; 5 *fieldworkers* with sophomore status in college at $75 per week. International students encouraged to apply.

Benefits College credit, preemployment training, formal ongoing training, on-site room and board at no charge, laundry facilities, travel reimbursement.

Contact Dr. Jeffrey Glick, Director of Operations, American Youth Foundation–Camp Miniwanca, Department SJ, 8845 West Garfield, Shelby, Michigan 49455; 616-861-2262, Fax 616-861-5244. Application deadline: April 1.

From the Employer *All staff attend seven-day staff training prior to summer camp program start. Focus is on team building, safety procedures, child guidance, facilitation, and leadership development. Staff considering 4-Trails (wilderness program) leadership positions attend a one-week wilderness skill-training workshop covering technical skills (canoeing, backpacking, bicycling), campcraft, group facilitation, trip planning, and wilderness safety. Support staff have continuing education opportunities on a weekly basis focusing on leadership development, community service, interpersonal skills, etc. In preparing program participants for a changing world, Miniwanca provides extensive training to help its staff facilitate the AYF mission. Using proven methodologies of community building and experiential learning, staff are equipped to model and guide campers in creating a summer of fun with a purpose: achievement of personal best, balanced living, and service to others.*

BAY CLIFF HEALTH CAMP
Big Bay, Michigan 49808

General Information Residential therapy camp serving 200 handicapped children ages 3–17 during one 7-week session. Established in 1934. Owned by Bay Cliff Health Camp. 170-acre facility located 300 miles north of Milwaukee. Features: beautiful natural area; location on Lake Superior; indoor heated swimming pool and sauna; beautiful sand beach; proximity to state and national parks; farm atmosphere.

Profile of Summer Employees Total number: 125; average age: 25; 30% male, 70% female, 5% minorities, 10% high school students, 50% college students, 5% retirees, 15% local residents, 10% teachers. Nonsmokers only.

Employment Information Openings are from June 18 to August 13. Jobs available: 5 *unit leaders* with teaching experience and special education degree (preferred) at $1800–$2300 per season; 50 *counselors* (minimum age 18) with one year of college completed (preferably in the study of special education, therapy, nursing, or human services) at $1200–$1500 per season; 8 *roving counselors* (minimum age 18) with one year of college completed (preferably in the study of special education, therapy, nursing, or human services) at $1200–$1500 per season; 3 *certified hearing therapists* at $2000–$2500 per season; 1 *certified music* *therapist* at $1800–$2300 per season; 4 *certified occupational therapists* at $2500 per season; 4 *certified physical therapists* at $2500 per season; 10 *certified speech therapists* at $2000–$2500 per season; 10 *student therapists* with formal school affiliation and ability to work under a supervising therapist at $600; 3 *nurses* with RN or LPN license at $2000–$2500 per season; 1 *nurse's aide* with student nurse status at $1000–$1250 per season; 1 *licensed dentist* at $3000 per season; 1 *licensed dental assistant* at $1200 per season; 1 *licensed dental hygienist* at $1500 per season; 2 *arts and crafts instructors, experience preferred,* with ability to plan and implement classes for all camp units at $1500 per season; 1 *nature instructor, experience preferred,* with ability to plan and implement classes for all camp units at $1500 per season; 1 *recreation instructor, experience preferred,* with ability to plan and implement classes for all camp units at $1500; 4 *waterfront staff members* with WSI or lifeguard certification at $1200 per season; *vision therapist* (instructor) at $2000 per season; 1 *experienced head cook* at $200–$275 per week; 1 *experienced assistant cook* at $175–$225 per week; 1 *baker* at $1500 per season; 12 *kitchen and dining room aides* (minimum age 16) at $900–$1200 per season; 3 *laundry/housekeeping personnel* at $1000–$1500 per season; 2 *linen-room personnel* at $1000–$1300 per season; 4 *experienced maintenance personnel* (minimum age 18) at $1000–$1300 per season; 1 *secretary* with good clerical skills and a pleasant, enthusiastic personality at $1200 per season.

Benefits   College credit, on-site room and board at no charge, laundry facilities, travel reimbursement, an opportunity to gain experience working with handicapped children.

Contact   Tim Bennett, Camp Director, Bay Cliff Health Camp, 310 West Washington Avenue, Suite 300, Marquette, Michigan 49855; 906-228-5770, Fax 906-228-5771. Application deadline: May 15.

From the Employer   *Bay Cliff Health Camp provides an opportunity to work with children who have many different kinds of handicaps in a therapy-based program. The program focuses on serving the whole child, creating opportunities to learn functional and daily living skills. Work and learn with talented people from across the United States and enjoy a personally and professionally rewarding experience.*

CAMP WALDEN
5607 South River Road
Cheboygan, Michigan 49721

General Information   Residential coeducational camp serving children ages 7–16. Established in 1959. Owned by Larry Stevens and Tom Lurie. Affiliated with American Camping Association, Private Independent Camps, Camp Horsemanship Association. 160-acre facility located 8 miles west of Cheboygan. Features: proximity to Mackinaw Island and Bridge and Michigan's upper peninsula; canoeing, biking, and backpacking in the Great Lakes area; 8 outdoor tennis courts and 2 large athletics fields; beautiful wooded camp environment and lake for sailing, skiing, and windsurfing; 25 horses with English and Western programs; fine arts and crafts facilities for jewelry, ceramics, weaving, silk-screening, painting, and sculpting.

Profile of Summer Employees   Total number: 100; average age: 23; 50% male, 50% female. Nonsmokers only.

Employment Information   Openings are from June 15 to August 20. Jobs available: *riding instructor* with CHA certification or equivalent experience; *certified windsurfing instructor; certified sailing instructor; certified kayaking instructor; certified waterskiing instructor; experienced tennis instructor; certified archery instructor; experienced gymnastics instructor; theater instructor* with training, acting, and directing experience; *experienced dance instructor; experienced fencing instructor; experienced arts and crafts instructor; experienced natural science instructor; experienced mountain-biking instructor; experienced backpack/*

canoe/trip instructor; swimming instructor with lifeguard and/or WSI certification. All positions offered at $1000–$2000 per season. International students encouraged to apply (must apply through Bunacamp).

Benefits College credit, formal ongoing training, on-site room and board at no charge, travel reimbursement.

Contact Larry Stevens and Tom Lurie, Co-Directors, Camp Walden, Department SJ, 31070 Applewood Lane, Farmington Hills, Michigan 48331; 810-661-1890, Fax 810-661-1891. Application deadline: May 15.

From the Employer *We have a seven-day precamp orientation that includes international staff members.*

CEDAR LODGE
47138 52nd Street
Lawrence, Michigan 49064

General Information Residential coeducational camp serving 44 campers in a relaxed, loosely structured program with a special emphasis on horsemanship from the beginner to show jumper. Established in 1964. Affiliated with American Camping Association, Association for Horsemanship Safety and Education. 160-acre facility located 105 miles west of Chicago. Features: private lake; location in the heart of fruit country; rustic setting; open-screened wooden cabins; 5 miles of riding trails; 3 riding rings and large boxstall barn.

Profile of Summer Employees Total number: 11; average age: 20; 25% male, 75% female, 95% college students, 5% retirees, 5% local residents. Nonsmokers only.

Employment Information Openings are from June 20 to August 20. Jobs available: 1 *swimming instructor* at $800–$1300 per season; 1 *riding instructor* at $800–$1300 per season; 1 *arts and crafts instructor* at $800–$1000 per season; 1 *music/dance/drama instructor* at $800–$1000 per season; 1 *biking/trip instructor* at $800–$1000 per season; *sports instructor* at $800–$1000 per season; 1 *kitchen assistant* at $800–$1200 per season.

Benefits College credit, preemployment training, formal ongoing training, on-site room and board at no charge, laundry facilities, precamp certification for riding and swimming instructors.

Contact Amy Edwards, Program Director, Cedar Lodge, Department SJ, P.O. Box 218, Lawrence, Michigan 49064; 616-674-8071, Fax 616-674-8078. Application deadline: June 5.

CRYSTALAIRE CAMP
1327 South Shore Road East
Frankfort, Michigan 49635

General Information Small, coeducational, loosely structured residential camp that is noncompetitive and nonsectarian, emphasizing individual growth. Established in 1921. Owned by David B. Reid. Affiliated with American Camping Association. 145-acre facility located 35 miles west of Traverse City. Features: location on Crystal Lake; proximity to Sleeping Bear National Lake; rustic setting; extensive use of Lake Michigan Wilderness beaches.

Profile of Summer Employees Total number: 30; average age: 22; 50% male, 50% female, 5% minorities, 20% high school students, 65% college students, 5% retirees, 10% international, 5% local residents. Nonsmokers only.

Employment Information Openings are from June 20 to August 22. Jobs available: 14 *counselors* with lifesaving training and art, sailing, trip, and sports skills at $900–$1500 per season; 1 *experienced riding instructor* with ability to manage Western-style riding program at $950–$1600 per season; 3 *experienced sailing/windsurfing instructors* with lifesaving training at $950–$1600 per season; 1 *art specialist* with ability to organize art program (teacher preferred) at $1000–$1800 per season; 1 *nurse* with RN, LPN, or EMT license at $1200–$2200 per season; 1 *trip coordinator* with ability to organize wilderness camping trips, train staff, and maintain bicycles, tents, and camping equipment at $950–$2000 per season; 2 *experienced cooks* at $1200–$2500 per season; 1 *experienced waterfront director* with WSI certification at $1200–$2000 per season; 1 *stable helper* at $60–$150 per week; 5 *junior counselors* (high school students) at $500–$700 per season; *sports specialist* with experience in competitive and noncompetitive sports and games at $1000–$1500 per season; *experienced assistant director/program director* with ability to conduct programs for small and large groups at $1500–$2500 per season.

Benefits College credit, preemployment training, formal ongoing training, on-site room and board at no charge, CPR/first aid training, vegetarian menu.

Contact David B. Reid, Director, Crystalaire Camp, 1327 South Shore Road East, Frankfort, Michigan 49635; 616-352-7589. Application deadline: June 20.

From the Employer *We offer a one-week precamp orientation and training with the opportunity to work in a somewhat unstructured situation with good support and guidance from administration. We put considerable emphasis upon creativity, encouraging staff to develop new programs and approaches.*

DOUBLE JJ RESORT RANCH
P.O. Box 94
Rothbury, Michigan 49452

General Information Resort ranch exclusively for adults. Golf club open to the public. Established in 1937. Owned by Joan and Bob Lipsitz. Affiliated with Circle Michigan, West Michigan Tourist Association, White Lake, Muskegon, Grand Rapids Chamber of Commerce. 1,000-acre facility located 20 miles north of Muskegon. Features: heated pool and spa; private lake; beautiful wooded acres; location near sand dunes of Lake Michigan; 18-hole championship golf course; horseback riding.

Profile of Summer Employees Total number: 100; average age: 25; 50% male, 50% female, 2% minorities, 5% high school students, 50% college students, 5% retirees, 8% international, 30% local residents.

Employment Information Openings are from May 1 to November 1. Jobs available: 9 *talented entertainers* (guitarists and singers) with outgoing personality at $130 per week; 6 *waiters/waitresses* at $130 per week; 5 *experienced prep cooks/bakers* at $130 per week; 20 *lawn maintenance personnel* at $130 per week; 1 *experienced disc jockey* at $130 per week; 6 *housekeepers* at $130 per week; 8 *experienced wranglers* at $130 per week; 6 *snack bar/bar staff members* (minimum age 21) at $130 per week; 2 *dishwashers* at $130 per week; 1 *dining room manager* with waiter/waitressing experience at $150 per week; 6 *office staff members* with computer experience and ability to answer phones and make reservations at $130 per week; 6 *pro shop/gift shop staff members* at $130 per week; 10 *golf course personnel* at $130 per week; 10 *golf course groundskeepers* at $130 per week.

Benefits College credit, on-site room and board at no charge, laundry facilities, use of all facilities.

Contact Joan Lipsitz, Owner, Double JJ Resort Ranch, Department SJ, P.O. Box 94, Rothbury, Michigan 49452; 616-894-4444, Fax 616-893-5355. Application deadline: April 1.

From the Employer *The Double JJ provides a fun-filled all-inclusive vacation package. Staff are encouraged to "work hard and play hard" and to participate in shows a nd entertainment.*

EL RANCHO STEVENS
2332 East Dixon Lake Road
Gaylord, Michigan 49735

General Information Family resort specializing in horses, waterskiing, and children's programs, serving 80 people weekly. Established in 1947. Owned by Steven S. Stevens. Affiliated with West Michigan Tourist Association, Gaylord Chamber of Commerce, Michigan Lodging Association. 1,000-acre facility located 3 miles southeast of Gaylord. Features: heated pool; indoor recreation room; lake (DNR stocked); tennis court and archery range; dining room; 500 acres of riding trails.

Profile of Summer Employees Total number: 25; average age: 25; 20% male, 80% female, 10% minorities, 10% high school students, 75% college students, 10% retirees, 25% local residents. Nonsmokers preferred.

Employment Information Openings are from May 29 to September 5. Jobs available: 5 *waitresses/waiters* at $150–$180 per week; 2 *experienced cooks* at $150–$200 per week; 2 *kitchen helpers* at $150–$180 per week; 3 *housekeepers* at $150–$180 per week; 1 *waterskiing instructor/boat driver* (minimum age 18) with knowledge of water safety rules at $150–$180 per week; 2 *experienced riding instructors/trail guides* (minimum age 18) at $150–$180 per week; 3 *children's counselors* at $150–$180 per week; 1 *recreational director* with ability to work with people of all ages at $150–$180 per week; 2 *bartenders/barmaids* (minimum age 18) at $150–$180 per week; 2 *office personnel* with good phone, typing, and bookkeeping skills at $150–$180 per week.

Benefits College credit, on-site room and board at no charge, travel reimbursement.

Contact Personnel Department, El Rancho Stevens, P.O. Box 495, Gaylord, Michigan 49735; 517-732-5090. Application deadline: May 15.

From the Employer *El Rancho is a small family-run operation. Staff and guests are on a first-name basis and share each other's company. This atmosphere enables the guests to feel at home and the staff to develop meaningful friendships. While all our employees have a primary job, we expect everyone to work as a team and help out as needed.*

LAKE OF THE WOODS AND GREENWOODS CAMPS
Decatur, Michigan 49045

General Information Private residential camps for children ages 7–15 in a recreational environment. Established in 1935. Owned by Marc Seeger. Affiliated with American Camping Association, Midwest Association of Private Camps. 50-acre facility located 20 miles southwest of Kalamazoo. Features: modern facilities; location in southwestern Michigan on beautiful ¼-mile lake frontage.

Profile of Summer Employees Total number: 65; average age: 21; 50% male, 50% female, 2% minorities, 90% college students, 5% international, 2% teachers. Nonsmokers preferred.

Employment Information Openings are from June 12 to August 15. Year-round positions also offered. Jobs available: 8 *swimming instructors* with lifeguard training and WSI certification at $1200 per season; 3 *sailing instructors* at $1150 per season; 3 *riding instructors* at $1200 per season; 1 *computer instructor* with Basic, Logo, and PASCAL experience (preferred) at $1150 per season; 7 *waterskiing instructors* with boat-driving experience at $1150 per season; 2 *tennis instructors* at $1150 per season; 1 *golf instructor* at $1150 per season; 1 *gymnastics instructor* at $1150 per season; 2 *arts and crafts instructors* at $1150 per season; 1 *dramatics instructor* at $1150 per season; 1 *dance/aerobics instructor* at $1150 per season; 2 *sports coaches* at $1150 per season; 2 *nurses* with RN license (preferred) at $2500 per season; 2 *experienced office persons* at $1150 per season; *kitchen personnel* (cooks and assistants) at $140–$350 per week; *riflery instructor* (minimum age 19) at $1150 per season;

archery instructor (minimum age 19) at $1150 per season; *rowing/canoe instructor* (minimum age 19) at $1150 per season; *model rocketry instructor* (minimum age 19) at $1150 per season; *ceramics instructor* (minimum age 19) at $1150 per season.

Benefits College credit, preemployment training, on-site room and board at no charge.

Contact Marc Seeger, Owner/Director, Lake of the Woods and Greenwoods Camps, Department SJ, 1765 Maple Street, Northfield, Illinois 60093; 708-446-2444, Fax 708-446-7342. Interviews will be conducted at selected Midwest universities in the spring.

From the Employer *At a six-day precamp orientation, employees learn how to interact and relate to children as well as how to handle situations that may come up at camp. Generally, 2 counselors and 10 campers share a modern cabin with electricity, hot water, bathrooms, and a shower in each cabin. Our campers stay four or eight weeks, which allows the staff enough time to develop a fantastic rapport with the campers.*

MICHILLINDA BEACH LODGE
5207 Scenic Drive
Whitehall, Michigan 49461

General Information Modified American-plan resort with 50 guest units overlooking Lake Michigan. Established in 1928. Owned by Donald E. Eilers. Affiliated with West Michigan Tourist Association, Michigan Lodging Association, American Hotel Association. 22-acre facility located 25 miles north of Muskegon. Features: location on Lake Michigan Beach; tennis courts; swimming and wading pools; miniature golf.

Profile of Summer Employees Total number: 35; average age: 18; 33% male, 67% female, 50% high school students, 50% college students, 90% local residents. Nonsmokers preferred.

Employment Information Openings are from June 15 to September 6. Spring break positions also offered. Jobs available: 10 *housekeeping staff members* at $4.25–$6 per hour; 6 *kitchen staff members* at $4.35–$6 per hour; 5 *bellpersons* at $4.25–$5.50 per hour; 3 *grounds maintenance staff members* at $4.25–$6 per hour; 9 *dining room staff members* at $4.50–$6 per hour.

Benefits College credit, preemployment training, laundry facilities, bonus in place of tips, on-site rooms are available for $30 a month (for women only), on-site meals available at $1.50 for breakfasts and $2.50 for dinners.

Contact Don Eilers, General Manager, Michillinda Beach Lodge, Department SJ, 5207 Scenic Drive, Whitehall, Michigan 49461; 616-893-1895, Fax 616-893-1805. Application deadline: April 1.

From the Employer *Michillinda Beach Lodge is a unique summer resort with emphases on family activities and atmosphere. The staff takes part in a 2½-day orientation program before the start of our season. Workshops on team building, communication, and guest relations, as well as specific training for each position, provide well-rounded training for all staff members. During our season a close working relationship exists between all staff members as we serve the needs of our guests.*

SUNNY BROOK FARM RESORT
South Haven, Michigan 49090

General Information American plan resort that caters to families, offering a variety of facilities, meals, activities, and lodging for a full week's vacation. Established in 1914. Owned by Dennis G. Ott. Affiliated with West Michigan Tourists Association. 120-acre facility located 45 miles south of Grand Rapids. Features: 3 heated pools; tennis courts;

driving range; proximity to Lake Michigan (3 miles); fun park next door; proximity to 40-mile hiking and biking trail.

Profile of Summer Employees Total number: 30; average age: 20; 50% male, 50% female, 15% minorities, 15% high school students, 75% college students, 5% international, 25% local residents, 10% teachers. Nonsmokers preferred.

Employment Information Openings are from June 5 to September 8. Spring break positions also offered. Jobs available: 7 *waitresses/waiters* at $2000–$3000 per season; 2 *cooks* at $2000–$3000 per season; 3 *desk clerks* with a major in business or hotel management (preferred) at $2000–$2500 per season; 2 *lifeguards* with lifesaving certification (required) and CPR certification (preferred) at $2000–$2500 per season; 3 *kitchen helpers* at $2000–$2500 per season; 4 *children's counselors* with lifesaving certification (required) and CPR certification (preferred) at $2000–$2500 per season; 2 *maintenance helpers* at $2000–$2500 per season; 2 *yard workers* at $1800–$2000 per season; 1 *night watch person* at $2000–$2500 per season; 3 *refreshment stand workers* at $2000–$2500 per season; 1 *assistant maintenance foreman* at $2000–$3000 per season.

Benefits On-site room and board at $60 per week, laundry facilities, bonus given to employees who stay the entire summer through closing (equal to approximately ½ of their room and board).

Contact Mary C. Ott, Sunny Brook Farm Resort, 68300 County Road 388, South Haven, Michigan 49090; 616-637-4796. Application deadline: May 1.

THE TIMBERS GIRL SCOUT CAMP
8195 Timbers Trail Drive
Traverse City, Michigan 49684

General Information Trip camp offering four 2-week sessions for 100 girls ages 12–18. Established in 1962. Owned by Fair Winds Girl Scout Council. Affiliated with Girl Scouts of the United States of America, American Camping Association. 262-acre facility located 6 miles west of Traverse City. Features: beautiful tourist area; 3 beautiful lakes; proximity to Grand Traverse Bay resort area; 48-foot climbing wall; initiatives course; waterfront with windsurfing, sailing, canoeing, and swimming; backpacking and biking trips.

Profile of Summer Employees Total number: 50; average age: 20; 100% female, 5% minorities, 95% college students, 5% international, 2% local residents. Nonsmokers preferred.

Employment Information Openings are from June 1 to August 26. Spring break, winter break, Christmas break positions also offered. Jobs available: 11 *level one counselors* with ability to pass 20-minute swimming test at $855–$1200 per season; 11 *level two counselors* with ability to pass 20-minute swimming test at $1035–$1400 per season; 1 *business manager* with driver's license and bookkeeping and typing experience at $1170–$1600 per season; 1 *arts and crafts instructor* with expertise in woodworking, stained glass, silk-screening, and nature crafts at $1125–$1600 per season; 1 *waterfront director* with WSI and LGT certification at $1170–$1600 per season; 1 *small craft director* with LGT and small craft instructor certification or equivalent at $1170–$1600 per season; 1 *trip outfitter* at $1125–$1400 per season; 1 *assistant camp director* at $1350–$2000 per season; 1 *head cook* at $1575–$1900 per season; 1 *assistant cook* at $1170–$1700 per season; 2 *kitchen aides* at $765–$1000 per season; 1 *pack-out supervisor* at $1125–$1600 per season; 1 *assistant ranger* at $1035–$1300 per season; 1 *camp nurse* with RN or EMT license at $205 per week; 2 *initiatives directors* at $1125–$1400 per season.

Benefits College credit, preemployment training, on-site room and board at no charge, laundry facilities, health insurance.

Contact Joann Downing, Director of Outdoor Education, The Timbers Girl Scout Camp, Department SJ, 2029-C South Elms Road, Swartz Creek, Michigan 48473; 313-230-0244.

YMCA CAMP ECHO AND THE OUTDOOR DISCOVERY CENTER

2000 West 32nd Street
Fremont, Michigan 49412

General Information Residential coeducational camp serving 250 youngsters in two-week sessions. Emphasis is on building self-esteem through YMCA principles. Outdoor education center operates during nonsummer months for Michigan schools and interest groups. Established in 1899. Owned by YMCA Camp Echo. Operated by McGaw YMCA. 460-acre facility located 40 miles north of Grand Rapids. Features: peninsula with 460 acres; cabins with porches overlooking lake; forest and field areas; nature trail; extended horse and bike trails; separate beaches for sailing, canoeing, waterskiing, and swimming instruction; low and high elements ropes courses.

Profile of Summer Employees Total number: 75; average age: 22; 50% male, 50% female, 40% minorities, 25% high school students, 75% college students, 5% international, 75% local residents, 5% teachers. Nonsmokers preferred.

Employment Information Openings are from April 20 to September 15. Jobs available: 15 *senior counselors* with standard first aid and CPR certification at $105–$120 per week; 1 *aquatic director* with lifeguard, first aid, and CPR certification at $125–$150 per week; 1 *arts and crafts director* with standard first aid and CPR certification at $110–$125 per week; 1 *office manager* with lifeguard, first aid, and CPR class C licenses at $125–$150 per week; 4 *adventure trip leaders* with lifeguard, first aid, and CPR class C licenses at $150–$200 per week; 2 *wilderness site leaders* with lifeguard, first aid, and CPR certification at $130–$150 per week; 1 *wrangler* with CHA training and first aid and CPR certification at $130–$150 per week; 1 *assistant wrangler* with standard first aid and CPR certification at $120–$140 per week; 5 *health officers* with RN or LPN license and CPR and standard first aid certification at $250 per week; 1 *van driver* with standard first aid and CPR class C license at $100–$125 per week; 3 *cooks* with CPR certification and experience with large groups at $100–$300 per week; 3 *sail/canoe/waterskiing directors* with standard first aid, CPR, and lifeguard certification at $110–$130 per week; 12 *outdoor education staff members* at $110 per week.

Benefits College credit, preemployment training, on-site room and board at no charge, use of facility, YMCA membership.

Contact Christopher Hart, Director, YMCA Camp Echo and the Outdoor Discovery Center, Department SJ, 1000 Grove Street, Evanston, Illinois 60201; 708-475-7400, Fax 708-475-7959.

MINNESOTA

CAMP BUCKSKIN

Box 389
Ely, Minnesota 55731

General Information Residential camp offering two 32-day sessions for youth with academic and/or social skill difficulties (learning disabilities, ADD/ADHD, and emotional/behavioral difficulties). Established in 1959. Owned by Mr. and Mrs. R. S. Bauer. Affiliated with American Camping Association. 165-acre facility located 80 miles northeast of Duluth. Features: location in the scenic Superior National Forest; extensive lakeshore for swimming and canoeing activities; separate canoe trip program in Boundary Waters Canoe Area wilderness; variety of environments for nature program (lakeshore, river, pond, marsh, woodlands, and meadows); well-equipped library for program and staff use; several large sports fields.

Profile of Summer Employees Total number: 75; average age: 22; 50% male, 50% female, 5% minorities, 12% high school students, 70% college students, 10% international, 10% local residents, 20% teachers. Nonsmokers only.

Employment Information Openings are from June 5 to August 20. Jobs available: 8 *counselors/swimming instructors* with WSI certification, lifeguard training, standard first aid, and CPR (preferred) at $1050–$1400 per season; 10 *counselors/canoeing instructors* with lifeguard training, standard first aid, and CPR (preferred) at $1050–$1400 per season; 6 *experienced counselors/nature and environment instructors* with certification in programs such as NOLS and Nature Quest (preferred) at $1050–$1400 per season; 6 *counselors/arts and crafts instructors* with creativity and ability to teach and enthuse others (preferred) at $1050–$1400 per season; 3 *experienced counselors/archery instructors* with certification from organizations like the National Archery Association at $1050–$1400 per season; 3 *counselors/riflery instructors* with gun and range safety training with the National Rifle Association, military, or similar agency (preferred) at $1050–$1400 per season; 8 *reading teachers* with license in elementary or secondary education and special education certification (preferred) at $1350–$1650 per season; 2 *office assistants* with good typing skills and phone ability (computer experience a plus) at $1050–$1350 per season; 5 *kitchen assistants* with a positive attitude and ability to work with others at $900–$1050 per season; 8 *trip counselors* with lifeguard, CPR, and standard first aid training at $1150–$1450 per season; 2 *registered nurses* with RN license.

Benefits College credit, preemployment training, formal ongoing training, on-site room and board at no charge, possible internships, increased responsibilities and compensation for returning staff, travel stipend for returning staff.

Contact Thomas Bauer, Director, Camp Buckskin, Department SJ, 3811 West Broadway, Minneapolis, Minnesota 55422; 612-536-9749. Application deadline: May 30.

From the Employer *Buckskin staff members participate in a nine-day training program that includes behavioral intervention and management techniques, social-skill goal attainment program, teaching techniques for various learning styles, and communication and leadership skills. This training helps the staff—undergraduate or graduate students or workers in the field—increase their knowledge and effectively facilitate the positive growth and development of our campers.*

CAMP COURAGE
8046 83rd Street, NW
Maple Lake, Minnesota 55358

General Information Programs offered for physically disabled children and adults, including adventure camping for the deaf and speech therapy for speech/language-impaired children. Established in 1955. Owned by Courage Center. Affiliated with American Camping Association. 300-acre facility located 50 miles west of Minneapolis. Features: 2 lakes; pool; gymnasium; forest areas; accessible site; horses.

Profile of Summer Employees Total number: 100; average age: 22; 50% male, 50% female, 5% minorities, 10% high school students, 80% college students, 1% retirees, 1% international, 60% local residents.

Employment Information Openings are from June 5 to August 29. Year-round positions also offered. Jobs available: 6 *waterfront personnel* with WSI/lifeguard certification at $125–$150 per week; 36 *counselors* at $125–$150 per week; 3 *nurses* with RN, LPN, or GN license at $300–$430 per week; 20 *program specialists* with appropriate certification for area at $125–$150 per week; 10 *speech clinicians* with M.S. in speech pathology/communications disorders at $300–$450 per week.

Benefits College credit, preemployment training, formal ongoing training, on-site room and board at no charge, laundry facilities, health insurance, tuition reimbursement, scholarships.

Contact Roger Upcraft, Program Manager, Camp Courage, Department SJ, 8046 83rd Street NW, Maple Lake, Minnesota 55358; 612-963-3121. Application deadline: May 31.

From the Employer *By working for Camp Courage, employees gain preprofessional training in the medical and educational fields. The staff-camper ratio is approximately 1:2.*

CAMP MISHAWAKA FOR BOYS/GIRLS
P.O. Box 368
Grand Rapids, Minnesota 55744

General Information Residential brother-sister camp for boys and girls. Established in 1910. Owned by Camp Mishawaka. Affiliated with American Camping Association, Midwest Association of Private Camps, Grand Rapids Chamber of Commerce. 200-acre facility located 5 miles south of Grand Rapids. Features: beautiful facility; secluded setting with easy access to town; 4 tennis courts; 5,000-acre lake with 1,800 feet of shoreline; 3 large sports fields.

Profile of Summer Employees Total number: 40; average age: 29; 63% male, 37% female, 4% minorities, 20% college students, 6% retirees, 3% international, 7% local residents. Nonsmokers preferred.

Employment Information Openings are from June 12 to August 19. Jobs available: 12 *cabin counselors (boys' and girls')* with WSI certification and general skills in tennis, swimming, canoeing, sailing, arts and crafts, boating, and music at $600–$850 per season; 1 *riding director* with HSA certification at $850–$1000 per season. International students encouraged to apply.

Benefits College credit, preemployment training, on-site room and board at no charge, travel reimbursement, use of facilities during time off, cordial atmosphere, interesting trips.

Contact Steve Purdum, Executive Director, Camp Mishawaka for Boys/Girls, Department SJ, P.O. Box 368, Grand Rapids, Minnesota 55744; 218-326-5011, Fax 218-326-9228. Application deadline: May 15.

CAMP THUNDERBIRD FOR BOYS/CAMP THUNDERBIRD FOR GIRLS
Route 2, Box 225
Bemidji, Minnesota 56601

General Information Separate residential facilities serving 150 girls and 200 boys from forty U.S. cities and five other countries. Established in 1946. Owned by Camp Thunderbird, Inc. Affiliated with American Camping Association, Greenpeace/Defender of Wildlife, Nature Conservancy. 700-acre facility located 12 miles south of Bemidji. Features: pristine pine and hardwood forest; 7-mile shoreline on serene, crystal-clear, sand-bottom lake; extensive riding and hiking trails; low ropes teams course with climbing/rappelling wall; 3 athletic fields; volleyball and basketball courts; 7 outdoor asphalt tennis courts.

Profile of Summer Employees Total number: 200; average age: 24; 55% male, 45% female, 5% minorities, 12% high school students, 60% college students, 2% retirees, 10% international, 3% local residents, 8% teachers. Nonsmokers preferred.

Employment Information Openings are from June 1 to August 12. Jobs available: 35

cabin counselors (minimum age 19) with freshman year of college completed, experience working with children, high-energy, caring attitude, ability to assist or teach in several camp activities, and outdoor orientation; 2 *certified riflery instructors* (minimum age 21) with DNR or NRA certification and teaching experience (required); 1 *arts and crafts specialist* (minimum age 21) with experience as an art teacher or student status preferred (completion of junior year required); 3 *experienced horseback specialists* (minimum age 21) with experience in Western and English Hunt Seat specialties, completion of junior year of college, and CHA or HSA certification preferred, but will send to clinic for certification; 1 *waterfront director* (minimum age 25) with WSI certification, college degree, and knowledge of various water sports; 10 *swimming instructors* (minimum age 22) with WSI certification and teaching experience (preferred); 4 *certified sailing instructors* (minimum age 21) with sailing and lifeguard certification; 2 *unit directors* (minimum age 22) with experience encompassing staff supervision and direct leadership of children in outdoor recreation/camp activities and college degree; 1 *program director* (minimum age 21) with experience encompassing staff supervision and direct leadership of children in outdoor recreation/camp activities and college degree; 1 *trip director* (minimum age 21) with experience in diverse kinds of wilderness trips and equipment use and college degree; 15 *wilderness and trip leaders* (minimum age 21) with certifications in CPR, lifeguard, and advanced first aid (must be comfortable and confident living in the wilderness); 3 *nurses* with RN or LPN license; 10 *kitchen personnel* (minimum age 19) with ability to assist with kitchen operations, food preparation, dishwashing, and cleanup and one year of college completed; 2 *office personnel* (minimum age 20) with bookkeeping and computer knowledge, ability to handle camper/ staff cash accounts, sophomore year of college completed, and average or above-average typing skills. International students encouraged to apply.

Benefits   College credit, preemployment training, on-site room and board at no charge, laundry facilities, travel reimbursement, medical services, families accepted.

Contact   Carol A. Sigoloff, Camp Thunderbird for Boys/Camp Thunderbird for Girls, Department SJ, 10976 Chambray Court, St. Louis, Missouri 63141; 314-567-3167, Fax 314-567-7218. Application deadline: April 30.

From the Employer   *Thunderbird staff members have a unique opportunity to have an impact on our campers. Our staff's talent, experience, and cultural and geographic diversity contribute to an enthusiastic, caring community. Staff members will be exposed to the positive, noncompetitive atmosphere for which we are known. The leadership training and life-skill development offered at Camp Thunderbird are of significant career value.*

DEEP PORTAGE CONSERVATION RESERVE
Route 1, Box 129
Hackensack, Minnesota 56452

General Information   Environmental education and resource management demonstration for school classes, in-house summer camps, families, tourists, natural resource professionals, and nature-related hobby groups. Established in 1973. Owned by Cass County. Operated by Deep Portage Conservation Foundation. Affiliated with Alliance for Environmental Education, National Audubon Society, Izaak Walton League. 6,107-acre facility located 50 miles north of Brainerd. Features: 6,107-acre demonstration working forest; resort area with over 400 lakes in a 35-mile radius; 30 miles of recreational trails; proximity to Chippewa National Forest (with largest breeding population of bald eagles in the lower 48 states); interpretive center with museum, wildflower garden, and bookstore; 27,000-square foot conference center with classrooms, theater, and overnight accommodations for 120 people.

Profile of Summer Employees   Total number: 14; average age: 22; 50% male, 50% female, 10% minorities, 10% high school students, 70% college students, 10% international.

Employment Information Openings are from June 5 to August 25. Year-round positions also offered. Jobs available: 12 *instructor/naturalists* with college training in related fields at $80–$160 per week.

Benefits Preemployment training, formal ongoing training, on-site room and board at no charge, laundry facilities.

Contact Arlene Naylon, Program Administrator, Deep Portage Conservation Reserve, Department SJ, Rt. 1, Box 129, Hackensack, Minnesota 56452; 218-682-2325.

From the Employer *Deep Portage employees experience a variety of leadership responsibilities as they interact with our diverse client base. In the course of a week, they may teach several classes to middle school children, lead an evening campfire, host a teacher's workshop, and interpret the forest management plan to a group of senior citizens.*

FRIENDSHIP VENTURES/CAMP FRIENDSHIP
10509 108th Street, NW
Annandale, Minnesota 55302

General Information Residential camp serving children and adults with developmental disabilities. Established in 1964. Owned by Friendship Ventures. Affiliated with American Camping Association. 100-acre facility located 60 miles north of Minneapolis. Features: location on a large lake; 80 wooded acres; resort-style camping; challenge/adventure course; hayride and hiking trails; tent-camping sites, including an island.

Profile of Summer Employees Total number: 100; average age: 20; 25% male, 75% female, 5% minorities, 15% high school students, 85% college students, 10% international, 20% local residents, 5% teachers. Nonsmokers preferred.

Employment Information Openings are from June 1 to August 31. Winter break, Christmas break positions also offered. Jobs available: 2 *experienced laundry/housekeeping staff members;* 60 *counselors* at $140 per week; 1 *waterfront director* with WSI and lifeguard certification at $150 per week; 3 *waterfront lifeguards* with lifeguard WSI and lifeguard certification (preferred) at $140 per week; 1 *experienced boating director* with knowledge of outboard motors, canoes, rowboats, and pontoon boats at $140 per week; 3 *experienced travel guides* with leadership skills at $140 per week; 1 *canteen manager* with record-keeping skills at $140 per week; 2 *seasonal support personnel* with computer, typing, and filing experience at $140 per week; 4 *nurses* with RN, LPN, or GN license or B.S.N. degree; 3 *weekend counselors* with physical strength, mental alertness, and at least one year of college completed at $100 per week; 12 *junior counselors* with physical and emotional strength, mental alertness, creativity, flexibility, and high school student status (successful volunteer experience may be substituted for the age requirement) at $75 per week; 2 *arts and crafts specialists* with current major in therapeutic recreation, occupational therapy, or art education/therapy or experience planning and implementing arts and crafts activities/projects at $140 per week; 1 *music specialist* with current major in music, music therapy, or special education and experience planning and implementing activities at $140 per week; 1 *outdoor specialist* with current major in an environmental, outdoor, or education field at $140 per week; 1 *recreation specialist* with current major in recreation, physical education, or adaptive physical recreation and leadership skills involving group activities at $140 per week; 1 *public-relations assistant* with current major in journalism, photography, or related field and experience with a 35mm camera at $140 per week; 2 *experienced dining hall staff members.*

Benefits College credit, preemployment training, formal ongoing training, on-site room and board at no charge, laundry facilities.

Contact Joanne Fieldseth, Director of Seasonal Personnel, Friendship Ventures/Camp

Friendship, Department SJ, 10509 108th Street, NW, Annandale, Minnesota 55302; 612-274-8376, Fax 612-274-3238. Application deadline: May 1.

From the Employer   *All staff members go through orientation prior to work, which includes team building, emergency water safety, health care, and job position training. This is a tremendously rewarding and challenging experience. Join staff members from all over the United States and our guest staff from other countries.*

GRAND VIEW LODGE GOLF AND TENNIS CLUB
South 134 Nokomis Avenue
Nisswa, Minnesota 56468

General Information   Resort that caters to families and business conventions. Established in 1919. Owned by ETOC Corp. Affiliated with Minnesota Resort Association. 900-acre facility located 140 miles north of Minneapolis. Features: historic main lodge and 60 cabins; full-service conference center; 1,500 feet of beach; 2 golf courses, 11 tennis courts, jacuzzi, and indoor pool; great hiking and biking trails; beautiful lakes for swimming, boating, and fishing.

Profile of Summer Employees   Total number: 200; average age: 21; 10% minorities, 20% high school students, 70% college students, 10% retirees, 20% international, 20% local residents.

Employment Information   Openings are from April 20 to October 20. Jobs available: 25 *dining room personnel* at $165–$185 per week; 5 *experienced bartenders* at $175–$195 per week; 5 *beach staff members* with knowledge of boats and motors at $165–$185 per week; 15 *housekeepers* at $195–$220 per week; 3 *skilled desk clerks* at $185–$205 per week; 3 *children's program instructors* at $155–$175 per week. International students encouraged to apply.

Benefits   Formal ongoing training, on-site room and board at $150 per month, laundry facilities, partial room rebate if work contract is completed, use of resort facilities at little or no charge, interaction with people from around the world.

Contact   Paul Welch, Operations Manager, Grand View Lodge Golf and Tennis Club, Department SJ, South 134 Nokomis Avenue, Nisswa, Minnesota 56468; 218-963-2234, Fax 218-963-2269.

From the Employer   *We're looking for outgoing students who are motivated to learn a variety of jobs and who can be flexible according to our guests' needs and demands. Staff members are particularly needed late in the season (through October 17).*

MENOGYN–YMCA WILDERNESS ADVENTURES
HC 64, Box 492
Grand Marais, Minnesota 55604

General Information   Wilderness base camp specializing in canoeing, backpacking, and rock-climbing trips in wilderness areas of North America. Established in 1922. Owned by YMCA of Metropolitan Minneapolis. Affiliated with American Camping Association, Young Men's Christian Association. 80-acre facility located 32 miles north of Grand Marais. Features: location near Canada bordering the Boundary Waters Canoe Area Wilderness; rustic base camp facility with very limited modern conveniences; rock-climbing programs along north shore of Lake Superior; extensive wilderness canoe trips in Northeast Minnesota, Ontario, and Manitoba; backpacking on Isle Royale, Superior Hiking Trail, the Rocky Mountains, and Alaska; fleet of 85 wood, aluminum, and plastic canoes.

Profile of Summer Employees   Total number: 42; average age: 22; 50% male, 50% female,

5% minorities, 90% college students, 5% international, 75% local residents. Nonsmokers only.

Employment Information Openings are from June 1 to August 30. Spring break, winter break, Christmas break positions also offered. Jobs available: 24 *trail counselors* with CPR, first aid, and lifeguard training at $110–$145 per week; 1 *experienced cook* with references at $2000–$3000 per season; 1 *program director* with CPR, first aid, and lifeguard training at $120–$145 per week; 3 *in-camp staff members* with CPR, first aid, and lifeguard training at $110–$145 per week; 1 *nurse* with current license at $1200–$2000 per season; 1 *maintenance person* with CPR, first aid, and lifeguard training at $1200–$2000 per season.

Benefits Formal ongoing training, on-site room and board at no charge.

Contact David L. Palmer, Executive Director, Menogyn–YMCA Wilderness Adventures, Department SJ, 4 West Rustic Lodge Avenue, Minneapolis, Minnesota 55409; 612-823-5282, Fax 612-823-2482. Application deadline: March 15.

From the Employer *A ten-day staff training session begins for the summer season on June 2. It is imperative that all summer staff members attend this training, which includes wilderness skills development, first aid, accident prevention, cultural sensitivity, blood borne pathogens training, and sexual abuse sensitivity training.*

NELSON'S RESORT
7632 Nelson Road
Crane Lake, Minnesota 55725

General Information Family resort with conventions in the fall. Established in 1931. Owned by Gloria N. Pohlman. Affiliated with Minnesota Resort Association, Minnesota Arrowhead, Northeastern Division of Minnesota Department of Tourism, Crane Lake Commercial Club. 84-acre facility located 75 miles north of Hibbing. Features: 28 cabins with extensive freshwater lake frontage; dining room/cocktail lounge; gift shop; marina; proximity to Voyageur National Park and Boundary Waters Canoe Area; professional fishing guides with access to 60 miles of Canadian/United States border lakes, hiking trails, and mountain bikes.

Profile of Summer Employees Total number: 32; average age: 20; 44% male, 56% female, 25% college students, 2% retirees, 1% international, 6% local residents.

Employment Information Openings are from May 1 to October 15. Jobs available: 6 *waiters/waitresses* at $800–$900 per month; 5 *cabin staff members* at $800–$900 per month; 3 *dock attendants* at $800–$900 per month; 1 *bellperson* at $800–$900 per month; 3 *kitchen helpers* at $800–$900 per month; 1 *store clerk* at $800–$900 per month; 1 *bartender* at $800–$1000 per month.

Benefits On-site room and board at $300 per month, laundry facilities, use of facilities, bonus.

Contact G. N. Pohlman, Owner, Nelson's Resort, Department SJ, 7632 Nelson Road, Crane Lake, Minnesota 55725; 218-993-2295. Application deadline: April 30.

From the Employer *We supply the use of a boat and motor, with repair and gas charges only, for staff use. Staff members can explore Voyageurs National Park and the Boundary Waters Canoe Area, which allows motor use at our entrance. Employees may also enter Canada, where both Canadian and U.S. customs are available. We train our waitstaff in wine service and the serving and preparation of five-course meals for our semi-formal dining room. Employees gain extensive training in all levels of the hospitality industry.*

PRESBYTERIAN CLEARWATER FOREST
Route 1, Box 397
Deerwood, Minnesota 56444

General Information Residential summer camp serving young people ages 8–17. Established in 1955. Owned by Presbyterian Clearwater Forest, Inc. Affiliated with Presbyterian Camp and Conference Association. 1,016-acre facility located 120 miles north of Minneapolis/St. Paul. Features: 3½ miles of lake frontage; 10 miles of hiking/skiing trails; large stone buildings.

Profile of Summer Employees Total number: 25; average age: 22; 50% male, 50% female, 5% minorities, 2% high school students, 78% college students, 20% retirees, 5% international, 10% local residents. Nonsmokers preferred.

Employment Information Openings are from June 1 to August 30. Jobs available: 12 *camp counselors* at $115–$130 per week; 3 *kitchen assistants* at $100–$120 per week; 2 *maintenance assistants* at $100–$120 per week; 1 *waterfront director* at $130–$160 per week.

Benefits Preemployment training, formal ongoing training, on-site room and board, laundry facilities, health insurance.

Contact Peter Claypoole, Director, Presbyterian Clearwater Forest, Department SJ, Route 1, Box 397, Deerwood, Minnesota 56444; 218-678-2325. Application deadline: May 1.

STRAW HAT PLAYERS
Center for the Arts— Moorhead State University
Moorhead, Minnesota 56563

General Information Summer stock theater producing five shows in a ten-week season, the largest of its type in operation in the region. Established in 1963. Owned by Moorhead State University. Affiliated with American College Theater Festival, Communication and Theater Association of Minnesota, American Theater in Higher Education. 20-acre facility located 1 mile east of Fargo, North Dakota. Features: 900-seat proscenium theater; 350-seat thrust theater; scene shops, costume shops, and dance studio; access to university facilities: library, pool, and athletic center; largest metropolitan area between Minneapolis and Seattle.

Profile of Summer Employees Total number: 60; average age: 25; 60% male, 40% female, 5% minorities, 5% high school students, 70% college students, 40% local residents. Nonsmokers preferred.

Employment Information Openings are from May 30 to August 15. Jobs available: 40 *acting company members* at $75–$200 per week; 5 *theater technicians* at $100–$300 per week; 1 *musical director* with extensive professional experience at $200–$300 per week; 1 *choreographer* with M.F.A. or professional experience at $150–$250 per week; *guest designers* with M.F.A. or professional experience at $150–$250 per week; 1 *properties master* at $150–$250 per week; 3 *costume stitchers* at $100–$250 per week. International students encouraged to apply.

Benefits College credit, preemployment training, formal ongoing training, on-site room and board at no charge, laundry facilities, dormitory housing available.

Contact Director of Theater, Straw Hat Players, Department SJ, Moorhead State University, Moorhead, Minnesota 56563; 218-236-4613, Fax 218-236-2168. Application deadline: January 2.

TOM & WOODS' MOOSE LAKE WILDERNESS CANOE TRIPS
P.O. Box 358
Ely, Minnesota 55731
General Information Wilderness canoe/fishing outfitter for trips into the Boundary Waters Canoe Area Wilderness and Quetico Parks. Established in 1966. Owned by Lyle Williams. Affiliated with Chamber of Commerce of Ely, NACLO, Ely Outfitters Association. 8-acre facility located 125 miles north of Duluth. Features: 1,500 lakes nearby; 1.3 million acres available for trips.
Profile of Summer Employees 60% male, 40% female, 10% high school students, 60% college students, 50% local residents. Nonsmokers preferred.
Employment Information Openings are from May 1 to September 31. Jobs available: *general staff* at $1400 per month.
Benefits Preemployment training, on-site room and board at $375 per month, laundry facilities, use of boats and canoes on days and evenings off.
Contact Lyle Williams, Tom & Woods' Moose Lake Wilderness Canoe Trips, P.O. Box 358, Ely, Minnesota 55731; Fax 218-365-6393.

VALLEYFAIR FAMILY AMUSEMENT PARK
1 Valleyfair Drive
Shakopee, Minnesota 55379
General Information Family amusement park offering a variety of entertainment attractions. Established in 1976. Owned by Cedar Fair Limited Partnership. 68-acre facility located 20 miles south of Minneapolis/St. Paul. Features: located along the Minnesota River; more than two dozen thrilling rides and an equal number of special attractions.
Profile of Summer Employees Total number: 1,200; average age: 18; 50% male, 50% female.
Employment Information Openings are from May 1 to September 30. Jobs available: 200 *ride hosts/hostesses;* 270 *food hosts/hostesses;* 90 *merchandise attendants;* 140 *game attendants;* 1 *accounting clerk;* 1 *employee relations person;* 1 *marketing assistant;* 25 *park-service attendants;* 28 *security officers;* 40 *admissions cashiers;* 40 *ticket takers; landscaper; mechanic's assistant;* 4 *seasonal group-sales representatives;* 4 *personnel clerks.* All positions offered at $2500–$3500 per season. International students encouraged to apply.
Benefits College credit, preemployment training, free admission to the park with Valley Fair identification, free admission passes for relatives and friends, free uniforms and laundry service, possible internships for certain positions.
Contact Camille Schaffer, Personnel Office, Valleyfair Family Amusement Park, Department SJ, 1 Valleyfair Drive, Shakopee, Minnesota 55379; 612-445-7600, Fax 612-445-1539. Application deadline: August 30.

WIDJIWAGAN–YMCA WILDERNESS ADVENTURES
3788 North Arm Road
Ely, Minnesota 55731
General Information Summer wilderness trips for teens as well as school-year wilderness environmental education. Established in 1929. Owned by YMCA of Greater St. Paul. Affiliated with American Camping Association, Young Men's Christian Association, Association for Experiential Education. 400-acre facility located 250 miles north of St. Paul. Features: location in the Superior National Forest; setting one-half mile from the Boundary

Waters Canoe Area (a 700,000-acre wilderness on the Minnesota-Canada border); hand-hewn log cabin camper housing; wilderness lake and forest setting.

Profile of Summer Employees Total number: 70; average age: 23; 60% male, 40% female, 5% minorities, 60% college students, 2% international, 2% local residents. Nonsmokers only.

Employment Information Openings are from June 5 to August 31. Year-round positions also offered. Jobs available: 50 *trail leaders* with CPR, first aid, and lifeguard certification at $1200–$2000 per season. International students encouraged to apply (must apply through YMCA International office).

Benefits Preemployment training, formal ongoing training, on-site room and board at no charge, laundry facilities.

Contact Rolf Thompson, Executive Director, Widjiwagan–YMCA Wilderness Adventures, Department SJ, 1761 University Avenue West, St. Paul, Minnesota 55104-3599; 612-645-6605, Fax 612-646-5521. Application deadline: February 10.

From the Employer *We offer opportunities for extensive wilderness leadership of teenagers, including backpacking and canoe trips in the Boundary Waters Canoe Area, Quetico Provincial Park, Isle Royale National Parks, Northern Ontario, and western mountain ranges.*

YMCA CAMP IHDUHPI
Box 37
Loretto, Minnesota 55357

General Information Residential camp serving 150 boys and girls weekly. Established in 1930. Owned by YMCA of Metropolitan Minneapolis. 200-acre facility located 25 miles west of Minneapolis. Features: beautiful Minnesota location; high adventure center; horse program; extensive waterfront program.

Profile of Summer Employees Total number: 50; average age: 21; 50% male, 50% female, 15% minorities, 30% high school students, 70% college students, 5% international, 50% local residents. Nonsmokers only.

Employment Information Openings are from June 12 to August 28. Year-round positions also offered. Jobs available: 1 *program director* at $1500–$1800 per season; 2 *unit directors* at $1400–$1700 per season; 1 *waterfront director* with WSI certification at $1400–$1700 per season; 1 *riding director* at $1350–$1600 per season; 1 *experienced ropes-course director* at $1350–$1600 per season; 20 *counselors* at $1150–$1400 per season; 1 *nurse* with RN license/LPN at $1600–$1800 per season; 3 *cooks* at $1400–$1700 per season; 1 *nature director* at $1200–$1450 per season; 1 *arts and crafts director* at $1200–$1450 per season; 1 *trip director* at $1200–$1500 per season.

Benefits College credit, preemployment training, formal ongoing training, on-site room and board at no charge, laundry facilities.

Contact Brian Kirk, Executive Director, YMCA Camp Ihduhpi, Department SJ, Box 37, Loretto, Minnesota 55357; 612-479-1146, Fax 612-479-1333. Application deadline: April 1.

From the Employer *Camp Ihduhpi provides CPR and first aid training during a seven-day staff training period before campers arrive. Each cabin has 2 counselors and up to 9 campers. The camp has a good sailing program, including sailboats and sail boards. We also have kayaks for waterfront activities. As part of the Minneapolis YMCA, Camp Ihduhpi offers summer employees help in finding a job in the YMCA.*

MISSOURI

LIONS DEN OUTDOOR LEARNING CENTER
3602 Lions Den Road
Imperial, Missouri 63052
General Information Residential camp providing traditional experiences to persons with developmental disabilities through an emphasis on group interaction and development. Several sessions are open to persons regardless of ability. Established in 1972. Operated by St. Louis ARC. Affiliated with American Camping Association. 300-acre facility located 25 miles southwest of St. Louis. Features: high and low ropes course; winterized cabins; swimming pool; lake frontage; nature area with small farm; trails and a large playing field.
Profile of Summer Employees Total number: 60; average age: 22; 30% male, 70% female, 15% minorities, 5% high school students, 85% college students, 20% international, 65% local residents.
Employment Information Openings are from June 1 to August 10. Jobs available: 10 *experienced activity specialists* (minimum age 19) at $1200–$1800 per season; 50 *experienced counselors* (minimum age 18) with knowledge of developmental disabilities (preferred) at $1140–$1500 per season; *experienced unit director* with two–three years of college completed, knowledge of behavior management techniques, and good communication skills at $1640–$1890 per season; *nurse* with RN, LPN, or equivalent license at $3350–$5000 per season. International students encouraged to apply.
Benefits Preemployment training, on-site room and board at no charge.
Contact Linda Oxendale, Summer Camp Director, Lions Den Outdoor Learning Center, Department SJ, 1816 Lackland Hill Parkway, Suite 200, St. Louis, Missouri 63146; 314-569-2211, Fax 314-569-0778. Application deadline: April 30.

From the Employer *Our staff collects memories to last a lifetime at Camp Lions Den. Sessions emphasizing a person-centered approach serve youth and adults of all abilities— primarily persons with developmental disabilities. We welcome and embrace diversity, creativity, and energy in our staff and campers. An extensive precamp training prepares staff for a remarkable summer.*

MONTANA

GLACIER PARK, INC.
Glacier National Park
East Glacier Park, Montana 59434-0147
General Information National park concessioner. Established in 1912. Affiliated with The Dial Corporation. Situated on 1 million acres. Features: 1,000 miles of hiking trails; glaciers; forest; wildlife; location in Big Sky Country (one of the few pristine regions remaining in the United States).
Profile of Summer Employees Total number: 936; average age: 20; 50% male, 50% female, 20% minorities, 90% college students, 10% retirees, 2% international, 15% local residents, 2% teachers. Nonsmokers preferred.
Employment Information Jobs available: *waiters/waitresses; buspersons; bartenders;*

front-office clerks; cashiers; night auditors; bell porters; room attendants; housepersons; porters; line cooks; kitchen workers; gift shop and camp store clerks; reservation clerks; general office personnel; accounting clerks; undergardeners; laundry workers; warehouse clerks; truck drivers; bus drivers/tour guides (minimum age 21) with or with ability to qualify for a Class A chauffeur's license; *dormitory supervisors.* All positions offered at $1000 per season. International students encouraged to apply.

Benefits Preemployment training, formal ongoing training, on-site room and board at $56 per week, laundry facilities, travel reimbursement, opportunity for internships (accounting, culinary arts, hotel/restaurant, music/drama), employee cafeterias, group tour gratuity share or bonus program for many positions, chance to meet students from every state and from abroad.

Contact Mr. Ian B. Tippet, Director of Facilities, Glacier Park, Inc., Dial Corporation Mail Station 0924, Phoenix, Arizona 85077; 602-248-2620, Fax 602-207-5589.

LAZY K BAR RANCH
P.O. Box 550
Big Timber, Montana 59011

General Information One hundred thirteen-year-old operating cattle and horse ranch accommodating selected guests for seventy-two summers. Established in 1880. Owned by Van Cleve family. Affiliated with Dude Ranchers' Association. 22,000-acre facility located 100 miles west of Billings. Features: swimming pool; rural setting in an isolated, unspoiled mountain environment; authentic ranch; horses; fossil fields; local rodeos.

Profile of Summer Employees Total number: 19; average age: 20; 60% male, 40% female, 45% high school students, 40% college students, 5% retirees, 5% international, 5% local residents.

Employment Information Openings are from June 10 to September 5. Jobs available: 1 *experienced head cook* with ability to cook for 65–70 people at $650–$850 per month; 1 *second cook/baker* at $450 per month; 3 *waiters/waitresses* at $425–$450 per month; 2 *housekeepers* at $425–$450 per month; 1 *laundry worker* at $450 per month; 1 *split-shift worker* at $450 per month; 1 *storekeeper* at $450 per month; 1 *choreperson* with experience with milk cows at $450 per month; 3 *experienced wranglers* at $450 per month; 1 *experienced children's wrangler* at $450 per month; 1 *experienced head wrangler* (salary negotiable); 1 *dishwasher* at $425 per month; 1 *winter caretaker* with desire for solitude and experience with chainsaws and other tools (position available from September 12 to June 12) at $444 per month. International students encouraged to apply.

Benefits College credit, on-site room and board at no charge, laundry facilities, riding on days off, square dancing bonus, excellent tips.

Contact Lazy K Bar Ranch, Department SJ, P.O. Box 550, Big Timber, Montana 59011; 406-537-4404. Application deadline: March 1.

From the Employer *Staff members are housed 2 to a cabin. There is a recreation cabin for staff. Employees and guests come from all over the world.*

NINE QUARTER CIRCLE RANCH
5000 Taylor Fork Road
Gallatin Gateway, Montana 59730

General Information Family-oriented dude ranch hosting 75 guests weekly. Established in 1946. Owned by Kim and Kelly Kelsey. Affiliated with Dude Ranchers' Association, State Chamber of Commerce. 1,000-acre facility located 60 miles south of Bozeman. Features:

mountain setting; log cabin buildings; isolated stream-side location; thousands of acres of national forest land surrounding ranch; swimming pool; view of Yellowstone National Park. **Profile of Summer Employees** Total number: 20; average age: 21; 40% male, 60% female, 90% college students, 10% retirees. Nonsmokers preferred.

Employment Information Openings are from June 1 to September 15. Jobs available: 4 *cabin cleaners/servers;* 2 *kitchen helpers/dishwashers;* 2 *baby-sitters* with first aid and adult, child, and infant CPR certification; 1 *laundry worker;* 2 *second cooks;* 2 *ranch hands* with first aid and adult, child, and infant CPR certification; *maintenance workers.* All positions offered at $600 per month.

Benefits College credit, on-site room and board at no charge, laundry facilities, use of horses on days off, participation in ranch activities such as square dances, movies, and games.

Contact Kim and Kelly Kelsey, Nine Quarter Circle Ranch, Department SJ, 5000 Taylor Fork Road, Gallatin Gateway, Montana 59730; 406-995-4276. Application deadline: April 1.

From the Employer *We are located in a beautiful mountain setting 7 miles from the northwest corner of Yellowstone Park. Employees are encouraged to interact with both coworkers and guests. Here, they will make lifelong friendships while learning many skills. Please, no international applicants.*

ST. MARY LODGE & RESORT
Glacier National Park
St. Mary, Montana 59417

General Information One of Montana's most notable full-service high country resorts. Established in 1932. Owned by Roscoe Black. 100-acre facility located 89 miles east of Kalispell. Features: located at the east entrance to Glacier National Park; 600 miles of hiking trails; internationally famous dining room; proximity to Canada.

Profile of Summer Employees Total number: 180; average age: 21; 40% male, 60% female, 5% high school students, 85% college students, 10% retirees, 20% local residents. Nonsmokers preferred.

Employment Information Openings are from May 1 to October 1. Year-round positions also offered. Jobs available: 26 *experienced waiters/waitresses* at $760 per month; 12 *pantry/fry cooks, experience preferred,* at $824–$840 per month; 5 *gas station attendants* at $792 per month; 15 *housekeepers* at $824 per month; 10 *gift shop clerks, experience preferred,* at $792 per month; 3 *sporting-goods clerks* at $792 per month; 6 *bartenders/ cocktail servers, experience preferred,* at $760 per month; 4 *pizza parlor staff members* at $792–$824 per month; 9 *supermarket staff members* at $792 per month; 4 *front-desk clerks* at $792 per month; 10 *maintenance personnel* at $792 per month; 14 *dishwashing/kitchen personnel* at $792 per month; 11 *deli cooks* at $792 per month; 4 *experienced accounting/ secretarial staff members* at $792 per month; 5 *clerical staff members* at $792 per month; *hosts/buspersons* at $760 per month.

Benefits College credit, on-site room and board at $245 per month, laundry facilities, guaranteed year-end bonuses, retail discount, internships.

Contact Rocky Black, Resort Manager, St. Mary Lodge & Resort, Department SJ, P.O. Box 1808, Sun Valley, Idaho 83353; 208-726-6279. Application deadline: April 10.

63 RANCH
P.O. Box 979
Livingston, Montana 59047

General Information Working cattle and dude ranch operating from June through September with capacity for 30 guests. Established in 1929. Owned by Sandra C. Cahill. Affiliated with Dude Ranchers' Association, National Wildlife Federation, Federation of Fly Fishermen, Montana Farm Bureau, Gallatin Outfitters Association, Trout Unlimited. 2,000-acre facility located 120 miles west of Billings. Features: location in Big Sky country bordering national forest and wilderness; clean air and water; proximity to Yellowstone National Park and blue-ribbon trout streams; location far from town; 100 miles of trails.

Profile of Summer Employees Total number: 15; average age: 25; 47% male, 53% female, 5% high school students, 45% college students, 10% retirees, 10% local residents. Nonsmokers only.

Employment Information Openings are from June 1 to September 20. Jobs available: 1 *experienced head cook* with ability to run a kitchen and cook for 50 people at $1000 per month; 1 *experienced second cook* at $800 per month; 1 *dishwasher* at $600 per month; 2 *waiters/waitresses* at $600 per month; 1 *kitchen helper* at $600 per month; 1 *experienced head housekeeper* at $800 per month; 2 *cabin cleaners* at $600 per month; 1 *chore boy/girl* with physical strength (lifting involved) at $600 per month.

Benefits On-site room and board at no charge, laundry facilities, workmen's compensation and possible end-of-season bonus, use of ranch facilities during time off, transportation to and from town and airport.

Contact Sandra C. Cahill, President, 63 Ranch, Department SJ, P.O. Box 979, Livingston, Montana 59047; 406-222-0570. College students need not apply unless they can stay until September 15.

From the Employer *Our crew may work harder than they have ever worked in their lives while having more fun. You will meet people from all over the world and get to know them with a little effort. Lifelong friendships are made between crew and guests. Nature is all around for learning about anything from geology, butterflies, or birds to the ranch life of country people. We are located far from the nearest town, which is small. Generally, 1½ hours should be planned for a round-trip into town. Employees will need to be self-sufficient.*

SWEET GRASS RANCH
Melville Route, Box 161
Big Timber, Montana 59011

General Information Working cattle ranch that accepts 20 guests to live ranch life. Established in 1926. Owned by Bill and Shelly Carroccia. Affiliated with National Register of Historic Places, Dude Ranchers' Association, National Cattlemen's Association. 20,000-acre facility located 120 miles northwest of Billings. Features: beautiful, unspoiled scenery; clear lake and streams for fishing.

Profile of Summer Employees Total number: 8; average age: 21; 50% male, 50% female, 100% college students, 25% local residents. Nonsmokers preferred.

Employment Information Openings are from June 1 to September 10. Jobs available: 2 *cooks* with experience or training as a baker and ability to work well with others at $600 per month; 2 *cabin staff members* with organizational and interpersonal skills and attention to cleanliness at $450 per month; 4 *wranglers* with horse experience (must enjoy working with people) at $500 per month.

Benefits On-site room and board at no charge, laundry facilities, tips.

Contact Mrs. William Carroccia, Owner, Sweet Grass Ranch, Department SJ, Melville

Route, Box 161, Big Timber, Montana 59011; 406-537-4497. Application deadline: February 15.

From the Employer　*Generally, 2 staff members share a cabin. Staff members have the opportunity to ride one day a week and to take at least one pack trip.*

YELLOWSTONE PARK SERVICE STATIONS
Yellowstone National Park
Gardiner, Montana 59030

General Information　Operator of automotive service facilities in Yellowstone National Park. Established in 1947. Affiliated with National Park Hospitality Association, Adopt-A-Highway Program. Located 90 miles south of Bozeman. Features: proximity to Grand Teton National Park and several national forests; world's greatest concentration of geysers; outdoor work; Yellowstone Lake (the largest Alpine lake in the United States); spectacular waterfalls, mountains, and canyons.

Profile of Summer Employees　Total number: 95; average age: 23; 68% male, 32% female, 5% minorities, 63% college students, 4% retirees, 1% international, 10% local residents. Nonsmokers preferred.

Employment Information　Openings are from May 1 to October 15. Jobs available: 50 *service station attendants* with good communication skills at $178 per week; 18 *automobile mechanics* with ASE certification or current enrollment in ASE program at $240 per week; 3 *accounting clerks* with ability to operate 10-key adding machine by touch, computer skills, and communication skills at $182 per week; 1 *warehouse helper* with good driving record and communication skills at $182 per week.

Benefits　College credit, preemployment training, on-site room and board at $58 per week, laundry facilities, health insurance, employee assistance program, employee recreation program, accident insurance, advancement potential in subsequent seasons.

Contact　Bill Berg, Director of Business Operations, Yellowstone Park Service Stations, P.O. Box 11, Department WDW, Gardiner, Montana 59030-0011; 406-848-7333, Fax 406-848-7731. Application deadline: May 1.

From the Employer　*The crew size at each of our locations varies from 4 to 15, and the experience typically fosters long friendships and a strong sense of community. Employees live in some of the world's finest country for hiking, rafting, fishing, photography, mountaineering, geyser gazing, and wildlife viewing.*

NEW HAMPSHIRE

BROOKWOODS FOR BOYS/DEER RUN FOR GIRLS
Chestnut Cove Road
Alton, New Hampshire 03809

General Information　Residential religious camps serving 250 campers in two-, four-, six- and eight-week sessions. Established in 1944. Owned by Christian Camps and Conferences-Brookwoods-Deer Run. Affiliated with Christian Camps and Conference, Inc., American Camping Association. 250-acre facility located 100 miles north of Boston. Features: frontage on Lake Winniprauke; rustic wilderness environment; beautiful lodge and recreational hall; exquisite surrounding wilderness area; well-rounded program activities.

Profile of Summer Employees   Total number: 100; average age: 28; 50% male, 50% female, 10% minorities, 10% high school students, 90% college students, 10% international, 20% local residents, 10% teachers. Nonsmokers only.

Employment Information   Openings are from June 15 to August 22. Spring break, winter break positions also offered. Jobs available: *trip staff* with CPR and first aid certification at $1000–$1200 per season; *waterfront staff* with WSI, LGT certification at $1000–$1200 per season; *general counselors* at $1000–$1200 per season; *riding instructor* (minimum age 21) with CHA certification at $1200–$1300 per season; *riflery instructor* with NRA certification at $1100–$1200 per season; *waterskiing instructor* with LGT certification at $1100–$1200 per season. International students encouraged to apply.

Benefits   Preemployment training, formal ongoing training, on-site room and board at no charge, travel reimbursement.

Contact   Miles M. Strodel, Executive Director, Brookwoods for Boys/Deer Run for Girls, Chestnut Cove Road, Alton, New Hampshire 03809; 603-875-3600, Fax 603-875-4606. Application deadline: May 1.

From the Employer   *We foster a warm, caring, evangelical environment that encourages young people to establish strong relationships with each other. We promote high standards, strong family values, and sensitive, positive leadership. Leadership training begins ten days before camp.*

CAMP ALBANY
RFD 1
Conway, New Hampshire 03818

General Information   Residential Girl Scout camp serving 100 girls ages 6–12 in one- and two-week sessions. Established in 1984. Owned by Swift Water Girl Scout Council. Affiliated with American Camping Association. 100-acre facility located 150 miles north of Boston. Features: location in White Mountains of New Hampshire; waterfront with panoramic view of Mt. Chocorua; sandy beach on beautiful Iona Lake; cabin sleeping.

Profile of Summer Employees   Total number: 35; average age: 20; 100% female, 5% minorities, 70% college students, 10% international, 20% local residents. Nonsmokers preferred.

Employment Information   Openings are from June 15 to August 22. Jobs available: 1 *experienced program director* at $2300–$3700 per season; 1 *health director* with RN license at $1600–$2800 per season; 1 *experienced waterfront director* with WSI and LGT certification at $1600–$2800 per season; 4 *waterfront assistants* with WSI and LGT certification at $1200–$1600 per season; 5 *experienced unit leaders* at $1600–$2100 per season; 15 *unit assistants* with child supervisory experience at $1200–$1600 per season; 1 *food supervisor* with menu planning and quantity cooking experience at $2300–$3700 per season; 2 *experienced cooks* at $1600–$2600 per season; 1 *experienced arts director* at $1600–$2600 per season.

Benefits   Preemployment training, on-site room and board at no charge, laundry facilities, health insurance.

Contact   Ms. Nancy Frankel, Director of Outdoor Education, Camp Albany, Department SJ, 88 Harvey Road, #4, Manchester, New Hampshire 03103; 603-627-4158. Application deadline: June 15.

From the Employer   *Albany offers an extensive seven-day precamp training session dealing with program planning and developing self-esteem and leadership in young girls.*

CAMP CODY FOR BOYS
Ossipee Lake Road
Freedom, New Hampshire 03836

General Information Multispecialty programs of play and skill development in all land and water sports, shop, arts and sciences, and adventure trips for 195 boys ages 7–16. Established in 1926. Owned by Camp Cody, Inc. Operated by Camp Cody for Boys. Affiliated with American Camping Association, New Hampshire Camp Directors' Association. 140-acre facility located 90 miles north of Boston, Massachusetts. Features: superb site near ocean at edge of White Mountain National Forest; warm sand-bottom 8-mile lake with 1 mile of shoreline; state-of-the-art facilities and equipment; many acres of athletics fields; over 50 buildings, including social hall, gymnasiums, labs, and fully-equipped cabins; indoor/outdoor and nighttime sports.

Profile of Summer Employees Total number: 100; average age: 24; 90% male, 10% female, 15% minorities, 10% high school students, 75% college students, 5% retirees, 20% international, 10% local residents, 30% teachers. Nonsmokers preferred.

Employment Information Openings are from June 19 to August 21. Jobs available: *experienced swimming instructors and assistants* at $800–$1500 per season; *canoe and kayak trip leaders* with high skill levels, trip abilities, and emergency skills at $900–$2000 per season; *experienced coaches and assistants* with coaching knowledge of land team and individual sports at $800–$2000 per season; *outdoor-skills and trip leaders* with experience in natural sciences/nature/ecology, camp craft, scouting, overnight backpacking, emergency skills, and bicycle trips at $800–$2000 per season; *art and science instructors* with experience in woodshop, model rocketry, computers, videos, photography/darkroom, ham radios, and fishing at $800–$2000 per season; *general counselors and assistants* with ability to assist in different areas and work well with youngsters at $700–$1500 per season; *experienced nurse* with RN license at $2000–$2500 per season; *chef's assistants* with experience in food handling and group feeding, including salads, bakery, and general skills; *office staff* with general ability in typing, computers, phone skills, and mailings; *housekeeping staff; nannies* (for director's family); *groundskeepers* with general grounds experience in lawn care, carpentry, and plumbing; *food-service workers* (dishwashers, waitstaff, cleaning crew, and chef's helpers); *maintenance workers* with general mechanical ability for sanitation, trash collection, repairs, construction, and automotive work. International students encouraged to apply.

Benefits College credit, preemployment training, formal ongoing training, on-site room and board at no charge, laundry facilities, travel reimbursement, health insurance, use of facilities, wonderful local vacation areas, no state taxes or deductions.

Contact Alan J. Stolz, Director, Camp Cody for Boys, Department SJ, 5 Lockwood Circle, Westport, Connecticut 06880; 203-226-4389/938-2173, Fax 203-938-2833.

From the Employer *Camp Cody has both a national and international clientele and staff participating in our eight-week season. During our one-week preseason staff orientation program, we conduct certifications and training in areas such as driver's safety, water safety, CPR, first aid, area tours, and full program orientations with many other certifications available. We have fully equipped cabins with electricity, cubbies, and bathrooms, and our employees enjoy an approximate 1:3 staff-camper ratio. Terrific camaraderie exists among our workers, who take pleasure in the surrounding area and our elaborate facilities. We also have a busy trip program extending across the northeast and Canada, with intercamp social and sports exchanges and an excellent dining room. There are limited preseason and postseason opportunities. We are served locally via Trailways bus and Portland/Portsmouth airports. Private autos are permitted.*

CAMP KENWOOD–EVERGREEN
Potter Place, P.O. Box 501
Andover, New Hampshire 03216

General Information Residential camp serving boys and girls. Established in 1930. Owned by Judy and Arthur Sharenow. Affiliated with American Camping Association, Private Independent Camps, New Hampshire Camp Directors' Association. 160-acre facility located 100 miles northwest of Boston, Massachusetts. Features: setting in mountain valley; beautiful pond; rolling hills; 11 tennis courts; major indoor gymnasium.

Profile of Summer Employees Total number: 100; average age: 23; 50% male, 50% female, 2% minorities, 20% high school students, 70% college students, 10% international, 10% local residents, 5% teachers. Nonsmokers preferred.

Employment Information Openings are from June 20 to August 20. Jobs available: 2 *waterfront directors* with college degree, WSI, and lifeguard certification at $2500 per season; 1 *tennis director* with club teaching experience at $3000 per season; 1 *arts and crafts instructor* with college degree at $2000 per season; 1 *experienced drama director* with college degree at $2000 per season; 4 *swimming instructors* with WSI and lifeguard certification at $1200–$1500 per season; 1 *experienced gymnastics instructor* with college degree at $1200–$1500 per season; *general athletics counselors* at $1100–$1800 per season.

Benefits Preemployment training, on-site room and board at no charge, laundry facilities, travel reimbursement.

Contact Arthur Sharenow, Director, Camp Kenwood–Evergreen, 10 Partridge Road, Lexington, Massachusetts 02173; 617-862-7537.

From the Employer *Kenwood-Evergreen is a friendly environment in which to work. We try to create a family atmosphere for our staff members as well as our campers. Very few new staff members come to Kenwood or Evergreen for only one summer—it becomes a life pattern for many.*

CAMP MERRIMAC
Route 2
Contoocook, New Hampshire 03229

General Information Residential camp serving over 200 highly motivated boys and girls. Established in 1919. Owned by Robert M. Martin. Affiliated with American Camping Association, New England Camping Association. 400-acre facility located 10 miles northwest of Concord, Massachusetts. Features: magnificent lake; pollen-free air; location 72 miles from Boston; modern cabins; pine forest location; 4 large sports fields.

Profile of Summer Employees Total number: 100; average age: 21; 60% male, 40% female, 40% college students, 40% international. Nonsmokers only.

Employment Information Openings are from June 25 to August 28. Jobs available: 1 *experienced archery instructor* at $800–$1200 per season; 1 *experienced riflery instructor* at $800–$1200 per season; 3 *swimming instructors* with WSI certification at $800–$1200 per season; 1 *canoe instructor* at $800–$1200 per season; 2 *waterskiing instructors* at $800–$1200 per season; 1 *sailing instructor* at $800–$1200 per season; 1 *athletic director* at $800–$1400 per season; 1 *head of waterfront* with WSI certification at $800–$2000 per season; 2 *soccer instructors* at $800–$1200 per season; 2 *softball instructors* at $800–$1200 per season; 2 *basketball instructors* at $800–$1200 per season; 4 *group leaders* at $1200–$1500 per season; 1 *fine arts instructor* at $800–$1200 per season; 1 *crafts instructor* at $800–$1200 per season; 3 *science instructors* at $1200–$1400 per season; 6 *bus drivers* at $800–$1200 per season; *tennis instructors* at $800–$1200 per season. International students encouraged to apply.

Benefits College credit, preemployment training, on-site room and board at no charge, laundry facilities, workmen's compensation insurance.
Contact Robert M. Martin, President, Camp Merrimac, Department SJ, 46 Standish Drive, Scarsdale, New York 10583; 914-725-1215, Fax 914-723-7105. Application deadline: March 1.

From the Employer *At a three-day preprogram orientation, all employees participate in workshops on safety and accident prevention, cultural sensitivity, and the facilitation of group interaction. Generally, 2 staff members and 6 campers share a cabin.*

CAMP TEL NOAR
Hampstead, New Hampshire 03841

General Information Jewish coeducational cultural residential camp serving 265 children. Established in 1952. Operated by Cohen Foundation. Affiliated with American Camping Association, New Hampshire Camping Association, Private Independent Camps. 60-acre facility located 50 miles north of Boston, Massachusetts. Features: unique housing; spring-fed lake; 8 tennis courts; beautiful multipurpose gym with stage.
Profile of Summer Employees Total number: 95; average age: 19; 16% high school students, 82% college students, 2% international. Nonsmokers preferred.
Employment Information Openings are from June 25 to August 24. Jobs available: 3 *arts and crafts instructors* at $1350–$1800 per season; 1 *arts and crafts program director* at $2000–$2500 per season; 1 *music program director* at $2000–$2500 per season; 2 *canoe instructors* at $1350–$2000 per season; 2 *sailing instructors* at $1350–$2000 per season; 3 *swimming instructors* with WSI and lifeguard training certification at $1350–$2000 per season; 1 *swimming program director* with WSI and lifeguard training certification at $2000–$2500 per season; 1 *athletics program director* at $2000–$2500 per season; 1 *waterskiing program director* at $1500–$1900 per season; 1 *archery instructor* at $1500–$1900 per season.
Benefits College credit, formal ongoing training, on-site room and board at no charge, laundry facilities, gratuities.
Contact Marty Wiadro, Director, Camp Tel Noar, Department SJ, 131 Victoria Road, Sudbury, Massachusetts 01776; 508-443-3655, Fax 508-881-1006. Application deadline: April 1.

CAMP TEVYA
Brookline, New Hampshire 03033

General Information Jewish coeducational cultural camp serving 325 campers. Established in 1940. Operated by Cohen Foundation. Affiliated with American Camping Association, New Hampshire Camping Association, Association of Independent Camps. 650-acre facility located 65 miles north of Boston, Massachusetts. Features: outstanding waterfront.
Profile of Summer Employees 16% high school students, 82% college students, 2% international. Nonsmokers preferred.
Employment Information Openings are from June 22 to August 24. Jobs available: 3 *arts and crafts instructors* at $1350–$1800 per season; 1 *arts and crafts head* at $2000–$2500 per season; 1 *music head* at $2000–$2500 per season; 2 *canoe instructors* at $1350–$2000 per season; 2 *sailing instructors* at $1350–$2000 per season; 3 *swimming instructors* at $1350–$2000 per season; 1 *swimming head* at $2000–$2500 per season; 1 *athletics head* at $2000–$2500 per season; 1 *waterskiing head* at $1500–$1900 per season; 1 *archery instructor* at $1500–$1900 per season; 1 *photography head* at $1350–$2000 per season; 1 *drama head* at $1500–$2000 per season.

Benefits College credit, formal ongoing training, on-site room and board at no charge, laundry facilities, gratuities.
Contact Judi Rapaport, Director, Camp Tevya, Department SJ, 14 Bonito Road, Framingham, Massachusetts 01701; 508-788-1585, Fax 508-881-1002. Application deadline: April 1.

CAMP WALT WHITMAN
Pike, New Hampshire 03780

General Information Coeducational residential camp serving 280 campers and offering a strong general program. Established in 1948. Owned by Jancy and Bill Dorfman. Affiliated with American Camping Association, Private Independent Camps. 300-acre facility located 120 miles north of Boston, Massachusetts. Features: location in White Mountains on a crystal-clear lake; 11 clay tennis courts; beautiful playing fields; excellent indoor facilities and modern cabins; beautiful natural environment.

Profile of Summer Employees Total number: 150; average age: 21; 50% male, 50% female, 5% high school students, 60% college students, 2% retirees, 10% international, 5% teachers. Nonsmokers only.

Employment Information Openings are from June 15 to August 22. Jobs available: 20 *experienced general counselors* at $900–$1400 per season; 6 *experienced sports coaches* at $1200–$1800 per season; 6 *experienced tennis instructors* at $1000–$1800 per season; 6 *swimming instructors* with WSI certification at $1000–$1800 per season; 3 *experienced hiking and camping specialists* at $1000–$1800 per season; 6 *experienced kitchen and maintenance personnel* at $1200–$2500 per season; 2 *experienced dance/gymnastics instructors* at $1200–$1800 per season; 3 *experienced art/woodshop instructors* at $1200–$1800 per season; 3 *experienced sailing, canoeing, and windsurfing instructors* at $1000–$1800 per season.

Benefits College credit, preemployment training, formal ongoing training, on-site room and board at no charge, travel reimbursement, health insurance, staff recreation program, staff lounge and kitchen, accessibility to Boston, Montreal, and the Maine seacoast for days off.
Contact Jancy Dorfman, Director, Camp Walt Whitman, Department SJ, P.O. Box 558, Armonk, New York 10504; 800-657-8282, Fax 914-273-6186.

From the Employer *A one-week staff orientation prepares new staff members for their role at camp, while positive support throughout the summer helps build a variety of skills necessary for working with children. Staff members typically come from across the United States and abroad, enjoying a unique sense of camaraderie that for many leads to a lifetime of friendship.*

INTERLOCKEN CENTER FOR EXPERIENTIAL LEARNING
RR 2, Box 165
Hillsboro, New Hampshire 03244

General Information Residential international summer camp serving 130 campers from a variety of countries in a creative cross-cultural atmosphere. Also offers 28 domestic and international small group travel programs that focus on performing arts, adventure/ wilderness, cycling, photojournalism, language, environment, and community service. Established in 1961. Owned by Richard Herman. Affiliated with Association for Experiential Education, American Camping Association. 500-acre facility located 75 miles northwest of Boston, Massachusetts. Features: wilderness area; full ropes course; lakefront; boating.

Profile of Summer Employees Total number: 45; average age: 26; 50% male, 50% female,

20% minorities, 40% college students, 20% international. Nonsmokers only.
Employment Information Openings are from June 20 to August 25. Jobs available: 4 *experienced sports staff members; 3 experienced applied arts staff members; 3 experienced performing arts staff members; 35 experienced travel leaders* with experience working with high school age students as well as expertise in program focus and geographic location at $175 per week; *3 experienced music staff members; 2 experienced environmental study staff members; 4 experienced leadership training staff members.* International students encouraged to apply.
Benefits Preemployment training, on-site room and board at no charge, laundry facilities.
Contact Judi Wisch, Staffing Coordinator, Interlocken Center for Experiential Learning, Department SJ, RR 2, Box 165, Hillsboro, New Hampshire 03244; 603-478-3166, Fax 603-478-5260. Application deadline: March 1.

From the Employer *All summer camp counselors and travel leaders participate in a ten-day staff orientation at Interlocken's residential camp in New Hampshire. Counselors get to use their creative abilities and spirit along with their particular program expertise. Many travel leaders start out as counselors at the camp, where they gain experience in experiential education, before taking on the responsibility for co-leading 13–15 high school-age students on a travel adventure.*

NEW ENGLAND HOCKEY AND FIGURE SKATING CAMP
Route 2
Contoocook, New Hampshire 03229
General Information Residential camp with a focus on ice hockey and figure skating instruction. Established in 1970. Affiliated with American Camping Association. 225-acre facility located 10 miles west of Concord. Features: magnificent ice rink; freshwater lake; tennis courts; 3 large sports fields; archery and riflery range; miniature golf and driving range.
Profile of Summer Employees 50% male, 50% female, 100% college students. Nonsmokers only.
Employment Information Openings are from June 26 to August 26. Jobs available: 10 *figure-skating counselors.* All applicants must have gold or high level figures (preferred). All positions offered at $600–$1200 per season.
Benefits College credit, on-site room and board at no charge, laundry facilities.
Contact Werner Rothschild, New England Hockey and Figure Skating Camp, Department SJ, 14 Joyce Lane, Woodbury, New York 11797; 516-364-8050.

From the Employer *We offer a three-day orientation program and are 1¼ hours from Boston. Generally, 2 staff members share a cabin with 6 to 7 campers.*

ROCKYWOLD–DEEPHAVEN CAMPS INC. (RDC)
Pinehurst Road, P.O. Box B
Holderness, New Hampshire 03245
General Information Family vacation camp providing its guests with a unique family living experience offering rustic simplicity, high-quality services, and a beautiful natural setting. Established in 1897. Owned by Rockywold–Deephaven Camps, Inc. Affiliated with American Camping Association, Squam Lake Association. 115-acre facility located 45 miles north of Concord. Features: location at the southern edge of the White Mountains on Squam Lake; 8 tennis courts, basketball court, and sports field; unlimited miles of hiking trails; 1½ miles of shore front, with a large fleet of canoes, kayaks, rowboats, and sailboats.

Profile of Summer Employees Total number: 80; average age: 23; 50% male, 50% female, 5% minorities, 70% college students, 5% retirees, 5% international, 10% local residents, 5% teachers. Nonsmokers only.

Employment Information Openings are from May 20 to October 15. Jobs available: 22 *housekeeping personnel* with a positive and flexible attitude and high work standards at $176–$280 per week; 20 *food service personnel* with a positive and flexible attitude and high work standards at $176–$360 per week; 10 *grounds/maintenance personnel* with experience in soft-surface tennis court maintenance and carpentry at $176–$280 per week; 5 *recreation staff members* with experience in tennis, water sports, and working with various age groups at $200–$250 per week; 6 *office staff members* with word-processing and money handling skills and experience working with the public at $184–$280 per week. International students encouraged to apply.

Benefits Preemployment training, on-site room and board at no charge, laundry facilities, possible end-of-season bonus, limited use of recreational facilities and equipment.

Contact John Jurczynski, General Manager, Rockywold–Deephaven Camps Inc. (RDC), Department SJ, P.O. Box B, Holderness, New Hampshire 03245; 603-968-3313. Application deadline: March 15.

WA-KLO
Thorndike Lake, Jaffrey Center
Jaffrey, New Hampshire 03452

General Information Private camp for girls accommodating 125 campers. Established in 1938. Owned by Ethel T. Kloberg and Marie J. Jensen. Affiliated with American Camping Association, New Hampshire Camp Directors' Association. 150-acre facility located 70 miles northwest of Boston, Massachusetts. Features: location on beautiful Thorndike Lake, at the base of Mount Monadnock; excellent facilities for all land and water sports; large gymnasium; dance studio, arts and crafts workshop, and fitness room.

Profile of Summer Employees Total number: 35; average age: 20; 10% male, 90% female, 80% college students, 50% international. Nonsmokers preferred.

Employment Information Openings are from June 15 to August 15. Jobs available: *swimming instructor* with lifeguard and WSI certification; *sailing instructor; waterskiing instructor; nurse; tennis instructor; riding instructor; windsurfing instructor; dance instructor; drama instructor; kayaking instructor; gymnastics instructor; pet care instructor; tutor; arts and crafts instructor; piano instructor; bugle instructor; golf instructor.* All positions offered at $1200–$1500 per season. International students encouraged to apply.

Benefits College credit, preemployment training, on-site room and board, health insurance, tuition reimbursement, 24-hour leave each week, free evenings.

Contact Ethel T. Kloberg, Owner/Director, Wa-Klo, Department SJ, 3638 Lorrie Drive, Oceanside, New York 11572; 516-678-3174, Fax 516-594-9234. Application deadline: June 1.

From the Employer *Wa-Klo welcomes staff members from all over the world. The warm, friendly atmosphere that exists at camp provides a happy and worthwhile experience for all.*

NEW JERSEY

APPEL FARM ARTS AND MUSIC CENTER
Elmer-Shirley Road
Elmer, New Jersey 08318
General Information Residential camp offering instruction in the fine and performing arts. Established in 1960. Owned by Appel Farm Arts and Music Center. Affiliated with American Camping Association, National Guild of Community Schools. 176-acre facility located 30 miles south of Philadelphia, Pennsylvania. Features: extensive visual arts studios, including film animation, fine arts, and photography facilities; rural area with playing fields; air-conditioned 300-seat theater; 2-acre organic garden; Olympic-size swimming pool; over a dozen air-conditioned rehearsal and practice studios.
Profile of Summer Employees Total number: 90; average age: 26; 40% male, 60% female, 20% minorities, 15% college students, 20% international, 10% local residents, 40% teachers. Nonsmokers only.
Employment Information Openings are from June 21 to August 24. Jobs available: 3 *experienced dance instructors* (over age 21) with expert knowledge of modern, jazz, and ballet dancing at $1100–$1400 per season; 10 *music instructors* (over age 21) with extensive experience in electronic music, rock, woodwinds, piano, strings, percussion, voice, and brass at $1100–$1500 per season; 3 *experienced photography instructors* (over age 21) at $1100–$1300 per season; 2 *experienced video instructors* (over age 21) at $1100–$1300 per season; 2 *registered nurses* with RN license, NJ certification preferred, at $1500–$2000 per season; 5 *experienced theater instructors* (over age 21) with directing experience at $1100–$1400 per season; 3 *technical theater personnel* (over age 21) with experience in stage craft, set design, costumes, and lighting at $1100–$1500 per season; 10 *art instructors* (over age 21) with extensive experience in painting, drawing, printmaking, sculpture, weaving, film animation, and ceramics at $1100–$1500 per season; 4 *swimming instructors* (over age 20) with lifeguard training or WSI certification at $1100–$1500 per season; 3 *sports staff members* (over age 20) with experience in tennis and noncompetitive sports at $1100–$1400 per season; 1 *community-outreach coordinator* (over age 20) with organizational ability and office work experience at $1100–$1300 per season; 1 *food service manager* with experience running camp kitchen, serving 250–300, stewardship, supervising workers, and cooking at $3000 per season.
Benefits On-site room and board at no charge, laundry facilities, weeklong staff orientation, opportunity to work in a community of artists, rehearsal/studio space.
Contact Rena Levitt, Camp Director, Appel Farm Arts and Music Center, P.O. Box 888, Elmer, New Jersey 08318; 609-358-2472, Fax 609-358-6513.

From the Employer *Our staff becomes part of a network of professional artists and arts educators across the country and around the globe.*

CAMP MERRY HEART/EASTER SEALS
RD 2, O'Brien Road
Hackettstown, New Jersey 07840
General Information Residential camp for disabled persons ages 5–60, day camp for nondisabled children ages 5–12, and TREC program for disabled persons. Established in 1949. Operated by Easter Seal Society of New Jersey. Affiliated with American Camping

Association. 121-acre facility located 3 miles west of Hackettstown. Features: pool; lake for boating and fishing; cabins; accessibility for disabled persons.

Profile of Summer Employees Total number: 55; average age: 21; 50% male, 50% female, 25% minorities, 10% high school students, 75% college students, 25% international, 10% local residents. Nonsmokers only.

Employment Information Openings are from June 13 to August 30. Christmas break positions also offered. Jobs available: 1 *swimming instructor* with WSI/lifeguard certification at $1110–$1300 per season; 1 *nature specialist* with ecology background at $1110–$1300 per season; 1 *recreation specialist* with therapeutic background at $1110–$1300 per season; 1 *boating specialist* with small craft certification at $1110–$1300 per season; 20 *counselors* (female) with college-student status and special education background at $1050–$1200 per season; 20 *counselors* (male) with college-student status and special education background at $1050–$1200 per season; 2 *cooks* with knowledge of cooking for groups at $2000–$3000 per season; 1 *experienced program specialist* at $2000–$3000 per season; 2 *nurses* with RN license, first aid, and CPR certification at $2000–$3000 per season. International students encouraged to apply.

Benefits College credit, preemployment training, formal ongoing training, on-site room and board at no charge, laundry facilities.

Contact Mary Ellen Ross, Director of Camping, Camp Merry Heart/Easter Seals, Department SJ, RD 2, O'Brien Road, Hackettstown, New Jersey 07840; 908-852-3896, Fax 908-852-9263. Application deadline: May 15.

From the Employer *Staff members participate in an orientation where they learn to work with people in the diverse situations encompassed by our various programs.*

CAMP NEJEDA
Saddleback Road
Stillwater, New Jersey 07875-0156

General Information Residential summer camp serving 84 campers with diabetes per week. Established in 1958. Owned by Camp Nejeda Foundation, Inc. Affiliated with American Camping Association. 72-acre facility located 50 miles west of New York City. Features: modern cabins; lake for boating and fishing; 20' x 60' pool; extensive hiking trails; indoor tennis and floor hockey; basketball court; field hockey and softball fields.

Profile of Summer Employees Total number: 50; average age: 19; 40% male, 60% female, 8% minorities, 10% high school students, 30% college students, 2% retirees, 16% international, 4% local residents. Nonsmokers preferred.

Employment Information Openings are from June 26 to August 20. Jobs available: 8 *nurses* with RN license or equivalent at $375 per week; 24 *senior counselors* (minimum age 18) at $1150 per season; 8 *junior counselors* (minimum age 17) at $800 per season; 5 *kitchen staff members* (minimum age 17) at $1000 per season; 1 *dietician* with RD license or eligibility at $2500–$3000 per season; 1 *dietary assistant* with RD eligibility or applicable major at $1500 per season; 1 *second cook* with institutional experience at $1500 per season. International students encouraged to apply.

Benefits Formal ongoing training, on-site room and board at no charge, laundry facilities.

Contact Camp Director, Camp Nejeda, P.O. Box 156, Stillwater, New Jersey 07875-0156; 201-383-2611, Fax 201-383-9891. Application deadline: March 31.

From the Employer *At a one-week training session, staff members learn extensive information on the care and management of diabetes, including emergency procedures and the special problems of these campers. By being part of the staff at Camp Nejeda, you will gain a sense of achievement in understanding and helping the diabetic child accept responsibility for the lifelong care of diabetes. Generally, 2 counselors and 8 campers share a cabin. All counseling staff are also program staff. Having an ability or skill in an activity is a requirement.*

CAMP VACAMAS
256 Macopin Road
West Milford, New Jersey 07480

General Information Camp serving the needs of children from low- and moderate-income families. Established in 1924. Operated by Camp Vacamas Association. Affiliated with American Camping Association. 500-acre facility located 45 miles west of New York City. Features: beautiful natural surroundings; new indoor/outdoor theater; new indoor basketball court; location 1 hour from New York City.

Profile of Summer Employees Total number: 160; average age: 21; 40% male, 60% female, 30% minorities, 5% high school students, 95% college students, 30% international, 15% local residents. Nonsmokers preferred.

Employment Information Openings are from June 15 to August 27. Year-round positions also offered. Jobs available: *experienced head counselor* (minimum age 21) with M.S.W. degree or equivalent at $2000–$3000 per season; *camper counselor* with M.S.W. or B.A. degree in psychology or sociology at $1800–$2000 per season; *teen coordinator* (minimum age 21) with education degree at $1800–$2000 per season; *waterfront director* (minimum age 21) with LGT certification and experience with staff supervision at $1800–$2000 per season; *experienced teen trip leaders* with college senior status at $1300–$1500 per season; *experienced teen theater arts director* with B.A. degree at $1200–$1500 per season; *teen leadership-in-training person* with B.A. degree and three years of camp experience at $1200–$1500 per season; *experienced creative arts director* at $1400 per season; *experienced woodshop/construction instructor* (minimum age 21) at $1000 per season; *nature/campcraft instructor* with outdoors experience at $1000 per season; *library counselor* with B.A. degree in education or psychology at $1000 per season; *ropes-course instructor* with college junior status and experience in rock climbing at $1000–$1200 per season; *experienced farm/garden director* at $900 per season; *head nurse* with RN license at $3000 per season; *nurse* with RN or LPN license at $2000–$3000 per season; *bunk counselor* at $1000 per season. International students encouraged to apply.

Benefits College credit, preemployment training, formal ongoing training, on-site room and board at no charge, laundry facilities, travel reimbursement.

Contact Michael H. Friedman, Executive Director, Camp Vacamas, 256 Macopin Road, West Milford, New Jersey 07480; 201-838-1394, Fax 201-838-7534. Application deadline: May 31.

From the Employer *Camp Vacamas is committed to offering a high-quality, residential camping experience to low- and moderate-income families. All fees are based on a sliding scale. The program is organized on a decentralized, noncompetitive philosophy geared toward the individuality of each child. Camp Vacamas is a multicultural community committed to serving a diverse population in every aspect—by gender, religion, ethnicity, culture, race, and socioeconomic level.*

JEWISH COMMUNITY CENTER
411 East Clinton Avenue
Tenafly, New Jersey 07670
General Information Day camp serving approximately 600 children ages 3–12 and special needs children. Established in 1980. Owned by Jewish Community Center on the Palisades. Located 10 miles west of New York City. Features: 3 outdoor pools; fully equipped gym; large sports field; low ropes course; 2 state-of-the-art playgrounds.
Profile of Summer Employees Total number: 180; average age: 23; 60% male, 40% female, 5% minorities, 40% high school students, 45% college students, 1% international, 90% local residents, 15% teachers. Nonsmokers preferred.
Employment Information Openings are from June 26 to August 18. Year-round positions also offered. Jobs available: *music specialist; drama specialist; arts and crafts specialist; ropes-course specialist; karate specialist; gymnastic specialist; nature specialist* with college degree. All positions offered at $2000–$3000 per season. International students encouraged to apply.
Benefits Preemployment training, membership for the summer.
Contact Ophrah Listokin, Camp Director, Jewish Community Center, Department SJ, 411 East Clinton Avenue, Tenafly, New Jersey 07670; 201-567-8963, Fax 201-569-7448.

From the Employer *We are a nonprofit social service agency serving a membership of 3,000 families. We are open year-round and run the camp both on our grounds and off-site.*

NEW JERSEY 4-H CAMPS
50 Nielson Road
Sussex, New Jersey 07461
General Information Two residential camp facilities with a total weekly capacity of 300 campers ages 9–13. Established in 1951. Owned by Rutgers University. Operated by Rutgers Cooperative Extension System. 700-acre facility located 70 miles northwest of New York City. Features: 6-acre lake; farm animals (working farm); proximity to Stokes State Forest, High Point State Park, and the Delaware River; access to the Applachian Trail for hiking trips.
Profile of Summer Employees Total number: 30; average age: 19; 40% male, 60% female, 10% minorities, 35% high school students, 35% college students, 10% international, 10% local residents. Nonsmokers preferred.
Employment Information Openings are from June 27 to August 20. Jobs available: 2 *waterfront supervisors* (minimum age 18) with lifeguard certification at $230–$250 per week; 4 *certified lifeguards* at $180–$210 per week; 2 *experienced boating/canoeing instructors* (minimum age 18) with lifeguard certification at $180–$210 per week; 2 *chefs* with kitchen, ordering, and supervisory experience at $230–$260 per week; 2 *experienced cooks* at $180–$200 per week; 2 *experienced assistant cooks* at $170–$180 per week; 4 *health directors* (minimum age 18) with Red Cross advanced first aid and CPR certification (as a minimum) at $270–$370 per week; 2 *experienced horseback-riding instructors* (minimum age 18) at $200–$230 per week; 2 *animal science instructors* (minimum age 18) with experience working with farm animals at $200–$230 per week; 2 *nature instructors* (minimum age 18) at $200–$230 per week; 1 *hiking/camping instructor* (minimum age 18) with Red Cross standard first aid and CPR certification at $200–$230 per week; 1 *fishing instructor* (minimum age 18) at $200–$230 per week; 2 *crafts shop managers* (minimum age 18) with experience maintaining inventories at $200–$230 per week; 1 *experienced horse-care person* at $170–$180 per week. International students encouraged to apply.
Benefits College credit, preemployment training, formal ongoing training, on-site room and

board at no charge, laundry facilities, health insurance, first aid training, 1½ days off each week, possible end-of-season bonus.

Contact   Kevin Mitchell, Director, 4-H Outdoor Education Centers, New Jersey 4-H Camps, Department SJ, 50 Nielson Road, Sussex, New Jersey 07461; 201-875-4715, Fax 201-875-1289. Application deadline: June 15.

From the Employer   *The New Jersey Camps provide a four-day orientation for all employees. You will receive training and certification in CPR and participate in workshops on safety, supervision, overall camp orientation, and team-building skills. Special sessions are provided to aid in developing lesson plans, diversity, and enhancing your teaching skills. Separate housing is provided for all staff members.*

PALISADES INTERSTATE PARK COMMISSION
P.O. Box 155
Alpine, New Jersey 07620

General Information   State park serving the cultural, historical, environmental, and recreational needs of the general public. Established in 1900. Owned by Palisades Interstate Park Commission. Affiliated with New Jersey Recreation and Park Association. 2,500-acre facility located 2 miles west of New York City. Features: over 30 miles of hiking/cross-country skiing trails and 20 miles of scenic roads; 4 major picnic areas; 2 boat basins and 1 boat launching ramp; 2 historic sites; 3 refreshment stands; bookstore/giftshop; 11-mile frontage along the Hudson River and Palisades Cliffs.

Profile of Summer Employees   Total number: 30; average age: 20; 60% male, 40% female, 20% minorities, 49% high school students, 50% college students, 1% retirees, 100% local residents. Nonsmokers preferred.

Employment Information   Openings are from April 1 to November 30. Jobs available: 3 *boat basin stewards* with knowledge of the Hudson River at $5.50–$11 per hour; 2 *assistant boat stewards* with knowledge of the Hudson River at $5.50–$11 per hour; 12 *fee collectors/ parking attendants* at $5.50–$6.50 per hour; 2 *historic site assistants* with strong interest in history, research, giving tours, and related activities at $5.50–$6.50 per hour; 10 *maintenance workers* at $5.50–$6.50 per hour.

Benefits   College credit, opportunity to meet many interesting people.

Contact   Jennifer A. March, Palisades Interstate Park Commission, Department SJ, P.O. Box 155, Alpine, New Jersey 07620; 201-768-1360, Fax 201-767-3842. Applications accepted year-round.

SOMERSET COUNTY PARK COMMISSION
ENVIRONMENTAL EDUCATION CENTER
190 Lord Stirling Road
Basking Ridge, New Jersey 07920

General Information   Environmental education programs for children, adults, and families, including nature day camps during the summer. Established in 1970. Owned by Somerset County Park Commission. Affiliated with National Association for Interpretation, Alliance for New Jersey Environmental Education. 430-acre facility located 35 miles west of New York City. Features: location within the Great Swamp Basin; 8½ miles of trails and boardwalk; 18,000-square-foot education building.

Profile of Summer Employees   Total number: 5; average age: 20; 50% male, 50% female, 100% college students, 80% local residents. Nonsmokers preferred.

Employment Information   Openings are from June 16 to August 31. Jobs available: 5

seasonal naturalists with college degree or upperclassman status at $240 per week.
Contact Ross A. Zito, Manager of Environmental Science, Somerset County Park Commission, Somerset County Park Commission Environmental Education Center, Department SJ, 190 Lord Stirling Road, Basking Ridge, New Jersey 07920; 908-766-2489. Application deadline: March 1.

TRAIL BLAZER CAMPS
RD 5, Box 657
Montague, New Jersey 07827
General Information Residential camp serving underprivileged campers in a rustic outdoor setting. Established in 1887. Owned by Trail Blazers. Affiliated with American Camping Association. 1,000-acre facility located 60 miles northwest of New York City. Features: surrounded by 30,000 acres of state park and forest; 55-acre lake; backpacking and camping. **Profile of Summer Employees** Total number: 60; average age: 21; 40% male, 60% female, 40% minorities, 60% college students, 5% retirees, 10% international, 50% local residents. Nonsmokers preferred.
Employment Information Openings are from June 15 to August 24. Jobs available: 35 *counselors* with one year of college completed at $850–$1100 per season; 5 *waterfront staff members* with WSI, ALS, and lifeguard certification at $850–$1100 per season; 3 *maintenance staff members* at $850–$1100 per season; 3 *infirmary staff members* with RN, EMT, or LPN license at $1500–$3500 per season; 7 *kitchen staff members* at $850–$1200 per season; 2 *secretaries* at $850–$1100 per season; *waterfront director* with WSI and lifeguard certification at $1500 per season; 2 *head cooks* at $1500–$1700 per season.
Benefits College credit, preemployment training, formal ongoing training, on-site room and board at no charge, travel reimbursement, potential scholarships for returning staff.
Contact Brad Gerstle, Camp Director, Trail Blazer Camps, 275 7th Avenue, 15th Floor, New York, New York 10001; 212-691-2720, Fax 212-691-4743. Application deadline: May 1.

From the Employer *Trail Blazer Camps offer the challenge of a lifetime for current/future educators, social workers, and environmentalists. Trail Blazers is a decentralized camping program for disadvantaged youth. This rugged, rustic camp emphasizes interpersonal skills, outdoor living skills, and small camp units and includes an intensive two-week training period.*

NEW MEXICO

BRUSH RANCH CAMPS FOR GIRLS AND BOYS
Tererro, New Mexico 87573
General Information Residential camp serving 80 girls ages 8–16 and 50 boys ages 8–14 with camp programs in a noncompetitive atmosphere. Established in 1957. Owned by Scott and Kay Rice. Affiliated with American Camping Association, Western Association of Independent Camps, Camp Horsemanship Association. 290-acre facility located 35 miles east of Santa Fe. Features: beautiful environment; well-maintained camp and grounds; log cabins and buildings in the mountains; heated swimming pool; 4 tennis courts; 2 miles of Pecos River.

Profile of Summer Employees   Total number: 49; average age: 23; 50% male, 50% female, 1% high school students, 90% college students, 1% local residents. Nonsmokers preferred. **Employment Information**   Openings are from June 16 to August 15. Jobs available: 2 *dance instructors* at $1000–$1500 per season; 2 *drama instructors* at $900–$2500 per season; 1 *music instructor* at $1000–$1200 per season; 3 *art instructors* at $1000–$1200 per season; 3 *swimming instructors* with WSI certification at $1000 per season; 2 *fencing instructors* at $1000–$1250 per season; 2 *tennis instructors* at $1000–$1250 per season; 2 *riding instructors (English-style)* at $1000–$1500 per season; 1 *shooting instructor* at $1000–$1200 per season; 3 *certified ropes challenge-course instructors* at $1000–$1500 per season; 2 *nature instructors* at $1000–$1100 per season; 1 *archery instructor* at $1000–$1200 per season; 1 *fishing instructor* with fly-fishing experience at $1000–$1500 per season; *mountain-biking instructor* at $1000–$1300 per season. **Benefits**   College credit, preemployment training, on-site room and board at no charge, travel reimbursement, cost-sharing or full tuition for training courses after first summer. **Contact**   Scott Rice, Owner/Director, Brush Ranch Camps for Girls and Boys, Department SJ, P.O. Box 5759, Santa Fe, New Mexico 87502-5759; 505-757-8821, Fax 505-757-8822. Application deadline: May 10.

CAMP MARY WHITE
Mayhill, New Mexico 88339
General Information   Residential camp for Girl Scouts and non-Girl Scouts from the third grade. Established in 1927. Owned by Girl Scouts. Operated by Zia Girl Scout Council. Affiliated with American Camping Association. 200-acre facility located 45 miles east of Alamogordo. Features: riding trails; backpacking trails; location at 8,000-foot elevation in the Sacramento Mountains. **Profile of Summer Employees**   Total number: 25; average age: 23; 1% male, 99% female, 40% minorities, 99% college students. Nonsmokers preferred. **Employment Information**   Openings are from June 2 to July 28. Jobs available: 9 *assistant counselors* at $600 per season; 1 *business manager* at $900–$950 per season; 1 *nurse* at $1000–$1100 per season; 1 *program director* at $900–$950 per season; 1 *riding director* at $900–$950 per season; 2 *assistant riding directors* at $800 per season; 7 *counselors* at $800–$850 per season; 1 *wrangler* at $650–$700 per season. **Benefits**   College credit, preemployment training, formal ongoing training, on-site room and board at no charge, laundry facilities, health insurance. **Contact**   Diana Miracle, Camping Services Coordinator, Camp Mary White, Department SJ, P.O. Box 202, Alamogordo, New Mexico 88310; 505-437-2921. Application deadline: May 1.

PHILMONT SCOUT RANCH
Cimarron, New Mexico 87714
General Information   Camp and family conference center offering mountain backpacking with a wide variety of outdoor and historical experiences. Established in 1938. Owned by Boy Scouts of America. Affiliated with American Camping Association. 137,493-acre facility located 200 miles northeast of Albuquerque. Features: mountain/high-country location with an elevation of from 6,500 to 12,441 feet; wilderness atmosphere for low-impact camping; conference facilities for the whole family; 32 staffed camps in the backcountry, each offering a program specialty ranging from archaeology to western lore; more than 300 miles of trails for ten-day mountain backpacking treks; large headquarters area, including museums, dining halls, trading post, supply issue, health lodge, and commissary.

Profile of Summer Employees Total number: 725; average age: 21; 75% male, 25% female, 2% high school students, 82% college students, 1% retirees, 1% international, 3% local residents. Nonsmokers preferred.

Employment Information Openings are from May 25 to August 25. Winter break positions also offered. Jobs available: *bookkeeping clerk and clerks/typists; food services staff (production manager, cook, assistant cook, backcountry cook, food services manager, food services assistant manager, food services staff, and snack bar clerks); commissary staff (manager, backcountry manager, and clerk); truck driver* (minimum age 21) with experience driving a two-ton truck over dirt roads; *trading post managers and clerks for headquarters, craft lodge, and backcountry; quartermaster staff (equipment and tent repair manager, tent repair helper, and warehouse clerk); custodial staff (custodian, housekeeper, and lawn maintenance personnel); seasonal registrars; security supervisor and staff; conservation staff (director of conservation, associate director of conservation, conservation crew foreman, trail crew foreman, assistant trail crew foreman, trail construction supervisor, and staff members); logistic services manager, assistant manager, and staff; transportation manager; headquarters activities manager and staff; headquarters services manager, assistant manager, and staff; postmaster; news and information staff (manager, assistant manager, photo lab manager, and photographers); medical/health lodge staff (administrator, medics, medical secretary, nurse, and health lodge drivers); headquarters maintenance staff; chief ranger, associate chief ranger, Rayado trek coordinator, mountain trek coordinator, training rangers, and approximately 160 rangers; backcountry manager; camp directors; program counselors* with knowledge of and experience in one or more of the following: adobe construction, archaeology, black powder weapons, blacksmithing, burro packing and racing, challenge events, environmental ecology and nature studies, fishing and flytying, gold mining and panning, mountain technology, Indian ethnology, logging skills, mountain biking, mountain living and homesteading, no-trace camping, riflery, rock climbing, search and rescue, shotgun instruction, trapping, and Western lore; *museum shop clerks and guides; ranch staff (supervisors and wranglers); training center office staff; support services manager and staff; tent city managers and assistant managers; family programs staff (manager, assistant manager, nursery leader, and leaders for activities for various age groups); crafts lodge manager and staff.* All positions offered at $450 per month.

Benefits College credit, preemployment training, formal ongoing training, on-site room and board at no charge, laundry facilities, health insurance, working with other people who have high values and service motivation, developing close friendships with people from throughout the United States and other countries, opportunities for growth and inspiration.

Contact Seasonal Personnel, Philmont Scout Ranch, Department SJ, Philmont Scout Ranch, Cimarron, New Mexico 87714; 505-376-2281. Application deadline: May 30 (most hiring takes place by March 1).

From the Employer *Planned, organized staff recreation activities are conducted each day. Informative and cultural staff events are scheduled throughout the season. All staff are encouraged to hike/backpack in the backcountry on days off. Most staff are housed 2 people to a 10' x 12' wall tent with a platform, beds, and electrical outlet.*

NEW YORK

ADIRONDACK MOUNTAIN CLUB
P.O. Box 867
Lake Placid, New York 12946
General Information Nonprofit conservation organization. Established in 1878. Owned by Adirondack Mountain Club. 640-acre facility located 135 miles north of Albany. Features: hundreds of miles of wilderness trails; 640-acre wilderness property includes Mt. Jo and Heart Lake; New York's highest peaks adjacent to property; ten minutes from Lake Placid, site of 1932 and 1980 Olympics; staff housing; backcountry lodges and mountain facilities; location adjacent to largest wilderness area in eastern United States.
Profile of Summer Employees Total number: 40.
Employment Information Openings are from June 10 to September 4. Year-round positions also offered. Jobs available: 10 *Adirondak Loj/Information center staff members* at $142 per week; 20 *backcountry trail crews and crew leaders* at $175 per week; 5 *John Brook Lodge crew* at $187 per week; 4 *backcountry educators* (summit stewards) at $240 per week; 1 *naturalist* at $220 per week; 1 *maintenance person* at $142 per week; 2 *reservations/front desk staff members* at $163 per season.
Benefits Preemployment training, formal ongoing training, on-site room and board, laundry facilities, variable room and board cost.
Contact Willie Janeway, North County Director, Adirondack Mountain Club, Department SJ, P.O. Box 867-P, Lake Placid, New York 12946-0867; 518-523-3480, Fax 518-523-3518. Application deadline: February 15.

From the Employer *Positions offer training for and an introduction to possible careers in resource management, public education, lodge operations, and stewardship.*

ADIRONDACK WOODCRAFT CAMPS
Rondaxe Road, P.O. Box 219
Old Forge, New York 13420
General Information Residential coeducational camp and environmental education center offering teaching, learning, and outdoor activities. Established in 1925. Owned by the Leach family. 400-acre facility located 60 miles north of Utica. Features: 2 private wilderness lakes, 2 miles of pristine riverfront; secluded location in the famous Adirondacks; location surrounded by hundreds of miles of prime hiking and canoeing routes; 4 separate waterfronts; basketball courts, tennis courts, large fields, and low ropes course.
Profile of Summer Employees Total number: 30; average age: 22; 70% male, 30% female, 10% minorities, 10% high school students, 55% college students, 5% retirees, 20% international, 15% local residents. Nonsmokers preferred.
Employment Information Openings are from May 3 to August 30. Jobs available: 16 *counselors* with experience working with children at $850–$1200 per season; 2 *kitchen assistants* at $110–$130 per week; 1 *office assistant* with typing, computer, and good communication skills at $120–$150 per week; 2 *experienced wilderness trip leaders* at $1000–$1400 per season; 4 *waterfront staff members* with WSI, lifeguard, and BLS certification at $900–$1400 per season.
Benefits Preemployment training, on-site room and board at no charge, laundry facilities, tuition reimbursement.

Contact   Chris Clemans, Program Director, Adirondack Woodcraft Camps, Department SJ, P.O. Box 219, Old Forge, New York 13420; 315-369-6031. Application deadline: May 1.

From the Employer   *Our staff members share a unique opportunity to work with a small population in a pristine wilderness setting.*

ANTONIO'S RESORT
Dale Lane
Elka Park, New York 12427

General Information   Family resort providing a variety of activities for guests. Established in 1973. Owned by Nat Manzella. 7-acre facility located 40 miles south of Albany. Features: access to downhill and cross-country skiing; indoor/outdoor sports, including basketball, racquetball, bocci, shuffleboard, volleyball, and softball; restaurant/lounge; indoor/outdoor pools, jacuzzi, and steam showers.

Profile of Summer Employees   Total number: 35; average age: 20; 50% male, 50% female, 25% college students, 75% international. Nonsmokers preferred.

Employment Information   Openings are from May 1 to October 1. Spring break, winter break, Christmas break, year-round positions also offered. Jobs available: 2 *social directors* with knowledge of sports and social games at $155 per week; 2 *child counselors* with knowledge of sports and social games at $155 per week; 2 *pool attendants* with junior Red Cross certification at $205 per week; 3 *maintenance/grounds persons* at $205 per week; 2 *office personnel* at $205 per week; 4 *housekeepers* at $150 per week; 1 *laundry person/ floater* at $205 per week; 1 *cocktail waitress/waiter* at $140 per week; 6 *waiters/waitresses* at $140 per week; 2 *subwaitresses/subwaiters* at $140 per week; 5 *kitchen helpers* at $205 per week; 2 *dish and pot washers* at $205 per week; 1 *floater* at $205 per week; 1 *host/office person* at $205 per week. International students encouraged to apply.

Benefits   College credit, on-site room and board at $67 per week, end-of-season bonus.

Contact   Cathy Manzella, Personnel Receptionist, Antonio's Resort, Department SJ, Dale Lane, Elka Park, New York 12427; 518-589-5197.

BRANT LAKE CAMP
Route 8
Brant Lake, New York 12815

General Information   Eight-week private residential camp for boys ages 7–15 with a capacity of 330 campers. Also two- and three-week sessions for 41 teenage girls in dance, arts, and sports—particularly tennis. Established in 1917. Owned by Robert S. Gersten, Karen Gerstenzang-Meltzer, and Richard Gersten. Affiliated with American Camping Association, New York State Camp Directors' Association. Located 80 miles north of Albany. Features: located on 5-mile-long crystal-clear lake; 16 tennis courts; 4 baseball fields; 5 basketball courts; 2 soccer fields; 3 art studios.

Profile of Summer Employees   Total number: 150; average age: 23; 85% male, 15% female, 10% minorities, 5% high school students, 70% college students, 2% retirees, 20% international, 5% local residents, 20% teachers. Nonsmokers preferred.

Employment Information   Openings are from June 20 to August 20. Jobs available: 15 *general staff members* (college-age) at $900–$1400 per season; 9 *athletics specialists* (college-age) at $1000–$1400 per season; 6 *waterfront staff members* (college-age) with WSI certification/lifeguard training at $1100–$1400 per season; 2 *group heads/athletics directors* with experience teaching/coaching at $1800–$2500 per season.

Benefits   Preemployment training, on-site room and board at no charge.

Contact Richard Gersten, Director, Brant Lake Camp, Department SJ, 19 East 80th Street, New York, New York 10021; 212-734-6216, Fax 212-734-6270. Application deadline: April 1.

From the Employer *There is a four-day precamp orientation program, including CPR training and an opportunity to take lifeguard certification. Generally, 2 counselors and 8 boys share a bunk. We provide transportation out of camp three nights per week.*

BUCK'S ROCK CAMP
193 North Detroit Avenue
North Massapequa, New York 11758

General Information Creative arts camp primarily devoted to the development of talents and the potential of boys and girls ages 11–16. Established in 1942. Owned by Stanley K. Simon and Ed Budd. Operated by Ron Danzig. Affiliated with American Camping Association, Connecticut Camping Association. 165-acre facility located 75 miles northwest of New York City. Features: horses; facilities for theater, dance, and music; large sporting fields; extensive horseback-riding trails; Olympic-size swimming pool.

Profile of Summer Employees Total number: 170; average age: 28; 50% male, 50% female, 10% minorities, 76% college students, 10% international, 5% local residents. Nonsmokers preferred.

Employment Information Openings are from June 25 to August 25. Jobs available: *fine arts instructor* at $1000–$1700 per season; *woodworking instructor* at $1000–$1700 per season; *weaving instructor* at $1000–$1500 per season; *photography instructor* at $1000–$1500 per season; *ceramics instructor* at $1000–$1500 per season; *sewing instructor* at $1000–$1500 per season; *silversmithing instructor* at $1000–$1700 per season; *creative writing instructor* at $1000–$1500 per season; *commercial art instructor; printing instructor* at $1000–$1500 per season; *stage design and construction personnel* at $1000–$1500 per season; *music instructor* at $1000–$1500 per season; *videotaping instructor* at $1200–$1500 per season; *sports instructor* at $1000–$1500 per season; *farming instructor* at $1000–$1500 per season; *waterfront staff* at $1000–$1500 per season; *computer science instructor* at $1000–$1500 per season; *kitchen staff* at $1000–$1500 per season; *dining room personnel* at $1000–$1500 per season; *maintenance staff* at $1000–$1500 per season; *guidance counselors* at $1000–$1500 per season; *registered nurses* at $1000–$1700 per season. International students encouraged to apply.

Benefits Formal ongoing training, on-site room and board at no charge, laundry facilities, travel reimbursement, health insurance.

Contact Stan Simon, Director, Buck's Rock Camp, Department SJ, 193 North Detroit Avenue, North Massapequa, New York 11758; 516-293-8711. Application deadline: December 1.

From the Employer *At a six-day preprogram orientation, all employees participate in workshops on safety and accident prevention, cultural sensitivity, and the facilitation of group interaction. In addition, workshops are provided for staff development as well as for preparing counselors for interacting with campers. Generally, 2–4 staff members share a cabin.*

CAMP BACO FOR BOYS/CAMP CHE–NA–WAH FOR GIRLS

Route 28N
Minerva, New York 12851

General Information Residential camp serving 160 girls and 190 boys in a traditional eight-week program. Established in 1923. Owned by Baco/Che-Na-Wah Equities Corporation. Affiliated with American Camping Association, New York State Camping Directors Association, Gore Mountain Chamber of Commerce. 100-acre facility located 225 miles north of New York City. Features: location in the beautiful Adirondack Mountains with scenic views of the High Peaks; private lake; 14 tennis courts (8 at Baco and 6 at Che-Na-Wah); weight-training and gymnastics building; indoor and outdoor basketball courts; indoor and outdoor theaters.

Profile of Summer Employees Total number: 110; average age: 20; 20% high school students, 80% college students. Nonsmokers only.

Employment Information Openings are from June 27 to August 20. Jobs available: 4 *swimming instructors* with WSI, LGT, and BLS certification at $800–$2000 per season; 3 *tennis instructors* with college team playing or coaching experience at $1400–$2500 per season; 1 *experienced gymnastics instructor* with college team experience at $1400–$2500 per season; 2 *music instructors* with ability to accompany on the piano at $1400–$2500 per season; 2 *ceramics instructors* at $1400–$2500 per season; 2 *sailing/windsurfing instructors* with LGT, BLS, and American Red Cross small crafts instructor certification at $1400–$2500 per season; 2 *canoeing instructors* with LGT, BLS, and American Red Cross small crafts instructor certification at $1400–$2500 per season; *experienced basketball instructor* at $1400–$2500 per season; *soccer instructor* at $1400–$2500 per season; *baseball/softball instructor* at $1400–$2500 per season; *instructors* (various sports) at $1400–$2500 per season; *hiking/pioneering instructor* with first aid or CPR certification at $1400–$2500 per season.

Benefits College credit, formal ongoing training, on-site room and board at no charge, laundry facilities, transportation provided five evenings per week for off-duty counselors, transportation provided to public bus on counselors' days off.

Contact Bob Wortman, Director, Camp Baco for Boys/Camp Che–Na–Wah for Girls, Department SJ, 80 Neptune Avenue, Woodmere, New York 11598; 516-374-7757, Fax 516-295-1377. Application deadline: May 30.

CAMP EAGLE COVE

P.O. Box 267
Inlet, New York 13360

General Information Residential camp serving 200 campers from the end of June to mid-August. Established in 1943. Owned by Donald E. Ross. Affiliated with American Camping Association, Camp Horsemanship Association. Situated on 35 acres. Features: 4 tennis courts (2 lighted); extensive lake frontage; 2 large sports fields with a little league stadium; 4 basketball courts (2 lighted); large recreation building; horse riding facility.

Profile of Summer Employees Total number: 100; average age: 25; 55% male, 45% female, 20% minorities, 80% college students, 5% international, 5% local residents. Nonsmokers preferred.

Employment Information Jobs available: *counselors*.

Benefits College credit, preemployment training, formal ongoing training, on-site room and board at no charge, laundry facilities.

Contact   Helen L. Ross, Owner, Camp Eagle Cove, Department SJ, Camp Eagle Cove, P.O. Box 1066, Boca Raton, Florida 33429-1066; 800-251-2267. Application deadline: June 1.

From the Employer   *Camp Eagle Cove offers a 5½-day staff institute for its employees to develop leadership skills and participate in workshops on safety, risk management, multicultural differences, and interpersonal communication with young people. Our diverse range of people gives our employees an opportunity to meet people from several foreign countries and many states in the United States.*

CAMP ECHO LAKE
Warrensberg, New York 12885

General Information   Coeducational summer program based on one 8-week session for children ages 7–16. Established in 1946. Owned by Morry, Amy, George, and Tony Stein. Affiliated with American Camping Association. 150-acre facility located 200 miles north of New York City. Features: sprawling campus in a completely wooded setting; spring-fed lake; tennis courts (12 hard surface, 4 clay, 12 lighted); numerous high-quality sports fields; modern cabins; project adventure course with both high and low elements.

Profile of Summer Employees   Total number: 180; average age: 21; 55% male, 45% female, 5% high school students, 75% college students, 15% international, 5% local residents. Nonsmokers only.

Employment Information   Openings are from June 16 to August 20. Jobs available: 2 *experienced group leaders* at $1300 per season; 20 *cabin specialists* with a love of working with children at $900 per season; 5 *waterfront personnel* with CPR and lifeguard certification at $1000 per season; 2 *gymnastics instructors* at $1000 per season; 8 *experienced tennis instructors* at $1000 per season; 1 *experienced woodshop director* at $1000 per season; 8 *experienced athletics instructors* at $1000 per season; 2 *experienced video instructors* at $1000 per season; 1 *experienced food-service person* at $150–$200 per week; *basketball and baseball directors* at $1200 per season.

Benefits   College credit, preemployment training, on-site room and board at no charge, laundry facilities, travel reimbursement, health insurance, internships.

Contact   Dawn Ewing, Staff Recruiter, Camp Echo Lake, Department SJ, 221 East Hartsdale Avenue, Hartsdale, New York 10530; 800-544-5448, Fax 914-472-9142. Application deadline: April 1.

From the Employer   *We feel strongly that all employees should be comfortable with our value system. Toward this end, our staff members participate in a five-day precamp orientation, program at which time our philosophy is reinforced along with discussions of each individual camper, goals for each age group, and methodology. Instead of relying on lectures and demonstrations, our orientation is based on experiences in building relationships and establishing the type of mutual confidence and support that form the very foundation of a successful staff experience.*

CAMP JEANNE D'ARC
154 Gadway Road
Merrill, New York 12955

General Information   Residential camp for 120 girls ages 6–17. Established in 1922. Owned by Fran McIntyre. Affiliated with American Camping Association, New York State Camp Directors' Association, Camp Directors' Roundtable. 230-acre facility located 30 miles west of Plattsburgh. Features: two-story Swiss chalet-type cabins with fireplace and living room; indoor plumbing and electricity; mile-long 28-station fitness trail; located on a 14-mile crystal-clear lake.

Profile of Summer Employees Total number: 50; average age: 21; 5% male, 95% female, 10% minorities, 10% high school students, 75% college students, 10% international, 15% local residents, 10% teachers. Nonsmokers preferred.

Employment Information Openings are from June 22 to August 19. Jobs available: 3 *riding instructors* at $1000–$1400 per season; 2 *waterskiing instructors* at $1000–$1200 per season; 1 *riflery instructor* with NRA rifle instructor certification at $1000–$1200 per season; 2 *tennis instructors* at $1000–$1200 per season; 1 *canoeing instructor* at $1000–$1200 per season; 1 *sailing instructor* at $1000–$1200 per season; 1 *music/guitar instructor* at $1000–$1200 per season; 1 *dance instructor* at $1000–$1200 per season; 1 *drama instructor* at $1000–$1200 per season; 2 *arts and crafts instructors* at $1000–$1200 per season; 2 *outdoor camping counselors* at $1000–$1200 per season; 2 *other land sports instructors* at $1000–$1200 per season; 2 *other water sports instructors* at $1000–$1200 per season; 3 *swimming instructors* with WSI certification at $1000–$1200 per season. International students encouraged to apply.

Benefits Preemployment training, on-site room and board at no charge, laundry facilities, travel reimbursement.

Contact Brian P. McIntyre, Assistant Director, Camp Jeanne D'Arc, 165 Narrows Road, Merrill, New York 12955; 518-425-3311, Fax 518-425-6673. Application deadline: June 15.

From the Employer *Every summer Jeanne d'Arc's campers and counselors come from many different states and countries. During our extensive precamp training and orientation, all counselors are trained in first aid and CPR. Waterfront counselors are offered lifeguard training certification.*

CAMP LOYALTOWN-AHRC

Glen Avenue
Hunter, New York 12442

General Information Summer residential recreational vacation camp for mentally retarded and developmentally disabled children and adults of all ages and functional levels. Established in 1974. Owned by Camp Loyaltown, Inc. Operated by Association for the Help of Retarded Children (Nassau County Chapter). Affiliated with United Way. 240-acre facility located 150 miles north of New York City. Features: location in the Catskill Mountains, adjacent to ski resorts; peaceful and idyllic setting; extensive and fully equipped recreation program; heated swimming pool; Special Olympics coaches' training; short walk to the village of Hunter, New York, and equally short walk into forest-covered mountains.

Profile of Summer Employees Total number: 125; average age: 20; 50% male, 50% female, 10% minorities, 3% high school students, 90% college students, 30% international, 5% teachers. Nonsmokers preferred.

Employment Information Openings are from June 19 to August 20. Jobs available: 1 *waterfront director* with WSI certification at $1900–$2200 per season; 4 *certified lifeguards* at $1400–$1600 per season; 80 *cabin counselors* with a major in special education or related field at $1100–$1500 per season; 2 *arts and crafts instructors* at $1400–$1600 per season; 6 *kitchen assistants* at $1200–$1500 per season; 4 *office staff members* with knowledge of office procedures and typing and clerical skills at $1200–$1600 per season; 4 *cooks* with experience in ordering, preparing, and serving large quality meals; 1 *dance instructor* at $1400–$1600 per season; 1 *drama instructor* at $1400–$1600 per season; 1 *music instructor* at $1400–$1600 per season; 1 *nature instructor* at $1400–$1600 per season; 1 *cooking instructor* at $1400–$1600 per season; 1 *sewing instructor* at $1400–$1600 per season; 1 *athletics instructor* at $1400–$1600 per season; 1 *woodshop instructor* at $1400–$1600 per season; 1 *recreation instructor* at $1400–$1600 per season; 1 *ceramics instructor* at $1400–$1600 per season. International students encouraged to apply.

Benefits　College credit, preemployment training, formal ongoing training, on-site room and board at no charge, laundry facilities, workmen's compensation.

Contact　Mr. Paul H. Cullen, Director of Camping, Camp Loyaltown-AHRC, Department SJ, 189 Wheatley Road, Brookville, New York 11545; 516-626-1000, Fax 516-626-1493. Application deadline: May 30.

From the Employer　*Camp Loyaltown is a highly structured vacation resort for developmentally disabled children and adults. Our staff receive five days of precamp training, which includes training in Special Olympics sports, handicap sensitivity, ways to best help disabled individuals overcome their limitations, and team building. Also, a great deal of time is allocated for the staff to get to know the strengths, weaknesses, and characteristics of the campers with whom they will be working before their arrival. Camp Loyaltown has a high counselor-camper ratio, where the youngest children and the most severely disabled campers have a 1:1 counselor-camper relationship. As the maturity, independence, and responsibility level rises, this ratio increases as high as 7:3. Generally, 3 counselors share a cabin with 5–8 campers, except for campers who require one-on-one care. Of the 728 campers, over 90 percent return year after year. The staff return rate ranges from 33 to 49 percent, indicating the high level of satisfaction and enthusiasm of our counselors in this intensely rewarding, demanding program.*

CAMP MADISON
201 Powder Mill Bridge Road
Kingston, New York 12401

General Information　Residential camp for boys and girls who are members of the Madison Square Boys and Girls Club. Established in 1984. Owned by Madison Square Boys and Girls Club. Affiliated with American Camping Association. 118-acre facility located 100 miles north of New York City. Features: 2 outdoor tennis courts; softball field; theater; 2 lakes; computers; hiking trails.

Profile of Summer Employees　Total number: 50; average age: 22; 50% male, 50% female, 60% minorities, 10% high school students, 90% college students, 30% international, 10% local residents. Nonsmokers preferred.

Employment Information　Openings are from June 15 to August 30. Year-round positions also offered. Jobs available: 23 *general camp counselors* at $900–$1100 per season; 3 *lifeguards* with lifeguard, BLS, CPR, and first aid certification at $1000–$1200 per season; 2 *nurses* with RN, LPN, EMT, or PA (New York state licensed) at $2500–$4000 per season; 1 *outdoor educator* at $1000–$1400 per season; 1 *computer instructor* at $1000–$1400 per season.

Benefits　Preemployment training, formal ongoing training, on-site room and board at no charge, laundry facilities.

Contact　Jack Thomas, Camp Director, Camp Madison, Department SJ, 301 East 29th Street, New York, New York 10016; 212-532-5751, Fax 212-779-2169. Application deadline: April 15.

CAMP NORTHWOOD
RR 1, Box 214
Remsen, New York 13438-9632

General Information　Residential camp serving highly functional learning disabled (ADD) children ages 8–18 during a seven-week session. Established in 1976. Owned by Gordon and

Donna Felt. Affiliated with American Camping Association, American Waterskiing Association. 15-acre facility located 220 miles northwest of New York City. Features: proximity to Adirondack State Park; outstanding facilities; 9-mile lake.

Profile of Summer Employees Total number: 70; average age: 23; 55% male, 45% female, 10% minorities, 20% college students, 20% international, 15% local residents, 25% teachers. Nonsmokers only.

Employment Information Openings are from June 28 to August 22. Jobs available: 12 *lifeguards* with American Red Cross lifeguard training at $1100–$1700 per season; 5 *swimming instructors* with American Red Cross WSI certification at $1100–$1700 per season; 2 *nurses* with RN or LPN license at $2500–$4000 per season; 2 *experienced tennis instructors* at $1000–$1500 per season; *sailing instructors* at $1000–$1500 per season.

Benefits College credit, preemployment training, on-site room and board at no charge, laundry facilities.

Contact Gordon Felt, Director, Camp Northwood, Department SJ, 175 East 96th Street #28E, New York, New York 10128; 212-369-9235, Fax 212-369-9326. Application deadline: June 15.

From the Employer *All staff members participate in a one-week orientation program prior to camper arrival. Workshops on learning disabilities, behavior/group management, scheduling, first aid, and more are presented by top professionals. There is a 2:1 camper-counselor ratio, which provides opportunities for highly individualized instruction in a noncompetitive, success-oriented environment.*

CAMP OF THE WOODS
Route 30
Speculator, New York 12164

General Information Nondenominational Christian family camp serving over 750 people and Christian girls' camp serving 72 girls ages 8–16. Established in 1900. Owned by Gospel Volunteers, Inc. Affiliated with Christian Camping International, American Camping Association. 120-acre facility located 90 miles north of Albany. Features: located in the Adirondack Mountains; beautiful lakefront with a quarter-mile natural sand beach; 1,500-seat auditorium; full recreational facilities and program.

Profile of Summer Employees Total number: 250; average age: 20; 45% male, 55% female, 5% minorities, 45% high school students, 45% college students, 2% retirees, 1% international, 1% local residents. Nonsmokers only.

Employment Information Openings are from May 10 to September 6. Year-round positions also offered. Jobs available: 50 *counselors/teachers* with ability to provide leadership and programming for children in preschool through high school at $500–$1200 per season; 10 *recreation leaders* with tennis, hiking, rafting, and team sports experience at $600–$1500 per season; 10 *waterfront staff members* with WSI certification (director), lifeguard training, and CPR training (staff) at $600–$1500 per season; 45 *musical performance staff members* (instrumental/vocal; double as waitstaff) at $600–$1500 per season; 45 *food-service personnel* at $500–$2000 per season; 50 *operational personnel (dishwashers, maintenance staff, and housekeepers)* at $500–$1200 per season; 10 *office/clerical staff members* at $600–$1000 per season; 15 *supervisors* (all departments) at $1500–$2100 per season; 3 *nurses* with RN, LPN, or EMT license at $1500–$2100 per season.

Benefits College credit, preemployment training, on-site room and board at no charge, laundry facilities.

Contact Ardith Murray, Personnel Director, Camp of the Woods, Department SJ, Route 30,

Speculator, New York 12164; 518-548-4311, Fax 518-548-4324. Application deadline: March 15.

From the Employer *Both Camp of the Woods and Tapawingo Camp for Girls offer unique opportunities for Christians to minister to others while continuing to grow personally through Bible studies, opportunities to hear leading Christian speakers, and interaction with missionaries stationed throughout the world.*

CAMP POK-O-MACCREADY
100 Mountain Road
Willsboro, New York 12996

General Information Traditional camp in the beautiful Adirondacks serving 230 boys and girls. Established in 1905. Owned by Jack Swan. Affiliated with American Camping Association. 450-acre facility located 20 miles southwest of Burlington, Vermont. Features: 2½ mile lake; 5 tennis courts; athletics fields; working farm from the 1830s; wilderness trips by land and water in the Adirondacks; arts and crafts; blacksmithing; 32 horses, horsemaster's program, and horse shows each Sunday.

Profile of Summer Employees Total number: 60; average age: 20; 51% male, 49% female, 2% high school students, 85% college students, 10% international.

Employment Information Openings are from June 20 to August 17. Jobs available: 1 *Indian crafts/dancing instructor;* 2 *swimming instructors* with WSI and lifeguard certification; 1 *lacrosse instructor;* 1 *woodworking instructor;* 1 *pottery instructor.* All positions offered at $700–$1300 per season.

Benefits On-site room and board at no charge, laundry facilities, travel reimbursement, additional work available May and June.

Contact Jack Swan, Director, Camp Pok-O-MacCready, Department SJ, 100 Mountain Road, Willsboro, New York 12996; 518-963-8366.

From the Employer *We offer a seven-day precamp orientation and nine 3-day trip leaders' clinics. There is also an opportunity to work at an outdoor education center before camp begins.*

CAMP SEQUOIA
Rock Hill, New York 12775

General Information Camp providing an environment where children can feel good about themselves and grow in many ways. Established in 1932. Owned by Len Shapiro. Affiliated with American Camping Association, American Waterskiing Association, United States Tennis Association. 300-acre facility located 90 miles northwest of New York City. Features: proximity to local town; indoor gymnasium with seating for 500; entertainment center for rainy-day activities; gymnastic pavillion and 500-seat theater; fitness center for weight training.

Profile of Summer Employees Total number: 200; average age: 22; 50% male, 50% female, 90% college students, 2% retirees, 5% international, 3% teachers. Nonsmokers preferred.

Employment Information Openings are from June 21 to August 21. Jobs available: 8 *swimming instructors* with WSI, CPR, and BLS certification at $800–$1000 per season; 8 *certified lifeguards* at $800–$1000 per season; 3 *experienced waterskiing instructors* with lifeguard certification at $800–$1000 per season; 8 *experienced outdoor education instructors* with CPR and BLS certification at $700–$1000 per season; 16 *arts instructors* (ceramics, fibers, woodworking, and photography) with extensive art background at $800–$1200 per season; 24 *experienced athletics instructors* (basketball, softball, volleyball, hockey, soccer, and tennis) with extensive playing background at the varsity level at $700–$1200 per season; *experienced theater staff* (directors, choreographers, and technical personnel) at $800–$1200 per season; 40 *general counselors* with ability and dedication to helping youngsters grow at $700–$1000 per season; 3 *horseback-riding instructors* with CHA, CPR, and BLS certification at $1000–$1200 per season; 2 *fitness/weight/gymnastics training counselors* with strong background in fitness/weight/gymnastics training and CPR certification at $700–$1000 per season.

Benefits   College credit, on-site room and board at no charge, laundry facilities, travel reimbursement, participation in camp activities and opportunity to take advantage of all programs with children, opportunities to travel, transportation on nights off.

Contact   Mark Zides, Director, Camp Sequoia, Department SJ, Box 1045, Woodstock, New York 12498; 914-679-5291. Application deadline: April 1.

CAMP SEVEN HILLS
Olean Road
Holland, New York 14080

General Information   Residential Girl Scout camp serving 150–200 girls ages 6–17 per week. Established in 1927. Owned by Girl Scout Council of Buffalo/Erie. Affiliated with American Camping Association, Girl Scouts of the United States of America. 600-acre facility located 45 miles south of Buffalo. Features: large indoor riding arena and outstanding English riding program with 22 horses; sports complex with tennis and basketball courts; 2 small lakes; Olympic-size swimming pool; proximity to Niagara Falls and Toronto, Canada; high and low ropes course; hills, meadows, and woodlands.

Profile of Summer Employees   Total number: 60; average age: 21; 2% male, 98% female, 5% minorities, 10% high school students, 77% college students, 5% international, 95% local residents. Nonsmokers preferred.

Employment Information   Openings are from June 25 to August 21. Jobs available: 1 *program director* with extensive camping and Girl Scout background at $2000–$2200 per season; 1 *health supervisor* with RN, LPN, or EMT license (New York) at $2000–$2500 per season; 1 *waterfront director* (minimum age 21) with WSI and lifeguard certification at $1800–$1900 per season; 5 *waterfront assistants* with WSI and lifeguard certification at $1100–$1500 per season; 10 *unit leaders* with camp experience (college age and Girl Scout background helpful) at $1200–$1400 per season; 15 *assistant unit leaders* with experience working with children at $1000–$1125 per season; 2 *riding instructors* with riding ability and knowledge of simple horse medications at $1300–$1400 per season; 1 *experienced arts and crafts director* at $1400–$1550 per season; 1 *experienced ropes-course specialist* with Project Adventure/ropes-course certification and group dynamics experience at $1400–$1550 per season; 1 *counselor-in-training director* with extensive Girl Scout camp experience and experience teaching older adolescents at $1400–$1550 per season; *head counselor* with camping experience, knowledge of Girl Scout program, and experience supervising and training staff at $1900–$2000 per season; 1 *stable manager* with extensive knowledge of barn management and equine care at $1200–$1500 per season; 1 *handyperson* with valid driver's license, knowledge of basic carpentry, and some maintenance skills at $700–$800 per season; *boating director* with current WSI, CPR/BLS certification, and certification in the fundamentals of canoeing and/or boating at $1800–$1900 per season; *assistant waterfront director* with current lifeguard training, first aid, and CPR certification at $1500–$1600 per season; *assistant boating director* with current lifeguard training, first aid, and CPR certification at $1500–$1600 per season; *junior counselor* (minimum age 17) with camp experience and successful completion of CIT program at $700–$800 per season; *activity specialist* with

specialization in sports/recreation, nature, arts and crafts, drama, and campcraft and ability to supervise adults and instruct classes at $1400–$1500 per season; *riding director* with riding ability, knowledge of horses, simple medications, and proper care at $1800–$1900 per season; *kitchen supervisor* with experience in food preparation and knowledge of operating simple kitchen equipment at $1600–$1700 per season; *assistant cook* with experience in food preparation for large groups and ability to meet deadlines at $1500–$1600 per season; *kitchen aide* with ability to work under supervision and as a team player at $600–$700 per season; *camp aide* with ability to work with limited supervision, valid driver's license, and reliable transportation at $700–$800 per season. International students encouraged to apply.
Benefits College credit, preemployment training, on-site room and board at no charge, laundry facilities, health insurance, tuition reimbursement, workmen's compensation, disability insurance, time off.
Contact Janet M. DePetrillo, Director of Outdoor Program, Camp Seven Hills, Department SJ, 70 Jewett Parkway, Buffalo, New York 14214; 716-837-6400, Fax 716-837-6407. Application deadline: June 1.

From the Employer *Staff members receive training in child abuse reporting, rabies prevention, and first aid. Employees also work together on the ropes course and learn different techniques in counseling.*

CAMP SOLITUDE
West Shore
Lake Placid, New York 12946
General Information Adirondack-style resort serving 15 guests per week, catering to families and groups. Established in 1896. Owned by Kelsall Family. Affiliated with Saranac and Lake Placid Chamber of Commerce. 20-acre facility located 30 miles west of Burlington, Vermont. Features: hiking trails; canoes and paddle boats; swimming, fishing, and waterskiing; rustic, log cabin-style lodge, recreation hall, guest house, and barn—all with scenic views of Lake Placid and natural surroundings; near many renowned Olympic attractions, including Whiteface Mountain; 15–20 old pianos, including a baby grand and grand Steinway.
Profile of Summer Employees Total number: 6; average age: 25; 50% male, 50% female, 20% high school students, 60% college students. Nonsmokers preferred.
Employment Information Openings are from June 1 to October 1. Jobs available: 2 *cooks* with first aid certification (preferred); 3 *maintenance persons/boat drivers* with lifeguarding and/or first aid certification; 2 *housekeeping personnel* with first aid certification (preferred). International students encouraged to apply.
Benefits On-site room and board at no charge, laundry facilities, travel reimbursement, tips, 20 percent commission for recruiting new guests, 20 percent of the total income divided among employees.
Contact Jay Kelsall, Camp Solitude, Department SJ, P.O. Box 26702, San Francisco, California 94126; 510-652-2677.

From the Employer *Camp Solitude is located on the boat-access-only shore of Lake Placid, site of the 1932 and 1980 winter Olympic games. Our employees have the opportunity to acquire technical skills such as boat handling, construction, landscaping, plumbing, and electrical work. Employees also have a chance to interact with the public in activity coordination, public relations, and marketing.*

CAMP WABENAKI
Lake Stahahe (S-3)
Southfields, New York 10975
General Information   Residential camp serving approximately 100 boys, mostly from underprivileged backgrounds, in each of three summer sessions. Established in 1932. Owned by State of New York. Operated by Boys Brotherhood Republic of New York, Inc. Affiliated with American Camping Association, Palisades Camping Association. Located 50 miles north of New York City. Features: freshwater lake; natural wooded environment; sports activities fields; proximity to New York City; arts and crafts facility; historical paths and trails.
Profile of Summer Employees   Total number: 30; average age: 23; 87% male, 13% female, 40% minorities, 26% high school students, 30% college students, 10% retirees, 37% international, 63% local residents. Nonsmokers preferred.
Employment Information   Openings are from June 22 to August 26. Jobs available: *general counselors; WSI lifeguards; nurse; second cook; music counselors; arts and crafts counselors.* All positions offered at $800 per season. International students encouraged to apply.
Benefits   On-site room and board at no charge.
Contact   Mr. Ralph Hittman, Executive Director, Boys Brotherhood Republic, Camp Wabenaki, Department SJ, 888 East 6th Street, New York, New York 10009; 212-686-8888.

From the Employer   *Camp Wabenaki counselors have the opportunity to act as role models for impressionable, underprivileged children, giving positive lessons that will remain with the children for their lifetimes.*

CAROUSEL DAY SCHOOL
9 West Avenue
Hicksville, New York 11801
General Information   Summer day camp for children ages 3–14. Established in 1956. Owned by Gene and Jane Formica. Affiliated with American Camping Association, Long Island Association of Private Schools and Day Camps. Located 30 miles east of New York City. Features: 2 pools; new basketball court; gymnasium for nursery school children; 3 playgrounds; Kids Kourt; 5 sports fields.
Profile of Summer Employees   Total number: 100; average age: 19; 90% college students. Nonsmokers preferred.
Employment Information   Openings are from June 28 to August 22. Jobs available: 4 *swimming instructors and lifeguards* with WSI, Nassau County, and CPR/BLS certification at $1500–$1900 per season; 4 *sports instructors/counselors* with knowledge of basketball coaching and skills in soccer and baseball at $825–$1100 per season; 1 *nature instructor* with ability to develop a nature science program at $825–$1100 per season; 30 *general counselors* with ability to relate to children at $825–$1200 per season; 1 *director/instructor for crafts program* with ability to order, supervise, and implement crafts programs at $2500 per season. International students encouraged to apply but must apply through Camp Counselors USA (415-617-8390).
Benefits   College credit, preemployment training, formal ongoing training.
Contact   Mike Epstein, Carousel Day School, Department SJ, 9 West Avenue, Hicksville,

New York 11801; 516-938-1137. Application deadline: May 10 (apply early for best choice of jobs).

From the Employer *The staff members participate in workshops to facilitate group interaction, safety, and cultural sensitivity. Training is also provided in specific program areas.*

CORTLAND REPERTORY THEATRE, INC.
37 Franklin Street
Cortland, New York 13045

General Information Professional summer theater producing five shows and offering sixty performances during a thirteen-week schedule. Established in 1972. Owned by Cortland County. Affiliated with Actors' Equity Association, Finger Lakes Association, Cortland Chamber of Commerce. 1-acre facility located 30 miles south of Syracuse. Features: historic Pavilion Theatre; proximity to scenic Little York Lake; location in beautiful Dwyer Memorial County Park; mild summer weather; picnic dinner baskets with wine at the Pavilion before each show; easy access from Interstate 81.

Profile of Summer Employees Total number: 50; average age: 28; 55% male, 45% female, 10% minorities, 5% high school students, 25% college students, 2% retirees, 20% local residents.

Employment Information Openings are from May 26 to August 30. Jobs available: 1 *experienced box office manager* with strong customer service orientation and a car at $140–$150 per week; 1 *box office clerk, experienced preferred,* with a strong customer service background and a car at $130–$140 per week; 1 *company manager* with a car, organization skills, and interest in theater at $140–$150 per week; *technical interns* with college experience and a commitment to exploring a theater career at $800–$1000 per season; *acting interns* with ability to perform in person at spring auditions at $500–$600 per season; 1 *experienced equity stage manager* with AEA membership at $240–$265 per week; 1 *props master/mistress* with college or professional experience and a car at $200 per week; 1 *costume designer* with professional experience or M.F.A. degree; 1 *scene designer* with professional experience or M.F.A. degree; 1 *lighting designer* with professional experience or M.F.A. degree at $200–$250 per week; 1 *house manager* with customer service background, volunteer coordinator experience, problem-solving skills, and a car at $100–$150 per week; 1 *technical director* with professional experience or M.F.A. degree at $250–$275 per week; 1 *master carpenter* with professional experience or M.F.A. degree at $200–$225 per week; 1 *master electrician* with professional experience or B.F.A. degree at $185–$195 per week; 1 *costumer* with experience sewing, cutting, and running a shop or B.F.A. degree at $200–$250 per week.

Benefits College credit, on-site room and board at no charge.

Contact Jana Mack, Managing Director, Cortland Repertory Theatre, Inc., Department SJ, P.O. Box 783, Cortland, New York 13045; 607-753-6161. Application deadline: March 15.

DRIFTWOOD ON THE OCEAN
Montauk Highway, Route 27
Montauk, New York 11954

General Information Seasonal oceanfront resort facility. Established in 1954. Owned by Driftwood Apartment Corporation. Affiliated with American Hotel and Motel Association, New York State Hotel and Motel Association, East Hampton Chamber of Commerce. 9-acre facility located 120 miles east of New York City. Features: oceanfront property.

Profile of Summer Employees   Total number: 15; average age: 25; 20% male, 80% female, 40% minorities, 40% international, 60% local residents.
Employment Information   Openings are from May 15 to October 15. Jobs available: 4 *chamberpersons, experienced preferred,* at $225 per week.
Benefits   On-site room and board, laundry facilities.
Contact   William Brinkman, Managing Agent, Driftwood on the Ocean, Department SJ, Box 5, Montauk, New York 11954; 516-668-5744. Application deadline: June 15.

FIVE RIVERS CENTER
Game Farm Road
Delmar, New York 12054
General Information   Environmental education center serving schools and families. Established in 1973. Owned by New York State Department of Environmental Conservation. 330-acre facility located 5 miles west of Albany. Features: 6 nature trails; classrooms; exhibit room; picnic area.
Profile of Summer Employees   Total number: 2; average age: 27; 50% male, 50% female. Nonsmokers only.
Employment Information   Openings are from June 21 to August 30. Year-round positions also offered. Jobs available: 2 *naturalist interns* at $100 per week.
Benefits   College credit, preemployment training, formal ongoing training, on-site room and board at no charge, travel reimbursement.
Contact   A. Sanchez, Five Rivers Center, Game Farm Road, Delmar, New York 12054; 518-475-0291. Application deadline: February 1.

From the Employer   *We provide training in natural history skills, environmental education methods, and teaching techniques. Participants gain experience in teaching and observing classes on a wide range of nature and environmental topics.*

THE FRESH AIR FUND
Sharpe Reservation, Van Wyck Lake Road
Fishkill, New York 12524
General Information   Five residential camps serving 2,800 inner-city children each summer. Established in 1947. Owned by The Fresh Air Fund. Affiliated with American Camping Association, New York State Outdoor Education Association, Child Welfare League of America. 3,000-acre facility located 65 miles north of New York City. Features: 2 lakes and a swimming pool; 14 miles of trails through wooded terrain; proximity to New York City; model farm, planetarium, and wildlife refuge.
Profile of Summer Employees   Total number: 300; average age: 20; 55% male, 45% female, 35% minorities, 3% high school students, 90% college students, 15% international, 30% local residents. Nonsmokers preferred.
Employment Information   Openings are from June 20 to August 20. Jobs available: 175 *general counselors* (minimum age 19) with some college and experience with children at $1300–$1800 per season; 22 *experienced village leaders* at $1700–$2200 per season; 5 *waterfront directors* (minimum age 21) with WSI certification and three years of experience at $2100–$2800 per season; 20 *waterfront assistants* with lifeguard certification at $1500–$1900 per season; 35 *program specialists* (photography, video, music, sewing, pioneering, nature, and arts and crafts) with ability to teach specialty at $1500–$1900 per season; 9 *nurses* with RN license at $3300–$3800 per season.
Benefits   College credit, preemployment training, formal ongoing training, on-site room and

board at no charge, laundry facilities, travel reimbursement, three-day breaks between twelve-day sessions, transportation to nearby town during free time.

Contact Thomas S. Karger, Associate Executive Director, The Fresh Air Fund, 1040 Avenue of the Americas, New York, New York 10018; 800-367-0003, Fax 212-302-7875. Application deadline: June 1.

From the Employer *The Fresh Air Fund's Career Awareness Camp, which opened for the summer of 1994, provides a unique opportunity for campers ages 12–15 to assess their interests and strengths, to explore a variety of career alternatives, and to understand the importance of staying in school. The camp's daily activities and educational projects are experiential and participatory.*

FROST VALLEY YMCA CAMPS
2000 Frost Valley Road
Claryville, New York 12725

General Information Frost Valley strives to develop self-esteem and healthy life-styles through traditional camp activities. Established in 1886. Operated by the Frost Valley Association. Affiliated with American Camping Association, Young Men's Christian Association. 4,800-acre facility located 100 miles northwest of New York City. Features: international campers and staff; diverse camper population; beautiful mountain environment; focus on environmental issues; composting and recycling facility; adventure trips for teenagers; extensive high, low, and group ropes courses.

Profile of Summer Employees Total number: 160; average age: 20; 50% male, 50% female, 15% minorities, 15% high school students, 65% college students, 2% retirees, 15% international, 5% local residents. Nonsmokers only.

Employment Information Openings are from June 19 to August 26. Year-round positions also offered. Jobs available: 10 *experienced unit leaders* (minimum age 21) at $1300–$1800 per season; 40 *experienced counselors* (minimum age 19) at $900–$1300 per season; 5 *waterfront staff members* with lifeguard, CPR, and first aid certification at $1000–$1300 per season; 5 *riding staff members* with experience teaching Western riding at $1000–$1300 per season; 2 *licensed nurses* at $2500–$3500 per season; 3 *experienced art instructors* at $1000–$1300 per season; 10 *trip leaders* with experience in canoeing, biking, and hiking at $140–$180 per week; 3 *experienced sports staff members* at $1000–$1300 per season; 8 *program area directors* with ability to supervise staff and develop programs in various areas, including riding, waterfront, art, sports, and health, at $1300–$2200 per season.

Benefits College credit, preemployment training, on-site room and board at no charge, laundry facilities, travel reimbursement.

Contact Peter M. Swain, Director of Camping, Frost Valley YMCA Camps, Department SJ, 2000 Frost Valley Road, Claryville, New York 12725; 914-985-2291, Fax 914-985-0056. Application deadline: March 31.

From the Employer *Frost Valley is a leader in innovative camp programs, including welcoming campers with disabilities, economic need, and from other cultures into a mainstream experience, introducing wellness concepts·and adventure-based programs. Frost Valley takes pride in building camaraderie and teamwork within cabin groups.*

GIRL'S VACATION FUND
370 Lexington Avenue
New York, New York 10017

General Information Residential camp serving 120 inner-city girls weekly in rustic wilderness environment. Established in 1935. Owned by Girls' Vacation Fund. Affiliated with United Way, American Camping Association. 500-acre facility located 150 miles north of New York City. Features: 8-acre private lake; low-ropes course elements; small farm animals; adjoins 5,000 acres of state forest and trails.

Profile of Summer Employees Total number: 45; average age: 21; 5% male, 95% female, 50% minorities, 88% college students, 2% international, 5% local residents, 5% teachers. Nonsmokers preferred.

Employment Information Openings are from June 25 to August 18. Jobs available: 4 *lifeguards/swim instructors* at $200–$300 per week; 3 *cooks* at $350–$500 per week; 2 *nurses/EMTs* at $300–$500 per week; 2 *trip directors* at $200–$250 per week; 1 *naturalist* at $200 per week; 24 *cabin co-counselors* at $150–$175 per week.

Benefits College credit, preemployment training, on-site room and board at no charge, laundry facilities.

Contact Ms. Eva Lewandowski, Girl's Vacation Fund, Department SJ, 370 Lexington Avenue, New York, New York 10017; 212-532-7050.

From the Employer *We provide a six-day orientation on safety, lesson planning, multicultural sensitivity, group dynamics, activity preparation, and our overnight backpacking trip. The camper-staff ratio is 3:1, but the cabin counselor-camper ratio is 1:4 or 1:5. There are 2 cabin counselors and 8–10 campers per sleeping cabin.*

GOLDEN ACRES FARM AND RANCH RESORT
CR 14
Gilboa, New York 12076

General Information Kosher family farm and ranch resort catering to young professional families with children. Established in 1950. Owned by Patricia and Jerry Gauthier. Affiliated with New York State Hospitality and Tourism Association, American Camping Association, Schoharie County Chamber of Commerce. 600-acre facility located 60 miles southwest of Albany. Features: dude ranch with indoor riding arena and extensive trails; location in central Catskill Mountains; indoor and outdoor pools and hot tubs; childcare for children ages 3 months to 16 years; lake with rowboats and paddleboats.

Profile of Summer Employees Total number: 100; average age: 21; 40% male, 60% female, 5% minorities, 51% college students, 2% retirees, 30% international, 10% local residents, 2% teachers. Nonsmokers preferred.

Employment Information Openings are from May 27 to September 5. Jobs available: 13 *experienced counselors* at $168 per week; 3 *experienced nursery counselors* at $168 per week; 1 *social director* with driver's license at $175–$250 per week; 4 *front-desk clerks* with computer, cash, and credit card experience at $175–$250 per week; 3 *bellhops/maintenance personnel* (minimum age 21) with driver's license and mechanical abilities at $175–$250 per week; 1 *head housekeeper* with supervisory skills at $250–$350 per week; 11 *chamber staff members* with clean and neat appearance at $168–$180 per week; 1 *experienced bartender/ barmaid* with cash-handling references at $150–$275 per week; 20 *experienced food-service assistants* at $168–$250 per week; 1 *experienced baker* at $250–$350 per week; 8 *experienced wranglers* at $168–$225 per week.

Benefits College credit, on-site room and board at $67 per week, laundry facilities, use of resort facilities, opportunity to meet people from all over the world, staff outings.

Contact Patricia Gauthier, Golden Acres Farm and Ranch Resort, Department SJ, County Road 14, Gilboa, New York 12076; 607-588-7329, Fax 607-588-6911. Application deadline: May 1.

JOHN DREW THEATER OF GUILD HALL
158 Main Street
East Hampton, New York 11937

General Information Presenting organization for the performing arts in a 387-seat theater. Established in 1931. Operated by Guild Hall of East Hampton, Inc. Affiliated with Association of Performing Arts Presenters, Actors' Equity Letter of Agreement. Located 80 miles east of New York City. Features: resort community and ocean beaches; culturally diverse community of well-known stars, writers, and poets.

Profile of Summer Employees Total number: 12; average age: 22; 25% male, 75% female, 85% college students, 90% local residents.

Employment Information Openings are from May 23 to September 5. Jobs available: 3 *experienced box office staff members* at $7 per hour; 2 *experienced technical staff members* at $275–$325 per week; 3 *interns* with backstage experience required of technical interns (administrative and production interns should be outgoing and willing to work long hours) at $70 per week; *administrative staff* at $275–$325 per week.

Benefits College credit, preemployment training.

Contact Brigitte Blachere, General Manager, John Drew Theater of Guild Hall, 158 Main Street, East Hampton, New York 11937; 516-324-4051, Fax 516-324-2722. Application deadline: March 30 (positions are filled on a rolling basis).

From the Employer *We offer a chance to meet and work with well-known artists in the performing and visual arts field. Staff and interns work with many different designers and are exposed to a wide range of tastes and choices in theater production.*

KUTSHER'S SPORTS ACADEMY
Monticello, New York 12701

General Information Residential coeducational sports camp featuring an elective instructional program for 500 campers, with arts and crafts, woodworking, dance, drama, computers, and photography. Established in 1968. Owned by the Kutsher family. Affiliated with American Camping Association, Association of Independent Camps. 100-acre facility located 90 miles northwest of New York City. Features: large fieldhouse with indoor tennis and basketball courts; beautiful lake; nice living conditions; scenic countryside; excellent athletic facilities; top level coaches to run programs.

Profile of Summer Employees Total number: 160; average age: 21; 69% male, 31% female, 20% minorities, 100% college students, 25% international, 20% teachers. Nonsmokers preferred.

Employment Information Openings are from June 23 to August 20. Jobs available: *counselors* with a specialty in at least one sport or college/high school athletics experience at $725–$1200 per season; *experienced coaches* at $1800–$3000 per season; *nurses* at $2000–$2500 per season.

Benefits College credit, preemployment training, formal ongoing training, on-site room and board at no charge, laundry facilities, travel allowance.

Contact Robert Trupin, Executive Director, Kutsher's Sports Academy, Department SJ, 2 Snowflake Lane, Westport, Connecticut 06880; 203-454-4991.

From the Employer *Counselors work under the direction of high school and college coaches so they can learn a great deal about their sports and make themselves better teachers and players. In the bunk areas, counselors are directed by experienced division leaders.*

NEW YORK SECTION–THE AMERICAN CAMPING ASSOCIATION
12 West 31st Street
New York, New York 10001

General Information   Employment clearinghouse for camps offering a free referral service for college students and faculty, teachers, and school administrators who desire a summer job outdoors.

Profile of Summer Employees   35% male, 65% female, 65% college students, 5% retirees. Nonsmokers preferred.

Employment Information   Openings are from June 30 to August 31. Jobs available: *waterfront staff* with WSI and scuba certification; *certified archery and riflery instructors; certified swimming instructors; certified lifeguards; land sports instructors* (team and individual); *performing arts staff* (theater, dance, and music); *arts and crafts instructors; gymnastics instructors; food service personnel; office personnel; administrative staff* (program directors and unit leaders); *nature specialist* (camp craft, science, and backpacking); *computer/ ham radio instructors; bilingual tutors; general counselors.*

Benefits   College credit, preemployment training, on-site room and board.

Contact   Sonia Sewell, Staff Placement, New York Section–The American Camping Association, 12 West 31st Street, New York, New York 10001; 212-268-7822, Fax 212-594-1684. There is no deadline, but earlier applicants have a better chance of obtaining a position.

From the Employer   *We handle applicants living in the northeastern region of the United States for residential and day camps in New York and New Jersey only.*

NORTH SHORE HOLIDAY HOUSE
74 Huntington Road
Huntington, New York 11743

General Information   Residential camp serving girls from low-income homes. Established in 1914. Owned by North Shore Holiday House. Affiliated with Townwide Fund of Huntington. 5-acre facility located 25 miles east of New York City. Features: pool; gazebo for dances and rainy days; 2 ball fields; large main building.

Profile of Summer Employees   Total number: 22; average age: 19; 100% female, 50% minorities, 20% high school students, 80% college students, 33% international, 20% local residents. Nonsmokers preferred.

Employment Information   Openings are from June 24 to August 20. Jobs available: 5 *bunk counselors* at $800–$950 per season; 1 *arts and crafts staff member* at $1000–$1500 per season; 1 *music staff member* at $1000–$1500 per season; 1 *dance staff member* at $1000–$1500 per season; 1 *swimming instructor* (minimum age 21) with WSI and lifeguard certification at $1500 per season.

Benefits   College credit, preemployment training, formal ongoing training, on-site room and board at no charge, laundry facilities.

Contact   Marty Gordon, Director, North Shore Holiday House, Department SJ, 3 Marine Street, Huntington, New York 11743; 516-549-6892. Application deadline: May 1.

OFFENSE-DEFENSE FOOTBALL CAMP
State University of New York at Stony Brook
Stony Brook, New York 11794

General Information Residential and day camp offering instruction in full-gear contact football to boys ages 8–18. Established in 1969. Owned by Mike Meshken. Affiliated with New England Camping Association. 200-acre facility located 25 miles east of New York City. Features: college campus in country setting; pool; weight room; coaching by 60 college coaches and several NFL players.

Profile of Summer Employees Total number: 80; average age: 23; 88% male, 12% female, 20% college students, 3% retirees. Nonsmokers preferred.

Employment Information Openings are from June 20 to July 10. Jobs available: 2 *swimming instructors* with WSI certification; 15 *counselors* with ability to work well with children at $100–$150 per week; 20 *football coaches* with experience as a high school or college football coach at $200–$300 per week; 3 *experienced student athletics trainers* at $150–$200 per week; 4 *certified athletics trainers* at $275–$400 per week.

Benefits College credit, preemployment training, formal ongoing training, on-site room and board, laundry facilities.

Contact Mike Meshken, President, Offense-Defense Football Camp, Department SJ, P.O. Box 317, Trumbull, Connecticut 06611; 800-243-4296. Application deadline: April 1.

From the Employer *Counselors live in private rooms on the same floor with campers, sharing large bathrooms on each floor.*

POINT O'PINES CAMP
Route 8
Brant Lake, New York 12815

General Information Eight-week traditional residential girls' camp with professional sports instruction as well as arts, performing arts, and horsemanship for 275 campers. Established in 1957. Owned by James and Margaret Sue Himoff. Affiliated with American Camping Association, American Quarter Horse Association. 523-acre facility located 76 miles north of Albany. Features: extensive freshwater lake frontage; 1 indoor and 12 outdoor tennis courts (red clay and Har-Tru surfaces); indoor sports recreational building; newly built indoor dance/gymnastics building; 3 outdoor sports fields; new fitness center; 500-acre horse farm, 3 horseback riding rings, and extensive riding trails.

Profile of Summer Employees Total number: 145; average age: 22; 10% male, 90% female, 10% minorities, 80% college students, 10% international, 5% local residents. Nonsmokers only.

Employment Information Openings are from June 20 to August 22. Jobs available: 23 *waterfront staff members* with extensive water sports experience; 14 *tennis staff members* with experience as college team player or professional instructor; 6 *athletics staff members* with experience as college team player or professional instructor; 6 *gymnastics/dance staff members* with experience as college team player or instructor; 6 *arts and crafts staff members* with professional teaching experience and/or a major in art; 2 *video/radio instructors* with at least two years of experience in operating equipment; 4 *experienced English horseback-riding instructors* with at least two years of teaching experience; 2 *photography staff members* with college or professional experience; 6 *experienced waterskiing instructors;* 3 *experienced sailing instructors;* 2 *experienced boating instructors;* 4 *experienced outdoor adventure staff members* with extensive training in safety; 1 *music director* with experience as piano accompanist for theater (must be able to transpose); 1 *experienced* *drama director;* 1 *drama technical person* with at least two years of experience in college or community theater.

Benefits College credit, preemployment training, formal ongoing training, on-site room and board at no charge, laundry facilities, travel reimbursement, separate staff laundry and lounge, weekly scheduled recreation programs for off-duty staff.

Contact Sue Himoff, Director, Point O'Pines Camp, 40 East 78th Street, New York, New York 10021; 212-288-0246, Fax 212-628-8011. Application deadline: March 30.

From the Employer *We have an extensive preseason aquatic school that teaches basic lifesaving, CPR, and water safety instruction as well as tennis and wilderness adventure skills. Point O'Pines takes pride in providing the finest experience in residential camping. Our excellent facilities, experienced and mature staff, professional instructors, great food, and warm, caring environment all contribute to a safe, supportive, fun-filled summer for both campers and staff.*

REGIS-APPLEJACK
P.O. Box 245
Paul Smith's, New York 12970

General Information Nonsectarian friendly coed camps for children ages 6–12 (Regis) and ages 13–17 (Applejack Teen Camp). Established in 1946. Owned by Humes family. Affiliated with American Camping Association, National Waterski Association, National Archery Association. 100-acre facility located 20 miles west of Lake Placid. Features: location in Adirondack Mountain Park on the shore of 7½-mile long St. Regis Lake; large boating/sailing program with 55 boats; cabins have 3–4 bedrooms, rustic living rooms with fireplaces, and bathrooms; 7 all-weather tennis courts, and 2 large athletic fields; extensive arts center for dramatics, dance, arts and crafts, and photography.

Profile of Summer Employees Total number: 80; average age: 23; 50% male, 50% female, 10% minorities, 70% college students, 1% retirees, 10% international, 20% local residents, 25% teachers. Nonsmokers only.

Employment Information Openings are from June 23 to August 25. Jobs available: *counselors* (minimum age 19)*; aquatic specialists* (minimum age 19) with lifeguard, WSI, first aid, BLS, and CPR certification; *boating department head; sailing instructors; waterski instructors; athletics staff; tennis counselors and head; arts & crafts instructors; drama instructors; wilderness trip leaders* (minimum age 19) with first aid, BLS, and CPR certification; *mountain biking counselors; office secretary/manager; nurses* with NY state license; *cooks; maintenance staff.* All positions offered at $900–$1500 per season.

Benefits College credit, preemployment training, on-site room and board, laundry facilities, travel reimbursement, opportunity to meet campers and staff from all over the United States and the world, no cost for laundry facilities.

Contact Michael N. Humes, Regis-Applejack, 107 Robinhood Road, White Plains, New York 10605; 914-997-7039, Fax 914-761-8228.

From the Employer *The beauty and grandeur of being in the midst of the Adirondack Mountains with a ¾-mile private waterfront on a pristine lake is unequaled. Come share a special, exciting, challenging adventure in a diverse, multicultural community where our focus is on human values, individual development, self-reliance, encouraging exchange, interaction, and group unity.*

STAGEDOOR MANOR THEATRE AND DANCE CAMP
Karmel Road
Loch Sheldrake, New York 12759

General Information Residential coeducational camp serving 240 campers in performing arts. Established in 1975. Owned by Stagedoor Enterprises, Inc. Affiliated with American Camping Association. 25-acre facility located 100 miles west of New York City. Features: close to town and health club; former resort hotel converted into a camp; indoor and outdoor pools; nearby lake for boating; 5 theater spaces, 3 television studios and 5 dance studios; location in the Catskill Mountains just 2 hours from New York City.

Profile of Summer Employees Total number: 115; average age: 25; 50% male, 50% female, 50% college students, 25% international, 2% local residents. Nonsmokers preferred.

Employment Information Openings are from June 23 to August 28. Jobs available: 6 *experienced theater directors* with B.A. degree at $2000–$2500 per season; 6 *pianists* with excellent sight reading ability and musical theater experience at $1600–$2200 per season; 3 *choreographers* with musical theater experience at $1600–$2200 per season; 10 *technicians* with theater experience at $1600–$2200 per season; 3 *designers* with theater experience at $1600–$2200 per season; 3 *swimming guards* with American Red Cross lifeguard training at $1400–$2000 per season; 3 *nurses* with RN or LPN license at $1600–$3000 per season; 2 *office managers* with administrative experience at $1600–$2500 per season; 4 *group leaders* with camp management experience at $1600–$2200 per season; 2 *head counselors* with camp management experience at $2000–$2500 per season; 2 *office assistants* with typing and bookkeeping skills at $1000–$1400 per season; 2 *groundspersons* with gardening, painting, and housekeeping skills at $1000–$1200 per season; 30 *counselors* with college student status and involvement in theater, sports, or other program areas at $850–$1200 per season; 2 *tennis counselors* at $1000–$1200 per season. International students encouraged to apply.

Benefits College credit, preemployment training, formal ongoing training, on-site room and board at no charge, laundry facilities, classes offered during time off, recreational facilities available for use during off hours, including tennis, horseback riding, and swimming.

Contact Konnie Kittrell, Production Director, Stagedoor Manor Theatre and Dance Camp, Department SJ, 215 Jones Cove Road, Cosby, Tennessee 37722; 615-487-3666, Fax 615-487-3666. Application deadline: May 15.

From the Employer *Staff members share rooms in separate quarters from campers. Staff members may take classes during their free periods. There is nearby public transportation to New York City. Employees have the opportunity to connect with a network of professional theatrical contacts.*

SURPRISE LAKE CAMP
Cold Spring, New York 10516

General Information General residential camp for Jewish children ages 7–15½. Established in 1902. Affiliated with United Jewish Appeal Federation, Association of Jewish Sponsored Camps, American Camping Association. 750-acre facility located 60 miles north of New York City. Features: half-mile-long private lake; beautifully wooded area; rugged terrain; mountain hiking trails; 4 outdoor tennis courts; numerous outdoor playing fields; 1,000-seat amphitheater.

Profile of Summer Employees Total number: 200; average age: 19; 50% male, 50% female, 15% high school students, 50% college students, 30% international, 5% teachers. Nonsmokers preferred.

Employment Information Openings are from June 21 to August 22. Jobs available: 12

lifeguards with Red Cross lifeguard training at $500–$1400 per season; 3 *arts and crafts instructors* at $400–$1400 per season; 2 *drama instructors* at $400–$1400 per season; 1 *experienced low-ropes instructor* at $400–$1400 per season; 1 *experienced archery instructor* at $400–$1400 per season; 2 *nature instructors* at $400–$1400 per season; 1 *Israeli dance instructor* at $400–$1400 per season; 1 *physical fitness instructor* at $400–$1400 per season; 1 *photography instructor* at $500–$1400 per season; 1 *tennis instructor* at $500–$1400 per season; 10 *experienced unit supervisors* with ability to supervise 40–50 kids and 6–8 counselors at $1600 per season; *kitchen workers* at $250–$1400 per season; *experienced counselors* at $500–$1500 per season; *experienced driver* with clean driving record at $1000–$1500 per season; *nurses* with RN or LPN (NY license preferred) at $1800–$2300 per season.

Benefits   Preemployment training, on-site room and board at no charge, laundry facilities, travel reimbursement, weekly staff activities.

Contact   Recruitment Coordinator, Surprise Lake Camp, Department SJ, 50 West 17th Street, New York, New York 10011; 212-924-3131, Fax 212-924-5112.

TOP OF THE PINES
250 West 57th Street, Room 1209
New York, New York 10019

General Information   Residential camp serving 80 urban youths ages 7–13 in each of the four sessions. Established in 1991. Owned by Palisades Interstate Park Commission. Operated by Camp Vacamas Association of New York and New Jersey. Affiliated with American Camping Association. Located 50 miles north of New York City. Features: freshwater lake frontage; extensive hiking trails; use of entire Harriman State Park facility; Bear Mountain State Park.

Profile of Summer Employees   Total number: 25; average age: 21; 70% male, 30% female, 30% minorities, 80% college students, 10% international, 1% local residents. Nonsmokers preferred.

Employment Information   Openings are from June 15 to August 31. Year-round positions also offered. Jobs available: *general counselors* at $1100 per season; *waterfront specialists* with American Red Cross lifeguard or WSI certification at $1100–$1300; *kitchen staff* at $1100–$1800 per season; *nurse* with New York RN license at $2000–$3000. International students encouraged to apply.

Benefits   College credit, on-site room and board at no charge.

Contact   Michael H. Friedman, Executive Director, Top of the Pines, 250 West 57th Street, Room 1209, New York, New York 10019; 212-765-4420, Fax 201-838-7534. Application deadline: May 15.

From the Employer   *Staff members participate in an intensive, extensive five-day precamp orientation that includes workshops on health and safety issues, programming, multicultural education, positive group facilitation, and environmental awareness. The camp maintains a camper-counselor ratio of 8:1.*

TRAILMARK OUTDOOR ADVENTURES
Nyack, New York 10960

General Information   Travel adventure program in New England, Prince Edward Island, the Pacific Northwest, and the American Southwest. Established in 1984. Owned by Rusty and Donna Pedersen. Located 18 miles north of New York City.

Profile of Summer Employees   Total number: 35; average age: 23; 50% male, 50% female, 20% high school students, 80% teachers. Nonsmokers only.
Employment Information   Openings are from June 15 to August 20. Jobs available: 30 *trip leaders* with knowledge of first aid and CPR at $100–$300 per week.
Benefits   On-site room and board at no charge, opportunity to participate in a variety of outdoor activities such as rock climbing, mountain biking, rafting, and canoeing.
Contact   Rusty Pedersen, Director, Trailmark Outdoor Adventures, 16 Schuyler Road, Nyack, New York 10960; 914-358-0262, Fax 914-358-2488. Application deadline: June 15.

From the Employer   *Staff participate in a one-week staff training program that includes field work. Staff are recruited from around the United States to create a diversity of thoughts and experiences. Close contact on a regular basis with the owner/director provides opportunity for communication and a better understanding of the program.*

WILLOW HILL FARM CAMP
RD 1, Box 341
Keeseville, New York 12944
General Information   Residential camp serving 36 horse-oriented young people. Established in 1975. Owned by Julie and Gerald Edwards. Affiliated with Ausable Valley Chapter of United States Pony Club. 500-acre facility located 150 miles north of Albany. Features: 3 riding rings; 2 dressage arenas; 2 cross-country courses; 2 jumping fields; unlimited riding trails; 70 horses (1 per rider).
Profile of Summer Employees   Total number: 7; average age: 30; 20% male, 80% female. Nonsmokers only.
Employment Information   Openings are from June 28 to August 29. Jobs available: *riding instructor/counselor* at $600–$1100 per season; *cook* at $150 per week.
Benefits   On-site room and board at no charge, laundry facilities, health insurance.
Contact   Julie Edwards, Director, Willow Hill Farm Camp, Department SJ, 75 Cassidy Road, Keeseville, New York 12944; 518-834-9746. Application deadline: February 1.

From the Employer   *High school students attending school here or college students on long breaks often work from September to June. Generally, 2 staff members and 8 campers share a cabin.*

YMCA CAMP CHINGACHGOOK
Pilot Knob Road
Kattskill Bay, New York 12844
General Information   Coed residential camp serving 225 campers and offering one- and two-week sessions. Established in 1913. Owned by Capital District YMCA. Affiliated with American Camping Association. 200-acre facility located 60 miles north of Albany. Features: location in Adirondack Park on Lake George; extensive high ropes course; waterfront focus; access to thousands of acres of State Forest Preserve bordering camp.
Profile of Summer Employees   Total number: 100; average age: 20; 55% male, 45% female, 5% minorities, 20% high school students, 75% college students, 15% international, 30% local residents. Nonsmokers preferred.
Employment Information   Openings are from May 1 to November 1. Jobs available: 45 *general camp staff members* at $500–$4500 per season; 35 *counselors* at $900–$1500 per season; 6 *adventure trip leaders* at $1200–$2000 per season. International students encouraged to apply.
Benefits   College credit, preemployment training, formal ongoing training, on-site room and

board at no charge, use of camp boats, camping gear, and climbing gear on days off.
Contact   Chris Gamble, Program Director, YMCA Camp Chingachgook, Department SJ, Katskill Bay, New York 12844; 518-656-9462, Fax 518-656-9362. Application deadline: May 15.

From the Employer   *Employment at a summer camp is the kind of experience that lasts a lifetime. Camp Chingachgook's location on Lake George—considered by many to be one of the loveliest spots in North America—complements the experience. In addition, the camp has undergone $3 million of improvements over the last five years. The purpose of Camp Chingachgook is to provide children with a safe, enriching program that encourages the growth of the whole person—spirit, mind, and body. Our staff is the motivating force in helping campers develop healthy life-styles and genuine self-respect.*

YMCA/YWCA CAMPING SERVICES–CAMPS GREENKILL/ MCALISTER/TALCOTT
Big Pond Road
Huguenot, New York 12746

General Information   Residential camps serving general population. Camps are split into two age groups: 6–10 and 11–15. Established in 1906. Owned by YMCA of Greater New York. Affiliated with American Camping Association. 1,000-acre facility located 85 miles northwest of New York City. Features: private lakes and high ropes course; easy access to Pocono and Catskill Mountains, rafting on the Delaware River, and New York City attractions.

Profile of Summer Employees   Total number: 80; average age: 21; 50% male, 50% female, 20% minorities, 8% high school students, 60% college students, 20% international, 10% local residents. Nonsmokers preferred.

Employment Information   Openings are from June 15 to August 25. Jobs available: 30 *general counselors* at $90–$110 per week; 3 *aquatic directors* (minimum age 21) with WSI, LGT, CPR, BLS, and first aid certification at $160–$180 per week; *unit director* with leadership and camp experience at $130–$150 per week; 6 *swimming instructors* with WSI certification at $120–$140 per week; 10 *kitchen staff members* at $125–$135 per week; 2 *high-ropes instructors* at $125–$135 per week; 2 *rock-climbing instructors* at $125–$135 per week; 2 *certified small craft instructors* at $125–$135 per week; *nurses* with RN or LPN certification at $275–$350 per week. International students encouraged to apply.

Benefits   College credit, preemployment training, formal ongoing training, on-site room and board at no charge, laundry facilities, travel reimbursement.

Contact   Jerry Huncosky, Director of Camping, YMCA/YWCA Camping Services–Camps GreenKill/McAlister/Talcott, Department SJ, P.O. Box B, Huguenot, New York 12746; 914-856-4382, Fax 914-858-7823. Application deadline: June 1.

From the Employer   *The YMCA offers a culturally diverse camp atmosphere focusing on activities in an overall values education environment. A seven-day precamp orientation includes skills training.*

NORTH CAROLINA

CAMP GOLDEN VALLEY
Route 2, Box 766
Bostic, North Carolina 28017
General Information Residential camp for girls ages 6–18 with a Girl Scout program emphasis and a capacity for 160 girls per session. Established in 1972. Owned by Pioneer Girl Scout Council. Affiliated with American Camping Association. 620-acre facility located 85 miles northwest of Charlotte. Features: beautiful North Carolina Mountains; rustic but modern facilities (treehouse, platform tents, and cabin units); canoes and paddleboats; 15-acre lake; horseback-riding facility; sports field, tennis courts, and hiking trails.
Profile of Summer Employees Total number: 25; average age: 20; 100% female, 25% minorities, 25% college students, 4% international, 80% local residents.
Employment Information Openings are from January 1 to May 30. Jobs available: 1 *assistant director and program director* (minimum age 21) with residential camp experience at $175–$205 per week; *camp nurse* (minimum age 21) with RN license (North Carolina) at $175–$200 per week; 1 *waterfront director* (minimum age 21) with WSI certification (ARC or equivalent) and lifeguard training at $135–$165 per week; 4 *waterfront assistants* (minimum age 18) with lifeguard training at $110–$140 per week; 5 *unit leaders* (minimum age 21) with experience as camp counselor, teacher, or youth leader at $135–$165 per week; 13 *unit assistants* (minimum age 18) with Girl Scout or youth leader experience at $110–$140 per week. International students encouraged to apply.
Benefits Preemployment training, on-site room and board at no charge, laundry facilities, accident insurance, American Red Cross first aid/CPR certification.
Contact Jill B. Rhinehart, Resident Camp Director, Camp Golden Valley, Department SJ, 324 North Highland Street, Gastonia, North Carolina 28052-2194; 704-864-3245, Fax 704-864-9020. Application deadline: May 1.

From the Employer *Camp Golden Valley offers a one-week staff training program that includes first aid and CPR certification. The camp administration will work with staff on internships or class credits.*

CAMP KANATA
13524 Camp Kanata Road
Wake Forest, North Carolina 27587
General Information Coeducational residential YMCA camp for children ages 6–15. Established in 1954. Operated by Durham YMCA. Affiliated with American Camping Association. 188-acre facility located 10 miles north of Raleigh. Features: 3 zip lines; 2 spring-fed lakes; seventeen cabins; 7,000-square-foot gymnasium; ropes course; 2 ball fields.
Profile of Summer Employees Total number: 42; average age: 20; 50% male, 50% female, 2% minorities, 30% high school students, 70% college students, 4% international, 35% local residents. Nonsmokers preferred.
Employment Information Openings are from June 7 to August 14. Jobs available: 37 *cabin counselors* with child work experience at $1000–$1300 per season; 2 *nurses* with RN license at $3000 per season; 1 *experienced arts and crafts director* at $1300 per season; 1 *program director* (minimum age 20) with creativity and camp experience at $2100–$2400 per season; 1 *staff-trainee director* (minimum age 20) with camp experience at $2100–$2400 per season; 1 *waterfront director* (minimum age 20) with camp experience and WSI,

lifeguard instructor, or YMCA certification at $1800–$2200 per season; 1 *waterskiing coordinator* (minimum age 21) with camp and maintenance experience at $1200–$1400 per season; 1 *ropes-course director* (minimum age 20) with camp experience and ropes-course training at $1400 per season.

Benefits Preemployment training, on-site room and board at no charge, laundry facilities.
Contact Richard R. Hamilton, Director, Camp Kanata, Department SJ, 13524 Camp Kanata Road, Wake Forest, North Carolina 27587; 919-556-2661. Application deadline: April 15.

From the Employer *At Camp Kanata, the individual child is our focus, helping to develop initiative, self-esteem, self-confidence, and physical skills in every camper. For our staff, we offer a two-day precamp ropes-course orientation class. There are 2 counselors and 10 campers per cabin.*

CHEROKEE KOA KAMPGROUND
Star Route, Box 39
Cherokee, North Carolina 28719

General Information Resort campground for recreational vehicles and tent campers who are visitors to the Great Smoky Mountains National Park and Cherokee Indian Reservation. Established in 1973. Owned by Sontag, Inc. Operated by Kampgrounds of America (KOA). 35-acre facility located 4 miles north of Cherokee. Features: swimming pool and 2 hot tubs; lighted tennis court; snack bar; trout fishing ponds stocked twice weekly; location on the Cherokee Indian Reservation in the Great Smoky Mountains; 400 camping spaces and 79 camping cabins; free shuttle buses to area attractions.

Profile of Summer Employees Total number: 54; average age: 22; 40% male, 60% female, 40% minorities, 20% high school students, 30% college students, 20% retirees, 33% international, 60% local residents. Nonsmokers preferred.

Employment Information Openings are from May 15 to October 31. Jobs available: 4 *front desk attendants* with fluency in English at $4.25–$6 per hour; 4 *cashiers* with fluency in English at $4.25–$5 per hour; 4 *food service/snack bar staff members* with fluency in English at $4.25–$5.25 per hour; 1 *night security person* at $4.25–$5.25 per hour; 2 *housekeeping/cleaning staff members* at $4.25–$6.50 per hour; *reservations agent* at $4.50–$6.50 per hour. International students encouraged to apply.

Benefits On-site room and board at $50 per week, laundry facilities, opportunity to meet campers from all over the United States and Europe, 30 percent discount at the snack bar.
Contact Walter Schumacher, Cherokee KOA Kampground, Department SJ, Star Route, Box 39, Cherokee, North Carolina 28719; 704-497-9711, Fax 704-497-6776. Application deadline: May 1.

From the Employer *All resort facilities are available to off-duty staff, including the free shuttle bus to town four times a day and great fishing.*

FALLING CREEK CAMP FOR BOYS
P.O. Box 98
Tuxedo, North Carolina 28784

General Information Privately owned camp in the western North Carolina mountains seeking to provide boys ages 7–16 with the maximum opportunity for growth and fun. Established in 1969. Owned by Charles W. McGrady. Affiliated with American Camping Association. 1,000-acre facility located 12 miles south of Hendersonville. Features: beautiful mountain setting that is remote yet accessible from highways; 2 horseback riding rings with barn and stable; 40-foot artificial climbing wall; high and low elements ropes course; miles of horseback-riding, mountain-biking, and hiking trails; brand new lodge.

Profile of Summer Employees Total number: 90; average age: 24; 90% male, 10% female, 90% college students, 10% international, 10% teachers. Nonsmokers preferred.

Employment Information Openings are from May 30 to August 20. Jobs available: 3 *swimming instructors* with WSI and lifeguard certification at $1625–$1800 per season; 1 *experienced riflery instructor* at $1625–$1800 per season; 1 *experienced archery instructor* at $1625–$1800 per season; 2 *arts and crafts instructors* at $1625–$1800 per season; 3 *land sports counselors* at $1625–$1800 per season; 3 *experienced tennis instructors* at $1625– $1800 per season; 2 *camp nurses* with RN (North Carolina) at $1800–$2400 per season; 2 *mountaineering staff members* with experience in rock climbing and backpacking trips at $1625–$1800 per season; 2 *canoeing staff members* with experience in white water in closed and open boats at $1625–$1800 per season; 2 *horseback-riding staff members* with experience in English-saddle instruction at $1625–$1800 per season; 1 *nature counselor* with background in biology, zoology, or ecology at $1625–$1800 per season.

Benefits College credit, preemployment training, on-site room and board, optional laundry service.

Contact Donnie Bain, Director, Falling Creek Camp for Boys, Department SJ, P.O. Box 98, Tuxedo, North Carolina 28784; 704-692-0262, Fax 704-696-1616. Application deadline: March 1 (applicants must apply early so an interview can be arranged).

GWYNN VALLEY
1080 Island Ford Road
Brevard, North Carolina 28712

General Information Noncompetitive creative residential camp for young boys and girls ages 5–12. Established in 1935. Owned by H. W. Boyd. Affiliated with American Camping Association. 350-acre facility located 30 miles southeast of Asheville. Features: 50-acre integrated working farm; swimming pool; spring-fed lake and streams; 300 wooded acres for hiking and camping; turn-of-the-century operational Grist Mill; location in the heart of the Blue Ridge Mountains.

Profile of Summer Employees Total number: 120; average age: 27; 50% male, 50% female, 5% minorities, 5% high school students, 60% college students, 5% retirees, 30% international, 5% local residents, 5% teachers. Nonsmokers only.

Employment Information Openings are from June 1 to August 20. Jobs available: *cabin counselors; swimming instructors; lifeguards; archery instructor; potter; ecology specialist; horseback-riding (English) instructor; miller; drama specialist; weaver.* All positions offered at $110–$200 per week.

Benefits College credit, preemployment training, on-site room and board at no charge, laundry facilities, partial camper tuition waivers, housing for married couples, possible reimbursement of certification costs.

Contact Gwynn Valley, Department SJ, 1080 Island Ford Road, Brevard, North Carolina 28712. Application deadline: March 1 (personal interview required for all applicants).

From the Employer *Gwynn Valley offers a supportive setting designed to foster personal growth and skills development in a beautiful, natural environment. Staff members should possess experience with groups of young children and an open attitude for working together to create a dynamic community for children.*

NOR'BANKS SAILING CENTER/OUTER BANKS SAILING AND WINDSURFING

1308 Duck Road
Duck, North Carolina 27949

General Information Water sports center with an emphasis on sailing and windsurfing. Operates as a U.S. Sailing Association certified sailing and windsurfing school. Established in 1979. Owned by Jonathan Britt. Affiliated with United States Sailing Association, Outer Banks Chamber of Commerce. 2-acre facility located 90 miles south of Virginia Beach. Features: location on the Currituck Sound (½ mile from Atlantic Ocean); over 40 square miles of open water for sailing and windsurfing; the best winds on the East Coast.

Profile of Summer Employees Total number: 10; average age: 21; 50% male, 50% female, 75% college students. Nonsmokers preferred.

Employment Information Openings are from May 10 to October 10. Year-round positions also offered. Jobs available: *windsurfing instructors* with U.S. Sailing certification, CPR, lifeguard certification, and USCG captain's license at $7–$9 per hour; *dock hands* with CPR and lifeguard certification at $6–$7 per hour; *retail help* with CPR certification at $5.50–$6 per hour; *sailing instructors* with U.S. Sailing certification, CPR, lifeguard certification, and USCG captain's license at $7–$9 per hour. International students encouraged to apply.

Benefits Use of water sports equipment and lessons, possibility of finding housing if search is done early.

Contact Jon Britt, Owner, Nor'Banks Sailing Center/Outer Banks Sailing and Windsurfing, 1308 Duck Road, Duck, North Carolina 27949; 919-261-4369. Application deadline: April 1.

From the Employer *During orientation a basic first aid and CPR course will be taught to all employees. Opportunities for certification in sailing and windsurfing may be available to interested employees. Any applicants who can stay through late September will have an advantage over others in obtaining a position and setting a pay scale.*

NORTH BEACH SAILING/BARRIER ISLAND SAILING CENTER

Box 8279 Duck Station
Kitty Hawk, North Carolina 27949

General Information Sailing center specializing in the rental and sale of windsurfing, sailing, and jet ski equipment and the teaching of proper use of equipment. Offers a line of clothing for enthusiasts. Established in 1985. Owned by William H. Miles Jr. Affiliated with American Windsurfing Industry Association, Outer Banks Chamber of Commerce, Windsurfing Instructors of America. Located 70 miles south of Virginia Beach, Virginia. Features: ocean and beaches; sailing and parasailing; windsurfing; swimming; jet skis, sea planes, and canoes; kayaks.

Profile of Summer Employees 50% male, 50% female, 10% high school students, 50% college students, 10% international, 15% local residents, 10% teachers. Nonsmokers preferred.

Employment Information Openings are from May 1 to October 15. Jobs available: 8 *experienced windsurfing instructors* with ability to relate to students in a positive manner at $250–$350 per week; 4 *experienced sailing instructors* with ability to relate to students in a positive manner at $250–$350 per week; 8 *rental/desk persons* with knowledge of sailing and windsurfing at $150–$200 per week; 3 *experienced retail salespersons* with sailing/windsurfing experience at $200–$300 per week; 1 *parasailing instructor* with Coast Guard captain's license at $550–$650 per week; 2 *experienced kayaking and canoeing instructors* (for teaching and renting duties). International students encouraged to apply.

Benefits Opportunity to learn to sail and windsurf.
Contact Bill Miles, President, North Beach Sailing/Barrier Island Sailing Center, Department SJ, Box 8279 Duck Station, Kitty Hawk, North Carolina 27949; 919-261-6262, Fax 919-261-1494. Application deadline: May 1.

ROLLING THUNDER RIVER CO.
P.O. Box 88
Almond, North Carolina 28702

General Information White-water rafting trips in North Carolina, Tennessee, and Georgia. Established in 1977. Owned by Ken Miller. Affiliated with America Outdoors, United States Forest Service, all local Chambers of Commerce. 7-acre facility located 60 miles west of Asheville. Features: horseback riding; proximity to Fontana Lake (less than 3 miles); proximity to some of the best mountain biking trails in the United States; great fishing; proximity to the Great Smoky Mountain National Park and the Appalachian Trail; location near several white-water rivers.
Profile of Summer Employees Total number: 15; average age: 20; 50% male, 50% female, 75% college students, 25% local residents.
Employment Information Openings are from May 15 to September 15. Jobs available: 15 *river guides* with advanced first aid, basic lifesaving, and CPR certification and company training; 2 *experienced photographers;* 1 *maintenance and repair person; reservation/office worker.*
Benefits College credit, preemployment training, on-site room and board at no charge, kitchen facilities.
Contact Beth Allison, Manager, Rolling Thunder River Co., Department SJ, P.O. Box 88, Almond, North Carolina 28702; 704-488-2030. Application deadline: March 31.

From the Employer *All employees participate in white-water training, which includes guiding techniques, safety and evacuation, history of rivers, and customer relations. Employees will improve their communication and cooperation skills through meeting and working with a diversity of people. Employees have the opportunity to participate in a multitude of outdoor activities in areas such as mountain biking, white-water paddling, rock climbing, hiking, swimming, and fishing.*

RUBIN'S OSCEOLA LAKE INN
P.O. Box 2258
Hendersonville, North Carolina 28793

General Information Summer resort hotel with eighty rooms, serving three meals daily. Established in 1941. Owned by Stuart Rubin. Affiliated with Hendersonville Chamber of Commerce, Asheville Chamber of Commerce, Henderson County Travel and Tourism. 16-acre facility located 1 mile south of Hendersonville. Features: original inn and newer lodge rooms; lake and pool; scenic attractions; sports.
Profile of Summer Employees Total number: 40; 50% male, 50% female. Nonsmokers preferred.
Employment Information Openings are from May 27 to October 23. Jobs available: 12 *waiters/waitresses;* 6 *buspersons;* 6 *housekeeping personnel;* 4 *desk clerks;* 3 *bellhops;* 1 *chauffeur;* 3 *kitchen aides.*
Benefits On-site room and board at no charge, bonus payable upon completion of contract.
Contact Stuart Rubin, Owner/Manager, Rubin's Osceola Lake Inn, Department SJ, 250 Palm Avenue, Palm Island, Miami Beach, Florida 33139; 305-534-8356.

UNITED METHODIST CAMPS
1307 Glenwood Avenue
Raleigh, North Carolina 27605

General Information Three campsites located in eastern North Carolina providing camping and outdoor experiences. Established in 1949. Owned by United Methodist Church. Affiliated with American Camping Association. Features: sailing and water experiences (featured at Don-Lee Camp, located 33 miles east of New Bern on the Neuse River); horseback riding and rustic camp with tent cabins (featured at Chestnut Ridge Camp, located 15 miles west of Durham); treehouses and canoeing (featured at Rockfish Camp, located 15 miles south of Fayetteville on a lake).

Profile of Summer Employees Total number: 150; average age: 19; 40% male, 60% female, 20% minorities, 10% high school students, 90% college students. Nonsmokers preferred.

Employment Information Openings are from June 1 to August 15. Jobs available: *cabin counselors* at $130–$165 per week; *nurses; lifeguards; sailing staff/canoeing instructors; naturalists* at $130–$160 per week; *arts and crafts instructors*. International students encouraged to apply.

Benefits Preemployment training, on-site room and board at no charge, laundry facilities, health insurance, accident insurance.

Contact Sue Ellen Nicholson, Director, Camping Ministries, United Methodist Camps, P.O. Box 10955, Raleigh, North Carolina 27605; 919-832-9560, Fax 919-834-7989. Application deadline: May 1.

WILDLIFE CAMPS
Hendersonville, North Carolina 28793

General Information Coeducational residential camp offering environmental education programs for youngsters ages 9–17. Established in 1971. Owned by National Wildlife Federation. Affiliated with American Camping Association. Situated on 1,000 acres. Features: comfortable cabins; view of the Blue Ridge Mountains; miles of hiking trails; rock-climbing and rapelling wall; volleyball and recreation field; waterfront location.

Profile of Summer Employees Total number: 45; average age: 23; 60% male, 40% female, 1% minorities, 95% college students, 1% international, 3% local residents. Nonsmokers preferred.

Employment Information Openings are from June 1 to August 25. Jobs available: 30 *counselors/instructors* with outdoor education experience and first aid certification at $1100–$1900 per season; 12 *backpacking leaders* with trip-leading experience and first-aid certification at $1400–$1600 per season; 1 *waterfront supervisor* with WSI certification at $1100 per season; 2 *nurses* with RN license at $3500 per season.

Benefits College credit, on-site room and board at no charge, laundry facilities, health insurance.

Contact Susan Johnson, Manager, Youth Programs, Wildlife Camps, 1400 16th Street, NW, Washington, D.C. 20036; 800-245-5484, Fax 703-442-7332. Application deadline: February 15.

From the Employer *These twelve-day sessions offer counselors/instructors an opportunity to educate and inspire children through environmental education. During the five-day staff training, instructors will have time to prepare lessons. Generally, 2 staff members and 14 campers share a cabin.*

YMCA BLUE RIDGE ASSEMBLY
84 Blue Ridge Circle
Black Mountain, North Carolina 28711

General Information Conference center serving families, teenagers, and adults. Established in 1906. Affiliated with Young Men's Christian Association. 1,200-acre facility located 17 miles east of Asheville. Features: location in the Appalachian woodlands of the Blue Ridge Mountains; athletics facilities, swimming pool, tennis courts, and hiking trails.

Profile of Summer Employees Total number: 90; average age: 20; 40% male, 60% female, 11% minorities, 5% high school students, 85% college students, 3% retirees, 14% international, 5% local residents. Nonsmokers preferred.

Employment Information Openings are from June 1 to August 19. Jobs available: 90 *collegiate staff members* at $850–$1100 per season.

Benefits College credit, preemployment training, formal ongoing training, on-site room and board at no charge, laundry facilities, travel reimbursement, tuition reimbursement, internships and programs, workmen's compensation insurance.

Contact Assistant Operations Director, YMCA Blue Ridge Assembly, Department SJ, 84 Blue Ridge Circle, Black Mountain, North Carolina 28711; 704-669-8422, Fax 704-669-8497. Application deadline: April 1.

YMCA CAMP CHEERIO
Camp Cheerio Road
Glade Valley, North Carolina 28627

General Information Residential camp serving 200 campers in one- and two-week sessions. A high adventure camp serving 15 campers per week is also offered, as well as a program for senior adults in the spring and fall. Established in 1960. Owned by High Point YMCA. Affiliated with American Camping Association, Young Men's Christian Association. 194-acre facility located 60 miles east of Winston-Salem. Features: beautiful mountain setting; 3-acre lake; swimming pool; 16 cabins with bathroom facilities; 23-room conference center; 4 tennis courts; 2 rappelling towers.

Profile of Summer Employees Total number: 90; average age: 20; 10% minorities, 40% high school students, 60% college students, 5% international, 10% local residents. Nonsmokers preferred.

Employment Information Openings are from June 1 to August 20. Year-round positions also offered. Jobs available: 16 *senior cabin counselors* with rising college sophomore status at $130–$150 per week; 16 *junior cabin counselors* with rising high school senior status at $95–$105 per week; 1 *aquatic director* (minimum age 21) at $165–$238 per week; 1 *rappelling director* (minimum age 21) at $130–$150 per week; *riding master* at $600 per month.

Benefits College credit, preemployment training, on-site room and board at no charge, laundry facilities, health insurance.

Contact Ron Austin, Brant Burgiss, or Keith Russell, YMCA Camp Cheerio, Department SJ, P.O. Box 6258, High Point, North Carolina 27262; 919-869-0195. Application deadline: March 1.

From the Employer *Camp Cheerio summer staff members are encouraged to attend a five-day training program that focuses on leadership skills, communication, and team building. A religious background is important since counselors are responsible for leading daily devotions in cabin groups. Counselors from Great Britain are asked to apply via the BUNACAMP office in London.*

NORTH DAKOTA

INTERNATIONAL MUSIC CAMP
International Peace Garden
Dunseith, North Dakota 58329
General Information   Residential camp serving 500 students per week in 24 different arts programs. Established in 1956. Owned by International Music Camp, Inc. Affiliated with American Camping Association, Canadian Music Educational Conference, U.S. Music Educational National Conference, Canadian and U.S. Band Associations. 120-acre facility located 117 miles north of Minot. Features: 2,000-seat concert hall; 500-seat performing arts center; 3 rehearsal halls; 3 dance studios; percussive arts center; 70 studios and classrooms.
Profile of Summer Employees   Total number: 200; 50% male, 50% female, 5% minorities, 35% college students, 5% retirees, 1% international, 20% local residents, 65% teachers. Nonsmokers preferred.
Employment Information   Openings are from June 5 to August 4. Jobs available: 4 *dishwashers* at $175 per week; 6 *cooks* at $200–$250 per week; 20 *deans/counselors* with college degree or college senior status at $200–$250 per week; 6 *secretaries* with ability to type 50 wpm and knowledge of computers at $175–$200 per week; 4 *music librarians* with instrumental knowledge at $175–$200 per week; *first aid technicians* with EMT or RN certification at $175–$250 per week; 11 *concessioners/housekeepers/maintenance persons* at $175 per week.
Benefits   On-site room and board at no charge, laundry facilities, opportunity to study privately with teaching staff and attend professional concerts at no charge.
Contact   Joseph T. Alme, Camp Director, International Music Camp, Department SJ, 1725 11th Street SW, Minot, North Dakota 58701; 701-838-8472, Fax 701-838-8472. Application deadline: February 28.

From the Employer   *We offer a preprogram orientation for all administrative staff members. Generally, 2 deans and 50 campers share a dormitory. We also have some programs available for graduate credit to those eligible.*

OHIO

CAMP BUTTERWORTH
8551 Butterworth Road
Maineville, Ohio 45039
General Information   Girls' residential camp providing the opportunity to have fun, try new activities, and live in the outdoors with girls from diverse backgrounds. Established in 1930. Owned by Great Rivers Girl Scout Council, Inc. Affiliated with American Camping Association, Girl Scouts of the United States of America. 160-acre facility located 20 miles northeast of Cincinnati. Features: location overlooking the Little Miami River; many scenic hiking trails; wide variety of wildlife found in wooded, rolling hills; location close to Cincinnati and expressway; swimming pool; platform tent units that enable campers and staff to truly experience the outdoors.
Profile of Summer Employees   Total number: 40; average age: 20; 5% male, 95% female,

10% minorities, 1% high school students, 75% college students, 1% retirees, 10% international, 75% local residents. Nonsmokers preferred.

Employment Information Openings are from June 9 to August 14. Year-round positions also offered. Jobs available: 1 *experienced camp director* (minimum age 25) with college degree at $3910–$4619 per season; 1 *health supervisor* with RN, EMT, PA, or MD certification at $2800–$4000 per season; 1 *experienced program director* (minimum age 21) at $1800–$2500 per season; 1 *experienced business manager* (minimum age 21) at $1800–$2350 per season; 1 *experienced equestrian director* (minimum age 21) at $1800–$2200 per season; 2 *experienced horseback-riding instructors* (minimum age 18) at $1400–$1650 per season; 1 *pool director* (minimum age 21) with lifeguard certification, WSI, and canoe experience (preferred) at $1800–$2200 per season; 2 *waterfront assistants* (minimum age 18) with lifeguard certification at $1450–$1800 per season; 2 *experienced naturalists/crafts consultants* (minimum age 18) at $1380–$1900 per season; 4 *experienced unit leaders* (minimum age 21) at $1600–$1900 per season; 10 *unit counselors* (minimum age 18) at $1380–$1600 per season; 1 *administrative assistant* (minimum age 17) at $1200–$1500 per season; 6 *kitchen staff members* at $1280–$3910 per season. International students encouraged to apply.

Benefits Preemployment training, on-site room and board at no charge, laundry facilities, health insurance.

Contact Cyndy Self, Outdoor Program Director, c/o Great Rivers Girl Scout Council, Inc., Camp Butterworth, Department SJ, 4930 Cornell Road, Cincinnati, Ohio 45242; 513-489-1025, Fax 513-489-1417. Application deadline: May 21.

From the Employer *Camp Butterworth employees develop outstanding communications and leadership skills through an extensive ten-day staff training program, as well as through in-service trainings throughout the summer.*

CAMP ECHOING HILLS
36272 County Road 79
Warsaw, Ohio 43844

General Information Camp experience for 120 mentally and physically disabled campers. Established in 1966. Affiliated with American Camping Association. 72-acre facility located 15 miles east of Coshooton. Features: swimming pool; basketball gym; fishing pond; multipurpose building (crafts and worship center); full service dining and kitchen area.

Profile of Summer Employees Total number: 60; average age: 20; 35% male, 65% female, 10% minorities, 20% high school students, 70% college students. Nonsmokers only.

Employment Information Jobs available: 40 *counselors* at $100–$125 per week; 20 *support staff members* at $80–$100 per week. International students encouraged to apply.

Benefits On-site room and board, laundry facilities, possibility of being sponsored up to $3500.

Contact Brian K. Betts, Camp Program Director, Camp Echoing Hills, Department SJ, 36272 County Road 79, Warsaw, Ohio 43844; 614-327-2311. Application deadline: May 1.

CAMP O'BANNON
9688 Butler Road NE
Newark, Ohio 43055

General Information Residential camp serving children ages 9–14 with the goal of increasing campers' self-esteem. Established in 1920. Owned by Camp O'Bannon of Licking County, Inc. Operated by United Way. Affiliated with American Camping Association.

169-acre facility located 45 miles east of Columbus. Features: swimming pool; low ropes course; cabins and platform tents; hiking trails.

Profile of Summer Employees Total number: 20; average age: 21; 40% male, 60% female, 20% high school students, 80% college students. Nonsmokers preferred.

Employment Information Openings are from June 10 to August 19. Jobs available: 4 *cabin counselors* (minimum age 19) with one year of college at $1100 per season; 3 *outpost counselors* (minimum age 19) with one year of college at $1100 per season; 1 *lifeguard* (minimum age 19) with WSI certification (preferred) at $1200 per season; 1 *arts and crafts counselor* (minimum age 19) with one year of college at $1100 per season; 1 *nature counselor* (minimum age 19) with one year of college at $1100 per season; 1 *cook* with ability to cook for 65 or more people at $1500–$1800 per season; 1 *nurse* with RN license at $1400 per season; 4 *co-counselors* (minimum age 17) at $1000 per season; 1 *assistant cook* (minimum age 17) at $900 per season; 1 *outpost director* (minimum age 21) with two years of college at $1500 per season; 1 *program director* (minimum age 21) with two years of college at $1500 per season; 1 *maintenance counselor* (minimum age 18) at $1000 per season; *camp director* (minimum age 21) with college degree (preferred) at $1800 per season.

Benefits College credit, preemployment training, on-site room and board at no charge, laundry facilities, health insurance.

Contact Ted Cobb, Camp Director, Camp O'Bannon, 62 West Locust Street, Newark, Ohio 43055; 614-349-9646. Application deadline: March 30.

From the Employer *Camp O'Bannon places the utmost importance on positive feelings and self-esteem in the developmental processes of our children. Camp O'Bannon provides a residential camping experience for referred children of Licking County and offers a tremendous experience for college students who hope to work with children.*

CAMP STONYBROOK
4491 East State Route 73
Waynesville, Ohio 45068

General Information Residential camp serving a diverse population of girls by providing a rustic, outdoor experience emphasizing physical fitness. Established in 1953. Owned by Great Rivers Girl Scout Council, Inc. Affiliated with American Camping Association, Girl Scouts of the United States of America. 315-acre facility located 35 miles north of Cincinnati. Features: many hiking trails; creek running through property; area rich in fossils; pool; par course and other sports facilities; outdoor tennis/volleyball courts.

Profile of Summer Employees Total number: 16; average age: 20; 5% male, 95% female, 12% minorities, 5% high school students, 75% college students, 5% international, 85% local residents. Nonsmokers preferred.

Employment Information Openings are from June 9 to August 14. Jobs available: 1 *experienced director* (minimum age 25) with college degree at $3910–$4619 per season; 3 *health supervisors* with RN, EMT, or PA license at $2800–$4000 per season; 1 *experienced program director* (minimum age 21) at $1800–$2500 per season; 1 *experienced business manager* (minimum age 21) at $1800–$2350 per season; 1 *pool director* (minimum age 21) with lifeguard and WSI certification and/or canoe experience (preferred) at $1800–$2200 per season; 2 *waterfront assistants* (minimum age 18) with lifeguard certification at $1450–$1800 per season; 1 *experienced naturalist/crafts consultant* (minimum age 18) at $1380–$1900 per season; 1 *unit leader* (minimum age 21) at $1600–$1900 per season; 2 *unit counselors* (minimum age 18) at $1380–$1600 per season; 6 *kitchen staff members* at $1280–$3910 per season. International students encouraged to apply.

Benefits Preemployment training, on-site room and board at no charge, laundry facilities, health insurance.

Contact Cyndy Self, Outdoor Program Director, c/o Great Rivers Girl Scout Council, Inc., Camp Stonybrook, Department SJ, 4930 Cornell Road, Cincinnati, Ohio 45242; 513-489-1025, Fax 513-489-1417. Application deadline: May 15.

HIDDEN HOLLOW CAMP
5127 Oppossum Run Road, Route 3
Bellville, Ohio 44813

General Information Traditional residential camp serving boys and girls ages 7–15 with activities such as swimming, nature hikes, trail rides, arts and crafts, archery, tennis, woodworking, dramatics, and pond canoeing. Established in 1940. Owned by Friendly House Community Center. Affiliated with American Camping Association, National Parks and Recreation Association. 561-acre facility located 11 miles north of Mansfield. Features: 10 log cabins and 3 dormitories; swimming pool; tennis court; riding trails; archery range; outdoor theater.

Profile of Summer Employees 50% male, 50% female, 20% minorities, 49% high school students, 51% college students, 85% local residents. Nonsmokers preferred.

Employment Information Openings are from July 4 to August 20. Jobs available: 15 *camp counselors* at $125 per week.

Benefits Preemployment training, on-site room and board at no charge.

Contact Bernard L. Dillon, Director, Hidden Hollow Camp, Department SJ, 380 North Mulberry Street, Mansfield, Ohio 44902; 419-522-0521. Application deadline: January 15.

YMCA CAMP TIPPECANOE
81300 YMCA Road
Tippecanoe, Ohio 44699

General Information Residential camp serving 80–120 campers per week, with an emphasis on horsemanship, waterfront activities, and the natural world. Established in 1957. Operated by Canton Area YMCA. Affiliated with American Camping Association, CHA–Camp Horsemanship Association, Ohio Outdoor Educators Association. 1,100-acre facility located 53 miles south of Canton. Features: nature lodge; large freshwater lake; scenic Allegheny Mountains; modern cabins and showerhouses; initiatives course (low challenges); 3 horse barns with 4 riding rings and miles of equestrian trails.

Profile of Summer Employees Total number: 25; average age: 22; 40% male, 60% female, 15% minorities, 5% high school students, 85% college students, 5% retirees, 15% international, 20% local residents. Nonsmokers preferred.

Employment Information Openings are from June 12 to August 19. Spring break, winter break, Christmas break positions also offered. Jobs available: 1 *ranch director* with CHA and first aid certification at $150–$200 per week; 2 *ranger directors* with first aid certification at $150–$200 per week; 1 *health director* with RN or EMT license at $150–$200 per week; 12 *cabin counselors* with caring demeanor and sensitivity to needs of campers at $100–$200 per week; 2 *foxfire ridge directors* with first aid and OLS certification at $150–$200 per week; 1 *nature director* at $125–$175 per week; 1 *craft director* at $125–$175 per week; 3 *lifeguards/waterfront staff members* with WSI or equivalent, boating, and first aid certification at $125–$175 per week; 4 *riding instructors* with CHA certification at $125–$175 per week. International students encouraged to apply.

Benefits Formal ongoing training, on-site room and board at no charge, laundry facilities.

Contact Mr. Jim Glunt, Executive Director, YMCA Camp Tippecanoe, Department SJ, 81300 YMCA Road, Tippecanoe, Ohio 44699; 614-922-0679. Application deadline: April 1.

From the Employer *YMCA Camp Tippecanoe offers memorable camping experiences where children can make new friends, try new activities, learn new skills, and take their first steps toward independence. Secure facilities, strong leadership, and high-quality programs are the benchmarks for Tippecanoe. Enriching the spirit, mind, and body of each camper is the goal of the camp staff. During our weeklong staff orientation, employees participate in a training experience that develops their communication, problem-solving, and leadership skills, as well as their risk management and programming talents.*

OREGON

CRATER LAKE LODGE COMPANY
Crater Lake National Park
Crater Lake, Oregon 97604
General Information Operates all concession facilities in Crater Lake National Park. Owned by Crater Lake Lodge, Inc. Located 83 miles northeast of Medford. Features: location at the south rim of Crater Lake at a 7,100-foot elevation in the Cascade Range; 40 cabin rooms, service station, 198-site campground, boat tours, food service, gift shop, and grocery store; many foreign visitors; the nation's deepest lake (1,932 feet).
Profile of Summer Employees Total number: 175; average age: 21; 40% male, 60% female, 2% minorities, 80% college students, 10% local residents.
Employment Information Openings are from June 12 to September 15. Year-round positions also offered. Jobs available: 100 *food service workers;* 6 *maintenance/janitorial/ registration personnel* with valid driver's license; 4 *experienced office workers* with accounting skills; 6 *boat tour operators* with Red Cross card; 26 *gift shop personnel* (retail); 10 *front desk personnel;* 15 *housekeeping staff members;* 3 *laundry staff members;* 2 *bellhops;* 8 *convenience store clerks;* 5 *campground staff members.* All positions offered at $4.75 per hour.
Benefits College credit, on-site room and board at $53 per week, laundry facilities, opportunities for advancement for returning employees.
Contact Personnel Manager, Crater Lake Lodge Company, Department SJ, P.O. Box 128, Crater Lake, Oregon 97604; 503-594-2511, Fax 503-594-2622. Application deadline: April 15.

From the Employer *While we hope that you will enjoy exploring Crater Lake, the Oregon Caves, the southern Oregon coast, and mountains on your days off, we expect you to work hard when you are scheduled to work. Each of us is committed to a team effort to provide a level of service that exceeds park visitors' expectations. All positions, regardless of level, have equal significance in ensuring that our guests have a truly memorable experience.*

YWCA CAMP WESTWIND
2353 North Three Rocks Road
Otis, Oregon 97368
General Information Coeducational residential camp with traditional activities for children ages 7–18 and adults. Established in 1936. Owned by YWCA. Affiliated with American

Camping Association. 500-acre facility located 90 miles west of Portland. Features: location on Pacific Ocean; environmentally rich site (estuary, rainforest, river, oceanfront, beaches, and tidepools); miles of hiking trails along the Pacific Ocean; hidden ocean coves; natural lakes and ponds (not for swimming).

Profile of Summer Employees   Total number: 35; average age: 20; 30% male, 70% female, 4% minorities, 2% high school students, 97% college students, 2% international, 70% local residents.

Employment Information   Openings are from June 12 to August 31. Jobs available: *teen leadership coordinator* (minimum age 21) with challenge course experience (preferred) and CPR/first aid certification at $115–$120 per week; *assistant horseback-riding instructor,* *experienced preferred,* with CPR/first aid certification at $95–$100 per week; *counselor* with CPR/first aid certification at $85–$90 per week; *nature/marine science specialist* (minimum age 21) with CPR/first aid certification at $90–$100 per week; *waterfront director* with lifeguarding and CPR/first aid certification and small craft instructor status at $100–$105 per week.

Benefits   College credit, preemployment training, on-site room and board at no charge.

Contact   Miriam Callaghan, Camp Administrator, YWCA Camp Westwind, Department SJ, 1111 Southwest Tenth Avenue, Portland, Oregon 97205; 503-223-6281, Fax 503-223-5988. Application deadline: June 5.

From the Employer   *At a ten-day preprogram staff training, all employees participate in workshops on inclusivity, behavior management, low elements challenge course, safety, accident prevention, and more. Generally, 1 staff member and 8 campers share a cabin. Camp sessions are six to seven days in length, with 24–36 hours of break between sessions for all employees.*

PENNSYLVANIA

BEACON LODGE CAMP FOR THE BLIND
RD 1, Mount Union
Mount Union, Pennsylvania 17066

General Information   Residential camp serving blind and visually impaired, deaf and hearing impaired, and special needs/physically disabled adults and children. Established in 1948. Operated by Lions/Lioness Clubs of Pennsylvania. Affiliated with Pennsylvania Recreation and Parks, Conference of Lions Camps of the U.S. 583-acre facility located 75 miles west of Harrisburg. Features: location beside the beautiful blue Juniata River; wooded area; modern facilities; fishing pond.

Profile of Summer Employees   Total number: 70; average age: 22; 30% male, 70% female, 13% high school students, 76% college students, 11% retirees, 49% local residents. Nonsmokers preferred.

Employment Information   Openings are from May 19 to August 18. Jobs available: 1 *outfitter* (minimum age 21) with experience in hiking and biking and valid driver's license at $1500 per season; 2 *nurses* with RN license at $3500 per season; 1 *canteen manager* with mature attitude and fast food restaurant experience at $1500 per season; 1 *lifeguard/pool supervisor* (minimum age 18, age 21 preferred) with WSI, CPR, and basic first aid certification at $1600–$1700 per season; 4 *lifeguards* with advanced lifesaving certification at $1400–$1500 per season; 1 *quartermaster* with camping experience at $1400–$1500 per season; 1 *crafts instructor* with demonstrable course work or experience in woodworking, macrame, pottery, ceramics, weaving, and candlemaking at $1400–$1600 per season; 1 *certified kayaking instructor* at $1500–$1700 per season; 1 *certified canoeing instructor* at $1500–$1700 per season; 1 *certified archery instructor* (minimum age 18) at $1500–$1700 per season; 1 *air-riflery instructor* (minimum age 18) with NRA air-riflery instructor certification at $1500–$1700 per season; 1 *trip counselor* (minimum age 18) with demonstrable experience in group trip planning at $1400–$1500 per season; 1 *program director* with B.A. degree in therapeutic recreation or related field at $1700–$1900 per season; 2 *unit directors* (minimum age 21) with a minimum of two years experience at Beacon Lodge at $1700–$1900 per season; 22 *general counselors* with scouting, camping, or similar experience and a genuine interest in working with people at $1300–$1500 per season.

Benefits   College credit, preemployment training, on-site room and board at no charge, laundry facilities.

Contact   Steve Arcona, Camp Director, Beacon Lodge Camp for the Blind, Department SJ, RD 1, Box 315, Mount Union, Pennsylvania 17066; 814-542-2511. Application deadline: April 15.

BRYN MAWR CAMP
RR 5, Box 410
Honesdale, Pennsylvania 18431

General Information   Camp serving 350 girls ages 5–15 for eight weeks. Year-round conference center and mountain retreat. Established in 1921. Owned by Herb Kutzen. Operated by Bryn Mawr Camp, Inc. Affiliated with American Camping Association, Wayne County Camping Association, Pocono Mountain Vacation Bureau. 135-acre facility located 105 miles north of New York City. Features: outstanding programs on 18 tennis courts; 2 heated swimming pools; 15,000-square-foot theater arts building capable of seating 1,000 people; 12,000-square-foot gymnasium facility; state-of-the-art ropes challenge course; extensive English riding program in 3 rings and trails.

Profile of Summer Employees   Total number: 150; average age: 22; 15% male, 85% female, 5% minorities, 2% high school students, 60% college students, 3% retirees, 15% international, 5% local residents, 10% teachers. Nonsmokers only.

Employment Information   Openings are from May 15 to September 30. Spring break, year-round positions also offered. Jobs available: 16 *swimming instructors* with WSI certification at $1000–$1600 per season; 2 *small craft instructors* with American Red Cross small craft license at $1000–$1400 per season; 4 *experienced waterskiing instructors* at $1000–$1500 per season; 20 *tennis instructors* at $800–$1600 per season; 4 *experienced arts and crafts instructors* at $800–$1600 per season; 3 *dance instructors* at $800–$1600 per season; 5 *English riding instructors* at $800–$1600 per season; 12 *kitchen assistants* at $1000–$1800 per season; 5 *laundry/light housekeeping personnel* at $1000–$1400 per season; 2 *office staff members* at $1000–$1600 per season; 7 *athletics instructors* at $800–$1600 per season; 4 *drama instructors* at $800–$1600 per season; 8 *gymnastics instructors* at $800–$1600 per season; 3 *piano/technical theater personnel* at $800–$1600 per season; 12 *general counselors* at $800–$1200 per season; 5 *ropes-challenge/outdoors counselors* at $1000–$1800 per season; 4 *registered nurses* at $1400–$2400 per season; 2 *nine-month recreation/marketing/sales internships* at $775–$1000 per month.

Benefits   College credit, preemployment training, formal ongoing training, on-site room and board at no charge, laundry facilities, travel reimbursement, staff uniforms, use of staff bicycles, planned staff days off, precamp and postcamp work, year-round employment possibility, skill bonuses, and travel allowances.

Contact   Herb Kutzen or Brad Finkelstein, Bryn Mawr Camp, Department SJ, 81 Falmouth

Street, Short Hills, New Jersey 07078; 201-467-3518, Fax 201-467-3750. Application deadline: May 15.

From the Employer   *Bryn Mawr Camp and Conference Center offers a unique learning experience for all of its staff. There is a strong sense of commitment and moral responsibility asked of each staff member. The guidance and leadership of our senior staff creates an exceptional learning environment.*

CAMP AKIBA
Reeders, Pennsylvania 18352
General Information   Private residential accredited camp offering an eight-week session. Established in 1926. Owned by Howard Gordon. Affiliated with American Camping Association, Pocono Mountain Vacation Bureau. 350-acre facility located 90 miles north of Philadelphia. Features: 21 tennis courts; 2 Olympic-size pools; 40-acre lake; in-line skating; 8 volleyball courts (4 sand); 2 miniature golf courses; 5 softball fields and 6 basketball courts.
Profile of Summer Employees   Total number: 200; average age: 20; 50% male, 50% female, 90% college students. Nonsmokers preferred.
Employment Information   Openings are from June 22 to August 17. Jobs available: 8 *pool instructors* with LGT and WSI certification at $1200–$1600 per season; 2 *lakefront personnel* with SCI certification or experience at $1100–$1500 per season; 10 *experienced tennis instructors* at $1200–$2000 per season; 150 *general counselors* with desire to work with children at $950–$1700 per season; 2 *riflery instructors* with experience handling .22 caliber rifles at $950–$1300 per season; 2 *experienced archery instructors* at $950–$1300 per season; 2 *experienced minibike/go-cart instructors* at $950–$1400 per season; 2 *experienced video/photo instructors* at $950–$1400 per season; 4 *experienced team sport instructors* at $950–$1500 per season; 4 *experienced individual sport instructors* at $950–$1500 per season; 2 *experienced arts and crafts instructors* at $1000–$1500 per season; 4 *experienced outdoor adventure instructors* with ability to teach ropes course, rappelling, and rafting at $950–$1500 per season; 2 *experienced jet-skiing instructors* at $950–$1400 per season; 2 *experienced waterskiing instructors* at $950–$1800 per season; 2 *experienced horseback-riding instructors* at $1000–$1400 per season. International students encouraged to apply.
Benefits   College credit, preemployment training, on-site room and board at no charge, laundry facilities, travel reimbursement, health insurance.
Contact   Marie B. Ray, Executive Director, Camp Akiba, Box 840, Bala Cynwyd, Pennsylvania 19004; 610-660-9555, Fax 610-660-9556. Application deadline: May 1.

From the Employer   *Camp Akiba, a brother-sister camp, has staff members representing most states and Europe. Our counselor-camper ratio is 1:3. We invite applications from undergraduate and graduate students as well as faculty to work in our outdoor educational environment.*

CAMP ARCHBALD
RR 2, Box 123
Kingsley, Pennsylvania 18826
General Information   Camp for girls ages 6–17 with the purpose of providing an opportunity to make friends, develop an appreciation of nature, learn new skills, and grow in self-confidence. Established in 1920. Owned by Scranton Pocono Girl Scout Council. Affiliated with American Camping Association. 288-acre facility located 35 miles north of Scranton. Features: 7-acre natural lake; large open fields; miniature golf course; horseback-riding

trails; 7 living areas for campers grouped by age levels; arts and crafts building.

Profile of Summer Employees   Total number: 40; average age: 20; 2% male, 98% female, 1% minorities, 25% high school students, 75% college students, 3% international. Nonsmokers preferred.

Employment Information   Openings are from June 13 to August 14. Spring break positions also offered. Jobs available: 1 *program director* with ability to supervise and coordinate all phases of camp program at $130–$150 per week; 1 *office manager* at $110–$130 per week; 1 *experienced food service manager* at $220–$275 per week; 1 *health care supervisor* with RN or EMT license and CPR certification at $175–$220 per week; 1 *waterfront director* with WSI, lifeguard, first aid, and CPR certification at $120–$150 per week; 1 *horseback-riding director* with instructor certification or documented experience at $120–$150 per week; 1 *arts and crafts/nature director* with knowledge of environmental education activities at $100–$125 per week; 7 *unit leaders* with camp and/or Girl Scout experience at $120–$150 per week; 2 *waterfront assistants* with WSI, lifeguard, first aid, and CPR certification at $100–$125 per week; 15 *assistant unit leaders* with camp and/or Girl Scout experience at $90–$110 per week; 1 *small craft director* with canoe instructor, first aid, and CPR certification, and knowledge of rowing and sailing at $100–$125 per week; 3 *cooks* with knowledge of food preparation.

Benefits   College credit, preemployment training, on-site room and board at no charge, laundry facilities, health insurance, time off as indicated in personnel policies.

Contact   Diane E. Bleam, Camp Director, Camp Archbald, Department SJ, 333 Madison Avenue, Scranton, Pennsylvania 18510; 717-344-1224, Fax 717-346-7259. Application deadline: June 1.

CAMP BALLIBAY
Box 1
Camptown, Pennsylvania 18815

General Information   Coeducational residential camp serving up to 155 children ages 6–16. Established in 1964. Owned by Gerard J. Jannone. Affiliated with American Camping Association. 500-acre facility located 50 miles northwest of Scranton. Features: excellent theater facility; 2 large dance studios; large well-appointed art complex; music building with practice rooms; audio and video studios (high-tech programs); pretty mountain surroundings.

Profile of Summer Employees   Total number: 42; average age: 23; 40% male, 60% female, 60% college students, 5% retirees, 15% international, 5% local residents. Nonsmokers preferred.

Employment Information   Openings are from June 22 to August 27. Jobs available: *theater directors; dance instructors* (all phases); *art instructors* (all areas); *music instructors* (vocal and instrumental); *video instructors; technical instructors* (lighting and sound); *costume instructors; WSI instructors; tennis instructors; golf instructors; riding instructors; supervisory staff; office staff.* All positions offered at $750–$2000 per season.

Benefits   On-site room and board at no charge, laundry facilities, travel reimbursement.

Contact   Mr. Gerard J. Jannone, Camp Ballibay, Department SJ, Box 1, Camptown, Pennsylvania 18815; 717-746-3223, Fax 717-746-3691.

CAMP CANADENSIS
Lake Road RR1, Box 150
Canadensis, Pennsylvania 18325

General Information   Coeducational residential camp offering an eight-week program for children ages 7–16. Established in 1941. Owned by Saltzman family. Affiliated with American

Camping Association. 1,000-acre facility located 90 miles west of New York City. Features: 75-acre lake; 2 heated pools; 16 tennis courts; 3 climbing walls; high ropes course; 12 miles of trails for hiking, mountain biking, and motorcycling; 5,000-square-foot fully equipped gymnastics building.

Profile of Summer Employees Total number: 135; average age: 21; 50% male, 50% female, 95% college students, 5% teachers. Nonsmokers preferred.

Employment Information Openings are from June 21 to August 19. Jobs available: 7 *swimming instructors* with WSI and lifeguard certification at $1000–$1400 per season; 30 *athletics instructors* with team experience at $1000–$1200 per season; 8 *ropes-course/climbing instructors* at $1000–$1200 per season; 5 *drama instructors* at $1000 per season; 7 *arts and crafts instructors* at $1000 per season; 8 *sailing/waterskiing/windsurfing instructors* at $1000 per season; 3 *experienced gymnastics instructors* at $1000 per season; 7 *experienced rafting/kayaking/scuba instructors* with lifeguard certification at $1000 per season; 14 *tennis instructors* with college team coaching experience at $1000–$1600 per season; 2 *archery instructors* at $1000 per season; 3 *riflery instructors* with NRA certification at $1000 per season; 3 *maintenance staff members* at $1000 per season; 3 *nurses* with RN license at $2000 per season; 20 *general counselors* at $1000 per season; 4 *photography/newspaper instructors* at $1000 per season; 2 *nature instructors* at $1000 per season.

Benefits College credit, preemployment training, on-site room and board at no charge, laundry facilities, all travel expenses with campers included.

Contact Terri/Steve Saltzman, Director, Camp Canadensis, Department SJ, Box 182, Wyncote, Pennsylvania 19095; 215-572-8222, Fax 215-572-8298.

From the Employer *Camp Canadensis has 130 staff members from throughout the United States as well as several international staff members. Usually, 2–3 staff members share a cabin with 8–10 campers. We have excellent facilities, including modern cabins and delicious meals. We have a five-day staff orientation program and offer five days off throughout the summer. Camp Canadensis has a friendly, comfortable working atmosphere.*

CAMP CAYUGA
Pocono Mountains, RD 1, Box 1180
Honesdale, Pennsylvania 18431

General Information Private coed nonsectarian sleepaway summer camp for children ages 5–16 specializing in first-time campers. Traditional noncompetitive program offering instruction in over fifty activities. Established in 1957. Owned by Brian and Trish Buynak. Affiliated with American Camping Association, Wayne County Camp Association, United States Tennis Association, American Red Cross, National Rifle Association, American Archery Association. 350-acre facility located 115 miles northwest of New York City. Features: 1 swimming pool for instruction and 1 heated pool for special events; private natural stream-fed lake used for sailing, canoeing, fishing, and swimming; Junior/Main campus (ages 5–13) and Teen campus (ages 14–16)—each with a special activity program; 45 modern cabins with bathrooms, showers, and electricity; 2 large indoor gymnasiums/recreational centers; 25-horse stable on premises, 7 miles of scenic trails, and 2 riding rings.

Profile of Summer Employees Total number: 110; average age: 23; 50% male, 50% female, 9% minorities, 98% college students, 2% retirees, 10% international, 2% local residents, 20% teachers.

Employment Information Openings are from June 19 to August 22. Jobs available: 10 *experienced swimming instructors* with WSI and lifeguard certification at $1200–$1600 per season; 5 *experienced sailing instructors* with lifeguard and ARC small craft certification at $1100–$1600 per season; 4 *experienced gymnastics instructors* with at least one year of college completed at $1100–$1300 per season; 4 *experienced ceramics instructors/pottery*

instructors with at least one year of college completed and kiln operating experience at $1100–$1300 per season; 4 *martial arts instructors, experience preferred,* with at least one year of college completed at $1100–$1300 per season; 3 *experienced riflery instructors* with NRA certification or equivalent and at least one year of college completed at $1100–$1300 per season; 4 *experienced drama instructors* with at least one year of college completed at $1000–$1300 per season; 4 *archery instructors, experience preferred,* with at least one year of college completed at $1100–$1300 per season; 8 *experienced tennis/field hockey/roller-skating instructors* with at least one year of college completed at $1100–$1300 per season; 3 *experienced Honda quad-riding instructors* with at least one year of college completed at $1100–$1300 per season; 3 *experienced computer instructors* with at least one year of college completed and Commodore computer knowledge at $1100–$1300 per season; 4 *experienced radio broadcasting instructors* with at least one year of college completed and disc jockey experience (preferred) at $1100–$1300 per season; 3 *experienced wrestling instructors* with at least one year of college completed at $1100–$1300 per season; 3 *windsurfing instructors* with lifeguard certification and at least one year of college completed at $1100–$1600 per season; 12 *experienced horseback-riding instructors* with at least one year of college completed and stable-care skills at $1100–$1300 per season; 3 *model rocketry instructors* with at least one year of college completed at $1000–$1300 per season; 3 *cheerleading instructors, experience preferred,* with at least one year of college completed at $1100–$1300 per season; 3 *experienced dance instructors* (ballet, jazz, tap, or folk) with at least one year of college completed at $1100–$1300 per season; 3 *basketball instructors, experience preferred,* with at least one year of college completed at $1100–$1300 per season; 5 *experienced waterfront directors* (minimum age 25) with WSI and lifeguard certification at $1500–$2500 per season; 4 *program directors* (minimum age 25) with coaching and camp experience (preferred) at $1500–$2500 per season; 4 *experienced athletics directors* (minimum age 25) with coaching and camp experience (preferred) at $1500–$2500 per season; 4 *experienced head counselors* (minimum age 25) with demonstrated supervisory skills at $1500–$2500 per season; 2 *lacrosse instructors, experience preferred,* with at least one year of college completed at $1100–$1300 per season; 3 *experienced video camera instructors* with at least one year of college completed at $1100–$1300 per season; 3 *golf instructors, experience preferred,* with at least one year of college completed at $1100–$1300 per season; 6 *experienced nurses* with RN, LPN, or EMT license at $1500–$2500 per season; 4 *arts and crafts instructors, experience preferred,* with at least one year of college completed at $1100–$1300 per season; 4 *experienced office personnel* with good organizational skills, excellent telephone manner, and administration skills at $1100–$1500 per season; 2 *experienced volleyball instructors* with at least one year of college completed at $1100–$1300 per season.
Benefits College credit, preemployment training, formal ongoing training, on-site room and board at no charge, laundry facilities, travel reimbursement, end-of-season bonus, free camp shirt, use of extensive facilities (gymnasiums, tennis courts, weight room, stables, and more), tips and gratuities permitted, free three-day winter camp ski reunion during winter break.
Contact Brian B. Buynak, Camp Director, Camp Cayuga, Department SJ, P.O. Box 452, Washington, New Jersey 07882; 908-689-3339, Fax 908-689-8209. Application deadline: June 1.

From the Employer *Over 100 high-caliber men and women are recruited from colleges across the United States and Europe. We have a diverse camper/staff population and a down-to-earth atmosphere. Generally, 2 counselors supervise each cabin. Free tuition is offered for families of program directors, athletics directors, head counselors, and nurses.*

CAMP CHEN-A-WANDA
RD 1
Thompson, Pennsylvania 18465

General Information Coeducational sleepaway camp serving 350 campers for an eight-week session. Established in 1939. Owned by Caryl and Morey Baldwin. Affiliated with American Camping Association, Wayne County Camping Association. 183-acre facility located 30 miles north of Scranton. Features: heated swimming pool; 7 lighted outdoor tennis courts; 6 large sports fields; 4 outdoor basketball courts and 1 indoor court; indoor fitness center; extensive frontage on Fiddle Lake.

Profile of Summer Employees Total number: 120; average age: 20; 54% male, 46% female, 10% high school students, 65% college students, 20% international. Nonsmokers preferred.

Employment Information Openings are from June 20 to August 24. Jobs available: 10 *waterfront specialists* (swimming, sailing, or waterskiing) with WSI certification; 4 *soccer specialists;* 4 *baseball specialists;* 4 *basketball specialists;* 3 *tennis specialists;* 2 *go-cart/quadrunner specialists;* 3 *arts and crafts specialists;* 2 *gymnastics specialists;* 2 *hockey specialists;* 2 *stage management/scenery staff members;* 2 *volleyball specialists;* 2 *ropes/rock-climbing/rappelling specialists.* All positions offered at $600–$1200 per season. International students encouraged to apply.

Benefits Preemployment training, on-site room and board at no charge, travel reimbursement.

Contact Morey Baldwin, Director, Camp Chen-A-Wanda, 8 Claverton Court, Dix Hills, New York 11747; 516-643-5878, Fax 516-643-0920. Application deadline: May 31.

From the Employer *Generally, 3 staff members and 10 campers share a cabin. Staff teams in basketball, soccer, and volleyball compete against other nearby camps.*

CAMP LAMBEC
13110 Old Lake Road
North Springfield, Pennsylvania 16430

General Information Lakefront camp providing worship and recreational activities for children ages 8–17 and family groups weekly; weekend and midweek retreats are scheduled in the off-season. Established in 1947. Owned by Camping Association of the Presbyteries of Northwest Pennsylvania. Operated by the Presbyteries of Beaver/Butler, Kiskimenitas, Lake Erie, and Shenango. Affiliated with American Camping Association, Christian Camping International, Presbyterian Camps and Conference Centers Association. 97-acre facility located 20 miles west of Erie. Features: 1,500 feet of frontage on Lake Erie; tennis court; asphalt and grass volleyball courts; children's playground; large sports fields; 3 picnic shelters.

Profile of Summer Employees Total number: 20; average age: 20; 40% male, 60% female, 90% college students, 10% international, 90% local residents. Nonsmokers only.

Employment Information Openings are from June 12 to August 15. Jobs available: 3 *lifeguards/sailing instructors* with WSI and lifeguard certification at $100–$175 per week; 3 *experienced cooks/kitchen aides* at $100–$175 per week; 1 *health supervisor* with first aid, EMT, or RN certification (salary depends on certification) at $100–$200 per week; 10 *support staff members (cabin counselors and maintenance assistants)* at $100–$125 per week. International students encouraged to apply.

Benefits Preemployment training, on-site room and board at no charge, laundry facilities, health insurance.

Contact Mrs. Idamarie Eckstein, Executive Director, Camp Lambec, Department SJ, 100

Venango Street, Mercer, Pennsylvania 16137-1109; 412-662-4481. Application deadline: April 30.

From the Employer *We are committed to helping our campers of all ages grow in religious faith. Our staff members must be committed Christians willing to participate in worship and lead Bible study activities. We emphasize faith, fellowship, and fun in all we do.*

CAMP LOG-N-TWIG
Dingman's Ferry, Pennsylvania 18328

General Information General coeducational recreation program serving up to 250 campers. Established in 1953. Owned by Morton and Ronne Tener. 125-acre facility located 110 miles north of Philadelphia. Features: 7 tennis courts; pool; man-made lake; indoor gymnasium; modern cabins (indoor showers and lavatories); many playing fiels.

Profile of Summer Employees Total number: 80; average age: 22; 50% male, 50% female. Nonsmokers preferred.

Employment Information Openings are from June 20 to August 21. Jobs available: *general counselors* at $900–$1100 per season; *specialty counselors* at $1000–$1300 per season; *nurse* at $2000 per season.

Benefits College credit, on-site room and board at no charge, laundry facilities.

Contact Dr. Morton Tener, Camp Log-n-Twig, 7700 Doe Lane, Laverock, Pennsylvania 19118; 215-887-9367. Application deadline: March 1.

CAMP NETIMUS
RD 1, Box 117A
Milford, Pennsylvania 18337

General Information Residential girls' camp with four- or eight-week sessions, offering thirty-six activities to help campers develop self-confidence and a positive self-image. Established in 1930. Owned by Camp Netimus, Inc. Affiliated with American Camping Association. 400-acre facility located 90 miles west of New York City. Features: northeastern Pennsylvania setting; cabins; well-equipped program facilities; ropes course; riding trails; proximity to the Delaware River; waterfalls, lake, and mountains.

Profile of Summer Employees Total number: 75; average age: 24; 10% male, 90% female, 6% minorities, 1% high school students, 4% college students, 5% retirees, 30% international, 5% local residents, 4% teachers. Nonsmokers preferred.

Employment Information Openings are from June 10 to August 20. Jobs available: 4 *swimming instructors* with WSI certification and lifeguard training; 2 *sailing instructors* with lifeguard training; 4 *fine arts instructors;* 2 *jewelry/metalcraft instructors;* 2 *waterskiing instructors* (minimum age 21) with lifeguard training; 4 *horseback-riding instructors* with first aid/CPR certification; 2 *nurses* with RN license; 1 *fencing instructor;* 1 *rock-climbing instructor;* 2 *stained glass instructors;* 2 *woodworking instructors;* 3 *canoeing instructors* with lifeguard training; 3 *outdoor/environmental instructors;* 2 *gymnastics instructors;* 3 *dance instructors* (jazz, modern, tap, and ballet); *trip instructors* with first aid, CPR, and lifeguard training; *rifle instructors* with first aid/CPR certification; *archery instructors* with first aid/CPR certification. All positions offered at $1000–$2500 per season. International students encouraged to apply.

Benefits College credit, preemployment training, formal ongoing training, on-site room and board at no charge, laundry facilities, transportation on day off, skill development (CPR, first aid, and lifeguard training), salary bonus for certifications and department heads.

Contact Donna Kistler, Director, Camp Netimus, Department SJ, RD 1, Box 117A,

Milford, Pennsylvania 18337; 800-225-0604, Fax 717-296-6128. Application deadline: April 30.

From the Employer *We care about the children and our staff by providing a family atmosphere that includes babies, grandparents, college students, teachers, those in the work world, couples, and international campers. Counselors enjoy the advantages of spending time in a healthy, fresh, beautiful environment while fine-tuning communication, teaching, and people skills. At our ten-day preprogram orientation, topics covered include safety, facilitating group interaction, program development, cabin techniques, and social events.*

CAMP NOCK-A-MIXON
249 Traugers Crossing Road
Kintnersville, Pennsylvania 18930

General Information Residential coeducational camp serving 350 youngsters ages 7–15 during a 7½-week session. Established in 1938. Owned by Mark and Bernice Glaser. Affiliated with American Camping Association. 115-acre facility located 48 miles north of Philadelphia. Features: 2 pools for instruction and recreation; 2 lakes for boating and sailing; 10 tennis courts; 3 indoor recreation halls; professional 18-hole mini-golf course; 7 basketball courts.

Profile of Summer Employees Total number: 120; average age: 19; 55% male, 45% female, 10% high school students, 80% college students, 5% teachers. Nonsmokers only.

Employment Information Openings are from June 20 to August 18. Jobs available: 30 *general counselors* at $800–$1100 per season; 30 *specialists and counselors* at $850–$1150 per season; 10 *swimming instructors* with WSI certification and/or lifeguard training at $1000–$2000 per season; 6 *tennis counselors* at $850–$1150 per season; 2 *drama directors* at $900–$1150 per season; 1 *crafts director* at $1200–$1800 per season; *division leaders* with college degree at $1600–$2400 per season.

Benefits Preemployment training, formal ongoing training, on-site room and board at no charge, laundry facilities, days off to visit nearby Philadelphia, New York City, and Atlantic City (all within 2 hours).

Contact Mark Glaser, Director, Camp Nock-A-Mixon, Department SJ, 16 Gum Tree Lane, Lafayette Hill, Pennsylvania 19444; 610-941-0128. Application deadline: May 1.

From the Employer *The average camper-counselor ratio is 4:1. All counselors live in cabins with campers who attend for the entire 7½- week program. There are no split-session campers. Staff orientation begins five days before campers arrive.*

CAMP SANDY HILL
Hickory Run State Park
Whitehaven, Pennsylvania 18661

General Information Residential and trip camp serving 120 children ages 7–16 weekly. Established in 1952. Owned by Morning Cheer Inc. Operated by Sandy Cove Ministries. Affiliated with American Camping Association, Christian Camping International. 100-acre facility located 100 miles north of Philadelphia. Features: 4 circles of cabins, each complete with a lodge; 2 tennis/basketball courts; 1 medium-size swimming pool; 3 playing fields; sand beach with lake access; large lodge.

Profile of Summer Employees Total number: 32; average age: 21; 50% male, 50% female, 10% minorities, 5% high school students, 80% college students, 20% international, 25% local residents, 20% teachers. Nonsmokers only.

Employment Information Openings are from June 15 to August 15. Jobs available:

counselors at $100 per week; *assistant counselors* at $50 per week; *trip counselors* at $125 per week; *cook* at $200 per week; *nurse* at $200 per week. International students encouraged to apply.

Benefits   College credit, preemployment training, formal ongoing training, on-site room and board at no charge, laundry facilities, opportunities for certification in first aid/CPR and lifeguarding.

Contact   Tim Nielsen, Director, Camp Sandy Hill, P.O. Box 13, North East, Maryland 21901; 410-287-5433, Fax 410-287-3196. Application deadline: June 1.

From the Employer   *All staff members are required to attend our seven-day precamp training. Working at Camp Sandy Hill allows our staff the opportunity to grow physically, mentally, socially, and spiritually.*

CAMP SUSQUEHANNOCK FOR BOYS
Box 71, RR 1
Brackney, Pennsylvania 18812

General Information   Residential camp for 175 boys ages 7–17 offering four- or eight-week sessions. Established in 1905. Owned by Edwin and George Shafer. Affiliated with American Camping Association, Camp Directors' Roundtable. 1,200-acre facility located 15 miles south of Binghamton, New York. Features: lake; 9 outdoor tennis courts; 3 baseball fields; 3 soccer fields; 3 basketball courts; 1 street-hockey court.

Profile of Summer Employees   Total number: 50; average age: 21; 90% male, 10% female, 5% minorities, 60% college students, 10% international. Nonsmokers only.

Employment Information   Openings are from June 13 to August 20. Jobs available: *swimming instructors* with WSI and lifeguard certification; 20 *sports counselors* with ability to teach one or more of the following: baseball, basketball, football, hockey, lacrosse, soccer, swimming, tennis, volleyball. All positions offered at $875–$1500 per season.

Benefits   College credit, preemployment training, on-site room and board at no charge, laundry facilities, travel reimbursement.

Contact   Edwin Shafer, Co-Owner, Camp Susquehannock for Boys, Department SJ, Box 71, RR 1, Brackney, Pennsylvania 18812; 717-967-2323, Fax 717-967-2631. Application deadline: April 1 (all applicants must fill out an application form).

From the Employer   *Our nine-week employment period includes one week of staff training. Extra pay is offered for precamp training. Generally, 2 counselors share a cabin with 10 campers.*

CAMP WATONKA
P.O. Box 127
Hawley, Pennsylvania 18428

General Information   Residential science camp for 120 boys offering hands-on experience in all areas of science combined with traditional camp activities. Established in 1963. Owned by Mr. and Mrs. Donald Wacker. Affiliated with American Camping Association, National Rifle Association, American Red Cross. 250-acre facility located 35 miles east of Scranton. Features: modern well-equipped science buildings and laboratories; extensive American Red Cross waterfront program; proximity to town and many well-known tourist areas; several large sports fields; modern, clean, and comfortable cabins; attracts campers and staff from many states and countries.

Profile of Summer Employees   Total number: 60; average age: 23; 95% male, 5% female,

10% minorities, 5% high school students, 55% college students, 20% international, 10% local residents, 40% teachers. Nonsmokers only.

Employment Information Openings are from June 20 to August 20. Jobs available: 15 *cabin counselors* with college junior or senior status at $1100–$1400 per season; 8 *science instructors* with college or graduate student status at $1100–$2500 per season; 3 *arts and crafts staff members* at $1100–$1400 per season; 8 *science supervisors* with teaching certification at $1500–$3000 per season; 2 *woodworking instructors* with teaching certification at $1500–$3000 per season; 3 *experienced minibike riding instructors* at $1100–$1400 per season; 5 *waterfront/water sports instructors* with ARC certification at $1100–$1500 per season; 1 *waterfront director* with ARC certification at $1500–$3000 per season.

Benefits Preemployment training, formal ongoing training, on-site room and board at no charge, laundry facilities.

Contact Donald P. Wacker, Director, Camp Watonka, Department SJ, P.O. Box 127, Hawley, Pennsylvania 18428; 717-857-1401. Application deadline: June 1.

From the Employer *A five-day orientation period will give new staff members the information they need to conduct a safe, meaningful program. All cabins have hot and cold water, showers, and toilets. There are 7 or 8 campers in each cabin with 2 counselors. Camp facilities are available for staff use as long as space is not taken away from campers.*

COLLEGE SETTLEMENT OF PHILADELPHIA
600 Witmer Road
Horsham, Pennsylvania 19044

General Information Residential and day camp serving mostly economically disadvantaged youths ages 7–14 from the Philadelphia metropolitan area. Established in 1922. Owned by The College Settlement of Philadelphia. Affiliated with American Camping Association, United Way of Southeastern Pennsylvania. 235-acre facility located 20 miles north of Philadelphia. Features: location in suburbs; outpost facility for trips; large swimming pool; high and low rope courses on site; diverse habitat, including pond, woods, fields, and meadows; adequate open space for recreation.

Profile of Summer Employees Total number: 60; average age: 21; 50% male, 50% female, 20% minorities, 10% high school students, 80% college students, 10% international, 10% local residents. Nonsmokers preferred.

Employment Information Openings are from June 10 to August 25. Year-round positions also offered. Jobs available: 12 *cabin counselors* at $1600 per season; 3 *unit leaders* at $1800 per season; 3 *trip leaders* with first aid and CPR certification at $1800–$2000 per season; 2 *environmentalists* at $1600–$1800 per season; 3 *swimming instructors* with WSI and LGT certification (preferred) at $1700–$1900 per season; 1 *provisions coordinator* at $1600–$1800 per season. International students encouraged to apply.

Benefits College credit, preemployment training, on-site room and board at no charge, laundry facilities, travel reimbursement.

Contact Wally Grummun, Director of Resident Programs, College Settlement of Philadelphia, Department SJ, 600 Witmer Road, Horsham, Pennsylvania 19044; 215-542-7974. Application deadline: May 1.

From the Employer *Summer employment at College Settlement provides a unique chance to create and be part of a community that is mindful of the needs of others, including showing respect, taking responsibility, and being resourceful.*

ENSEMBLE THEATRE COMMUNITY SCHOOL
Box 188
Eagles Mere, Pennsylvania 17731
General Information   Summer theater school serving high school students ages 14–18. Established in 1984. Located 40 miles north of Williamsport. Features: location in the Allegheny Mountains; intensive training and performances; ensemble-oriented approach; large residential Victorian housing for faculty and students; community arts facility for performances and classes; swimming, tennis courts, basketball facilities, and hiking trails.
Profile of Summer Employees   Total number: 12; average age: 24; 50% male, 50% female, 15% minorities, 33% college students. Nonsmokers preferred.
Employment Information   Openings are from June 20 to August 6. Jobs available: 1 *experienced acting instructor* with extensive training at $1200–$1700 per season; 1 *experienced acting instructor/director* with extensive training at $1200–$1700 per season; 1 *experienced movement instructor* with extensive training at $1200–$1700 per season; 1 *experienced music instructor* with extensive training at $1200–$1700 per season; 1 *experienced technical director* with extensive training at $1200–$1700 per season; 4 *college interns* with training and experience in theater and related arts at $300–$350 per season.
Benefits   College credit, preemployment training, on-site room and board at no charge, laundry facilities.
Contact   Seth Orbach, Associate Director, Ensemble Theatre Community School, 511 East 82nd Street, #4FW, New York, New York 10028; 212-794-4696. Application deadline: February 28.

From the Employer   *Our four-day faculty orientation emphasizes the creation of an adult ensemble. Special emphasis is on communicating clearly, developing trust, and teaching and learning from each other, which helps us to work effectively as a faculty group to ensure an ensemble with our students. Our unusual staff-student ratio (1:2) distinguishes our program and allows for small classes and the opportunity to give each student personal attention. In addition, all members of the faculty appear in an original children's theater production created by students and faculty. Full faculty members have their own rooms; interns share rooms with students.*

HARMONY HEART CAMP
RR 2, Box 246
Jermyn, Pennsylvania 18433
General Information   Christian outreach serving inner-city children from New York City; Newark, New Jersey; and Chester, Pennsylvania through a well-rounded camping program. Established in 1946. Owned by World Impact, Inc. Affiliated with Christian Camping International, Camp Horsemanship Association, Evangelical Council for Financial Accountability. 30-acre facility located 15 miles north of Scranton. Features: game room; full-size indoor gym; beautiful country setting; indoor and outdoor chapels; picnic grove; location on Heart Lake in the Pocono Mountains; swimming, boating, and fishing.
Profile of Summer Employees   Total number: 15; average age: 19; 50% male, 50% female, 20% minorities, 40% high school students, 60% college students, 1% international, 30% local residents. Nonsmokers only.
Employment Information   Openings are from June 18 to August 15. Jobs available: 2 *swimming instructors* with WSI certification or equivalent; 1 *camp nurse* with RN license (preferred); 1 *experienced horsemanship instructor;* 1 *crafts instructor; program staff;* 10 *support staff members.* All positions offered at $25 per week. International students encouraged to apply.

Benefits Preemployment training, on-site room and board at no charge.
Contact Jan Stewart, Programs Director, Harmony Heart Camp, Department SJ, RR 2, Box 246, Jermyn, Pennsylvania 18433; 717-254-6272. Application deadline: May 1.

From the Employer *Our positions are "summer missions" with our sponsoring organization, World Impact. We are looking for people who have a heart for inner-city children and are able to volunteer a summer to help out. A first aid course is usually included as part of our staff training.*

HERSHEYPARK
100 West Hersheypark Drive
Hershey, Pennsylvania 17033

General Information Facility producing seven residential shows, song and dance revues, and other types of family entertainment. Established in 1972. Owned by Hershey Entertainment Resort Company. 87-acre facility located 90 miles southwest of Philadelphia. Features: location in Chocolatetown, USA; 7 residential shows; professional production team; subsidized housing.
Profile of Summer Employees Total number: 75; average age: 21; 50% male, 50% female. Nonsmokers preferred.
Employment Information Openings are from May to September. Jobs available: 60 *experienced singing/dancing performers* at $310–$330 per week; 5 *experienced stage managers* at $300–$350 per week; 3 *experienced sound technicians* at $300–$330 per week; 6 *seamstresses/dressers* at $285 per week.
Benefits College credit, on-site room and board at $190 per month, laundry facilities, use of all park facilities, end-of-season bonus, equity eligibility.
Contact Stacy Benson, Assistant Entertainment Manager, Hersheypark, Department SJ, 100 West Hersheypark Drive, Hershey, Pennsylvania 17033; 717-534-3349, Fax 717-534-3192. Application deadline: February 15.

HIDDEN FALLS CAMP
Dingman's Ferry, Pennsylvania 18328

General Information Residential camp serving 65 girls in each of six 1-week sessions. Established in 1960. Owned by Girl Scouts of Delaware County. Affiliated with American Camping Association, Girl Scouts of the United States of America. 1,000-acre facility located 120 miles north of Philadelphia. Features: large outdoor pool; freshwater lake; horse ring and miles of trails; nature trails and activity areas; 6 units of platform tents.
Profile of Summer Employees Total number: 25; average age: 25; 100% female, 15% minorities, 5% high school students, 80% college students, 10% international, 90% local residents, 10% teachers. Nonsmokers preferred.
Employment Information Openings are from June 25 to August 15. Jobs available: *counselor* at $1000–$1400 per season; *lifeguard* with lifeguard training, community first aid, and CPR certification at $1200–$1500 per season; *nurse* with PA, RN, or LPN preferred at $2300–$2500 per season; *horseback-riding instructors* with documented experience at $1200–$1500 per season; *cook* at $1800–$2500 per season; *crafts/nature specialist* at $1000–$1200 per season.
Benefits College credit, preemployment training, on-site room and board at no charge, laundry facilities, access to all recreational facilities during time off.
Contact Laurie Estes, Director, Outdoor Program and Property, Hidden Falls Camp,

Department SJ, 594 South New Middletown Road, Media, Pennsylvania 19063; 610-874-3377, Fax 610-874-0760. Application deadline: June 15.

From the Employer *At our six-day staff training program, employees develop program skills and learn about the camp facility and resources. Topics include leadership, behavior management, and cultural diversity. Staff members live in units of platform tents with 20 campers and 4 staff members in a unit. There is also a separate staff tent and retreat.*

HIDDEN VALLEY CAMP
P.O. Box 98, Wallerville Road
Equinunk, Pennsylvania 18417

General Information Residential camp serving girls ages 7–17. Established in 1971. Owned by Rolling Hills Girl Scout Council. Affiliated with Girl Scouts of the United States of America, American Camping Association. 1,200-acre facility located 25 miles south of Hancock, New York. Features: 40-acre lake; proximity to Delaware River and Pocono Mountains; nearby stables; rugged terrain; beautiful scenery.

Profile of Summer Employees Total number: 25; average age: 20; 2% male, 98% female, 20% minorities, 10% high school students, 90% college students, 4% international, 10% local residents.

Employment Information Openings are from June 20 to August 20. Jobs available: 1 *business manager* (minimum age 23) at $1000 per season; 1 *program manager* (minimum age 23) at $2000 per season; 15 *unit leaders* (minimum age 21) at $1000 per season; 10 *unit assistants* (minimum age 18) at $800 per season; 1 *waterfront director* (minimum age 21) with WSI certification at $1000 per season; 1 *waterfront assistant* (minimum age 18) with lifeguard certification at $800 per season; 1 *boating director* (minimum age 21) with WSI and canoe certification at $950 per season; 1 *health supervisor* (minimum age 21) with RN, LPN, or EMT license at $1200 per season; 1 *cook* (minimum age 21) at $1200 per season; 1 *assistant cook* (minimum age 18) at $900 per season; 4 *kitchen aides* (minimum age 18) at $600 per season; 1 *experienced riding instructor* (minimum age 21) at $1000 per season.

Benefits Preemployment training, on-site room and board at no charge, laundry facilities, health insurance.

Contact Lani Jeffrey, Camping Services Manager, Hidden Valley Camp, Department SJ, 1171 Highway 28, North Branch, New Jersey 08876; 908-725-1226. Application deadline: May 31.

From the Employer *Hidden Valley employees gain new skills and develop personal strengths during precamp training. Certification training is available. Our staff members are important role models for young girls and can be responsible for making a real difference in their lives.*

JUMONVILLE
RR 2, Box 128
Hopwood, Pennsylvania 15445

General Information Residential Christian camp serving 250–300 youths per week. Established in 1941. Owned by Jumonville, Inc. Operated by United Methodist Church, Western Pennsylvania Conference. Affiliated with Christian Camping International, American Camping Association. 281-acre facility located 50 miles south of Pittsburgh. Features: 60-foot cross located on top of mountain; 4 outdoor tennis courts; 4 outdoor volleyball courts; outdoor swimming pool; challenge/ropes course; beautiful campus-type setting.

Profile of Summer Employees Total number: 30; average age: 19; 50% male, 50% female,

5% minorities, 10% high school students, 90% college students, 5% international, 10% local residents. Nonsmokers only.

Employment Information Openings are from June 1 to August 1. Year-round positions also offered. Jobs available: 5 *counselors* at $140 per week; 2 *adventure staff members* at $140 per week; 1 *arts and crafts instructor* at $126 per week; 1 *office assistant/business manager* at $126 per week; 1 *business manager/truck driver* at $126 per week; 2 *certified lifeguards* at $126 per week; 3 *snack shop workers* at $126 per week; 4 *dishroom staff members* at $126 per week; 2 *dining room staff members* at $126 per week; 1 *kitchen helper* at $126 per week; 1 *cookout staff member* at $126 per week; 2 *audio/visual specialists* at $126 per week; 2 *maintenance/housekeeping helpers* at $126 per week; 1 *multipurpose floater* at $126 per week; 1 *health-care staff member* with EMT, paramedic, LPN, or RN license at $126 per week; 1 *assistant program director* at $126 per week.

Benefits On-site room and board at no charge, laundry facilities, use of on-site recreational facilities.

Contact Larry Beatty, Executive Director, Jumonville, Department SJ, RR 2, Box 128, Hopwood, Pennsylvania 15445; 412-439-4912, Fax 412-439-1415. Application deadline: March 1.

From the Employer *Precamp training is provided for all work areas.*

LAKE OWEGO AND TIMBERTOPS CAMPS
Greeley, Pennsylvania 18425

General Information Residential camps serving boys and girls for four or eight weeks. Pine Forest is coed, Lake Owego is for boys, and Timbertops is for girls. Established in 1931. Owned by Marvin and Mickey Black. Affiliated with American Camping Association. 1,000-acre facility located 90 miles southwest of New York City. Features: 2 Olympic-size swimming pools; 75-acre lake; indoor gym with regulation basketball court; gymnastic pavilion; 12 all-weather tennis courts at each camp; 100-acre riding ranch with 24 horses (English and Western riding).

Profile of Summer Employees Total number: 250; average age: 21; 45% male, 55% female, 5% minorities, 90% college students, 1% retirees, 10% international. Nonsmokers only.

Employment Information Openings are from June 23 to August 19. Spring break, winter break, Christmas break, year-round positions also offered. Jobs available: 20 *athletics staff members* with high school or college varsity team experience at $600–$1500 per season; 15 *swimming instructors* with WSI certification at $600–$2500 per season; 10 *arts and crafts staff members* with a major in art at $600–$1000 per season; 6 *drama instructors* with a major in theater at $600–$2000 per season; 20 *tennis instructors* with USPTA or team experience at $600–$2400 per season; 20 *climbers* with all-around camp experience at $600–$1000 per season; *unit leaders* with college degree at $1000–$2000 per season; 1 *athletics director* with college degree at $1500–$2400 per season; 4 *drivers* (minimum age 21) with good driving record at $800–$1200 per season; 3 *experienced nature staff members* at $600–$1000 per season; 3 *experienced archery instructors* at $600–$1000 per season; 3 *riflery instructors* (minimum age 21) with NRA experience at $800–$1000 per season; 2 *waterskiing instructors* (minimum age 21) with WSI experience at $800–$1200 per season; 4 *gymnastics instructors;* 10 *sailing/canoeing instructors.*

Benefits College credit, preemployment training, formal ongoing training, on-site room and board at no charge, laundry facilities, five days off per summer, partial travel reimbursement.

Contact Mickey Black, Director, Lake Owego and Timbertops Camps, Department SJ, 151

Washington Lane, Jenkintown, Pennsylvania 19046; 215-887-9700, Fax 215-887-3901. Application deadline: June 15.

From the Employer *At our three camps, staff members acquire excellent opportunities to work with children. The camps provide a terrific atmosphere and invaluable preparation for future teachers. We welcome applicants from all specialty areas.*

LONGACRE EXPEDITIONS
RD 3, Box 106
Newport, Pennsylvania 17074
General Information Adventure travel program emphasizing group living skills and physical challenges. Established in 1981. Owned by Longacre Expeditions. 35-acre facility located 32 miles northwest of Harrisburg. Features: ropes course; climbing wall.
Profile of Summer Employees Total number: 50; average age: 25; 50% male, 50% female, 10% minorities, 40% college students, 10% local residents. Nonsmokers only.
Employment Information Openings are from May 15 to August 15. Jobs available: 2 *rock-climbing instructors* (minimum age 21) at $360–$450 per week; 2 *caving instructors* (minimum age 21) at $360–$450 per week; 8 *support and logistics staff members* (minimum age 21) at $150–$175 per week; 1 *equipment manager* (minimum age 21) at $175–$225 per week; 24 *assistant trip leaders* (minimum age 21) at $150–$175 per week.
Benefits Preemployment training, on-site room and board at no charge, Pro-Deal package.
Contact Roger Smith, Longacre Expeditions, RD 3, Box 106, Newport, Pennsylvania 17074; 717-567-6790.

From the Employer *There is an eight-day precamp staff training period emphasizing hard and soft skills. Individual advancement is expected of returning staff. First-time staff usually join us as assistant trip leaders and support personnel. In the following season, most graduate to trip leader. Continued advancement leads to positions as base camp manager or course director. We offer beginning and intermediate programs, including bicycle touring, backpacking, rock climbing, kayaking, and caving.*

NEW JERSEY CAMP JAYCEE
Ziegler Road
Effort, Pennsylvania 18330
General Information Residential camp serving 135 developmentally disabled campers per week. Established in 1975. Owned by New Jersey Jaycee Foundation. Operated by Association for Retarded Citizens of New Jersey. Affiliated with Association for Retarded Citizens of New Jersey, American Camping Association, New Jersey Jaycees. 185-acre facility located 18 miles southwest of Stroudsburg. Features: 2-acre lake; natural setting near Pocono Mountains; accessibility to New York City (1 hour); location near resort areas; extensive recreation areas.
Profile of Summer Employees Total number: 78; average age: 24; 50% male, 50% female, 10% minorities, 95% college students, 50% international, 50% local residents.
Employment Information Openings are from June 15 to August 15. Jobs available: 2 *swimming instructors* with WSI certification at $160–$190 per week; 2 *lifeguards* with Red Cross certification at $150–$180 per week; 6 *specialists* with experience pertaining to developmental disabilities and special campers at $150–$180 per week; 2 *nurses* with RN license at $2800–$3500 per season; 1 *licensed EMT* at $170–$220 per week; 1 *maintenance assistant* with driver's license and light maintenance experience at $160–$170 per week; 15 *counselors* with experience pertaining to developmental disabilities at $140–$160 per week.

Benefits Preemployment training, formal ongoing training, on-site room and board at no charge, laundry facilities, days off with transportation, beautiful staff hall.

Contact Ron Martin, Executive Director, New Jersey Camp Jaycee, Department SJ, 985 Livingston Avenue, North Brunswick, New Jersey 08902; 908-247-9670, Fax 908-214-1834. Application deadline: May 15.

From the Employer *To give our staff a sense of confidence, we provide five full days of training prior to campers' arrival. At New Jersey Camp Jaycee, you will learn to excel. In general, 2 staff members and 6 campers share a cabin.*

ONEKA
Tafton, Pennsylvania 18464

General Information Residential girls' camp serving 100 campers in 2-, 3½-, and 7-week sessions. Established in 1908. Owned by Dale and Barbara Dohner. Affiliated with American Camping Association, Camp Alert Network. 7-acre facility located 30 miles east of Scranton. Features: extensive freshwater lake frontage with an excellent waterfront area; all facilities centrally located and well maintained; picturesque, woodsy environment with 400 acres for hiking; courts for tennis and volleyball; rooms for ceramics and jewelry-making; darkroom; dances; canoe trips; overnighters.

Profile of Summer Employees Total number: 28; average age: 21; 5% male, 95% female, 5% high school students, 95% college students, 40% international, 15% local residents, 20% teachers. Nonsmokers preferred.

Employment Information Openings are from June 22 to August 23. Jobs available: 5 *swimming instructors/lifeguards* with LT, CPR, first aid, and WSI certification at $900–$1200 per season; 3 *canoeing/boating/sailing instructors* with LT, CPR, first aid, and WSI certification (preferred) at $900–$1200 per season; 2 *experienced arts and crafts instructors* at $900–$1200 per season; 2 *experienced tennis instructors* at $900–$1200 per season; 1 *experienced volleyball instructor* at $900–$1200 per season; 3 *experienced field sports/ hockey/soccer/softball instructors* at $900–$1200 per season; 1 *experienced campcraft instructor* at $900–$1200 per season; 1 *archery instructor* with good personal shooting skills (employee may be sent for further training) at $900–$1200 per season; 1 *music instructor* with piano-playing ability and knowledge of show tunes at $900–$1200 per season; 1 *drama instructor* with experience in directing and set design at $900–$1200 per season; 1 *assistant program director* with two years of camp experience at $1500–$2000 per season; 1 *program director* with three years of camp experience and good management and people skills at $1800–$2500 per season; 1 *aquatic director* with WSI and LTI certification at $1600–$2000 per season; 1 *nurse* with RN license at $1800–$2500 per season; 2 *maintenance helpers* (14–16 years old) at $600–$750 per season.

Benefits On-site room and board at no charge.

Contact Dale H. Dohner, Camp Director, ONEKA, Department SJ, 10 Oakford Road, Wayne, Pennsylvania 19087; 215-687-6260. Application deadline: March 31.

From the Employer *Precamp training includes sessions run by professionals in safety, law, education, and health care. ONEKA's small size and family atmosphere allow staff to be members of a unique, nurturing group. International staff lend cultural diversity to our small, close-knit family.*

PINE FOREST CAMPS
Box 242
Greeley, Pennsylvania 18425

General Information Residential camps serving children ages 6–16 offering four- and eight-week sessions. Established in 1931. Owned by Marvin and Mickey Black. Affiliated with American Camping Association. 1,000-acre facility located 88 miles north of New York City. Features: private lakes and modern swimming pool; location 1,800 feet above sea level in the forests of the Pocono Mountains; indoor gym and theater; 12 all-weather tennis courts.

Profile of Summer Employees Total number: 260; average age: 20; 50% male, 50% female, 2% minorities, 90% college students, 1% retirees, 10% international, 25% local residents. Nonsmokers preferred.

Employment Information Openings are from June 24 to August 20. Year-round positions also offered. Jobs available: 16 *tennis instructors* with high school or college varsity status at $1000–$2000 per season; 16 *general athletics instructors* with high school or college varsity status at $1000–$1500 per season; 6 *arts and crafts instructors* with a major in art at $800–$1500 per season; 4 *drama/theater instructors* with a major in theater at $800–$1500 per season; 8 *certified canoe/boating instructors* at $800–$2000 per season; 4 *certified sailing/windsurfing instructors* at $800–$2000 per season; 4 *experienced archery instructors* at $800–$1200 per season; 3 *drivers* (minimum age 21) with good driving record at $1000–$1200 per season; *overnight hikers* with scouting experience at $1000–$1200 per season; 2 *athletics directors* with college degree in physical education at $1500–$2500 per season; 6 *head counselors* with college degree at $1500–$2400 per season; 2 *lake directors* with college degree and WSI certification at $2000–$2500 per season; 2 *pool directors* with college degree and WSI certification at $2000–$2500 per season; 12 *swimming instructors* with WSI certification at $600–$2000 per season; 1 *nature director* with a major in nature studies/conservation or nature study experience at $1000–$1200 per season; *waterfront staff* with lifeguard or WSI certification at $800–$1500 per season.

Benefits College credit, preemployment training, formal ongoing training, on-site room and board, laundry facilities, travel reimbursement.

Contact Mickey Black, Director, Pine Forest Camps, 151 Washington Lane, Jenkintown, Pennsylvania 19046; 215-887-9700, Fax 215-887-3901. Application deadline: June 15.

PINEMERE CAMP ASSOCIATION
RD 8, Box 8001
Stroudsburg, Pennsylvania 18360

General Information Residential camp serving 205 children. Established in 1943. Owned by Pinemere Camp Association. Affiliated with Pinemere Camp Association, Jewish centers throughout the mid-Atlantic region. 180-acre facility located 45 miles north of Allentown. Features: 8¾-acre private lake; Olympic-size pool; 130' x 80' enclosed field house; athletic fields; staff lounge; ropes course.

Profile of Summer Employees Total number: 95; average age: 20; 50% male, 50% female, 5% minorities, 10% high school students, 57% college students, 20% international, 3% local residents, 5% teachers. Nonsmokers only.

Employment Information Openings are from June 21 to August 24. Jobs available: 2 *swimming instructors* with WSI certification at $800–$1200 per season; 1 *lifeguard instructor* with lifeguard instructor certification at $800–$1200 per season; 6 *experienced general counselors* at $800–$1000 per season; 1 *experienced ropes-course instructor* at $800–$1100 per season; 1 *CPR instructor* with CPR instructor certification at $800–$1100 per season; 1 *first aid instructor* with first aid instructor certification at $800–$1100 per season; 1 *experienced ceramics instructor* with working knowledge of kilns at $800–$1100 per season; 1 *experienced* *archery instructor* at $800–$1100 per season; 2 *riflery instructors* with NRA instructor certification at $800–$1100 per season; 1 *music instructor* with ability to play guitar or other portable instrument at $800–$1100 per season; 1 *experienced drama instructor* at $800–$1100 per season; 1 *gymnastics instructor* with beam and mat experience at $800–$1100 per season; 1 *canoe trip leader* (minimum age 21) with lifeguard certification at $800–$1400 per season; 1 *head waitress/waiter* with supervisory ability at $800–$1200 per season; *arts and crafts instructor* at $800–$1400 per season; *athletics director* at $800–$1500 per season; *tennis/basketball/soccer instructors* at $800–$1100 per season. International students encouraged to apply.

Benefits College credit, on-site room and board at no charge, laundry facilities, travel reimbursement, health insurance, possible end-of-season bonus, free snacks nightly, video in staff lounge nightly.

Contact Robert H. Miner, Executive Director, Pinemere Camp Association, Department SJ, 438 West Tabor Road, Philadelphia, Pennsylvania 19120; 215-924-0402.

ROCK CREEK FARM
RR 1, Box 54
Thompson, Pennsylvania 18465

General Information Residential camp serving 80 children in three-, six-, or nine-week sessions. Established in 1965. Owned by Elling Camps, Inc. Affiliated with American Camping Association, International Camping Association, Learning Disabilities Association of America. 96-acre facility located 30 miles north of Scranton. Features: swimming pond; boating pond; comfortable, clean cabins with bathrooms; tent camp area; small animal farm.

Profile of Summer Employees Total number: 60; average age: 25; 75% male, 25% female, 10% minorities, 50% college students, 1% retirees, 30% international, 1% local residents. Nonsmokers only.

Employment Information Openings are from June 12 to August 21. Jobs available: *swimming instructors* at $1200–$2000 per season; *group counselors* at $1200–$1500 per season; *activity counselors* with specialized skills in crafts, nature, and other areas at $1200–$2000 per season; *kitchen aides* at $1000–$1500 per season; *cooks* at $1500–$3000 per season; *nurses* with RN license at $2000–$3000 per season; *maintenance aides* at $1000–$1500 per season. International students encouraged to apply.

Benefits Preemployment training, on-site room and board at no charge, laundry facilities, travel reimbursement, workmen's compensation.

Contact Lloyd E. Elling, Director, Rock Creek Farm, Department SJ, RR#1, Box 54, Thompson, Pennsylvania 18465; 717-756-2706, Fax 717-756-3306. Application deadline: March 15.

From the Employer *A 48-hour training program is required prior to campers' arrival. Educational sessions continue throughout the summer. An end-of-season bonus is offered to all employees who complete the season satisfactorily. Generally, 2 staff members and 6 campers share a cabin.*

SHAVER'S CREEK ENVIRONMENTAL CENTER, PENNSYLVANIA STATE UNIVERSITY
201 Mateer Building
University Park, Pennsylvania 16802

General Information Environmental education day camp for children ages 6–11, adventure program for children ages 12–14, and environmental programs for the general public, as well as fairs and festivals within the community. Established in 1972. Owned by Pennsylvania State University. Affiliated with National Wildlife Federation, Alliance for Environmental Education, Pennsylvania Alliance for Environmental Education. 750-acre facility located 120 miles west of Harrisburg. Features: 72-acre lake for boating and aquatic study; Raptor Rehabilitation Center; hands-on environmental museum/exhibit room; herb and flower gardens; 25 miles of hiking trails; team building and low ropes course.

Profile of Summer Employees Total number: 6; average age: 21; 50% male, 50% female, 10% minorities, 90% college students, 10% international, 5% local residents. Nonsmokers preferred.

Employment Information Openings are from June 1 to August 25. Year-round positions also offered. Jobs available: 6 *environmental education interns* with first aid and CPR certification (preferred) at $100 per week. International students encouraged to apply.

Benefits College credit, preemployment training, formal ongoing training, on-site room and board at no charge, use of Pennsylvania State Health Clinic, use of Pennsylvania State University facilities.

Contact Doug Wentzel, Intern Coordinator, Shaver's Creek Environmental Center, Pennsylvania State University, Department SJ, 201 Mateer Building, University Park, Pennsylvania 16802; 814-863-2000. Application deadline: March 1.

From the Employer *Interns receive extensive training in natural and cultural history interpretation and in the care and handling of the center's live collection of turtles, snakes, and birds of prey. As part of a 15-member teaching staff, interns develop and lead a wide variety of hands-on environmental education programs for both children and adults. The internship program emphasizes personal and professional growth.*

SPORTS AND ARTS CENTER AT ISLAND LAKE
Island Lake Road
Starrucca, Pennsylvania 18462

General Information Residential camp serving 400 campers, ages 7–17, with emphasis on individualized programming and a well-rounded program in all sports and performing and visual arts. Established in 1985. Owned by Michael and Beverly Stoltz. Affiliated with American Camping Association, Wayne County Camping Association, Association of Independent Camps. 280-acre facility located 150 miles northwest of New York City. Features: 13 outdoor tennis courts; full athletics fields and gymnasium; indoor horseback-riding arena; miles of trails; outdoor pasture; fully equipped theater; 3 rehearsal studios; 3 fully equipped music studios; 2 modern dance studios.

Profile of Summer Employees Total number: 190; average age: 20; 50% male, 50% female, 10% minorities, 85% college students, 1% retirees, 20% international, 1% local residents, 5% teachers. Nonsmokers only.

Employment Information Openings are from June 22 to August 21. Jobs available: *experienced specialists* (in all areas) at $1000–$1500 per season; *experienced nurses* at $200–$500 per week; *doctors* at $300–$600 per week; *experienced department heads* at $1500–$3000 per season; *experienced head counselors* at $2500–$6000 per season; *swimming instructors* with WSI certification at $600–$1500 per month.

Benefits College credit, preemployment training, on-site room and board at no charge, laundry facilities, travel reimbursement.

Contact Matt or Mike Stoltz, Directors, Sports and Arts Center at Island Lake, Department SJ, P.O. Box 800, Pomona, New York 10970; 914-354-5517, Fax 914-362-3039. Application deadline: May 15.

SUNSET HILL CAMP
Chadds Ford, Pennsylvania 19317

General Information General activities day camp offering four 10-day sessions serving 200 girls each session. Owned by Girl Scouts of Delaware County. Affiliated with American Camping Association, Girl Scouts of the United States of America. 200-acre facility located 2 miles north of Chadds Ford. Features: pond and marsh walkway; meadows; forests; swimming pool; lodge.

Profile of Summer Employees Total number: 50; average age: 25; 1% male, 99% female, 16% minorities, 35% high school students, 60% college students, 1% international, 99% local residents, 5% teachers.

Employment Information Openings are from June 1 to August 1. Spring break positions also offered. Jobs available: *counselors* at $1100–$1450 per season; *lifeguard* at $1150–$1300 per season; *nurse* at $1700–$1900 per season; *crafts specialist* at $1000–$1200 per season; *nature specialist* at $1000–$1200 per season. International students encouraged to apply.

Benefits Preemployment training, off-site room/board at no cost.

Contact Laurie Estes, Director, Outdoor Program and Property, Sunset Hill Camp, Department SJ, 594 New Middletown Road, Media, Pennsylvania 19063; 215-874-3377. Application deadline: June 15.

THREE RIVERS SHAKESPEARE FESTIVAL
University of Pittsburgh, 1617 CL
Pittsburgh, Pennsylvania 15260

General Information Professional classical theater. Established in 1980. Owned by University of Pittsburgh. Operated by Theatre Arts Department. Features: proximity to country trails (1 hour); campus pool and gymnasium; 2 campus libraries.

Profile of Summer Employees Total number: 50; average age: 25; 70% male, 30% female, 75% college students, 15% local residents.

Employment Information Openings are from May 1 to July 15. Jobs available: *experienced actors; experienced technical crew; experienced costume crew; experienced assistant stage managers.* All positions offered at $175–$300 per week.

Benefits College credit, access to city facilities.

Contact Laura Worthen, Artistic Director, Three Rivers Shakespeare Festival, Department SJ, University of Pittsburgh, 1617 CL, Pittsburgh, Pennsylvania 15260; 412-624-1897, Fax 412-624-6338. Application deadline: January 1.

From the Employer *Individuals who are interested in entering professional theater may earn Equity Membership Candidate points while employed by the Festival under an agreement with Equity.*

WESTMINSTER HIGHLANDS
RD 3, Box 338
Emlenton, Pennsylvania 16373

General Information Religious camp for children ages 8–17. Water and bike trips and retreat rental facilities are also offered. Established in 1957. Owned by Presbyterian Church. Affiliated with American Camping Association, Christian Camping International, Presbyterian Camps and Conference Centers Association. 640-acre facility located 70 miles north of Pittsburgh. Features: 640-acre wooded site; swimming pool; ropes course with 15 elements and zip line; miles of hiking trails; beautiful forest chapel; fun bug watercraft pond.

Profile of Summer Employees Total number: 35; average age: 21; 50% male, 50% female, 90% college students, 1% international, 50% local residents. Nonsmokers only.

Employment Information Openings are from June 12 to August 6. Jobs available: 3 *lifeguards* with WSI or lifeguard certification at $100–$175 per week; 4 *experienced kitchen helpers* at $100–$175 per week; 1 *health supervisor* with Red Cross first aid certification, EMT, or RN license (salary depends on certification) at $105–$200 per week; 16 *support staff members/cabin counselors/maintenance helpers* at $100–$125 per week. International students encouraged to apply.

Benefits On-site room and board at no charge, laundry facilities, health insurance.

Contact Idamarie Eckstein, Executive Director, C.A.P.N.W.P., Westminster Highlands, Department SJ, 100 Venango Street, Mercer, Pennsylvania 16137-1109; 412-662-4481. Application deadline: April 30.

From the Employer *A one-week staff orientation preceeds the camper season. Staff members are free Saturday noon to Sunday noon. Christian commitment and ability to meet campers' spiritual needs are prime qualifications sought in applicants.*

RHODE ISLAND

ROCKY POINT AMUSEMENTS, INC.
1 Rocky Point Avenue
Warwick, Rhode Island 02889

General Information Family-oriented amusement park situated along the Narragansett Bay. Established in 1847. 144-acre facility located 10 miles south of Providence. Features: beautiful location; world's largest shore dinner hall; freefall ride (one of eight in the United States); New England's only corkscrew roller coaster; 20 adult rides; 11 kiddie rides.

Profile of Summer Employees Total number: 600; average age: 20; 60% male, 40% female.

Employment Information Openings are from May 1 to September 1. Jobs available: 150 *ride operators* (minimum age 18); 100 *cashiers; gate attendants;* 200 *food service personnel; assistant ride operators; office personnel; carpenters/mechanics/maintenance personnel; barmaids/bartenders.* International students encouraged to apply.

Benefits Preemployment training, formal ongoing training.

Contact Albert Albino, Operations Manager, Rocky Point Amusements, Inc., Department SJ, 1 Rocky Point Avenue, Warwick, Rhode Island 02889; 401-737-8000, Fax 401-738-3690. Application deadline: April 15.

YMCA CAMP FULLER
P.O. Box 432
Wakefield, Rhode Island 02880-0432

General Information Residential camp serving 200 campers each session with a focus on sailing (saltwater) and aquatic activities. General programs offered to campers ages 7–16. Established in 1887. Owned by Greater Providence YMCA. Affiliated with American Camping Association, YMCA. 40-acre facility located 40 miles south of Providence. Features: extensive saltwater pond frontage for sailing and windsurfing; ten 15-foot Gallilees; ten 15-foot Lasers; rock-climbing tower.

Profile of Summer Employees Total number: 70; average age: 20; 50% male, 50% female, 5% minorities, 20% high school students, 75% college students, 1% international, 50% local residents. Nonsmokers only.

Employment Information Openings are from June 15 to August 28. Jobs available: 10 *senior counselors* (minimum age 19) at $100–$140 per week; 1 *camp nurse* with RN license at $300–$350 per week; 2 *experienced division leaders* (minimum age 21) at $150–$200 per week.

Benefits Preemployment training, on-site room and board at no charge, laundry facilities, strengthening of self-confidence and reliability.

Contact Jerry Huncosky, Executive Director, YMCA Camp Fuller, Department SJ, 166 Broad Street, Providence, Rhode Island 02903; 401-521-1470, Fax 401-421-6431. Application deadline: April 30.

From the Employer *An eight-day orientation preceeds camper arrival.*

SOUTH CAROLINA

CAMP CHATUGA
Camp Chatuga Road
Mountain Rest, South Carolina 29664

General Information Residential coeducational camp serving 135 campers for six weeks. Established in 1956. Owned by Nield Gordon. Affiliated with American Camping Association, Association of Independent Camps. 60-acre facility located 100 miles north of Atlanta, Georgia. Features: private 18-acre lake; 20 cabins; 2 large playing fields; horseback-riding ring and stables; indoor recreational facilities; near the Chattooga Wild and Scenic River.

Profile of Summer Employees Total number: 45; average age: 22; 50% male, 50% female, 5% minorities, 10% high school students, 75% college students, 5% retirees, 5% international, 50% local residents. Nonsmokers only.

Employment Information Openings are from June 15 to August 8. Jobs available: *counselor* at $625–$1000 per season; *junior counselor; waterfront director* with WSI certification at $775–$1100 per season; *Western horseback-riding director* at $775–$1100 per season; *health supervisor* with CPR/first aid certification (RN preferred) at $800–$1100 per season; *nanny* at $800–$1000 per season; *program director* at $900–$1100 per season. International students encouraged to apply (must speak fluent English).

Benefits College credit, preemployment training, formal ongoing training, on-site room and board at no charge, laundry facilities, workmen's compensation insurance, off-camp trip.

Contact Kelly Moxley, Director of Personnel, Camp Chatuga, Department SJ, P.O. Box 111, Mountain Rest, South Carolina 29664; 803-638-3888, Fax 803-638-3728. Application deadline: March 1.

From the Employer *Our ten-day precamp staff training helps employees earn certifications in lifeguarding, CPR, and first aid. Staff members are given many opportunities to experience new activities.*

CAMP WABAK
P.O. Box 1227
Mauldin, South Carolina 29662-1227
General Information   Residential camp serving girls ages 7–16. Established in 1948. Owned by Old 96 Girl Scout Council, Inc. Affiliated with American Camping Association. 125-acre facility located 40 miles north of Greenville. Features: modern horseback-riding facility; swimming pool; lake for canoeing and fishing; low group-initiatives course; 2 large playing fields; several hiking trails.
Profile of Summer Employees   Total number: 25; average age: 21; 100% female, 10% minorities, 10% high school students, 90% college students, 5% international.
Employment Information   Openings are from June 6 to July 31. Jobs available: *unit leaders* (minimum age 21) with supervisory and program skills at $160–$190 per week; *unit assistants* (minimum age 18) at $130–$160 per week; *waterfront assistants* with lifeguard training certification at $130–$160 per week; *arts and crafts director* (minimum age 21) at $160–$190 per week; *canoeing instructor* with certification or documented skills and lifeguard training certification at $145–$175 per week. International students encouraged to apply.
Benefits   Preemployment training, on-site room and board at no charge, laundry facilities, health insurance, free transportation from airport, bus, or train station.
Contact   Melissa Cox, Outdoor Program Director, Camp Wabak, Department SJ, P.O. Box 1227, Mauldin, South Carolina 29662-1227; 803-297-5890, Fax 803-675-1616.

From the Employer   *During our precamp training session, all staff members participate in first aid and CPR training. A full day is spent on group initiatives and everyone participates in a high ropes-adventure session. Staff members have their own cabin with approximately 6 people per cabin.*

FRIPP ISLAND BEACH CLUB
300 Tarpon Boulevard
Fripp Island, South Carolina 29920
General Information   Private coastal resort island offering clientele a full range of recreational facilities. Established in 1965. Owned by The Fripp Company, Inc. Affiliated with Resort and Commercial Recreation Association. 3,100-acre facility located 17 miles east of Beaufort. Features: 8 pools and a beach club; championship golf course; 10-court racquet club; full-service marina; nature study day camp program for children ages 3–14.
Profile of Summer Employees   Total number: 45; average age: 21; 50% male, 50% female, 50% college students, 50% local residents. Nonsmokers preferred.
Employment Information   Openings are from April 1 to September 30. Spring break, year-round positions also offered. Jobs available: 9 *nature day camp counselors* with Red Cross lifesaving, CPR, and first aid certification and experience with children ages 3–16 at $4.25–$5.25 per hour; 2 *swimming instructors* with Red Cross lifesaving, CPR, and first aid certification and experience with children ages 6–16 at $4.25–$5.25 per hour; *pool staff* with Red Cross lifesaving, CPR, and first aid certification and experience with children ages 6–16 at $4.25–$5.25 per hour; *waitstaff, experience preferred,* at $2.75 per hour; *experienced retail staff* at $5 per hour. International students encouraged to apply.
Benefits   College credit, on-site room and board at $25 per week, use of club facilities.
Contact   Mr. Timothy Goulet, Recreation Director, Fripp Island Beach Club, 300 Tarpon Boulevard, Fripp Island, South Carolina 29920; 803-838-2165, Fax 803-838-2177. Application deadline: March 15.

From the Employer   *During your work experience, you will learn about South Carolina's coastal wildlife and their habitats.*

CAMP THUNDERBIRD
1 Thunderbird Lane
Lake Wylie, South Carolina 29710-8811
General Information Coeducational residential camp serving children ages 7–16 during one- and two-week sessions. Established in 1937. Owned by YMCA of Greater Charlotte. Affiliated with American Camping Association, Young Men's Christian Association. 110-acre facility located 12 miles south of Charlotte. Features: 1 mile of shoreline; beautifully maintained facilities; nature preserve on 110 acres; extensive land and water programs.
Profile of Summer Employees Total number: 130; average age: 20; 55% male, 45% female, 10% minorities, 25% high school students, 75% college students, 5% international, 15% local residents. Nonsmokers preferred.
Employment Information Openings are from June 5 to August 20. Year-round positions also offered. Jobs available: 2 *outpost instructors* with CPR or first aid training at $120 per week; 3 *outdoor living skills personnel* at $105–$120 per week; 4 *experienced waterskiing instructors* with CPR or first aid training at $105–$120 per week; 4 *challenge course instructors* with CPR or first aid training at $105–$120 per week; 5 *experienced English-style riding instructors* at $105–$120 per week; 1 *experienced horseback-riding chief* with CHA certification at $160–$200 per week; 2 *riflery instructors* at $105–$120 per week; 2 *archery instructors* at $105–$120 per week; 4 *swimming instructors* with lifeguard training (YMCA or ARC) and YMCA progressive instructor or WSI certification at $105–$120 per week; 4 *experienced canoeing instructors* with American Red Cross certification at $105–$120 per week; 5 *experienced sailing instructors* at $105–$120 per week; 2 *golf instructors* at $105–$120 per week; 4 *experienced gymnastics instructors* at $105–$120 per week; 3 *dance/aerobics/cheerleading/in-line skating instructors* at $105–$120 per week; 6 *general athletics instructors* at $105–$120 per week.
Benefits Preemployment training, on-site room and board at no charge.
Contact Sloane Frantz, Assistant Camp Director, Camp Thunderbird, Department SJ, 1 Thunderbird Lane, Lake Wylie, South Carolina 29710-8811; 803-831-2121, Fax 803-831-2977. Application deadline: February 28.

From the Employer *Counselors at Thunderbird provide leadership to children through instruction at an assigned activity and as a cabin counselor. All staff members attend one week of staff training prior to camp. Counselors, new and returning, gain experience, build friendships, and leave Thunderbird knowing that they made a difference to their campers.*

SOUTH DAKOTA

CUSTER STATE PARK RESORT COMPANY
HC 83, Box 74
Custer, South Dakota 57730
General Information Operator of four resorts offering services such as lodging, dining, groceries, gas, and souvenirs and gifts as well as activities that include trail rides, jeep tours, and cookouts. Established in 1919. Owned by Wild Phil's, Inc. Affiliated with South Dakota Restaurant Association, South Dakota Innkeepers' Association, National Tour Association. 73,000-acre facility located 30 miles south of Rapid City. Features: world's largest public buffalo herd; scenic mountain and plains area site; proximity to Mount Rushmore National Memorial (20 miles); location in the beautiful Black Hills; buffalo safari jeep tours to

observe wildlife and scenery; buffalo round-up, sorting, and branding every October.

Profile of Summer Employees Total number: 300; average age: 28; 35% male, 65% female, 15% minorities, 10% high school students, 50% college students, 20% retirees, 1% international, 20% local residents.

Employment Information Openings are from April 15 to October 30. Jobs available: 35 *sales clerks* at $515–$650 per month; 45 *waitpersons* at $515 per month; 10 *cooks/chefs* at $800–$1400 per month; 15 *cook's assistants* at $515–$650 per month; 8 *kitchen/food preparation personnel* at $515–$750 per month; 50 *housekeeping personnel* at $515–$750 per month; 17 *front desk/reservations personnel* at $515–$750 per month; 5 *hosts/hostesses* at $600–$800 per month; 6 *maintenance personnel* at $515–$1000 per month; 5 *jeep drivers* (minimum age 21) with clean driving record at $515–$800 per month; 8 *wranglers* at $515–$750 per month; 4 *bookkeepers* at $515–$800 per month; 5 *bartenders* (minimum age 21) at $515–$800 per month; 3 *manager trainees* with desire to learn the resort business at $515–$800 per month; 18 *dishwashers/buspersons* at $515–$650 per month.

Benefits College credit, formal ongoing training, on-site room and board at no charge, laundry facilities, tuition reimbursement, internships, scholarship bonuses.

Contact Phil Lampert, President, Custer State Park Resort Company, Department SJ, HC 83, Box 74, Custer, South Dakota 57730; 605-255-4541, Fax 605-255-4706. Application deadline: June 1.

PALMER GULCH RESORT/MT. RUSHMORE KOA
Hill City, South Dakota 57745

General Information Full-service resort located 5 miles west of Mount Rushmore. Established in 1972. Owned by Satellite Cable Services, Inc. Affiliated with South Dakota Campground Owners' Association, South Dakota Innkeepers' Association, Black Hills, Badlands, and Lakes Association. 150-acre facility located 25 miles south of Rapid City. Features: campsites and cabins; cafe; horses; 2 large heated pools and waterslide; shuttle buses; proximity to Mount Rushmore National Park, Black Elk Wilderness Area, Crazy Horse Memorial, and Custer State Park (site used in "Dances With Wolves").

Profile of Summer Employees Total number: 60; 50% male, 50% female, 5% minorities, 30% high school students, 40% college students, 30% retirees, 40% local residents. Nonsmokers preferred.

Employment Information Openings are from May 1 to October 1. Jobs available: 10 *registration office/store personnel* at $180–$200 per week; 10 *maintenance personnel* at $180–$225 per week; 3 *reservations staff members* at $180–$200 per week; 10 *housekeeping staff members* at $180–$200 per week; 4 *waterslide staff members* with lifesaving, CPR, or first aid certification at $180–$200 per week.

Benefits Formal ongoing training, on-site room and board at $20 per week, laundry facilities, free admission to Black Hills attractions, free use of resort recreation facilities, bonus given to employees who stay through Labor Day, special employee activities.

Contact Mr. Al Johnson, General Manager, Palmer Gulch Resort/Mt. Rushmore KOA, Department SJ, Box 295, Hill City, South Dakota 57745; 605-574-2525, Fax 605-574-2574. Early applicants are given preferential treatment.

From the Employer *Please, no international applicants.*

TENNESSEE

CHEROKEE ADVENTURES WHITEWATER RAFTING
Route 1, Box 605
Erwin, Tennessee 37650-9524
General Information Guided rafting, camping, and mountain-biking trips. Established in 1979. Owned by Dennis I. Nedelman. Affiliated with America Outdoors. 50-acre facility located 18 miles north of Johnson City. Features: 1¼ hours from Asheville, North Carolina; adjacent to Cherokee National Forest; proximity to the Nolichucky River; sand volleyball court.
Profile of Summer Employees Total number: 20; average age: 25; 60% male, 40% female, 40% college students, 2% international, 58% local residents. Nonsmokers preferred.
Employment Information Openings are from May 15 to August 31. Spring break positions also offered. Jobs available: 6 *raft guides* with responsible, outgoing personalities and Red Cross first aid/CPR certification (salary begins after training completed) at $400–$600 per month; 1 *grounds/maintenance person* at $4.25–$5 per hour; 2 *cooks/cleaning staff members* with ability to prepare lunches and perform general cleaning at $4.25–$5 per hour; 1 *reservationist/general office person* with good phone manner and the ability to type 50 wpm at $4.25–$5.50 per hour.
Benefits Free white-water training provided to guides, including safety, rescue, reading, and water-craft guiding, white-water trips, camping on the property available with common room and cooking area at $25 per month.
Contact Dennis I. Nedelman, President, Cherokee Adventures Whitewater Rafting, Department SJ, Route 1, Box 605, Erwin, Tennessee 37650-9524; 615-743-7733, Fax 615-743-5400. Application deadline: April 30.

From the Employer *Be part of an efficient, effective team interested in providing a quality white-water experience for all types of people. Employees at Cherokee Adventures interact daily with persons interested in the outdoors and experiencing adventure in their lives.*

GIRL SCOUT CAMP SYCAMORE HILLS
Box 40466
Nashville, Tennessee 37204
General Information Residential camp serving 180 girls per session with general and specialized programs. Established in 1959. Owned by Cumberland Valley Girl Scout Council. Affiliated with American Camping Association. 742-acre facility located 35 miles northwest of Nashville. Features: beautiful wooded rolling hills; new covered riding arena; unique dining barn; rappelling cliffs and hiking trails; new team challenge course; beautiful canoeable creek through camp.
Profile of Summer Employees Total number: 60; average age: 20; 1% male, 99% female, 2% minorities, 90% college students, 10% local residents. Nonsmokers preferred.
Employment Information Openings are from June 7 to July 31. Jobs available: 1 *assistant camp director* with Girl Scout residential camp experience at $180–$375 per week; 1 *unit coordinator* with Girl Scout residential camp experience at $130–$250 per week; 1 *business manager* with accounting training at $130–$250 per week; 1 *health supervisor* with RN or paramedic certification at $130–$350 per week; 3 *high-adventure staff members* with lifeguard training at $120–$275 per week; 8 *experienced equestrian counselors* at $110–$140 per week; 1 *waterfront director* with lifeguard and WSI certification at $130–$200 per week; 4

waterfront counselors with lifeguard training at $110–$140 per week; 2 *rappelling staff members* with at least two years of experience at $110–$200 per week; 2 *experienced arts and crafts staff members* at $110–$200 per week; 1 *certified canoeing director* at $120–$160 per week; 1 *nature director* with background in the field at $120–$160 per week; 9 *unit leaders* at $120–$160 per week; 18 *unit counselors* at $110–$135 per week; 1 *counselor-in-training director* with Girl Scout residential camp experience at $120–$160 per week. International students encouraged to apply.

Benefits Preemployment training, on-site room and board at no charge, laundry facilities, health insurance, free certification in some areas.

Contact Tricia Coleman, Outdoor Program Manager, Girl Scout Camp Sycamore Hills, Box 40466, Nashville, Tennessee 37204; 615-383-0490. Application deadline: May 27.

From the Employer *We offer a six-day staff training program focusing on building leadership skills and self-esteem in girls. First aid and CPR certification, as well as certifications in lifeguarding, archery, and canoeing are available for certain positions.*

TEXAS

CAMP BETTE PEROT
4411 Skillman, P.O. Box 64815
Dallas, Texas 75206

General Information Residential camp serving 150 Girl Scouts per session. Established in 1970. Owned by Texas Girl Scout Council. Affiliated with United Way, American Camping Association, National Recreation and Park Association. 1,500-acre facility located 100 miles southeast of Dallas. Features: extensive equestrian center; many horseback-riding trails; Olympic-size swimming pool; large sports field.

Profile of Summer Employees Total number: 35; average age: 21; 100% female, 8% minorities, 80% college students, 5% international, 90% local residents. Nonsmokers preferred.

Employment Information Openings are from June 1 to August 10. Spring break positions also offered. Jobs available: 2 *directors* (minimum age 25) with experience in hiring, training, and supervision at $275–$325 per week; 1 *program director* (minimum age 21) with leadership, outdoor training, program skills, and work experience with children as a teacher or counselor at $140–$175 per week; 2 *assistant directors* (minimum age 23) with planning, implementing outdoor living, and activity experience at $160–$200 per week; 2 *business managers* (minimum age 21) with training in business, experience in coordination of office activities, and sound judgment in purchasing at $125–$150 per week; 2 *health supervisors* (minimum age 21) with RN, PA, EMT, or LPN license and first aid/CPR certification at $175–$300 per week; 2 *experienced waterfront directors* (minimum age 21) with ARC lifeguard training and WSI certification at $130–$170 per week; 5 *lifeguards* (minimum age 18) with ARC lifeguard certification at $115–$135 per week; 1 *certified assistant equestrian director* (minimum age 25) at $140–$175 per week; 1 *experienced equestrian riding instructor* (minimum age 18) at $110–$140 per week; 1 *experienced equestrian staff member* (minimum age 18) with working knowledge of stable care, horses, and tack at $90–$120 per week; 7 *experienced unit leaders* (minimum age 21) at $125–$140 per week; 24 *experienced unit counselors* (minimum age 18) at $110–$130 per week. International students encouraged to apply.

Benefits Preemployment training, formal ongoing training, on-site room and board at no charge, laundry facilities, health insurance, 24–hour leave each week.

Contact   Carla R. Weiland, Outdoor Program Manager, Camp Bette Perot, Department SJ, 4411 Skillman, Dallas, Texas 75206; 214-823-1342, Fax 214-824-3324. Application deadline: March 30.

From the Employer   *Camp staff attends a seven- to ten-day training session that includes an overview of Girl Scouting, program planning, first aid and CPR training, safety management, diversity, group programming, and "what campers are like."*

CAMP EL TESORO
2700 Meacham Boulevard
Fort Worth, Texas 76137

General Information   Residential camp for boys and girls ages 6–16. Established in 1934. Owned by First Texas Council of Camp Fire. Affiliated with American Camping Association, Camps Associated for Mutual Progress, Granbury Chamber of Commerce. 228-acre facility located 45 miles southwest of Fort Worth. Features: 2 swimming pools; 20 horses with barn and arena; location on Brazos River; creek with suspension bridge; extensive hiking trails; screened and enclosed cabins.

Profile of Summer Employees   Total number: 50; average age: 21; 40% male, 60% female, 12% minorities, 8% high school students, 86% college students, 50% local residents, 3% teachers. Nonsmokers preferred.

Employment Information   Openings are from May 28 to August 15. Jobs available: 20 *cabin counselors* with one year of college at $75–$150 per week; 4 *horseback staff members* with CHA certification (preferred) at $80–$150 per week; 4 *waterfront staff members* with lifeguard, CPR, and first aid certification at $80–$150 per week; 4 *kitchen staff members* at $85–$150 per week; 1 *experienced program director* at $100–$225 per week; 3 *unit coordinators* with supervisory experience at $100–$225 per week; 1 *arts and crafts director* at $75–$200 per week; 4 *special needs staff members* with one year of college at $75–$150 per week.

Benefits   Preemployment training, on-site room and board at no charge, laundry facilities, health insurance.

Contact   Laurie Johnston, Camp Director, Camp El Tesoro, Department SJ, 2700 Meacham Boulevard, Fort Worth, Texas 76137; 817-831-2111, Fax 817-831-0929. Application deadline: May 1.

From the Employer   *Staff members are taught leadership skills, behavior management, child development, and recreational activities. Camping with El Tesoro provides an excellent opportunity to work with peers and children of all ages.*

CAMP FERN
Route 4, Box 584
Marshall, Texas 75670-9441

General Information   Residential camp providing fun, adventure, learning, self-esteem development, and lasting friendships. Established in 1934. Owned by Mrs. Peggy Rotzler. Affiliated with State of Texas Department of Health Resources, Camping Association for Mutual Progress, National Riflery Association, Camp Archery Association. 100-acre facility located 8 miles north of Marshall. Features: 100-acre private lake for swimming; ropes course with 10 low and 7 high elements; specialized clinics in basketball and skeet shooting; nature and campcraft with outpost camp in wilderness for backpacking and overnight camping; boxing and weight-training facilities; a 30-horse stable, jump course, 400 acres of trails, and an English horseback-riding program.

Profile of Summer Employees   Total number: 60; average age: 19; 100% college students. Nonsmokers preferred.

Employment Information   Openings are from June 1 to August 15. Jobs available: *waterfront staff* with WSI, lifeguard, and CPR certification; *certified ropes-course staff; English horseback-riding staff; riflery staff; crafts staff; tennis staff.* All positions offered at $400 per month. International students encouraged to apply.

Benefits   On-site room and board at no charge, laundry facilities.

Contact   Margaret R. Thompson, Director, Camp Fern, Route 4, Box 584, Marshall, Texas 75670-9441; 903-935-5420. Application deadline: April 5.

From the Employer   *Generally, our counselors have completed one year of college. They are required to attend a one-week precamp session and must be able to teach their activities. Log cabins house 2 counselors and 10 campers.*

CAMP LA JUNTA
P.O. Box 136
Hunt, Texas 78024

General Information   Private residential camp with a focus on individual lifetime activities serving 200 boys in two- or four-week terms. Established in 1928. Owned by Lawrence L. Graham. Affiliated with Camping Association for Mutual Progress. 150-acre facility located 75 miles northwest of San Antonio. Features: 1 mile of riverfront; traditional stone and wood floors in cabins; adjacent 500-acre game ranch; 6 athletics fields; 4 tennis courts; 150 tree-shaded acres.

Profile of Summer Employees   Total number: 50; average age: 21; 90% male, 10% female, 5% minorities, 100% college students, 5% international, 25% local residents. Nonsmokers only.

Employment Information   Openings are from June 1 to August 15. Jobs available: *junior counselors* (approximate age 18 and younger) at $450–$600 per month; *senior counselors* (approximate age 19 and older) at $550–$700 per month.

Benefits   Preemployment training, formal ongoing training, on-site room and board at no charge, laundry facilities.

Contact   Blake W. Smith, Director, Camp La Junta, Department SJ, P.O. Box 136, Hunt, Texas 78024; 210-238-4621, Fax 210-238-4333. Application deadline: May 1.

From the Employer   *Camp La Junta seeks to blend a staff of 50 qualified college students with 200 boys into a cohesive family during the summer. All staff members are hired for their interest in working with young people, their activity background, and commitment to excellence. Our primary goal is to instill a positive self-image in each boy. Throughout the summer, staff members are trained in reinforcement, patience, communication, and entertainment to improve their ability to be an uplifting influence on their boys. All staff members teach an activity and supervise a cabin of boys. A typical cabin houses 8–10 boys and 2 staff members. La Junta also places 6 staff members to work with the youngest campers.*

CAMP LOMA LINDA FOR GIRLS
Mo Ranch
Hunt, Texas 78024

General Information   Residential camp serving girls ages 10–15 in two 3–week terms. Established in 1949. Owned by Presbyterian Mo Ranch Assembly. Affiliated with American Camping Association. 434-acre facility located 90 miles west of San Antonio. Features: 1

mile of river front; 3 tennis courts; Mexican-tile swimming pool; riding trails; river slide; historic ranch buildings.

Profile of Summer Employees   Total number: 15; average age: 21; 10% male, 90% female, 15% minorities, 90% college students. Nonsmokers preferred.

Employment Information   Openings are from June 9 to August 2. Year-round positions also offered. Jobs available: 14 *counselors/instructors* at $700–$900 per season. International students encouraged to apply.

Benefits   Preemployment training, on-site room and board at no charge, laundry facilities.

Contact   Mike Busby, Personnel Director, Camp Loma Linda for Girls, Department SJ, Route 1, Box 158, Hunt, Texas 78024; 210-238-4455, Fax 210-238-4202. Application deadline: May 1.

From the Employer   *Mo Ranch is a camp and year-round conference center offering an opportunity to work with people encompassing a wide variety of ages from across the country. The beautiful Texas Hill Country offers numerous recreational, cultural, and historic opportunities, as does nearby Mexico.*

CAMP MANISON
Box 148, Drawer PG
Friendswood, Texas 77546-0148

General Information   Residential camp serving 75–125 boys and girls, with optional space training program available at an extra charge for children ages 6–16. Space training program includes off-site activities. Additionally, a day camp is offered for 50 boys and girls ages 6–13. Established in 1947. Owned by Mr. and Mrs. Tom Manison. Affiliated with American Camping Association, Camp Horsemanship Association. 80-acre facility located 35 miles south of Houston. Features: swimming pool; 2 tennis courts; 5 volleyball courts; shaded riding trails (Western horseback); rustic air-conditioned buildings; proximity to Johnson Space Center, a training site for astronauts (8 miles from camp).

Profile of Summer Employees   Total number: 30; average age: 20; 40% male, 60% female, 20% minorities, 90% college students, 20% local residents. Nonsmokers only.

Employment Information   Openings are from June 5 to August 10. Jobs available: 18 *cabin counselors/activity instructors* with activity training certification at $100–$125 per week; 2 *wranglers* with CHA certification at $150 per week; 2 *waterfront directors* with WSI certification at $125 per week; 2 *day camp coordinators* at $125 per week.

Benefits   Preemployment training, on-site room and board at no charge, laundry facilities, health insurance, congenial and challenging atmosphere.

Contact   Tom Manison, Director, Camp Manison, P.O. Box 148, Drawer PG, Friendswood, Texas 77546-0148; 713-482-1251, Fax 713-482-1253. Application deadline: February 1.

From the Employer   *Precamp training features interactive sessions with campers and returning staff, as well as CPR and first aid sessions. Generally, 2 staff members share a cabin with 4–10 campers.*

CAMP ROCKY POINT
4411 Skillman, P.O. Box 64815
Dallas, Texas 75206

General Information   Residential camp serving 90 girls per session. Established in 1950. Owned by Texas Girl Scout Council. Affiliated with United Way, American Camping Association, National Recreation and Park Association. 50-acre facility located 70 miles north of Dallas. Features: location on Lake Teroma; extensive waterfront; value-based program; stage area; large sports field.

Profile of Summer Employees   Total number: 25; average age: 21; 100% female, 8% minorities, 80% college students, 5% international, 90% local residents. Nonsmokers preferred.

Employment Information   Openings are from June 1 to August 10. Spring break positions also offered. Jobs available: 2 *directors* (minimum age 25) with experience in hiring, training, and supervising and administrative skills at $275–$325 per week; 1 *program director* (minimum age 21) with leadership and outdoor training, background training in a variety of program skills, and work experience with children as a teacher or counselor at $140–$175 per week; *assistant directors* (minimum age 23) with experience in planning and implementing outdoor living and camp activities at $160–$200 per week; *business managers* (minimum age 21) with training in business and office practices and sound judgment in purchasing and coordinating various business activities in a camp situation at $125–$150 per week; 2 *health supervisors* (minimum age 21) with RN, PA, EMT, or Nurse Practioner certification, standard first aid and CPR certification, ability to adapt to camp work situation, and knowledge of the physical needs of campers at $175–$300 per week; 2 *waterfront directors* (minimum age 21) with ARC lifeguard training or equivalent, WSI (preferred), and at least six weeks of pool-area experience at $130–$175 per week; 1 *lifesaver/guard* (minimum age 18) with current ARC lifeguard training certification or the equivalent at $115–$135 per week; 7 *unit leaders* (minimum age 21) with training in group leadership and staff supervision and the ability to teach and guide girls at $125–$140 per week; 24 *unit counselors* (minimum age 18) with leadership ability, ability to work with children, and experience as a group leader, camper, or teacher at $110–$130 per week. International students encouraged to apply.

Benefits   Preemployment training, formal ongoing training, on-site room and board at no charge, laundry facilities, health insurance, 24-hour leave each week.

Contact   Carla R. Weiland, Outdoor Program Manager, Camp Rocky Point, Department SJ, 4411 Skillman, Dallas, Texas 75206; 214-823-1342, Fax 214-824-3324. Application deadline: March 30.

From the Employer   *All camp staff attend a seven- to ten-day training session that includes an overview of Girl Scouting, program planning, first aid and CPR training, safety management, diversity, group programming, and "what campers are like."*

CAMP STEWART FOR BOYS
Route 1, Box 110
Hunt, Texas 78024-9714

General Information   Traditional camp offering a fun, challenging program to 250 boys for seventeen- or twenty-eight-day programs. Established in 1924. Owned by Mr. and Mrs. Silas B. Ragsdale Jr. Affiliated with Christian Camping International, Camp Association Mutual Progress, American Horse Show Association, American Tennis Association. 522-acre facility located 80 miles northwest of San Antonio. Features: 1-mile frontage on headwaters of Guadalupe River for all aquatic activities; 7 tennis courts; hardwood floor gymnasium; weight room; extensive riding trails and jump fields; climbing wall; challenge course; 7 baseball fields, 4 soccer fields, and 1 football field.

Profile of Summer Employees   Total number: 80; average age: 24; 90% male, 10% female, 10% minorities, 86% college students, 2% international, 2% local residents. Nonsmokers only.

Employment Information   Openings are from May 25 to August 15. Jobs available: 10 *riding instructors* with ability to take CHA clinic at Stewart (required) at $1000–$2000 per season; 8 *swimming instructors* with WSI certification at $1000–$2000 per season; 2 *tennis* *instructors* at $1000–$2000 per season; 2 *crafts instructors* at $1000–$2000 per season; 4 *sports personnel* at $1000–$2000 per season; 2 *riflery instructors* with NRA certification at $1000–$2000 per season; 2 *archery instructors* at $1000–$2000 per season; 3 *certified rock-climbing instructors* at $1000–$2000 per season; 2 *certified challenge-course instructors* at $1000–$2000 per season; 1 *band leader* at $1000–$2000 per season; 2 *secretaries* at $1000–$2000 per season; 12 *kitchen personnel* at $1000–$3000 per season; 24 *general counselors* with leadership ability and good moral character at $1000–$2000 per season. International students encouraged to apply.

Benefits College credit, preemployment training, on-site room and board at no charge, health insurance, clothing (shirts and shorts), accident insurance.

Contact Kathy C. Ragsdale, Co-director, Camp Stewart for Boys, Department SJ, Route 1, Box 110, Hunt, Texas 78024-9714; 210-238-4670, Fax 210-238-4737. Application deadline: April 1.

From the Employer *Staff members say they gain more from Stewart than any other experience. Preorientation certification is available at no cost. Our six-day orientation includes outstanding outside speakers, team building, how-to, and hands-on practice. Camp Stewart is well-known for its good food, facilities, and natural setting. Other summer camps in the area enhance staff members' social lives.*

HOCKADAY COED SUMMER SESSION
11600 Welch Road, P. O. Box 29900
Dallas, Texas 75229

General Information Residential and day camp serving over 800 students ages 4–18 with a focus on academic enrichment and creative exploration. Established in 1913. Affiliated with Independent Schools Association of the Southwest, National Association of Independent Schools. Situated on 100 acres. Features: 50,000-volume library; art center with studios and labs; science center with labs and lecture hall; outdoor and indoor pools; 10 tennis courts; 2 gyms with dance studio; 2 raquetball courts; weight room; 4 basketball courts.

Profile of Summer Employees Total number: 90; average age: 35; 20% male, 80% female, 5% high school students, 5% college students. Nonsmokers preferred.

Employment Information Openings are from June 6 to July 25. Jobs available: 4 *experienced boarding counselors* at $250–$350 per week; 4 *swimming instructors* with WSI certificate at $250–$350 per week; 20 *experienced academic instructors* with graduate degree (preferred) at $22–$25 per hour.

Benefits On-site room and board at no charge, laundry facilities, tuition reimbursement.

Contact Vige Barrie, Director, Hockaday Coed Summer Session, Department SJ, 11600 Welch Road, Dallas, Texas 75229; 214-363-6311 Ext. 274, Fax 214-363-0942. Application deadline: January 30 (early applicants are given preferential consideration).

LAZY HILLS GUEST RANCH
Ingram, Texas 78025

General Information Resort ranch catering to families and groups. Established in 1960. Owned by Bob and Carol Steinruck. Affiliated with Texas Hotel/Motel Association, Texas Restaurant Association, Kerrville Chamber of Commerce. 750-acre facility located 75 miles northwest of San Antonio. Features: junior Olympic swimming pool; 2 lighted tennis courts; hot tub; 3 large, spring-fed fishing ponds; game room with pool tables, Ping-Pong tables, and video games; children's playground; wading pool.

Profile of Summer Employees Total number: 10; average age: 20; 20% male, 80% female,

10% minorities, 25% high school students, 75% college students. Nonsmokers preferred.

Employment Information Openings are from May 1 to August 1. Year-round positions also offered. Jobs available: 1 *activities director* with enthusiasm and ability to work well with children and adults; 5 *waiters/waitresses;* 2 *wranglers;* 1 *office worker* with computer experience. All positions offered at $500–$600 per month.

Benefits College credit, on-site room and board at no charge, laundry facilities, tips.

Contact Beth Steinruck, Office Manager, Lazy Hills Guest Ranch, Department SJ, Box G, Ingram, Texas 78025; 210-367-5600, Fax 210-367-5667. Application deadline: March 1.

From the Employer *Employees meet people from around the world and enjoy the ranch facilities when time permits. Employees share dorm facilities.*

MO RANCH BOYS CAMP
Mo Ranch
Hunt, Texas 78024

General Information Residential camp and conference center serving boys ages 10–13 in one 3-week term. Established in 1949. Owned by Presbyterian Mo Ranch Assembly. 434-acre facility located 90 miles west of San Antonio. Features: 1 mile of riverfront; 3 tennis courts; Mexican-tile swimming pool; riding trails; river slide; historic ranch buildings.

Profile of Summer Employees Total number: 6; average age: 24; 90% male, 10% female, 20% minorities, 60% college students. Nonsmokers preferred.

Employment Information Openings are from July 6 to August 2. Year-round positions also offered. Jobs available: 6 *counselors/instructors* at $250–$300 per season. International students encouraged to apply.

Benefits Preemployment training, on-site room and board at no charge, laundry facilities.

Contact Mike Busby, Personnel Director, Mo Ranch Boys Camp, Department SJ, Route 1, Box 158, Hunt, Texas 78024; 210-238-4455, Fax 210-238-4202. Application deadline: May 1.

From the Employer *Mo Ranch, a boys' camp and year-round conference center, offers the opportunity to work with a wide variety of ages from all over the country. The beautiful Texas Hill Country offers numerous recreational, cultural, historical opportunities, as does nearby Mexico.*

PRUDE RANCH
P.O. Box 1431
Fort Davis, Texas 79734

General Information Western horsemanship program for boys and girls ages 7–15. Established in 1952. Owned by the Prude family. Affiliated with American Camping Association. 5,000-acre facility located 150 miles southwest of Odessa. Features: 1 horse per camper; 40 miles of riding trails; indoor Olympic-size pool; soccer, baseball, and game area; indoor activity building (5,000 square feet); rodeo arena; raft trips on Rio Grande.

Profile of Summer Employees 50% male, 50% female, 5% minorities, 10% high school students, 85% college students, 5% retirees, 5% international, 5% teachers.

Employment Information Spring break, Christmas break positions offered. Jobs available: *counselors; cooks; housekeepers.* International students encouraged to apply (must apply through Camp America).

Benefits Preemployment training, on-site room and board at no charge, laundry facilities, travel reimbursement, health insurance.

Contact Chipper Prude, Camp Director, Prude Ranch, Box 1431, Fort Davis, Texas 79734; 915-426-3202, Fax 915-426-3502.

SUPERCAMP
Texas Lutheran College
Seguin, Texas 78155
General Information Residential program for teens that includes life skills and academic courses designed to build self-confidence and lifelong learning skills. Established in 1981. Owned by Bobbi DePorter. Affiliated with American Camping Association, Society of Accelerated Learning and Teaching. Located 60 miles east of San Antonio. Features: dormitory rooms; ropes course; swimming pool.
Profile of Summer Employees Total number: 200; average age: 22; 50% male, 50% female, 80% high school students. Nonsmokers only.
Employment Information Jobs available: 12 *team leaders* at $500–$1000 per season; 1 *office manager;* 1 *licensed paramedic* at $700–$2800 per season; 1 *nurse* at $1000–$4000 per season.
Benefits Preemployment training, on-site room and board at no charge, laundry facilities, internships, experience working with teens in an educational and self-esteem building environment, excellent experience for education and psychology majors.
Contact Shelby Reeder, Human Resources Coordinator, SuperCamp, Department SJ, 1725 South Hill Street, Oceanside, California 92054; 800-527-5321, Fax 619-722-3507. Application deadline: May 1.

From the Employer *SuperCamp employees develop outstanding communications and leadership skills through an extensive five-day training program, where they can meet exciting new people from across the country. Staff members support teens through powerful, life-changing experiences and become familiar with new accelerated-learning techniques. Sessions are held on beautiful college campuses in six locations across the country, including California, Illinois, and Massachusetts.*

Y. O. ADVENTURE CAMP
HC 01 Box 555
Mountain Home, Texas 78058-9705
General Information Residential coeducational camp serving 80 campers per session. Established in 1976. Owned by Y. O. Ranch. Affiliated with American Camping Association, Camp Association for Mutual Progress, National Association of Experimental Education. 40,000-acre facility located 75 miles north of San Antonio. Features: high ropes course; horseback riding on 40,000 private acres; pool; 5 campsites; exotic wildlife, including giraffes and zebra; sand volleyball court.
Profile of Summer Employees Total number: 28; average age: 20; 50% male, 50% female, 10% high school students, 20% college students. Nonsmokers preferred.
Employment Information Openings are from May 21 to August 18. Year-round positions also offered. Jobs available: 8 *counselors* with CPR, first aid, and lifeguard training at $425 per month. International students encouraged to apply.
Benefits College credit, preemployment training, on-site room and board at no charge, laundry facilities.
Contact Director, Y. O. Adventure Camp, Department SJ, HC 01, Box 555, Mountain

Home, Texas 78058-9705; 210-640-3220, Fax 210-640-3348. Application deadline: March 20.

From the Employer *During our paid two-week orientation, counselors participate in workshops where they develop leadership, learn to teach various outdoor activities, and learn to work with campers on the high ropes course and climbing tower. Counselors also learn our daily schedule, emergency procedures, how to report possible child abuse, and how to deal with special camper situations. The program is adventurous, and our training reflects this theme.*

UTAH

FOUR CORNERS SCHOOL OF OUTDOOR EDUCATION
East Route
Monticello, Utah 84535
General Information Educational adventures using the spectacular Colorado Plateau as an outdoor classroom with three-day to two-week programs on natural and human history via raft, backpack, van, or skis. Established in 1985. 7-acre facility located 250 miles south of Salt Lake City. Features: rustic 1930's Mormon Homestead used for basecamp; situated in the heart of the Colorado Plateau near the Four Corners; archaeology, geology, and native culture sites nearby; major outdoor destinations such as Mesa Verde, Canyonlands, and the San Juan river (within 1 hour); 160,000-acre wonderland of high mesas, deep canyons, and winding rivers.
Profile of Summer Employees Total number: 6; average age: 21; 70% male, 30% female, 5% minorities, 5% high school students, 95% college students, 5% local residents, 5% teachers. Nonsmokers preferred.
Employment Information Openings are from March 15 to October 30. Jobs available: *outdoor education interns* with interest in a career in outdoor education and knowledge of the Southwest at $75 per week. International students encouraged to apply.
Benefits College credit, on-site room and board at no charge, laundry facilities, intern stipend of $75 per week, opportunities for hands-on outdoor education, paid opportunities to hike, backpack, and run rivers.
Contact Janet Ross, Director, Four Corners School of Outdoor Education, Department SJ, P. O. Box 1029, Monticello, Utah 84535; 801-587-2156, Fax 801-587-2193.

From the Employer *Through hands-on experience, interns gain knowledge of low-impact cultural and environmental techniques, outdoor education processes, and exploration logistics. Interns are involved in every aspect of operating an outdoor education organization.*

VERMONT

ALOHA CAMPS ALOHA HIVE–ALOHA
RR 1, Box 91A
Fairlee, Vermont 05045
General Information Residential camp serving 350–400 campers for 3½- or 7-week sessions. Established in 1905. Owned by The Aloha Foundation, Inc. Affiliated with American

Camping Association, Vermont Camping Association. 1,000-acre facility located 150 miles northwest of Boston, Massachusetts. Features: beautiful lakes; proximity to Hanover (New Hampshire) and the Green and White Mountains; tents or cabins; rustic but complete facilities.

Profile of Summer Employees Total number: 200; average age: 30; 40% male, 60% female, 3% minorities, 5% high school students, 65% college students, 2% retirees, 5% international, 5% local residents. Nonsmokers preferred.

Employment Information Openings are from June 20 to August 18. Jobs available: *waterfront personnel (swimming, canoeing, and sailing)* with lifeguard training at $1000 per season; *tennis, gymnastics, or land sports staff* at $1000 per season; 3 *nurses* at $1800 per season; 2 *riding instructors* at $1200 per season.

Benefits College credit, preemployment training, on-site room and board at no charge.

Contact Posie M. Taylor, Managing Director, Aloha Camps Aloha Hive–Aloha, Department SJ, RR 1, Box 91A, Fairlee, Vermont 05045; 802-333-9113, Fax 802-333-9216.

From the Employer *One of the real joys of working at the Aloha Camps is the diversity and abundance of talent found among the staff. Along with students and recent graduates, each camp has a strong core of senior staff who have been with the camp for years.*

CAMP CATHERINE CAPERS
Lake St. Catherine
Wells, Vermont 05774

General Information Residential camp for 60 girls ages 9–15 with a riding camp in June and a regular camp from the end of June to mid-August. Established in 1952. Owned by Camp Catherine Capers, Inc. Affiliated with American Camping Association, Camp Horsemanship Association, Vermont Camping Association. 100-acre facility located 30 miles south of Rutland. Features: 35 camp-owned horses; many local mountains and streams for hiking and tubing; 4 riding rings; outside hunt course; trails available for days of horse trips; all-weather tennis court; a warm, clean lake.

Profile of Summer Employees Total number: 30; average age: 24; 5% male, 95% female, 80% college students, 4% international, 30% local residents, 15% teachers. Nonsmokers only.

Employment Information Openings are from May 22 to August 29. Jobs available: 2 *riding instructors/counselors* with experience with children, teaching, and first aid/CPR certification at $1200–$1800 per season; 1 *infirmary assistant* with first aid/CPR certification and experience with children at $1500–$2000 per season; 1 *experienced photography instructor* with experience with children and first aid/CPR certification at $1200–$1400 per season; 1 *windsurfing and canoeing instructor* with lifeguard and CPR/first aid certification and experience with children at $1200–$1600 per season; 1 *certified archery instructor/counselor* with experience with children and first aid/CPR certification at $1200–$1400 per season; 1 *outdoor living skills instructor/counselor* with experience with children and first aid/CPR certification at $1200–$1400 per season; 1 *tennis instructor/counselor* with tournament playing and teaching experience, experience with children, and first aid/CPR certification at $1200–$1400 per season; 1 *experienced riding trail leader/counselor* with experience with children and first aid/CPR certification at $1400–$2000 per season; 1 *waterskiing/sailing instructor* (minimum age 21) with boat driving experience, experience with children, and first aid/CPR and LGT certification at $1400–$1600 per season; *sports coordinator* with first aid/CPR certification and ability to coordinate instructors, schedule groups, and lead recreation program at $1500–$1700 per season; *trip leader* (hiking) with advanced first aid certification or wilderness first aid experience and outdoor living skills at $1400–$2000 per season; *trip leader* (canoeing) with LGT certification, outdoor living skills, and experience smooth-water canoeing at $1400–$1800 per season.

Benefits College credit, preemployment training, on-site room and board at no charge, half of cost paid for certification/improvement clinics (balance paid in second year of employment), American Camping Association Membership.

Contact Audrey C. Nelson, Director, Camp Catherine Capers, Department SJ, Box 68, West Pawlet, Vermont 05775; 802-645-0216. Application deadline: March 1.

From the Employer *We hire leaders who can also be followers—positive, creative, honest counselors who are willing to increase their skills and awareness while undertaking general camp responsibilities. This experience will enhance your résumé in child growth and development fields, leadership, group dynamics, self direction, judgment, sales, marketing, poise and presentation skills, risk management, and quality control while giving you the opportunity to share fun with campers in the outdoors.*

CAMP FARNSWORTH
Route 113
Thetford, Vermont 05074

General Information Residential Girl Scout camp for girls ages 6–16 offering four 2-week sessions. Established in 1909. Owned by Swift Water Girl Scout Council. Affiliated with American Camping Association, Vermont Camping Association, Camp Horsemanship Association. 300-acre facility located 150 miles north of Boston. Features: location in the Green Mountains of Vermont; private 50-acre lake; 50-foot waterslide; low-ropes course; lake zip line; 2 riding rings.

Profile of Summer Employees Total number: 100; average age: 22; 1% male, 99% female, 5% minorities, 50% college students, 30% international, 20% local residents. Nonsmokers preferred.

Employment Information Openings are from June 15 to August 22. Jobs available: 2 *health directors* with RN, LPN, or EMT license at $1600–$2800 per season; 1 *experienced waterfront director* with WSI and LGT certification at $1600–$2800 per season; 8 *waterfront assistants* with WSI and LGT certification at $1200–$1600 per season; 12 *experienced unit leaders* at $1600–$2100 per season; 30 *unit assistants* with child supervisory experience at $1200–$1600 per season; 1 *counselor-in-training director* with camp supervisory experience at $1700–$2100 per season; 1 *horseback riding director* with CHA certification at $1600–$2600 per season; 4 *riding assistants* with instructor experience at $1200–$1600 per season; 1 *adventure director* with experience instructing low-ropes course at $1600–$2600 per season; 1 *experienced ecology director* at $1600–$2600 per season; 1 *experienced arts director* at $1600–$2600 per season; 3 *experienced arts assistants* at $1200–$1600 per season; 1 *food supervisor* with experience in menu planning and quantity cooking at $2300–$3700 per season.

Benefits Preemployment training, on-site room and board at no charge, laundry facilities, health insurance.

Contact Nancy Frankel, Director of Outdoor Education, Camp Farnsworth, Department SJ, 88 Harvey Road, #4, Manchester, New Hampshire 03103; 603-627-4158. Application deadline: June 15.

From the Employer *At an extensive seven-day precamp training program, staff members learn first aid, CPR, group development, and the progressive way to help groups make decisions. Many opportunities exist to meet and interact with people in a large staff.*

CAMP KINIYA
77 Camp Kiniya Road
Colchester, Vermont 05446

General Information Traditional residential camp serving girls 7–18. Established in 1919. Owned by Marilyn and John Williams. Affiliated with American Camping Association, New England Section of the American Camping Association, Vermont Camping Association. 100-acre facility located 12 miles north of Burlington. Features: 1 mile private beach on Lake Champlain; 100 acres of meadows, lawns, and woods; 2 miles of riding trails; cross-country course; 3 large sports fields; 10-acre hunting course; 5 outdoor tennis courts.
Profile of Summer Employees Total number: 60; average age: 27; 15% male, 85% female, 10% minorities, 5% high school students, 50% college students, 2% retirees, 30% international, 10% local residents, 20% teachers. Nonsmokers only.
Employment Information Openings are from June 16 to August 25. Jobs available: 1 *gymnastics instructor* with teaching experience at $1600 per season; 1 *drama head* with directing experience at $1600–$2000 per season; *sailing head and 1 counselor* with big lake or ocean experience and experience with 14'–18' boats at $1600–$2000 per season; 2 *tennis counselors* at $1400–$1800 per season; 2 *experienced hiking/trip leaders* with maturity and scouting skills at $1400–$1800 per season; 2 *canoeing counselors* with big lake/trip experience at $1400–$1800 per season; 2 *swimming instructors* with WSI certification at $1800 per month. International students encouraged to apply.
Benefits Preemployment training, formal ongoing training, on-site room and board at no charge, travel reimbursement.
Contact Marilyn and John Williams, Owners, Camp Kiniya, Department SJ, 77 Camp Kiniya Road, Colchester, Vermont 05446; 802-893-7849.

From the Employer *In a seven-day preprogram orientation, all employees participate in workshops on risk management, positive ways of working with children, cultural sensitivity, and the facilitation of group interaction. Staff members work as a team to provide a safe, healthy summer for the children and each other. Staff members share cabins with 4–8 campers. There is a 1:3 staff-camper ratio.*

CAMP LANAKILA
RR 1, Box 98
Fairlee, Vermont 05045

General Information Residential camp serving 100–200 campers for 3½- or 7-week sessions. Established in 1922. Owned by The Aloha Foundation, Inc. Affiliated with American Camping Association, Vermont Camping Association. Located 150 miles northwest of Boston, Massachusetts. Features: beautiful lake; proximity to Hanover, New Hampshire, and the Green and White Mountains; tents or cabins provided; rustic but complete facilities.
Profile of Summer Employees Total number: 250; average age: 30; 40% male, 60% female, 3% minorities, 5% high school students, 65% college students, 2% retirees, 5% international, 5% local residents. Nonsmokers preferred.
Employment Information Openings are from June 20 to August 17. Jobs available: *tennis/land sports staff; nurses.* International students encouraged to apply.
Benefits College credit, preemployment training, on-site room and board at no charge.
Contact Posie M. Taylor, Managing Director, Camp Lanakila, RR 1, Box 91A, Fairlee, Vermont 05045; 802-333-9113, Fax 802-333-9216.

From the Employer *One of the real joys of working at the Aloha Camps is the diversity and abundance of talent found among the staff. Along with students and recent graduates, each camp has a strong core of senior staff members who have been with the camp for years.*

CAMP THOREAU-IN-VERMONT
RR 1, Box 88, Miller Pond Road
Thetford Center, Vermont 05075-9601

General Information   Coeducational democratic community living for 150 campers and 60 staff members. Established in 1962. Owned by An Experience In People, Inc. Affiliated with American Camping Association, Vermont Camping Association, Camp Horsemanship Association. 280-acre facility located 30 miles north of White River Junction. Features: rural environment; campsite on a 64-acre lake; hiking in nearby White and Green Mountains.

Profile of Summer Employees   Total number: 60; average age: 25; 50% male, 50% female, 15% minorities, 8% high school students, 60% college students, 20% international, 10% local residents. Nonsmokers preferred.

Employment Information   Openings are from June 15 to August 22. Jobs available: 8 *counselors/swimming instructors* with WSI, LGT, first aid, and CPR/BLS certification at $1200–$2000 per season; 12 *counselors/lifeguards* with LGT, CPR/BLS, and first aid certification at $1200–$2000 per season; 6 *counselors/small craft instructors* with LGT and canoeing/sailing/kayaking instructor certification at $1200–$2000 per season; 3 *counselors/ riding instructors* with CHA and CPR/first aid certification at $1200–$2000 per season; 2 *experienced counselors/woodshop instructors* with CPR/first aid certification at $1200– $2000 per season; 3 *experienced counselors/arts and crafts instructors* with CPR/first aid certification at $1200–$2000 per season; 2 *experienced counselors/photography instructors* with CPR/first aid certification at $1200–$2000 per season; 4 *experienced counselors/sports instructors* with CPR/first aid certification at $1200–$2000 per season; 2 *experienced counselors/martial arts and fencing instructors* with belt and CPR/first aid certification at $1200–$2000 per season; 1 *experienced counselor/newspaper person* at $1200–$2000 per season; 2 *experienced counselors/drama instructors* at $1200–$2000 per season; 2 *experienced counselors/nature (small animals) instructors* with CPR/first aid certification at $1200– $2000 per season; 2 *experienced counselors/hiking and outdoor living instructors* with familiarity with area and CPR/first aid certification at $1200–$2000 per season; 2 *experienced counselors/low-ropes instructors* with CPR/first aid certification at $1200–$2000 per season; 2 *experienced counselors/evening programs instructors* with creativity to design activities for the entire camp at $1200–$2000 per season; *nurses* with RN license, ability to obtain Vermont RN license, and CPR certification at $3000–$3200 per season; *experienced maintenance staff* at $1200–$2500 per season; *office manager* with filing, simple bookkeeping, and telephone skills at $1200–$2500 per season.

Benefits   College credit, preemployment training, on-site room and board at no charge, laundry facilities, travel reimbursement, health insurance, opportunity to work with diverse, multicultural staff in several different program areas.

Contact   Gregory H. Finger, Director, Camp Thoreau-In-Vermont, Department SJ, 157 Tillson Lake Road, Wallkill, New York 12589-3213; 914-895-2974, Fax 914-895-1281. Application deadline: February 15.

CAMP THORPE, INC.
RR 3, Box 3314
Goshen, Vermont 05733

General Information   Summer camp for mentally and physically disabled children and adults. Established in 1927. Affiliated with Vermont Camping Association. 200-acre facility located 60 miles south of Burlington. Features: location in the Green Mountains; trout pond; playground; modern cabins; 43 camp buildings; overnight sites; 100' x 50' pool; multipurpose tennis court.

Profile of Summer Employees Total number: 30; average age: 22; 40% male, 60% female, 90% college students, 30% international, 70% local residents.

Employment Information Openings are from June 15 to August 20. Jobs available: 1 *program director* with B.S. degree at $1800–$2000 per season; 2 *head counselors* with two years of college completed at $1500–$1800 per season; 5 *specialists (art, nature, music, pool, and sports)* with one year of college completed at $1300–$1500 per season; 12 *general counselors* (minimum age 18) at $1200 per season; 1 *camp nurse* with RN, LPN, or EMT license at $2500–$3000 per season. International students encouraged to apply (must apply through Camp America).

Benefits College credit, preemployment training, on-site room and board at no charge, laundry facilities.

Contact Lyle P. Jepson, Director, Camp Thorpe, Inc., RR 3, Box 3314, Goshen, Vermont 05733; 802-247-6611. Application deadline: May 30.

From the Employer *A four-day orientation will introduce counselors to camp procedures, CPR and first aid training, reality therapy as a means of resolving conflict, and general program development using the experiences and strengths of the staff. Each counselor will share a cabin with 3–4 campers.*

CAMP WYODA
Lake Fairlee, RR 1, Box 284
Fairlee, Vermont 05045

General Information Residential camp for 80 girls in two-, four-, or seven-week sessions. Established in 1916. Owned by Kay N. Schlighting. Affiliated with American Camping Association, Vermont Camping Association. 200-acre facility located 18 miles north of Hanover, New Hampshire. Features: extensive freshwater lake frontage; clean lake with sandy bottom; swimming area; 3 riding rings in level valley; riding trail through woods and valley.

Profile of Summer Employees Total number: 35; average age: 21; 30% male, 70% female, 5% minorities, 60% college students, 10% international, 5% local residents, 20% teachers. Nonsmokers preferred.

Employment Information Openings are from July 1 to August 19. Spring break, winter break, Christmas break, year-round positions also offered. Jobs available: *swimming instructors* with WSI certification and swim team experience; *riding counselors* with teaching experience; *sailing counselor* with teaching experience; *drama counselor* with experience directing musicals; *tennis counselor* with teaching experience; *archery counselor* with teaching experience; *crafts counselor* with teaching experience. All positions offered at $900–$1100 per season. International students encouraged to apply.

Benefits College credit, preemployment training, on-site room and board at no charge, laundry facilities, travel reimbursement, health insurance, wholesome outdoor life, valuable experience gained living with children.

Contact Mary Kay Binder, Director, Camp Wyoda, 11 De Wolf Road, Old Tappan, New Jersey; 201-768-0371, Fax 201-664-5120.

From the Employer *Generally, 1 staff member and 3–4 campers share a cabin. Each week the counselors have an opportunity to go waterskiing and usually to have a riding lesson from the riding staff.*

CHALLENGE WILDERNESS CAMP
Bradford, Vermont 05033

General Information   Residential camp serving 60 boys ages 9–16 with outdoor skills and wilderness trips. Established in 1965. Owned by Dr. J. Thayer and Dr. Candice L. Raines. Affiliated with American Camping Association. 542-acre facility located 26 miles north of Hanover, New Hampshire. Features: backpacking and canoe trips; rugged, primitive setting; 15-acre private lake; 542-acre forest preserve.

Profile of Summer Employees   Total number: 12; average age: 21; 100% male, 60% college students, 40% international. Nonsmokers only.

Employment Information   Openings are from June 18 to August 24. Jobs available: 1 *waterfront director* with WSI certification/lifeguard training at $1200–$2000 per season; 1 *kayak instructor* with ACA or BCU certification at $1200–$2000 per season; 3 *rock-climbing instructors* with one 5.10 lead plus two 5.9 seconds at $1200–$2000 per season; 1 *experienced woodworking instructor* at $1200–$2000 per season; 1 *marksmanship instructor* with .22-caliber and military experience at $1200–$2000 per season; 1 *blacksmithing instructor* with ability to be trained at $1200–$2000 per season; 1 *food-services director* with outdoorsman and cooking skills at $1200–$2000 per season; 1 *kitchen assistant* with outdoorsman skills at $1200–$2000 per season.

Benefits   On-site room and board at no charge, laundry facilities.

Contact   Dr. J. Thayer and Dr. Candice L. Raines, Directors, Challenge Wilderness Camp, 300 North Grove Street #4, Rutland, Vermont 05701; 800-832-HAWK.

From the Employer   *All staff (including kitchen) live with 6–8 campers, teach basic outdoor skills, instruct in specialty area, lead backpack trips, and assist with white-water canoe trips. Must enjoy rugged, primitive environment, demonstrate high physical energy, present clean-cut positive role model, and have own vehicle at camp.*

HEART'S BEND WORLD CHILDREN'S CENTER
South Wardsboro and Grout Pond Roads
Newfane, Vermont 05345

General Information   International, coeducational residential programs for boys and girls ages 4 and up. Sessions are one to three weeks long and vary in emphasis, providing children and youth with appropriate skills, information, and understanding to take initiative and have positive impact in the creation of their own future. Established in 1970. Owned by Dr. Nina Meyerhof. Affiliated with American Camping Association. 100-acre facility located 14 miles north of Brattleboro. Features: location on a beautiful old Vermont farm; 8 horse stables and pastures; dairy cow, poultry, pigs, and sheep; vegetable, herb, and flower gardens; outdoor tennis court, amphitheater, and sports fields; painting/drawing/photography studio.

Profile of Summer Employees   Total number: 20; average age: 21; 40% male, 60% female, 10% high school students, 70% college students, 10% international, 10% local residents. Nonsmokers only.

Employment Information   Openings are from June 15 to August 31. Jobs available: 1 *experienced head chef* at $200–$300 per week; 1 *swimming instructor* (minimum age 21) with lifeguard, WSI, CPR, and first aid certifications at $100–$200 per week; 1 *visual arts/pottery instructor* at $100–$200 per week; 1 *nurse/activity counselor* with RN license at $100–$200 per week; 1 *farm and stable manager* at $100–$200 per week. International students encouraged to apply.

Benefits   Preemployment training, on-site room and board at no charge, laundry facilities.

Contact   Nina Meyerhof, Director, Heart's Bend World Children's Center, Department SJ,

P.O. Box 217, Newfane, Vermont 05345; 802-365-7797, Fax 802-365-7798. Application deadline: April 15.

From the Employer *Heart's Bend is an organic farm dedicated to becoming a model eco-community that provides all its participants with the inspiration, freedom, and nourishment to grow. Through extensive international connections and affiliation with the United Nations World Summit of Children, it is also an important communications hub for children and youth activists around the world. Our committed staff have the satisfying experience of making a real contribution to the creation of a healthier, happier, and more sustainable human society.*

KEEWAYDIN WILDERNESS CANOE TRIPS
Salisbury, Vermont 05769

General Information Five-week wilderness canoeing expeditions in Quebec and Labrador. Established in 1963. Owned by Keewaydin Foundation. Affiliated with American Camping Association. Located 40 miles south of Burlington. Features: 17-foot white-water canoes; Cree Indian guide; beautiful wilderness of Quebec.

Profile of Summer Employees Total number: 6; average age: 24; 90% male, 10% female, 20% college students, 20% international. Nonsmokers only.

Employment Information Openings are from June 15 to August 25. Jobs available: 2 *wilderness trip leaders* with EWS and first aid certification at $1200–$1600 per season.

Benefits Preemployment training, on-site room and board at no charge.

Contact Seth Gibson, Wilderness Trip Director, Keewaydin Wilderness Canoe Trips, P.O. Box 626P, Middlebury, Vermont 05753-0626; 802-388-2556, Fax 802-388-7522. Application deadline: March 1.

KILLOOLEET
Route 100
Hancock, Vermont 05748-0070

General Information Full-season, noncompetitive, coeducational camp serving 100 campers ages 9–14 for seven or more weeks. Emphasis is on developing techniques in group leadership and individual counseling. Established in 1927. Owned by John, Eleanor, and Katherine Seeger. 300-acre facility located 35 miles north of Rutland. Features: small private lake; 2 tennis courts; theater; flat campus for bike trips (bring your own or rent bikes); 12 horses with ring and trails; television studio.

Profile of Summer Employees Total number: 40; average age: 22; 55% male, 45% female, 7% minorities, 6% high school students, 65% college students, 15% international, 15% local residents, 10% teachers. Nonsmokers preferred.

Employment Information Openings are from December 1 to April 1. Jobs available: *group horseback-riding (English) staff* with Pony Club experience; *electronics staff; secretary; nature staff; video, control room, and editing staff.* All positions offered at $1000–$1500 per season. International students encouraged to apply.

Benefits Preemployment training, formal ongoing training, on-site room and board at no charge, laundry facilities, health insurance, reimbursement for half of travel costs.

Contact   Kate Spencer-Seeger, Director, Killooleet, Department SJ, 70 Trull Street, Somerville, Massachusetts 02145; 617-666-1484. Application deadline: April 1.

From the Employer   *All counselors spend ten days exploring Vermont with campers on foot, bike, horse, and canoe, both in day hikes and overnights. All counselors help run a cabin of 8–14 campers with 1 or 2 experienced counselors. Approximately two-thirds of the staff return each summer. Since the aim of the camp is to build supportive groups, the counselors find the staff to be encouraging.*

LOCHEARN CAMP FOR GIRLS
Lake Fairlee, P.O. Box 400
Post Mills, Vermont 05058

General Information   Private residential camp for girls ages 7–16 offering a comprehensive activity program with special emphasis on positive character development of children. Established in 1916. Owned by Rich and Ginny Maxson. Affiliated with American Camping Association, Vermont Camping Association, Association of Independent Camps. 51-acre facility located 150 miles north of Boston, MA. Features: 5 outdoor tennis courts (2 clay, 3 all-season); large all-purpose gamefield; lakeside cabins; central recreation hall, including 4 art studios, dance studio, and lakeside dining room; gymnastics center; 16 horses and riding complex with 2 large riding rings.

Profile of Summer Employees   Total number: 70; average age: 22; 10% male, 90% female, 10% high school students, 80% college students, 15% international, 10% teachers. Nonsmokers only.

Employment Information   Openings are from June 16 to August 21. Jobs available: 5 *field sports instructors* at $1200–$1400 per season; 3 *gymnastics instructors* at $1200–$1400 per season; 4 *tennis instructors* at $1200–$1400 per season; 4 *studio arts instructors* at $1200–$1400 per season; 2 *performing arts instructors* at $1200–$1400 per season; 2 *sailing instructors* at $1200–$1400 per season; 2 *leadership trainers* at $1400–$1600 per season; 2 *swimming instructors* at $1200–$1400 per season; 2 *canoe instructors* at $1200–$1400 per season; 1 *diving instructor* at $1200–$1400 per season. International students encouraged to apply (must speak English fluently).

Benefits   College credit, preemployment training, formal ongoing training, on-site room and board at no charge, laundry facilities, travel reimbursement.

Contact   Rich Maxson, Owner/Director, Lochearn Camp for Girls, Department SJ, Camp Lochearn on Lake Fairlee, Post Mills, Vermont 05058; 800-235-6659, Fax 802-333-4856. Application deadline: May 1 (best to apply as soon as possible).

From the Employer   *An eight-day orientation prepares staff to design and implement daily lesson plans and practice teach in their areas of expertise. Training on interpersonal issues and specific ways to foster moral development in children helps staff understand child development issues in substantial ways. Lochearn provides an ideal learning experience for anyone interested in a career in teaching or counseling. Academic credit is available. Ongoing training and support are provided throughout the season.*

POINT COUNTER POINT CHAMBER MUSIC CAMP
Lake Dunemore, Vermont 05733

General Information   Residential camp serving 50 campers who are string players and pianists for three-, four-, or seven-week sessions. Established in 1963. Owned by Paul and Margaret Roby. 2-acre facility located 55 miles south of Burlington. Features: beautiful lake; waterskiing; mountains; hiking trails.

Profile of Summer Employees Total number: 6; average age: 25; 34% male, 66% female, 16% minorities, 33% college students, 16% international, 27% local residents, 50% teachers. Nonsmokers preferred.

Employment Information Openings are from June 19 to August 15. Jobs available: 6 *activity counselors* with WSI, first aid, and CPR certification (preferred) at $1500–$1700 per season; 8 *music staff members (4 violinists, 1 violist, 2 cellists, and 1 pianist)* with performing and teaching experience at $2300–$2500 per season; *experienced cooks* at $2200–$3000 per season.

Benefits On-site room and board at no charge, one week of staff training before campers arrive.

Contact Paul Roby, Director, Point Counter Point Chamber Music Camp, P.O. Box 3181, Terre Haute, Indiana 47803; 812-877-3745. Application deadline: March 15.

From the Employer *Music staff is housed off campus. Counseling staff has 7–15 campers per cabin. Frequent student-staff concerts are given.*

WAPANACKI PROGRAM CENTER
RR 1, Box 1086 West Hill Road
Hardwick, Vermont 05843

General Information Residential summer camp with one-, two-, or three-week sessions for girls ages 6–17. Girl-adult partnership is stressed in small group activities based on Girl Scout principles. Established in 1992. Owned by Vermont Girl Scout Council. Affiliated with American Camping Association, Girl Scouts of the United States of America, Vermont Camping Association. 220-acre facility located 50 miles east of Burlington. Features: rolling meadows, coniferous and hardwood forests; brooks and wetland areas; arts and crafts and recreational buildings; 10-person cabins with running water and bathrooms; beautiful views from 1700-foot elevation; 22-acre swimming and boating lake; athletic fields.

Profile of Summer Employees Total number: 40; average age: 21; 5% male, 95% female, 4% minorities, 4% high school students, 95% college students, 1% retirees, 15% international, 3% local residents, 1% teachers.

Employment Information Openings are from June 28 to August 14. Jobs available: 1 *camp director* (minimum age 25) with administration/supervision abilities and resident camp experience (knowledge of Girl Scout program preferred) at $2500–$4000 per season; 1 *assistant camp director* (minimum age 21) with administration, supervision, and Girl Scout program abilities (camp experience preferred) at $1500–$2500 per season; 1 *business manager* (minimum age 21) with business training (typing, bookkeeping, and office practices), attention to detail, and a current driver's license at $900–$1400 per season; 1 *health supervisor* (minimum age 21) with RN, LPN, EMT, or physician's license and recent first aid training at $1500–$2500 per season; 1 *waterfront/boating director* (minimum age 21) with current WSI certification, CPR training, and experience as an aquatics instructor at $1500–$2500 per season; 2 *waterfront counselors* (minimum age 18) with current ALS or WSI certification and/or SCI certification at $900–$1400 per season; 4 *unit leaders* (minimum age 21) with experience with children in groups, supervisory background, and experience with Girl Scout and outdoor programs at $1000–$1600 per season; 12 *unit counselors* (minimum age 18) with ability to work with children, experience in Girl Scout programs, and outdoor skills at $700–$1100 per season; 1 *trip leader/director of counselors-in-training* (minimum age 21) with experience with children in groups, current ALS and SCI certification, and canoe trip experience at $900–$1400 per season; 1 *program director* (minimum age 21) with experience in camp supervising, working with groups, and teaching in specialized program areas at $1000–$1600 per season; 1 *cook* (minimum age 21) with menu-planning, purchasing, and quality food preparation experience and ability to supervise kitchen personnel at $2200–$3500 per season; 1 *assistant cook* (minimum age 18) with ability to assist quantity food preparation and experience in camp or school cooking at $1000–$1600 per season; 2 *kitchen helpers* (minimum age 16) with ability to work with people and a willingness to fulfill responsibilities as directed at $600–$1000 per season; 1 *maintenance person* (minimum age 18) with experience in minor building, grounds, and equipment repair at $1100–$1700 per season; *program specialists* (minimum age 18) with training and teaching experience in specialized program areas and experience working with groups and/or previous camp experience at $1000–$1600 per season.

Benefits College credit, preemployment training, formal ongoing training, on-site room and board at no charge, laundry facilities, travel reimbursement, health insurance, tuition reimbursement, first aid, CPR, and lifeguard training.

Contact Kathy Reise, Director of Program and Training, Wapanacki Program Center, Department SJ, 79 Allen Martin Drive, Essex Junction, Vermont 05452; 802-878-7131, Fax 802-878-3943. Application deadline: May 1.

WINDRIDGE TENNIS CAMP AT CRAFTSBURY COMMON
P.O. Box 27
Craftsbury Common, Vermont 05827

General Information Residential coeducational camp serving 110 campers with an emphasis on tennis along with traditional camp activities. Established in 1973. Owned by Ted Hoehn. Affiliated with Vermont Camping Association. 50-acre facility located 40 miles north of Montpelier. Features: 16 tennis courts (14 clay, 2 hard surface); fully equipped waterfront on 2-mile lake; soccer field; outdoor basketball court; Sunfish sailing program; wilderness setting.

Profile of Summer Employees Total number: 35; average age: 20; 50% male, 50% female, 10% minorities, 80% college students, 20% international, 10% local residents, 10% teachers. Nonsmokers only.

Employment Information Openings are from June 6 to August 24. Jobs available: 12 *tennis instructors* at $1200–$2500 per season; 3 *soccer instructors* at $1200–$2500 per season; 1 *waterfront director* at $2000–$3000 per season; 1 *lifeguard* at $1200–$2000 per season; 1 *photography instructor* at $1200–$2000 per season; 1 *nurse* at $400–$425 per week; 2 *sailing instructors* at $1200–$2000 per season. International students encouraged to apply.

Benefits On-site room and board at no charge, laundry facilities, exposure to first-class tennis coaching, opportunity for self-directed teaching and creation of programs in elective areas.

Contact Charles Witherell, Director, Windridge Tennis Camp at Craftsbury Common, Department SJ, P.O. Box 27, Craftsbury Common, Vermont 05827; 802-586-9646. Application deadline: February 15.

From the Employer *The Windridge Tennis Camp is known for its ability to make fun of the serious business of teaching tennis skills. All instructors participate in a thorough orientation program that provides guidance and confidence for teachers of all backgrounds. Instructors are also counselors who befriend their students and enjoy the social side of living with teenagers.*

WINDRIDGE TENNIS CAMP AT TEELA-WOOKET, VERMONT

Box 88, Route 12A
Roxbury, Vermont 05669
General Information Residential camp for boys and girls ages 9–15 specializing in tennis, riding, and soccer. Established in 1986. Owned by Ted Hoehn and Alden Bryan. Affiliated with The Windridge Camp at Teela-Wooket. 235-acre facility located 50 miles south of Burlington. Features: 21 clay and Har-Tru tennis courts; 2 soccer fields; 5 riding rings; 30' x 60' swimming pool; archery range; miles of beautiful trails for riding and biking.
Profile of Summer Employees Total number: 70; average age: 23; 50% male, 50% female, 5% minorities, 5% high school students, 65% college students, 20% international, 10% teachers. Nonsmokers only.
Employment Information Openings are from June 5 to August 23. Jobs available: *tennis instructor; riding instructors; soccer instructors; archery instructors.* All positions offered at $1155–$2000 per season. International students encouraged to apply.
Benefits On-site room and board at no charge, laundry facilities, travel reimbursement for some applicants.
Contact Cubby Momsen, Director, Windridge Tennis Camp at Teela-Wooket, Vermont, Department SJ, P.O. Box 4518, Burlington, Vermont 05406-4518; 802-658-0313, Fax 802-658-0288. Application deadline: April 1.

From the Employer *At a seven-day orientation program, all employees participate in teaching, training, and getting to know each other. For evenings away from camp, transportation is provided. During time off, employees can enjoy our separate staff lounge. Counselors have private quarters in a cabin for 4 campers. Spending the summer at Windridge Tennis Camp at Teela-Wooket is a valuable teaching experience for life after camp.*

VIRGINIA

BLUE RIDGE SUMMER SCHOOL

Dyke, Virginia 22935
General Information Coeducational academic summer school serving 55–65 students in academic course work and a remedial skills development program. Established in 1962. Owned by Blue Ridge School. Affiliated with National Association of Independent Schools, Virginia Association of Independent Schools. 1,000-acre facility located 18 miles northwest of Charlottesville. Features: 8 outdoor tennis courts; swimming pool; field house and gymnasium (weight room, basketball, and indoor tennis); 1,000 acres in foothills of Blue Ridge Mountains (Appalachian Trail and Shenadoah National Park); upper and lower ropes course for rappelling, rock climbing, and caving; extensive outdoor program, including hiking, camping, and canoeing.
Profile of Summer Employees Total number: 25; average age: 28; 60% male, 40% female. Nonsmokers preferred.
Employment Information Openings are from June 20 to August 9. Jobs available: 6 *interns* (minimum age 20) with academic background in various sports and activities at $1200–$1400 per season.
Benefits Preemployment training, on-site room and board at no charge, laundry facilities, small stipend.

Contact Director, Blue Ridge Summer School, Department SJ, The Blue Ridge Summer School, Dyke, Virginia 22935; 804-985-7724, Fax 804-985-7215. Application deadline: March 15.

CAMP CARYSBROOK/CAMP CARYSBROOK EQUESTRIAN CAMP/CAMP CARYSBROOK DAY CAMP
3500 Camp Carysbrook Road
Riner, Virginia 24149

General Information Traditional residential camp for girls ages 6–16 in two-, four-, six-, and eight-week sessions; equestrian camp for one or two weeks and a two-week day camp in late August. Established in 1923. Owned by Toni M. Baughman. Affiliated with American Camping Association, Association of Independent Camps, National Archery Association, Camp Horsemanship Association. 200-acre facility located 30 miles west of Roanoke. Features: 200 forested acres; spring-fed lake; 2 tennis courts; stable and riding rings with 5 miles of trails; archery range; rifle range.

Profile of Summer Employees Total number: 25; average age: 21; 2% male, 98% female, 10% minorities, 90% college students, 10% international, 5% local residents. Nonsmokers preferred.

Employment Information Openings are from June 12 to August 14. Jobs available: *experienced riding instructors* with CHA certification at $550–$1200 per season; *swimming instructors* with WSI or lifesaving certification at $550–$1200 per season; *canoeing instructors* with Red Cross canoe and lifesaving certification at $550–$1000 per season; *experienced tennis instructors* at $550–$1000 per season; *experienced team sports staff* at $550–$1000 per season; *experienced recreational sports staff* at $550–$1000 per season; *experienced fencing instructors* at $500–$1000 per season; *experienced dance instructors* at $550–$1000 per season; *experienced drama instructors* at $550–$1000 per season; *experienced arts and crafts instructors* at $550–$1000 per season; *experienced riflery instructors* at $550–$1000 per season; *experienced archery instructors* at $550–$1000 per season; *experienced climbing, rappelling, and caving instructors* at $550–$1000 per season; *experienced ecology instructors* at $550–$1000 per season; *experienced outdoor living skills instructors* at $550–$1000 per season. International students encouraged to apply.

Benefits Preemployment training, on-site room and board at no charge, chance to receive letters of recommendation.

Contact Toni M. Baughman, Director, Camp Carysbrook/Camp Carysbrook Equestrian Camp/Camp Carysbrook Day Camp, Department SJ, 2705 King Street, Alexandria, Virginia 22302; 703-836-7548, Fax 703-836-0725. Application deadline: June 1.

From the Employer *We have a seven-day precamp orientation with an emphasis on child development. Generally, 1 or 2 staff members and 4–6 campers share a cabin.*

CAMP FRIENDSHIP
P.O. Box 145
Palmyra, Virginia 22963

General Information Residential camp with a traditional program, specialized equestrian program, and adventure trips for teens in one- and two-week sessions. Established in 1967. Owned by Charles R. Ackenbom. Affiliated with American Camping Association, National Rifle Association, National Archery Association. 730-acre facility located 25 miles southeast of Charlottesville. Features: 4 tennis courts; 60-event ropes course; stables for 80 horses and indoor arena; gymnasium; beautiful location in Blue Ridge foothills; lake, river, and new swimming pool.

Profile of Summer Employees   Total number: 130; average age: 25; 50% male, 50% female, 5% minorities, 10% high school students, 50% college students, 10% international, 10% local residents. Nonsmokers only.

Employment Information   Openings are from June 7 to August 21. Year-round positions also offered. Jobs available: 55 *cabin counselors/trip leaders* with teaching skills at $1000–$1300 per season; 1 *waterfront director* with WSI certification at $1200–$1400 per season; 1 *experienced tennis instructor* at $1200–$1400 per season; 1 *experienced ropes-course director* at $1200–$1400 per season; 1 *creative arts director* with crafts and drama skills at $1200–$1400 per season; 8 *experienced riding counselors/instructors* at $1000–$1200 per season; 4 *village directors* with college degree and supervisory experience at $1600–$2000 per season; 11 *kitchen staff members* at $1000–$2000 per season; 3 *drivers/maintenance personnel* (minimum age 21) with driver's license at $1200–$1400 per season; 2 *nurses* with RN license; 2 *laundry staff members* with willingness to perform night work at $1200–$1400 per season.

Benefits   Preemployment training, on-site room and board at no charge, tuition reimbursement.

Contact   Linda Grier, Director, Camp Friendship, Department SJ, P.O. Box 145, Palmyra, Virginia 22963; 804-589-8950, Fax 804-589-3925. Application deadline: April 1.

From the Employer   *Certification workshops in lifeguarding, NRA rifle instruction, NAA archery instruction, riding instruction, and ropes-course instruction are offered during a comprehensive precamp training program. Year-round staff of 25 serve in key supervisory and advisory roles.*

CAMP HORIZONS
Route 3, Box 374
Harrisonburg, Virginia 22801

General Information   Summer residential camp for children ages 7–18. Corporate training center and retreat center for schools, churches, and universities in the spring and fall. Established in 1983. Owned by John Hall. Affiliated with American Camping Association, Virginia Council of Outdoor Adventure Education, International Camping Fellowship. 240-acre facility located 10 miles north of Harrisonburg. Features: 2 meeting rooms; outdoor swimming pool and private lake; riding trails; extensive high and low adventure initiative ropes course; beach volleyball court; 2 tennis courts.

Profile of Summer Employees   Total number: 25; average age: 21; 50% male, 50% female, 10% minorities, 100% college students, 50% international, 40% local residents. Nonsmokers only.

Employment Information   Openings are from April 1 to November 1. Jobs available: 4 *general waterfront counselors* with lifeguard, first aid, and CPR certification at $700–$900 per season; 12 *general activities counselors* with first aid, CPR certification, and experience in any combination of the following: swimming, French, Spanish, Japanese, ESL, drama, model rocketry, caving, and rock climbing at $700–$900 per season; 3 *general riding counselors* with first aid, CPR certification, and knowledge of horseback riding (Western-style) at $700–$900 per season; 1 *experienced program director* with bachelor's degree and skills in education, administration, and international education at $1100–$1400 per season; 2 *adventure coordinators* with bachelor's degree and skills in caving, rock climbing, canoeing, and ropes course at $1000–$1200 per season; *general counselors/kitchen staff* at $700–$900 per season. International students encouraged to apply.

Benefits   Preemployment training, on-site room and board at no charge, laundry facilities, travel reimbursement.

Contact   Larry Swenson, Camp Director, Camp Horizons, Department SJ, Route 3, Box 374, Harrisonburg, Virginia 22801; 703-896-7600, Fax 703-896-5455. Application deadline: March 1.

From the Employer   *Camp Horizons provides an excellent opportunity for staff members to live and work with people from around the world. There is also great potential for learning skills in a variety of areas since everyone does a little bit of everything.*

CAT'S CAP & ST. CATHERINE'S CREATIVE ARTS PROGRAM
6001 Grove Avenue
Richmond, Virginia 23226

General Information   Day camp concentrating on exploration of the visual and performing arts, with offerings in sports, horseback riding, and river exploration. Established in 1976. Owned by St. Catherine's School. Situated on 16 acres. Features: 6 outdoor tennis courts; theater; large sports fields; dance studio; gymnasium; photography lab; extensive art studios.

Profile of Summer Employees   Total number: 120; 50% male, 50% female. Nonsmokers preferred.

Employment Information   Openings are from June 20 to July 30. Jobs available: *instructors* with certification in dance, music, art, theater, physical education, or other visual or performing arts at $11 per hour; *assistants* with training or degree in education at $8–$10 per hour; *junior counselors* (ages 15–21) at $3.60–$4.25 per hour; *senior counselors* at $4.25 per hour; *canoeing instructors* at $11 per hour; *rappelling instructors* at $11 per hour; *nurse/ clerk* with RN license at $11 per hour.

Benefits   Lunch provided for full-day cafeteria staff.

Contact   Jan Holland, Director, Cat's Cap & St. Catherine's Creative Arts Program, 6001 Grove Avenue, Richmond, Virginia 23226; 804-288-2804 Ext. 45, Fax 804-285-8169.

From the Employer   *Generally, 1 teacher and 1 assistant conduct classes, with a maximum of 12 students. Cat's Cap welcomes applicants with interests in working with children and in the creative arts seeking to gain experience to help determine their vocational direction.*

4 STAR TENNIS ACADEMY AT THE UNIVERSITY OF VIRGINIA
Charlottesville, Virginia 22901

General Information   Residential tennis camp serving 90 students per week with private lessons and matchplay daily and other sporting events in the evenings. Established in 1974. Owned by Mike Eikenberry. Affiliated with United States Tennis Association. Located 100 miles south of Washington, DC. Features: 13 outdoor hard-surface tennis courts and 3 indoor synthetic tennis courts; indoor swimming pool and numerous athletics fields; 2 hours from Washington, DC; location at the University of Virginia in historic Charlottesville; housing in apartment-style air-conditioned dormitories; school cafeteria for dining.

Profile of Summer Employees   Total number: 30; average age: 22; 60% male, 40% female, 10% minorities, 70% college students, 10% local residents. Nonsmokers only.

Employment Information   Openings are from June 6 to August 15. Jobs available: 25 *tennis instructors/camp counselors* with advanced level tennis player status and some competitive experience at $900–$1400 per season; 1 *evenings activities director* with good organization and planning skills at $1800–$2250 per season; 1 *dormitory supervisor* with good organization and problem-solving skills at $1575–$2025 per season.

Benefits   On-site room and board at no charge, training in teaching tennis.

Contact   Ann Grubbs, Assistant Director, 4 Star Tennis Academy at the University of Virginia, Department SJ, P.O. Box 3387, Falls Church, Virginia 22043; 703-573-0890, Fax 703-573-0297. Application deadline: May 1.

From the Employer   *A five-day staff training session is held to teach staff how to teach tennis, conduct drills effectively, feed tennis balls, promote camp safety, handle problems, and more. During camp there are weekly staff workouts scheduled for staff members to improve their games.*

FREDERICKSBURG AND SPOTSYLVANIA NATIONAL MILITARY PARK
120 Chatham Lane
Fredericksburg, Virginia 22405

General Information   Historic park preserving and interpreting four Civil War battlefields in the Fredericksburg area. Established in 1927. Operated by United States Department of the Interior, National Park Service. 7,000-acre facility located 50 miles south of Washington, DC. Features: Fredericksburg Battlefield with visitor center and guided walking tour along Confederate battleline; Chancellorsville Battlefield with visitor center and guided walking tour at site of "Stonewall" Jackson's wounding; "Stonewall" Jackson shrine with tours; historic structure (Chatham) with exhibits; Wilderness Battlefield with guided tour; Spotsylvania Battlefield with tour.

Profile of Summer Employees   Total number: 8; average age: 27; 50% male, 50% female, 20% minorities, 60% college students, 30% local residents.

Employment Information   Openings are from June 1 to September 1. Spring break, Christmas break, year-round positions also offered. Jobs available: 8 *seasonal park historians;* 1 *seasonal cultural resource assistant;* 1 *seasonal natural resource assistant.* All positions offered at $7.32–$8.21 per hour.

Benefits   Preemployment training, on-site room and board at $30 per week, opportunity to meet and work with top Civil War scholars in the nation (several staff members have been published).

Contact   Gregory A. Mertz, Supervisory Historian, Fredericksburg and Spotsylvania National Military Park, 120 Chatham Lane, Fredericksburg, Virginia 22405; 703-373-6124, Fax 703-371-1907. Application deadline: January 15.

From the Employer   *A vast majority of the seasonal positions at Fredericksburg and Spotsylvania National Military Park are for historians or interpreters. The park has what is arguably the most complex military story interpreted in the entire National Park system— over 100,000 soldiers fell in four major battles fought within a 12-mile radius. Competition for positions is keen, and applicants should have a strong interest in and knowledge of the Civil War.*

LEGACY INTERNATIONAL'S SUMMER PROGRAM
Route 4, Box 265-D
Bedford, Virginia 24523

General Information   Residential coeducational leadership-training program for youths from all over the world offering training and workshops in conflict resolution, environmental leadership, global issues, cross-cultural relations, English as a second language, and issue-oriented theater. Established in 1979. Operated by Legacy International. Affiliated with American Camping Association. 86-acre facility located 15 miles northeast of Lynchburg. Features: rural setting; location in the foothills of the Blue Ridge Mountains (close to lakes and hiking trails); ropes course, pool, basketball, and volleyball courts; soccer field.

Profile of Summer Employees   Total number: 40; average age: 25; 40% male, 60% female, 10% minorities, 10% college students, 30% international, 1% local residents. Nonsmokers only.

Employment Information   Openings are from June 15 to August 20. Jobs available: 1 *experienced waterfront director* with first aid, CPR, and lifeguarding experience; 4 *experienced lead counselors* (male); 6 *experienced lead counselors* (female); 3 *experienced art instructors* with pottery-making skills; 1 *evening and special program coordinator* with performing arts background (preferred); 1 *summer office manager* with typing/word processing ability (50 wpm), organizational skills, and an interest in working with people; 1 *program assistant* with organizational and word-processing skills; 7 *kitchen staff members;* 1 *maintenance person* with valid driver's license; 1 *program support/set-up person* with valid driver's license; 2 *experienced adventure/outdoor skills instructors* with first aid and CPR certification and rock-climbing experience (preferred); 3 *experienced leadership instructors* with ability to teach such skills as event planning, setting priorities, and running meetings; 2 *experienced environmental educators;* 1 *experienced bookkeeper* with knowledge of LOTUS; 2 *experienced certified English as a second language instructors;* 2 *experienced performing arts instructors* with improvisational theater and script-writing skills; 2 *experienced ropes-course instructors;* 1 *housekeeper* with valid driver's license and motivational and organizational skills; 1 *sports and games coordinator* with ability to lead and guide large groups in various games and sports and familiarity with new games and noncompetitive sports; 1 *experienced global issues instructor* with background and knowledge in international relations. International students encouraged to apply.

Benefits   College credit, preemployment training, on-site room and board at no charge, laundry facilities, health insurance, travel reimbursement for international staff, negotiable stipend for non-interns, internships for college-level applicants (work-exchange program).

Contact   Leila Baz, Co-Director, Legacy International's Summer Program, Route 4, Box 265–D, Bedford, Virginia 24523; 703-297-5982, Fax 703-297-1860. Application deadline: May 1.

From the Employer   *Legacy provides a unique opportunity for staff to share their knowledge in new ways. It is a dynamic, cooperative, learning community with people representing many cultures, abilities, experiences, and viewpoints. Staff participate in a two-week training program, which includes Legacy's approaches in communication and counseling, group dynamics, facilitation, intercultural relations, and experiential education.*

OAKLAND SCHOOL AND CAMP
Boyd Tavern
Keswick, Virginia 22947

General Information   Residential and day camp for students ages 8–14 with academic problems. Established in 1950. Owned by Joanne Dondero. Affiliated with Virginia Association for Independent Special Education Facilities, Orton Dyslexia Society. 450-acre facility located 12 miles east of Charlottesville. Features: large open spaces and 450 mostly wooded acres; swimming pool; new gymnasium/recreation building; creek.

Profile of Summer Employees   Total number: 45; average age: 21; 50% male, 50% female. Nonsmokers preferred.

Employment Information   Openings are from June 13 to August 5. Year-round positions also offered. Jobs available: 2 *swimming instructors* with lifesaving certification at $1500–$2000 per season; 12 *counselors* at $1500–$1900 per season; 1 *pool director* with WSI certification at $2300–$2700 per season. International students encouraged to apply.

Benefits Preemployment training, on-site room and board at no charge.

Contact Resident Services Supervisor, Oakland School and Camp, Department SJ, Boyd Tavern, Keswick, Virginia 22947; 804-293-9059, Fax 804-296-8930. Application deadline: June 1.

From the Employer *The camp counseling staff receives an extensive training program prior to the opening of camp. They are given training in child behavior and techniques for working with young people. The camp has a reputation among past camp counselors for being well run. Successful summer employees are often hired for the year-round school.*

STUART HALL SUMMER SCHOOL
Box 210
Staunton, Virginia 24402-0210

General Information Coeducational college-preparatory summer school for advancement or remediation in major subject areas. Established in 1846. Owned by Stuart Hall Board of Trustees. Affiliated with Virginia Association of Independent Schools, National Association of Independent Schools. 17-acre facility located 40 miles west of Charlottesville. Features: 3 outdoor tennis courts; on- and off-campus athletics fields; indoor swimming pool; proximity to Blue Ridge Mountains; hiking, camping, and canoeing on or near James River.

Profile of Summer Employees Total number: 12; average age: 35; 50% male, 50% female, 33% college students, 75% local residents. Nonsmokers preferred.

Employment Information Openings are from June 12 to August 7. Jobs available: *experienced teachers; student teachers.*

Benefits On-site room and board at no charge, laundry facilities.

Contact Dr. Robert Cox, Head of Summer School, Stuart Hall Summer School, Department SJ, Box 210, Staunton, Virginia 24402-0210; 703-885-0356. Application deadline: April 1.

WOODBERRY FOREST SUMMER SCHOOL
P.O. Box 354
Woodberry Forest, Virginia 22989

General Information Coeducational boarding school for approximately 200 students grades 8–12. Established in 1888. Operated by Woodberry Forest School. Affiliated with Virginia Association of Independent Schools, Southern Association of Independent Schools. 1,300-acre facility located 35 miles north of Charlottesville. Features: modern science facility with greenhouses, aquariums, and computers; air-conditioned classrooms; 9-hole golf course; 7 tennis courts and 3 squash courts; fully-equipped field house; 2 swimming pools.

Profile of Summer Employees Total number: 50; 66% male, 34% female, 36% college students, 64% teachers. Nonsmokers preferred.

Employment Information Openings are from June 23 to August 6. Jobs available: *English intern* with three or four years of college (or recent graduate) at $230 per week; *math intern* with three or four years of college (or recent graduate) at $230 per week; *teacher (English or math)* at $2700 per season.

Benefits On-site room and board at no charge, laundry facilities, use of school facilities.

Contact James D. Reid, Director, Woodberry Forest Summer School, Department SJ, P.O.

Box 354, Woodberry Forest, Virginia 22989; 703-672-6047, Fax 703-672-9076. Application deadline: March 1.

From the Employer *Summer school college interns assist veteran faculty in classroom instruction and are given the opportunity to engage in their own classroom teaching. Interns also have considerable responsibility in the areas of dormitory life, afternoon athletics, the fine arts program, and other extracurricular activities. Most people find this an excellent opportunity to investigate the education profession as a career option.*

WASHINGTON

CAMP BERACHAH
19830 Southeast 328th Place
Auburn, Washington 98002

General Information Offers ten day camps (60 campers each), ten horse camps (20 campers each), junior and teen camps (300 campers each), and gymnastics camps (200 campers each). Established in 1975. Owned by Philadelphia Church/Multi-Church Board. Affiliated with Christian Camping International. 140-acre facility located 30 miles south of Seattle. Features: indoor Olympic-size pool; gymnasium; beautiful woods with 6 miles of riding trails; mountain bikes; obstacle course; horses.

Profile of Summer Employees Total number: 60; average age: 20; 30% male, 70% female, 5% minorities, 50% high school students, 20% college students, 25% local residents. Nonsmokers only.

Employment Information Openings are from June 1 to September 1. Year-round positions also offered. Jobs available: *counselors* at $75–$100 per week; 1 *recreation director* at $100–$125 per week; 1 *nurse* at $100–$125 per week; 1 *crafts director* at $100–$125 per week; *lifeguard* at $500–$600 per month.

Benefits College credit, preemployment training, on-site room and board at no charge, laundry facilities.

Contact James Richey, Program Director, Camp Berachah, Department SJ, 19830 Southeast 328th Place, Auburn, Washington 98002; 206-939-0488, Fax 206-833-7027. Application deadline: May 15.

From the Employer *All Camp Berachah employees undergo training sessions that include Red Cross CPR and first aid, gun safety, canoe use, general courage, discipline, and Bible study training. Some schools offer credit for working here. Working at Camp Berachah provides an excellent base for education, sociology, and recreation majors.*

CAMP NOR'WESTER
Route 1, Box 1700
Lopez, Washington 98261

General Information Coeducational residential camp serving 185 children ages 9–16 during two 4-week sessions. Established in 1935. Owned by Charles Curran. Affiliated with American Camping Association. 385-acre facility located 70 miles north of Seattle. Features: location on Lopez Island in Washington State's San Juan Islands; 4 miles of waterfront; live-in tents and teepees; Kwakiutl-style long house and 35-foot Haida-style canoe; authentic Northwest coast Native-American dances performed twice a season.

Profile of Summer Employees Total number: 85; average age: 21; 50% male, 50% female, 10% high school students, 90% college students. Nonsmokers preferred.

Employment Information Openings are from June 16 to August 25. Jobs available: 7 *waterfront instructors* with lifeguard training, advanced lifesaving, or emergency water safety certification at $850 per season; 12 *unit counselors* with lifeguard training certification (preferred) at $950 per season; 12 *assistant unit counselors* with lifeguard training certification (preferred) at $850 per season; 3 *activity directors* (waterfront, riding, and crafts) at $950 per season; 5 *riding instructors* at $850 per season; 6 *crafts instructors* at $850 per season; 2 *cooks* with food-handler's card at $1800–$2000 per season; 1 *kitchen manager* with food-handler's card at $1500–$1800 per season; 1 *registered nurse* at $2500–$3000 per season; 1 *program director* at $1500 per season; 1 *head counselor* at $1500 per season; 3 *rock-climbing/ropes-course instructors* at $850 per season; 1 *naturalist* at $850 per season; 2 *bike trip leaders* with advanced first aid or emergency water safety certification (preferred) at $900 per season; 1 *archery instructor* at $900 per season; 1 *drama instructor* at $900 per season; 2 *music leaders* at $900 per season; 1 *pool director* with WSI and LGT certification at $900 per season; 1 *store manager* at $900 per season; 2 *camp operations personnel* with experience with a chainsaw (preferred) at $850 per season; 1 *filmmaker* with resume and tape/film at $2000–$2500 per season; 1 *photographer* (black-and-white) with portfolio (preferred) at $900 per season; 4 *dishwashers* with food-handler's card at $850 per season; 4 *cook's assistants* with food-handler's card at $850 per season.

Benefits On-site room and board at no charge, laundry facilities, health insurance, full week of staff training, reimbursement for advanced certification in areas such as lifeguard training and EMT.

Contact Paul Henriksen or Christa Campbell, Directors, Camp Nor'Wester, Department SJ, Route 1, Box 1700, Lopez, Washington 98261; 206-468-2225, Fax 206-468-2472. Application deadline: February 15.

From the Employer *Campers and staff are housed separately. Our program emphasizes development of group living skills through outdoor living and challenge-oriented activities.*

CAMP SEALTH
13900 SW Camp Sealth Road
Vashon Island, Washington 98070

General Information Residential camp with a capacity of 350 campers offering eight summer sessions. Group living and informal education programs provided. Established in 1921. Owned by Central Puget Sound Council of Camp Fire. Affiliated with American Camping Association, Camp Fire Boys and Girls. 400-acre facility located 20 miles south of Seattle. Features: location on Vashon Island (between Seattle and Tacoma); 1½ miles of Puget Sound beach; beautiful, Pacific Northwest forest setting; several miles of hiking and riding trails; sports field; challenge course.

Profile of Summer Employees Total number: 100; average age: 20; 34% male, 66% female, 20% minorities, 10% high school students, 80% college students, 1% retirees, 2% international, 30% local residents, 5% teachers. Nonsmokers preferred.

Employment Information Openings are from June 12 to August 20. Spring break, winter break, Christmas break, year-round positions also offered. Jobs available: 45 *cabin counselors* at $1050 per season; 12 *unit leaders* at $1150 per season; 1 *riding director* at $1300 per season; 1 *assistant riding director* at $1150 per season; 1 *arts and crafts director* at $1150 per season; 1 *waterfront director* at $1300 per season; 1 *assistant waterfront director* at $1150 per season; 8 *experienced program specialists* with skills in waterfront, arts and crafts, archery, and nature activities at $975 per season; 2 *nurses* with RN license at $2400 per season; 2 *paramedics/EMTs* at $1800 per season; 1 *cook* at $2000 per season; 2 *assistant* *cooks* at $1800 per season; 10 *kitchen assistants* at $950 per season; 1 *driver* at $1050 per season.

Benefits College credit, preemployment training, on-site room and board at no charge, laundry facilities, health insurance.

Contact Jan Milligan, Director of Camping, Camp Sealth, 13900 Southwest Camp Sealth Road, Vashon Island, Washington 98070; 206-463-3174, Fax 206-463-6936. Application deadline: May 1.

From the Employer *Approximately 100 talented and dynamic staff members are needed each summer to combine their ideas and skills with Sealth's goals for child development. We welcome and encourage staff to contribute their skills and take initiative in offering creative programming, positive learning, and human relations experiences for campers ages 6–17.*

LONGACRE EXPEDITIONS
Seattle, Washington

General Information Adventure travel program emphasizing group living skills and physical challenges. Established in 1981. Owned by Longacre Expeditions. Located 30 miles north of Seattle.

Profile of Summer Employees Total number: 15; average age: 25; 50% male, 50% female, 10% minorities, 40% college students, 30% local residents. Nonsmokers only.

Employment Information Openings are from June 14 to July 31. Jobs available: 1 *mountaineering instructor* (minimum age 21) at $300–$400 per week; 1 *rock-climbing instructor* (minimum age 21) at $300–$400 per week; 3 *support and logistics staff members* (minimum age 21) at $150–$175 per week; 8 *assistant trip leaders* (minimum age 21) at $150–$175 per week.

Benefits Preemployment training, on-site room and board at no charge, Pro-Deal package.

Contact Roger Smith, Longacre Expeditions, RD 3, Box 106, Newport, Pennsylvania 17074; 717-567-6790.

From the Employer *There is an eight-day precamp staff training period highlighting hard and soft skills. Individual advancement is expected of returning staff. First-season staff usually join us as assistant trip leaders and support personnel. In the following season, most graduate to trip leader. Continued advancement leads to positions as base camp manager or course director. We offer intermediate and advanced programs, including mountaineering, sea kayaking, eco-service, backpacking, and rock climbing.*

ROSARIO RESORT
1 Rosario Way
Eastsound, Washington 98245

General Information Resort with a variety of facilities. Established in 1960. Owned by Rosario Hotel, Inc. Located 90 miles north of Seattle. Features: located amidst Washington State's San Juan Islands; beautiful natural environment; Moran Mansion (on National Register); spa facilities; proximity to Moran State Park; marina.

Profile of Summer Employees Total number: 75; average age: 22; 50% male, 50% female, 10% minorities, 10% high school students, 50% college students, 10% retirees, 20% local residents. Nonsmokers preferred.

Employment Information Openings are from May 15 to October 15. Year-round positions also offered. Jobs available: 30 *room attendants/laundry workers/laundry drivers* with physical stamina, attention to detail, and a commitment to stay the entire season (preference given for available housing) at $220–$240 per week; 10 *experienced wait persons* (bussers, cocktails servers, and bartenders) with physical stamina, neat appearance, and pleasant personality (should find own housing) at $4.90–$5.50 per hour; 10 *experienced cooks* (breakfast and dinner) at $260–$300 per week; 10 *dishwashers* with stamina, attention to detail, willingness to work, and commitment at $240–$250 per week; 10 *clerks* (desk, reservations, accounting, and cashiers) with computer and typing skills, phone experience, and an interest in working with people at $200–$240 per week; 6 *marina attendants* with outgoing personality, cashiering experience, and confidence around water at $200–$220 per week; 4 *attendants* (for spa and mansion) with cleaning skills at $220–$240 per week.

Benefits On-site room and board at $50 per week, laundry facilities, health insurance, one free meal while on duty, employee cafeteria for off-duty hours.

Contact S. E. Anthony, Personnel Director, Rosario Resort, Department SJ, 1 Rosario Way, Eastsound, Washington 98245; 206-376-2222, Fax 206-376-2289.

From the Employer *Rosario Resort and Spa is located on Orcas Island. A Washington state ferry takes you from Anacortes to the island. Rosario is 17 miles from the ferry landing. While in a relaxed island atmosphere, our business is as fast-paced as any city business. We house those willing to work as housekeepers and dishwashers first. You must be 18 to be eligible for our housing.*

YMCA CAMP SEYMOOR
9725 Cramer Road KPN
Gig Harbor, Washington 98329

General Information Residential camp serving 140 campers weekly and biweekly. Shorter minicamps of four days are also available. Established in 1906. Owned by YMCA of Tacoma–Pierce County. Affiliated with Young Men's Christian Association, American Camping Association. 150-acre facility located 18 miles northwest of Tacoma. Features: one-half mile of shoreline on Puget Sound; outdoor swimming pool; building with touch tanks for hands-on marine study; outpost trips for individuals of high school age; leadership program for high school age participants; low ropes initiative and group building cooperation course.

Profile of Summer Employees Total number: 50; average age: 21; 55% male, 45% female, 10% minorities, 10% high school students, 50% college students, 10% international, 50% local residents. Nonsmokers preferred.

Employment Information Openings are from June 15 to August 20. Christmas break, year-round positions also offered. Jobs available: 12 *cabin leaders* at $100–$130 per week; 1 *experienced pool manager* with WSI, American Red Cross advanced lifesaving, and American Red Cross lifeguarding certification at $150–$190 per week; 1 *experienced waterfront manager* with American Red Cross advanced lifesaving and American Red Cross lifeguarding certification at $160–$200 per week; 2 *program specialists (arts and crafts, outdoor education)* at $130–$170 per week; 4 *experienced trip leaders* with ability to lead bike, backback, canoe, and kayak trips at $130–$180 per week; 2 *outpost coordinators* with ability to outfit all extended trips and overnights, oversee pretrip meetings and menu planning, and share driving responsibilities at $140–$170 per week; 3 *unit leaders* at $150–$190 per week.

Benefits College credit, preemployment training, formal ongoing training, on-site room and board at no charge, laundry facilities, possible internships.

Contact Dan Martin, Assistant Director of Camping, YMCA Camp Seymoor, Department

SJ, 1002 South Pearl Street, Tacoma, Washington 98465; 206-564-9622, Fax 206-564-1211. Application deadline: May 31.

From the Employer   *YMCA Camp Seymour is a tradition-based camp. We believe in helping staff and campers grow through their experiences at Camp Seymour. Employees are given excellent training and the freedom to implement what they have learned.*

WEST VIRGINIA

CACAPON STATE PARK
Route 1
Berkeley Springs, West Virginia 25411
General Information   Destination recreation resort facility. Established in 1934. Owned by State of West Virginia. Operated by West Virginia Department of Natural Resources. 6,115-acre facility located 10 miles south of Berkeley Springs. Features: 49-room lodge; 30 cabins; 18-hole golf course designed by Robert Trent Jones; 6-acre lake for swimming, fishing, and boating; over 20 miles of hiking trails; 2 tennis courts.
Profile of Summer Employees   Total number: 40; average age: 21; 60% male, 40% female, 1% minorities, 30% high school students, 70% college students, 5% retirees, 99% local residents, 2% teachers. Nonsmokers preferred.
Employment Information   Openings are from May 1 to September 1. Year-round positions also offered. Jobs available: *assistant naturalist* at $4.65 per hour; 4 *park aides* at $4.25 per hour; 20 *attendants* at $4.25 per hour; 4 *lifeguards* with Red Cross beach front lifesaving, first aid, and CPR certification at $4.45 per hour.
Contact   Thomas D. Ambrose III, Cacapon State Park, Cacapon State Park, Route 1, Box 304, Berkeley Springs, West Virginia 25411; 304-258-1022, Fax 304-258-5323. Application deadline: January 15.

WISCONSIN

BIRCH TRAIL CAMP FOR GIRLS
P.O. Box 527
Minong, Wisconsin 54859
General Information   Residential camp serving 185 girls ages 8–15 in two- to four-week sessions including extensive wilderness trips. Established in 1959. Owned by Richard and Barbara Chernov. Affiliated with American Camping Association, Association for Experimental Education, Wilderness Education Association. 310-acre facility located 50 miles south of Duluth, Minnesota. Features: 2 climbing walls; low and high ropes course; 4,000-foot freshwater shoreline; 5 miles of mountain-biking trails.
Profile of Summer Employees   Total number: 90; average age: 21; 5% male, 95% female, 10% minorities, 10% high school students, 80% college students, 15% international, 5% local residents. Nonsmokers preferred.
Employment Information   Openings are from June 10 to August 15. Jobs available:

swimming instructors with WSI certification at $1000–$1500 per season; *wilderness trip leaders* (minimum age 20) with LGT certification at $1700–$1900 per season; *cabin counselors* (minimum age 17) at $1100–$1400 per season; *kitchen helpers* (minimum age 17) at $130–$150 per week; *housekeepers* (minimum age 17) at $130–$150 per week; *caretaker's assistant* (minimum age 17) at $130–$150 per week.

Benefits On-site room and board at no charge, laundry facilities, travel reimbursement, health insurance, internships.

Contact Richard Chernov, Owner/Director, Birch Trail Camp for Girls, Department SJ, 5146 North Woodburn, Milwaukee, Wisconsin 53217; 414-962-2548, Fax 414-962-1001. Application deadline: February 1.

From the Employer *At a nineteen-day preprogram orientation, all employees participate in workshops on safety and accident prevention, adventure-based experiential education, cultural sensitivity, and the facilitation of group interaction. Generally, 3 staff members and 8–10 campers share a cabin.*

BOYD'S MASON LAKE RESORT
P.O. Box 57
Fifield, Wisconsin 54524

General Information American-plan family resort that rents eighteen cabins, serves three meals daily, and performs daily maid service for up to 100 guests. Established in 1895. Owned by Richard Simon. Affiliated with Park Falls Area Chamber of Commerce, Wisconsin Innkeepers' Association. 2,600-acre facility located 400 miles north of Chicago, Illinois. Features: 4 private lakes; secluded Northwoods environment; miles of maintained hiking trails; swimming beach; playgrounds and supervised children's activities; extensive water sports (fishing, canoeing, boating, and sailing).

Profile of Summer Employees Total number: 22; average age: 26; 30% male, 70% female, 15% college students, 25% local residents.

Employment Information Openings are from May 10 to October 10. Jobs available: 5 *dining room attendants* at $170–$250 per week; 1 *children's recreation supervisor* with background in elementary education at $165 per week; 1 *dishwasher* at $170–$250 per week; 1 *pots and pans washer* at $170–$250 per week; 1 *swing cook* at $176–$260 per week; *receptionist* at $170.

Benefits On-site room and board at no charge, laundry facilities.

Contact Richard Simon, Manager/Owner, Boyd's Mason Lake Resort, Department SJ, P.O. Box 57, Fifield, Wisconsin 54524; 715-762-3469. Application deadline: May 1.

From the Employer *Our staff members have the unique opportunity of working in a secluded, wooded environment while being exposed to a wide diversity of people and experiences.*

CAMP ALGONQUIN
4151 Bryn Afon Road
Rhinelander, Wisconsin 54501

General Information Residential camp for 150 boys and girls ages 8–17 with a full recreation program and academic instruction/tutoring in reading, writing, and math. Established in 1975. Owned by Bob Stewart and partners. Affiliated with American Camping Association, National Water Ski Association, Association of Camp Nurses, Association of Independent Camps. 160-acre facility located 285 miles north of Chicago, Illinois. Features: large, beautiful main lodge; extensive freshwater lake frontage; large athletic field; recreation court and tennis court; unique art shop; all cabins are amongst large pine trees.

Profile of Summer Employees Total number: 55; average age: 20; 50% male, 50% female, 7% minorities, 5% high school students, 70% college students, 5% retirees, 20% international, 5% local residents. Nonsmokers preferred.

Employment Information Openings are from June 15 to August 25. Jobs available: 12 *certified teachers* (minimum age 21) with math, special education, and learning disabled experience at $1000–$1200 per season; 20 *general counselors* (minimum age 19) with knowledge of a variety of activities and games and first aid/CPR certification (preferred) at $900–$1100 per season; 1 *experienced waterfront director* (minimum age 20) with WSI or advanced lifesaving certification at $1000–$1600 per season; 1 *food service manager* (head cook) with experience in mass food preparation, menu planning, purchasing, inventory, and budget control at $1800–$2500 per season; 1 *experienced assistant cook* with ability to work closely with food service manager and supervise dining hall and/or dishwashing staff at $1200–$1500 per season; 2 *lifeguards and waterskiing /sailing instructors* with lifeguard certification and experience teaching skiing and/or sailing at $1000–$1200 per season; 1 *registered nurse* with Wisconsin license, adaptability, and desire for camp life at $2000–$2500 per season; 1 *certified art teacher* (drawing, painting, silk screening, sculpture, and pottery) at $1200–$1600 per season. International students encouraged to apply.

Benefits College credit, preemployment training, on-site room and board, travel reimbursement, use of camp facilities during time off, transportation into town provided on time off, use of health club membership.

Contact Debra Buley, Camp Algonquin, Department SJ, 4151 Bryn Afon Road, Rhinelander, Wisconsin 54501; 800-521-2074, Fax 309-691-5450. Application deadline: April 1.

From the Employer *We offer a unique blend of recreational and outdoor experiences with an emphasis on learning. We serve children with learning disabilities, attention deficit-hyperactivity disorder, and those who need or desire reinforcement and support in reading, writing, and math skills. Week-long staff training is provided. Staff members gain valuable work experience and form lasting friendships in a beautiful north woods setting.*

CAMP BIRCH TRAILS

601 South 32nd Avenue
Wausau, Wisconsin 54401

General Information Residential and day camp for girls ages 6–17 serving 80 campers weekly. Established in 1965. Owned by Birch Trails Girl Scout Council. Affiliated with Girl Scouts of the United States of America. 360-acre facility located 26 miles north of Wausau. Features: large sports field; 35-acre lake for swimming, canoeing, sailing, and paddle boats; rolling hills and woods surrounding a 35-acre lake.

Profile of Summer Employees Total number: 20; average age: 20; 10% male, 90% female, 20% high school students, 50% college students, 10% international, 20% local residents. Nonsmokers preferred.

Employment Information Openings are from June 4 to August 4. Christmas break positions also offered. Jobs available: 1 *experienced waterfront director* with lifeguard certification at $1300–$1500 per season; 2 *waterfront assistants* with lifeguard certification at $1100–$1300 per season; 12 *unit counselors* at $1000–$1300 per season; 1 *health supervisor* with advanced first aid certification at $1300–$1500 per season; 1 *experienced cook* at $1700–$2000 per season; 2 *kitchen assistants* at $850–$950 per season; 1 *experienced business manager* at $1200–$1350 per season. International students encouraged to apply.

Benefits Preemployment training, on-site room and board at no charge, laundry facilities, staff lounge, shower house, staff uniform.

Contact Ronetta L. Curran, Program Director, Camp Birch Trails, Department SJ, 601

South 32nd Avenue, Wausau, Wisconsin 54401; 715-848-2371, Fax 715-848-0687. Application deadline: April 1.

From the Employer *Employees are offered a five- or six-day precamp training session covering team building, first aid/CPR, songs, outdoor skill, and much more. Screened platform tents house campers and most staff members. Facilities include a staff recreation building, dining hall, trading post, administration building, and craft and nature centers.*

CAMP INTERLAKEN JCC
7050 Old Highway 70
Eagle River, Wisconsin 54521
General Information Residential coeducational camp serving 400 campers ages 8–16. Established in 1966. Owned by Jewish Community Center of Milwaukee. Affiliated with Jewish Community Centers of America, American Camping Association. 110-acre facility located 250 miles north of Milwaukee. Features: spring-fed lake; location in the magnificent Northwoods; family accommodations; complete waterfront program; 5 outdoor tennis courts.
Profile of Summer Employees Total number: 60; average age: 20; 50% male, 50% female, 5% minorities, 90% college students, 5% international. Nonsmokers preferred.
Employment Information Openings are from June 1 to August 25. Jobs available: 4 *experienced kitchen stewards* at $1500 per season; 1 *experienced gymnastics instructor* with instructor-level expertise at $1000–$1500 per season; 1 *trip director* with LGT, CPR, and first aid certification at $1700–$2200 per season; 1 *experienced sailing instructor* with LGT certification at $1200–$1800 per season; 2 *crafts instructors* with knowledge of ceramics, tie-dyeing, crafts, and painting preferred at $1200–$2000 per season; 1 *tennis instructor* with USTA certification at $1200–$2000 per season; *nurse* with LPN or RN license at $2000–$3000 per season.
Benefits Preemployment training, on-site room and board at no charge, travel reimbursement.
Contact Jon Levin, Director, Camp Interlaken JCC, Department SJ, 6255 North Santa Monica, Milwaukee, Wisconsin 53217; 414-964-4444, Fax 414-964-0922. Application deadline: March 1.

From the Employer *We provide a one-week precamp orientation period. Staff members enjoy ongoing training, interaction, and activities.*

CAMP LUCERNE
Route 1, Box 3150, County YY
Neshkoro, Wisconsin 54960-9329
General Information Residential camp serving 150 campers weekly. Established in 1947. Owned by United Methodist Church. Affiliated with American Camping Association, Christian Camping International. 530-acre facility located 40 miles west of Oshkosh. Features: clear 50-acre lake; woods; meadow; climate conducive to general camp activity; comfortable sleeping cabins; serene woodsy area.
Profile of Summer Employees Total number: 50; average age: 20; 50% male, 50% female, 10% minorities, 70% college students, 30% international, 10% local residents. Nonsmokers only.
Employment Information Openings are from June 4 to August 17. Jobs available: 12 *counselors* at $110–$120 per week; 1 *relief worker* with ability to assist in kitchen (primary responsibility) at $120 per week; 1 *maintenance person* with valid driver's license at $120–$140 per week; 1 *truck driver* with valid driver's license at $110–$125 per week; 2

waterfront personnel with lifeguard training at $115–$140 per week; 1 *waterfront director* with lifeguard training and WSI certification at $125–$140 per week; 1 *dishwasher* at $110–$120 per week; 1 *health supervisor* with first aid/CPR certification or RN license (preferred) at $160–$185 per week; 1 *dining room coordinator* at $110–$125 per week; 1 *assistant cook* at $115–$130 per week.

Benefits Preemployment training, on-site room and board at no charge, laundry facilities.

Contact Joel Jarvis, Director, Camp Lucerne, Department SJ, Route 1, Box 3150, County YY, Neshkoro, Wisconsin 54960-9329; 414-293-4488, Fax 414-293-4361. Application deadline: May 1.

CAMP NEBAGAMON FOR BOYS
P.O. Box 429
Lake Nebagamon, Wisconsin 54849

General Information Residential boys' camp for 220 campers from forty different communities and several countries. Established in 1929. Owned by Roger and Judy Wallenstein. Affiliated with American Camping Association, Midwest Association of Independent Camps, American Camping Association–Illinois Section. 70-acre facility located 35 miles southeast of Duluth, Minnesota. Features: beautiful setting in heart of the Northwoods; complete waterfront; 7 tennis courts; log cabin art building; well-equipped darkroom; spacious playing fields.

Profile of Summer Employees Total number: 125; average age: 20; 80% male, 20% female, 5% minorities, 27% high school students, 40% college students, 10% international, 18% local residents.

Employment Information Openings are from June 16 to August 16. Jobs available: 2 *waterfront directors* with WSI or Red Cross lifeguard certification at $1400–$2200 per season; 25 *senior cabin counselors* (college age) with skills in water and land sports, tennis, target skills, art, campcraft, and photography at $1000–$1150 per season; 1 *nurse* with RN license at $200–$225 per week; 2 *cooks* with experience cooking for large groups at $200–$225 per week; 2 *drivers* (minimum age 21) with clean driving record at $1400–$1700 per season; 25 *junior cabin counselors* (11th and 12th graders) with skills in water and land sports, tennis, target skills, art, campcraft, and photography at $800–$850 per season; 2 *swimming instructors* with WSI certification at $800 per season.

Benefits Preemployment training, formal ongoing training, on-site room and board at no charge, laundry facilities, travel reimbursement, health insurance, many options for time off, excellent opportunity to work with professional staff.

Contact Roger and Judy Wallenstein, Directors, Camp Nebagamon for Boys, 5237 North Lakewood, Chicago, Illinois 60640; 312-271-9500, Fax 312-271-9816. Application deadline: March 15.

From the Employer *Camp Nebagamon offers people of all ages the opportunity to join a child-centered camp community built on a philosophy of caring, recreation, and fun. Since 1929, our staff members have experienced professional growth and a sense of accomplishment. Our 70 percent return rate indicates satisfaction and fulfillment.*

CAMP SHEWAHMEGON
Drummond, Wisconsin 54832

General Information Residential camp for 80 boys ages 8–14. Established in 1934. Owned by Bill and Gerry Will. Affiliated with American Camping Association. 45-acre facility located 70 miles northwest of Duluth, Minnesota. Features: Lake Owen with natural sand beach; 3 tennis courts; nearby golf course; surrounded by Chequamegon National Forest; athletic field; basketball court; recreation lodge.

Profile of Summer Employees Total number: 30; average age: 20; 90% male, 10% female, 5% minorities, 20% high school students, 40% college students, 12% international, 10% local residents. Nonsmokers preferred.

Employment Information Openings are from June 14 to August 14. Jobs available: 8 *general staff members* at $1000–$2000 per season; *lifeguard* with ARC certification at $1200–$1800 per season; *campout trip leader* with campcraft experience and first aid certification at $1000–$1800 per season; *swimming instructors* with WSI certification at $1000–$2000 per season.

Benefits On-site room and board at no charge, laundry facilities.

Contact Bill Will, Director, Camp Shewahmegon, Department SJ, 1208 East Miner Street, Arlington Heights, Illinois 60004; 708-255-9710. Application deadline: June 1.

From the Employer *Staff orientation, training, and activity area set-up begins June 14 and ends a day before camper arrival. Each staff member is encouraged to contribute ideas for the program and is helped to develop activities for campers in accordance with the individual counselor's interests and expertise. It is expected that each staff member will participate in a number of supervisory and instructional program activities including weekly cookouts and at least two 3-day campouts. Each cabin consists of 4–7 boys and 1 counselor. Special activities for staff members include the opportunity to go white-water kayaking on the Brule River.*

CAMP TIMBERLANE FOR BOYS
AV 11400 Airport Road
Woodruff, Wisconsin 54568

General Information Noncompetitive residential camp offering four- and eight-week sessions serving 150 boys from across the country. Established in 1960. Owned by Leslie and Mike Cohen. Affiliated with American Camping Association, Midwest Association of Independent Camps, International Camping Fellowship. 250-acre facility located 250 miles north of Milwaukee. Features: 2,000 feet of secluded lake shoreline; location 5 miles from small but active town; 250 acres of secluded forest land; 4 tennis courts; 2 basketball courts; 50-foot tall rock-climbing wall.

Profile of Summer Employees Total number: 70; average age: 22; 80% male, 20% female, 10% minorities, 25% high school students, 60% college students, 5% local residents. Nonsmokers preferred.

Employment Information Openings are from June 15 to August 15. Jobs available: 2 *counselors/swimming instructors* with lifeguard or WSI certification at $1000–$1200 per season; 1 *counselor/sailing instructor* at $1000–$1200 per season; 2 *counselors/scuba diving instructors* with PADI advanced open water or divemaster certification at $1000–$1500 per season; 2 *counselors/waterskiing instructors* with teaching and boat-driving experience at $1000–$1500 per season; 2 *counselors/tennis instructors* at $1000–$1500 per season; 1 *counselor/photography instructor* with experience developing black-and-white film at $1000–$1500 per season; 1 *counselor/pottery instructor* with experience in wheel and kiln use at $1000–$1200 per season; 2 *counselors/horseback riding instructors* with significant English saddle experience at $1000–$1500 per season; 1 *counselor/guitar instructor* at $1000–$1500 per season; 1 *counselor/golf instructor* at $1000–$1500 per season; 6 *trip leaders* with canoeing background and standard first aid certification at $1000–$1500 per season; 2 *nurses* with RN, GN, or LPN license at $1200–$2500 per season; 1 *experienced assistant cook* at $1000–$2500 per season; 2 *maintenance persons* with carpentry skill at $1000–$2000 per season; 1 *driver* with good driving record at $1000–$1500 per season.

Benefits College credit, preemployment training, formal ongoing training, on-site room and board at no charge, travel reimbursement, health insurance, accommodation of special dietary needs.

Contact Mike Cohen, Director, Camp Timberlane for Boys, Department SJ, 12239 Northeast Shoreland Drive, Mequon, Wisconsin 53092; 414-243-5885, Fax 414-243-9195. Application deadline: May 31.

From the Employer *Live and work with children in a positive, healthy atmosphere in Wisconsin's beautiful Northwoods. We are looking for conscientious, fun-loving people with a strong interest in helping young boys develop skills in our activities and in group living. We emphasize making new friends and having fun.*

CLEARWATER CAMP FOR GIRLS
7490 Clearwater Road
Minocqua, Wisconsin 54548

General Information Traditional residential camp providing caring staff and high-quality camping experiences for girls ages 8–16. Established in 1933. Owned by Clearwater Camp, Inc. Affiliated with American Camping Association. 80-acre facility located 25 miles southeast of Rhinelander. Features: 3,600-acre Headwaters Lake; 5-acre island with 25 cabins for campers and staff; location surrounded by nature conservancy; sailing and waterfront area; location within 5 miles of a charming resort community.

Profile of Summer Employees Total number: 40; average age: 20; 2% male, 98% female, 2% high school students, 87% college students, 2% international, 1% local residents, 1% teachers. Nonsmokers preferred.

Employment Information Openings are from June 14 to August 14. Jobs available: 4 *sailing instructors* with experience handling C scows, Red Cross sailing USRA rating, and CPR certification at $1200–$2500 per season; 5 *swimming instructors* with CPR, WSI, and lifeguard certification at $1200–$2400 per season; 1 *experienced archery instructor* at $1200–$1300 per season; 2 *crafts instructors* with creativity and varied skills in weaving, pottery, and leather at $1100–$1300 per season; 2 *tennis instructors* with CPR certification and the ability to teach with enthusiasm at $1100–$1400 per season; 2 *experienced English-style riding instructors* with first aid, CPR, CHA, and HSA certification at $1100–$3500 per season; 4 *experienced canoeing instructors* with lifeguard or emergency water safety, CPR certification, and canoe certification (preferred) at $1100–$1400 per season; 2 *trip leaders* with campcraft, canoeing, and backpacking experience and first aid, CPR, and lifeguard or EWS certification at $1100–$1500 per season; 1 *drama instructor* with talent, ability to direct, and creativity at $1100–$1200 per season; 1 *windsurfing instructor* with lifeguard and EWS certification and windsurfing instructor rating (preferred) at $1100–$1200 per season; 2 *waterskiing instructors* with boat-driving experience and WSI, EWS, or lifeguard certification at $1100–$1400 per season; *experienced cook and assistant cook* at $1200–$3000 per season; 4 *kitchen staff members*; 5 *general counselors* with love for children, willingness and ability to assist youngsters, and EWS lifeguard, first aid, and CPR certification at $1100–$1300 per season. International students encouraged to apply.

Benefits College credit, preemployment training, on-site room and board at no charge, health insurance, tuition reimbursement, positive reference on résumé, added skill and confidence working with children.

Contact Sunny Moore, Director, Clearwater Camp for Girls, Department SJ, 7490 Clearwater

Road, Minocqua, Wisconsin 54548; 715-356-5030, Fax 715-356-3124. Application deadline: April 15.

From the Employer *At a carefully planned precamp training session encouraging personal growth, employees are instructed in CPR, first aid, leadership, and teaching skills. Located in an exquisite setting and caring community, Clearwater Camp impacts the lives of all involved. Friends from around the world gain a heightened sense of self worth.*

HOUSE IN THE WOOD
3300-1 Bay Road
Delavan, Wisconsin 53115
General Information Residential camp serving inner-city Chicago children. Established in 1910. Owned by Northwestern University Settlement. Affiliated with American Camping Association. 54-acre facility located 45 miles southwest of Milwaukee. Features: location on a peninsula on Lake Delavan; carpeted cabins with indoor plumbing; swimming, boating, sailing, campcraft, and cooperative games; nature center with farm animals; growing resort area; staff lounge and resource center.
Profile of Summer Employees Total number: 25; average age: 21; 60% male, 40% female, 40% minorities, 10% high school students, 70% college students, 25% international, 75% local residents.
Employment Information Openings are from June 10 to August 19. Christmas break positions also offered. Jobs available: 7 *cabin counselors* at $130–$140 per week; 2 *swimming counselors* with WSI/LGT certification at $130–$170 per week; 2 *boating counselors* with extensive experience in sailing and/or canoeing at $130–$160 per week; 1 *outdoor living skills counselors* with camping and outdoor cooking experience at $130–$140 per week; 1 *nature counselor* at $130–$140 per week; 1 *assistant cook* with experience in an institutional kitchen at $150–$160 per week.
Benefits Preemployment training, formal ongoing training, on-site room and board at no charge, laundry facilities, bonus for American Red Cross certification, free certification in CPR and first aid.
Contact Val Wright, Camp Director, House in the Wood, Department SJ, 3300-1 Bay Road, Delavan, Wisconsin 53115; 414-728-4015, Fax 414-728-4015. Application deadline: May 31.

From the Employer *House in the Wood offers an ongoing commitment to building communication, leadership, and group interaction skills in both campers and staff members. Training and individual skill evaluation is provided prior to and during the camping season. Staff members are provided ample opportunity to practice their new skills in a supportive atmosphere with campers and other staff members.*

LAKE GENEVA CAMPUS, GEORGE WILLIAMS COLLEGE EDUCATION CENTERS
P.O. Box 210
Williams Bay, Wisconsin 53191
General Information Educational conference center serving families and nonprofit agencies. Established in 1886. Owned by George Williams College Educational Centers. Affiliated with International Association of Conference Center Administrators, American Camping Association, Association for Experiential Educators. 200-acre facility located 50 miles east

of Milwaukee. Features: 1,200 feet of lake frontage; 18-hole golf course; 4 tennis courts; nature trails; sports fields.

Profile of Summer Employees Total number: 75; average age: 17; 40% male, 60% female, 60% high school students, 40% college students, 10% international. Nonsmokers preferred.

Employment Information Openings are from May 15 to October 15. Year-round positions also offered. Jobs available: 6 *lifeguards* (minimum age 18) with WSI certification, CPR, and advanced first aid at $4.75–$5 per hour; 3 *sailing instructors* (minimum age 18) with Red Cross sailing instructor certification and CPR training at $5–$6 per hour; 12 *housekeepers* at $4.75–$5 per hour; 30 *food service workers* at $4.75–$5 per hour; 2 *painters* at $5–$6 per hour; 5 *grounds crew* at $4.50–$5.50 per hour; 2 *front desk workers* (minimum age 18) at $5–$6 per hour; 2 *arts and crafts staff members* (minimum age 18) at $5–$6 per hour; 4 *preschool/day care staff* (minimum age 18) at $5–$6 per hour; 10 *golf course staff members* (minimum age 18) at $5–$6 per hour; 2 *swimming instructors* with WSI, CPR, and first aid certification at $5.50–$6.50 per hour; 7 *snack shop clerks* at $5–$5.50 per hour; 4 *conference center set-up crew* at $5–$5.50 per hour. International students encouraged to apply.

Benefits Formal ongoing training, on-site room and board at $52 per week, laundry facilities, health insurance.

Contact Richard Miller, Director of Personnel, Lake Geneva Campus, George Williams College Education Centers, Department SJ, P.O. Box 210, Williams Bay, Wisconsin 53191-0210; 414-245-5531, Fax 414-245-5652.

SALVATION ARMY WONDERLAND CAMP AND CONFERENCE CENTER
Camp Lake, Wisconsin 53109

General Information Residential camping program for Chicago-area Salvation Army, including camps for 500–700 low-income and at-risk young people and adults for six 8-day sessions. Established in 1924. Owned by The Salvation Army Metro Division. Affiliated with American Camping Association, Christian Camping International. 140-acre facility located 45 miles south of Milwaukee. Features: low-ropes course; rural area with 50 wooded acres for primitive camping and hiking; lake with boating and fishing; swimming pool with dive tank, children's pool with slide; nature center; 2 large sports fields, 6 tennis courts, and gymnasium.

Profile of Summer Employees Total number: 54; average age: 20; 50% male, 50% female, 5% minorities, 90% college students, 2% retirees, 5% international, 10% local residents. Nonsmokers only.

Employment Information Openings are from May 16 to August 31. Christmas break positions also offered. Jobs available: 1 *aquatics director* with WSI and LTI (preferred) certification at $140 per week; 1 *aquatics assistant* with WSI and LTI (preferred) certification at $135 per week; 6 *boys' counselors* (minimum age 19) with one year of college completed at $130 per week; 6 *girls' counselors* (minimum age 19) with one year of college completed at $130 per week; 4 *program unit directors* (minimum age 21) with two years of college completed at $140 per week; 1 *nature director* (minimum age 21) with two years of college completed at $140 per week; 1 *pioneer director* (minimum age 21) with two years of college completed at $140 per week; 1 *arts and crafts director* (minimum age 21) with two years of college completed at $140 per week; 1 *nurse* with BSN or RN license with CPR training at $300 per week; 1 *nurse's assistant* with student nurse status or experience in nursing at $140 per week; 2 *experienced cooks* at $150 per week; 6 *support counselors* with one year of college (preferred) at $130 per week. International students encouraged to apply.

Benefits College credit, preemployment training, on-site room and board at no charge, laundry facilities, Christian staff fellowship, leadership training.

Contact David Ditzler, Director of Camping Services, Salvation Army Wonderland Camp and Conference Center, Department SJ, 9241 Camp Lake Road, P.O. Box 222, Camp Lake, Wisconsin 53109-0222; 414-889-4305 Ext. 304, Fax 414-889-4307. Application deadline: April 15.

From the Employer *Leadership staff receive two weeks of training, and general staff receive one week. Training covers group cooperation, health and safety, camper characteristics by age, conflict resolution, camper discipline, and camper electives such as archery, boating, fishing, computers, and camping. Camper-staff ratio is 4:1. Counselors have 6–9 campers per cabin in units of three cabins and 5–7 staff members. Campers receive swimming lessons daily in Wonderlands pool complex. The camp offers off-camp trips for campers and staff—public zoo, dairy farm, water ski show, horse farm, and more. Staff and campers utilize talents in daily chapel meetings.*

TIWAUSHARA PROGRAM CENTER
2967 Brown Deer Court
Redgranite, Wisconsin 54970

General Information Girl Scout residential camp serving girls ages 7–17. Established in 1955. Owned by Fond du Lac Exchange Club. Operated by Wau-Bun Girl Scout Council. 180-acre facility located 30 miles west of Oshkosh. Features: wooded terrain; spring-fed lake; swimming pool; shower house; dining hall; orienteering course.

Profile of Summer Employees Total number: 25; average age: 22; 10% male, 90% female, 15% minorities, 15% high school students, 70% college students, 5% international, 10% local residents. Nonsmokers preferred.

Employment Information Openings are from June 11 to August 15. Jobs available: 1 *assistant camp director* with Girl Scout camp experience at $1400–$1575 per season; 1 *business manager* with bookkeeping experience at $995–$1170 per season; 1 *program director* with experience in organized camping at $1170–$1345 per season; 2 *program specialists* with skills in arts and crafts and ecology at $910–$1040 per season; 3 *lifeguards* with current Red Cross lifeguard certification at $900–$1300 per season; 1 *nurse* with RN or EMT license at $1300–$1700 per season; 8 *counselors* with experience as youth leaders at $900–$1200 per season; 1 *food supervisor* with large quantity cooking experience at $1400–$1700 per season; 1 *assistant cook* with large quantity cooking experience at $1000–$1350 per season; 2 *kitchen aides* with willingness to learn at $690–$900 per season. International students encouraged to apply.

Benefits College credit, on-site room and board at no charge, laundry facilities, health insurance, workmen's compensation.

Contact Miriam Somero, Field Executive/Program Services, Tiwaushara Program Center, Department SJ, 307 North Main Street, Fond du Lac, Wisconsin 54935; 414-921-8540, Fax 414-921-5892. Application deadline: May 15.

From the Employer *Tiwaushara Program Center offers employees the opportunity to fine-tune their leadership and communication skills while leading campers on a journey of self-discovery and participating in action-packed weeks of girl-planned activities.*

TOWERING PINES CAMP
5586 County D
Eagle River, Wisconsin 54521

General Information Residential camp serving 100 campers during a seven-week session. Established in 1946. Owned by Towering Pines, Inc. Affiliated with American Camping

Association, National Rifle Association, United States Tennis Association. 450-acre facility located 20 miles north of Rhinelander. Features: 2 lakes; Lake Superior outpost; Northwoods resort setting; development center for acclimation ecology program; modern facilities.

Profile of Summer Employees Total number: 30; average age: 20; 90% male, 10% female, 90% college students, 5% retirees. Nonsmokers preferred.

Employment Information Openings are from June 1 to August 20. Year-round positions also offered. Jobs available: *various recreation and instructional positions* at $750–$950 per season; *kitchen and maintenance staff* at $950–$1400 per season; *nurse* at $175–$200 per week.

Benefits College credit, preemployment training, on-site room and board at no charge, laundry facilities, travel reimbursement.

Contact John M. Jordan, Towering Pines Camp, 242 Bristol Street, Northfield, Illinois 60093; 800-882-7034.

From the Employer *Field study candidates are especially welcome. Special efforts are made to facilitate necessary requirements and evaluation. The ecology appreciation program, Acclimatization, was developed here and is still featured. Our sailing program is exceptional. Our sister camp, Woodland, provides extended camping resources utilized for special events and coed activities.*

WISCONSIN BADGER CAMP
Route 2, Box 351
Prairie du Chien, Wisconsin 53821

General Information Residential camp serving 75 developmentally challenged children and adults weekly. Established in 1966. Affiliated with American Camping Association, Platteville Chamber of Commerce, Prairie du Chien Chamber of Commerce. 620-acre facility located 80 miles west of Madison. Features: petting farm; in-ground swimming pool with ramp; special primitive camp; beautiful vistas of Mississippi River Valley; 20 miles of trails.

Profile of Summer Employees Total number: 50; average age: 20; 50% male, 50% female, 5% minorities, 5% high school students, 90% college students, 10% international, 20% local residents. Nonsmokers preferred.

Employment Information Openings are from May 30 to August 20. Jobs available: 17 *boys' counselors* at $1320–$1400 per season; 17 *girls' counselors* at $1320–$1400 per season; 2 *swimming directors* with lifesaving certification at $1320–$1375 per season; 1 *recreation director* at $1320–$1350 per season; 1 *arts and crafts director* at $1320–$1350 per season; 1 *nature/farm director* at $1320–$1350 per season; 1 *camping/fishing director* at $1320–$1350 per season; 2 *health-care staff members* with RN, GN, LPN, or EMT license or status as third-year nursing student at $200–$350 per week; 1 *dietary technician* with nutrition or dietetics student status at $1320–$1400 per season; 1 *head cook* with food-service degree or student status at $1300–$1500 per season; 3 *kitchen assistants* at $1320 per season; 2 *coordinators* with degree in special education at $1485–$1700 per season; 1 *program coordinator* with experience or degree in therapeutic recreation at $1485–$1700 per season; 1 *horseback-riding director* with experience or HSA certification at $100–$150 per week; 1 *secretary* at $1320 per season; 1 *maintenance person* at $1100–$1200 per season. International students encouraged to apply.

Benefits College credit, preemployment training, on-site room and board at no charge.

Contact Brent Bowers, Camp Director, Wisconsin Badger Camp, Department SJ, P.O. Box 240, Platteville, Wisconsin 53818; 608-348-9689. Application deadline: April 30.

From the Employer *Badger Camp employees gain extensive training and experience working with individuals who have developmental challenges. We do not turn campers away due to the severity of their disabilities. Staff members provide a safe and fun vacation for ten sessions each summer.*

WOODLAND
5113 County D
Eagle River, Wisconsin 54521
General Information Residential camp serving 70 girls. Established in 1940. Owned by Towering Pines, Inc. Affiliated with American Camping Association. 95-acre facility located 20 miles north of Rhinelander. Features: lake chain; Lake Superior sailing outpost; Northwoods setting; development center for acclimation ecology program; modern facilities.

Profile of Summer Employees 10% male, 90% female, 90% college students. Nonsmokers only.

Employment Information Openings are from June 15 to August 15. Jobs available: *activity instructors* at $750–$950 per season; *kitchen and service staff* at $950–$1500 per season; *nurse* at $175–$200 per week.

Benefits College credit, formal ongoing training, on-site room and board at no charge, travel reimbursement.

Contact John M. Jordan, Director, Woodland, 242 Bristol Street, Northfield, Illinois 60093; 708-446-7311. Application deadline: June 1.

From the Employer *At Woodland, field study candidates are valued. Special efforts are made to facilitate school requirements. The ecology appreciation program, Acclimatization, was developed here. Our sailing program is exceptional. Our brother camp, Towering Pines, supports extended camping resources for special events and coed activities.*

WOODSIDE RANCH RESORT
Highway 82
Mauston, Wisconsin 53948
General Information Full-service American plan dude ranch offering log cabins with fireplaces. Established in 1926. Owned by Feldmann family. Affiliated with Wisconsin Innkeepers' Association, Central Wisconsin River Country. 1,200-acre facility located 65 miles northwest of Madison. Features: pool; newly enlarged pond for paddle boats and row boats; 12 miles of marked hiking trails; buffalo herd; pony ring and play school for kids; weekly professional horse show (gymkhana).

Profile of Summer Employees Total number: 60; average age: 19; 40% male, 60% female, 5% minorities, 25% high school students, 25% college students, 5% international, 50% local residents.

Employment Information Openings are from June 1 to September 7. Christmas break, year-round positions also offered. Jobs available: 6 *horse-trail guides, experience preferred,* at $180–$200 per week; 6 *food-service personnel* at $180–$200 per week; 6 *bartenders/ country store clerks, experience preferred,* at $200–$220 per week; 1 *recreation director* at $250 per week; 1 *yard and pool maintenance person* at $200–$250 per week; 2 *housekeepers* at $180–$200 per week; 1 *experienced horse-drawn wagon teamster* at $200–$250 per week.

Benefits On-site room and board at no charge, laundry facilities, free use of most resort facilities: pool, tennis, mini-golf (if use does not conflict with guest use).

Contact   Rick Feldmann, Woodside Ranch, Woodside Ranch Resort, Department SJ, Highway 82, Mauston, Wisconsin 53948; 608-847-4275.

From the Employer   *Woodside Ranch offers students the chance to save most of their summer income. With free room and board provided, plus the use of most of the resort and recreation facilities, a student could have virtually an expense-free summer job. (A car is not necessary as Woodside Ranch will pick up and deliver employees at the bus and train stations.) We also encourage our employees to mingle with the guests, go to dances and evening entertainments, form friendships, and generally become part of the family.*

WYOMING

ABSAROKA MOUNTAIN LODGE
1231 East Yellowstone Highway
Wapiti, Wyoming 82450
General Information   Guest ranch on the eastern edge of Yellowstone National Park with lodging, meals, horseback riding, fishing, and other activities. Established in 1910. Owned by David and Cathy Sweet. Affiliated with American Automobile Association, Mobil Travel Guide. 7-acre facility located 40 miles west of Cody. Features: location 12 miles east of Yellowstone National Park; historical mountain lodge; 16 log cabins; horseback rides in Shoshone National Forest; mountain stream.
Profile of Summer Employees   Total number: 12; average age: 22; 50% male, 50% female, 10% high school students, 80% college students, 10% retirees, 25% local residents.
Employment Information   Openings are from May 1 to November 1. Jobs available: 2 *cooks, experience preferred,* at $350–$450 per month; 4 *waitstaff/cabin staff members* at $350 per month; 2 *experienced wranglers* at $350–$450 per month; 1 *maintenance person, experience preferred,* at $350 per month; 1 *front-desk person* at $350–$400 per month. International students encouraged to apply.
Benefits   On-site room and board at no charge, laundry facilities, salaries supplemented by gratuities, possible end-of-season bonus.
Contact   David Sweet, Owner, Absaroka Mountain Lodge, 1231 East Yellowstone Highway, Wapiti, Wyoming 82450; 307-587-3963. Application deadline: April 1.

CODY'S RANCH RESORT
2604 Yellowstone Highway
Cody, Wyoming 82414
General Information   Horseback-riding resort catering to families. Established in 1925. Owned by Bill Cody's Ranch Inn. Affiliated with American Automobile Association, United States Chamber of Commerce, Cody Country Chamber of Commerce. Located 100 miles south of Billings, Montana. Features: proximity to Yellowstone and Teton National Parks; 70 riding horses; 17 different trails, all located in Shoshone National Forest east of Yellowstone National Park.
Profile of Summer Employees   Total number: 20; average age: 25; 40% male, 60% female, 90% college students, 2% local residents. Nonsmokers preferred.
Employment Information   Openings are from April 15 to November 15. Year-round positions also offered. Jobs available: 5 *horse wranglers* with physical ability to perform

required duties and valid driver's license at \$300–\$500 per month; 2 *cooks* with some culinary experience at \$300–\$500 per month; 6 *housekeepers* at \$250–\$400 per month; 5 *waiters/waitresses* at \$250–\$400 per month; 2 *office assistants* at \$300–\$500 per month; 2 *wagon drivers* with draft horse driving experience, advanced first aid and CPR certification at \$300–\$500 per month.

Benefits   On-site room and board at no charge, laundry facilities, free horseback riding, end-of-season/contract bonus.

Contact   Mrs. William Cody, Owner, Cody's Ranch Resort, 2604 Yellowstone Highway, Cody, Wyoming 82414; 307-587-2097.

From the Employer   *Make new friends with employees from all over the United States and ranch guests from around the world. This is an opportunity for your personality to shine, to learn life skills, and to improve interpersonal communication skills.*

HATCHET MOTEL AND RESTAURANT
P.O. Box 316
Moran, Wyoming 83013

General Information   Motel with twenty-two logged units, a suite, restaurant, gift shop, and gas station. Established in 1953. Owned by Don Albrecht. Operated by Phil and Diane Mehlhaff, Managers. Affiliated with Jackson Chamber of Commerce, Wyoming Hotel/Motel Association, Wyoming Restaurant Association, American Automobile Association. 35-acre facility located 35 miles east of Jackson. Features: proximity to the Grand Tetons and Yellowstone Park; quiet surroundings; referral for float trips; horseback riding; hiking and fishing nearby.

Profile of Summer Employees   Total number: 18; average age: 23; 40% male, 60% female, 23% minorities, 15% high school students, 50% college students, 25% retirees, 10% local residents. Nonsmokers preferred.

Employment Information   Openings are from May 21 to September 15. Jobs available: 2 *station attendants* (morning and evening shift) at \$500 per month; 2 *desk attendants* (morning and evening shift) at \$500 per month; 2 *cooks* (morning and evening shift) at \$600 per month; 5 *kitchen helpers* (morning and evening shift) at \$500 per month; 5 *waiters/ waitresses* (morning and evening shift) at \$375 per month; 2 *housekeeping staff members* at \$500 per month; 1 *yard maintenance person* at \$500 per month; 2 *relief position personnel* at \$500 per month. International students encouraged to apply.

Benefits   College credit, preemployment training, formal ongoing training, on-site room and board at no charge, laundry facilities.

Contact   Phil and Diane Mehlhaff, Managers, Hatchet Motel and Restaurant, Department SJ, P.O. Box 316, Moran, Wyoming 83013; 307-543-2413. Application deadline: May 15.

From the Employer   *We offer all of our employees the chance to work in a beautiful setting and a congenial atmosphere under the direction of friendly and fair-minded employers.*

SIGNAL MOUNTAIN LODGE
Grand Teton National Park, P.O. Box 50
Moran, Wyoming 83013

General Information   Summer resort providing national park visitors with services such as lodging, food, marinas, gifts, guided fishing, groceries, and gasoline. Established in 1940. Owned by Rex Maughan. Affiliated with Jackson Hole Chamber of Commerce. 30-acre facility located 30 miles north of Jackson. Features: location on Jackson Lake at the foot of the Grand Tetons; proximity to Yellowstone National Park; new top-rate dormitories for employees.

Profile of Summer Employees   Total number: 130; average age: 28; 50% male, 50% female, 5% minorities, 60% college students, 15% retirees, 1% international, 5% local residents. Nonsmokers preferred.

Employment Information   Openings are from May 1 to October 20. Jobs available: 5 *front-desk and reservations persons* with typing and interpersonal skills at $4.35 per hour; 3 *experienced accounting personnel (day and night audit)* at $6 per hour; 6 *marina attendants* with ability to handle boat rentals, shuttle guests to and from boats, and pump gas at $4.35 per hour; 20 *lodging helpers* with ability to make beds, clean, and do laundry at $4.35 per hour; 5 *cooks* with experience planning fine-dining and coffee shop menus at $5–$6 per hour; 5 *pantry personnel* with ability to prepare salads and desserts at $5 per hour; 4 *employee dining room staff members* at $5–$6 per hour; 15 *experienced waiters/waitresses* at $2.21 per hour; 2 *experienced bartenders* at $4.35 per hour; 2 *cocktail waitpersons;* 4 *hosts/hostesses* at $4.35 per hour; 9 *buspersons/dishwashers* at $3.75–$4.35 per hour; 5 *experienced gift store sales clerks* at $4.35 per hour; *experienced convenience store attendants* at $4.35 per hour; 10 *experienced management and staff positions* with full-season availability. International students encouraged to apply (must be able to work from May until October).

Benefits   College credit, preemployment training, on-site room and board at $195 per month, laundry facilities, discounts in the restaurants, gift stores, and marinas, free river rafting trips, bonuses for some positions, proximity to religious services.

Contact   Sandy Nietling, Personnel Manager, Signal Mountain Lodge, Department SJ, P.O. Box 50, Moran, Wyoming 83013; 307-543-2831, Fax 307-543-2569. Application deadline: April 1 (it is best to apply in January and February).

TETON VALLEY RANCH CAMP
Jackson Hole, P.O. Box 8
Kelly, Wyoming 83011

General Information   Residential summer camp serving 125 campers each five-week session with a strong Western horseback-riding and backpacking program. Multi-day trips into the mountains on foot and horseback. Established in 1939. Affiliated with American Camping Association, Western Association of Independent Camps. Situated on 1,200 acres. Features: warm spring-fed pond; spectacular mountain country of Jackson Hole and Grand Teton National Park; hundreds of miles of riding and hiking trails; located on a longhorn cattle ranch with a herd of 45 horses; horse packtrips, hiking, gymkhana rodeo events, fly fishing, photography, leadership training, crafts and lapidary, ham radio, archery/riflery, outdoor skills, and a nature discovery program.

Profile of Summer Employees   Total number: 70; average age: 23; 50% male, 50% female, 10% high school students, 70% college students, 10% retirees, 10% teachers. Nonsmokers only.

Employment Information   Openings are from June 5 to August 22. Jobs available: 14 *boys' cabin counselors* (first five weeks of summer) with first aid and CPR certification at $400–$700 per season; 14 *girls' cabin counselors* (second five weeks of summer) with first aid and CPR certification at $400–$700; 5 *kitchen staff members* at $1100–$1500 per season; 2 *laundry workers* at $1300–$1500 per season. International students encouraged to apply.

Benefits   Preemployment training, on-site room and board at no charge, laundry facilities, travel reimbursement.

Contact Teton Valley Ranch Camp, Department SJ, P.O. Box 8, Kelly, Wyoming 83011; 307-733-2958, Fax 307-733-2978. Application deadline: April 15.

From the Employer *Teton Valley Ranch Camp is adjacent to Grand Teton National Park on the eastern edge of the famous Jackson Hole, looking across the valley to the towering Wyoming Teton mountain range. Staff arrive before campers for a weeklong training session. The counseling staff live in log cabins with another staff member or by themselves with 5–10 campers. Support staff also live in log cabins and are involved in all aspects of camp life.*

TOGWOTEE MOUNTAIN LODGE
P.O. Box 91
Moran, Wyoming 83013
General Information Mountain lodge serving a variety of clientele. Established in 1925. Owned by Dave and Judie Helgeson. Affiliated with American Hotel and Motel Association, National Federation of Independent Businesses, National Forest Recreation Association. 67-acre facility located 48 miles north of Jackson Hole. Features: remote location; near Yellowstone and Grand Teton National Parks, with hiking and backpacking in wilderness areas; mountain streams for fishing; horses on premises.
Profile of Summer Employees Total number: 40; average age: 25; 60% male, 40% female, 5% high school students, 50% college students. Nonsmokers preferred.
Employment Information Openings are from June 1 to October 29. Christmas break, year-round positions also offered. Jobs available: 3 *front-desk/reservations persons* with good math aptitude and an outgoing personality at $5–$6 per hour; 5 *housekeepers/laundry personnel* with neat appearance and efficient work habits at $4.50–$5 per hour; 7 *waitstaff (food servers)* with an outgoing personality and desire to perform a thorough job at $2.75–$3 per hour; 2 *experienced bartenders* at $4.50–$5 per hour; 3 *dishwashers* with ability to accomplish tasks neatly and quickly at $4.50–$5 per hour; 4 *experienced cooks* with neat and efficient work habits at $5.50–$7 per hour; 2 *gas attendants (clerks)* with good math skills and an outgoing personality at $4.50–$5.50 per hour; 1 *night auditor* with good math aptitude (should enjoy working nights) at $5–$6 per hour; 2 *general laborers* with efficient work habits at $4.50–$6 per hour.
Benefits On-site room and board at $300 per month, laundry facilities, health insurance, end-of-season bonus available.
Contact Peggy Pruitt, General Manager, Togwotee Mountain Lodge, Department SJ, P.O. Box 91, Moran, Wyoming 83013; 307-543-2847. Applications accepted year-round.

From the Employer *This is an opportunity to live in one of the most scenic areas of the United States while meeting people from all parts of the world. This is especially attractive for individuals who enjoy outdoor activities such as hiking, fishing, mountain climbing, cross-country skiing, and snowmobiling.*

YELLOWSTONE PARK SERVICE STATIONS
Yellowstone National Park
Yellowstone, Wyoming 82190
General Information YPSS operates automotive service facilities in Yellowstone National Park. Established in 1947. Affiliated with National Park Hospitality, Adopt-A-Highway Program. Located 90 miles south of Bozeman, Montana. Features: proximity to Grand Teton National Park and several national forests; world's greatest concentration of geysers; spectacular waterfalls, mountains, and canyons; Yellowstone Lake (the largest Alpine lake in the United States).

Profile of Summer Employees Total number: 95; average age: 23; 68% male, 32% female, 5% minorities, 63% college students, 4% retirees, 1% international, 10% local residents. Nonsmokers preferred.

Employment Information Openings are from May 1 to October 15. Jobs available: 50 *service station attendants* with good interpersonal skills at $178 per week; 18 *automobile mechanics* with ASE certification or current enrollment in an ASE program at $240 per week; 3 *accounting clerks* with ability to operate 10-key adding machine by touch plus computer and communication skills at $182 per week; 1 *warehouse helper* with good driving record and communication skills at $182 per week.

Benefits College credit, preemployment training, on-site room and board at $58 per week, laundry facilities, health insurance, employee assistance program, accident insurance, employee recreation program, outdoor work, advancement potential.

Contact Bill Berg, Director of Business Operations, Yellowstone Park Service Stations, P.O. Box 11–Department WDM, Gardiner, Montana 59030-0011; 406-848-7333. Application deadline: May 1.

From the Employer *The crew size at each of our locations varies from 4–15, and the experience typically fosters long friendships and a strong sense of community. Employees live in some of the world's finest country for hiking, rafting, fishing, photography, mountaineering, geyser gazing, and wildlife viewing.*

Canadian Listings

(Please note: Wages in the profiles that follow are in Canadian dollars.)

ALBERTA

HOMEPLACE GUEST RANCH & TRAIL TRIPS
RR #1
Priddis, Alberta T0L 1W0
General Information Guest ranch serving up to 14 persons, emphasizing horse-related activities and ranch life. Established in 1978. Owned by Mac Makenny. 4,000-acre facility located 60 miles west of Calgary. Features: proximity to the Rocky Mountains; 35 horses for beginners to experts; polo and rodeos in the summer; jacuzzi; lodge with private rooms, private baths, and Western living room.
Profile of Summer Employees Total number: 6; average age: 30; 50% male, 50% female, 20% college students, 20% retirees. Nonsmokers only.
Employment Information Openings are from May 1 to October 11. Christmas break positions also offered. Jobs available: *internal administrator* at $800–$1000 per month; *chef* at $800–$1200 per month; *wranglers* at $800–$1000 per month. International students encouraged to apply.
Benefits Formal ongoing training, on-site room and board at no charge, laundry facilities.
Contact Mac Makenny, Homeplace Ranch, Homeplace Guest Ranch & Trail Trips, Site 2, Box 6, Priddis, Alberta, Canada T0L 1W0; 403-931-3245, Fax 403-931-3245. Application deadline: April 31.

From the Employer *All employees participate in preseason and ongoing workshops on safety, accident prevention, and cultural sensitivity.*

JOHNSTON CANYON RESORT
P.O. Box 875
Banff, Alberta T0L 0C0
General Information Resort with forty-one units, serving 200 guests per night. Established in 1927. Operated by Johnston Canyon Company, Ltd. 6-acre facility located 200 miles west of Calgary. Features: 1 tennis court; hiking trails; near 7 waterfalls; large hot tub; tourist cabins, cafe, patio, and restaurant; proximity to Banff, a world-class resort town.
Profile of Summer Employees Total number: 35; average age: 23; 50% male, 50% female. Nonsmokers preferred.
Employment Information Openings are from May 15 to October 1. Jobs available: *waitstaff* at $6 per hour; *cabin cleaners/laundry help* at $6.50 per hour; *desk clerks* at $6.50 per hour; *gas jockey* at $6 per hour. International students encouraged to apply.
Benefits On-site room and board at $70 per week, laundry facilities, travel reimbursement, travel passes by tour bus to various highlights of the national parks.
Contact Stella Nokes, Manager, Johnston Canyon Resort, Box 875, Banff, Alberta, Canada

T0L 0C0; 403-762-4086/762-2971, Fax 403-762-4086. Application deadline: April 1 (prospective employees begin applying in January).

From the Employer   *Our resort is in the most beautiful area in Alberta. Good staff rapport and staff activities prevail.*

BRITISH COLUMBIA

APRIL POINT LODGE AND FISHING RESORT
April Point Road, Quandra Island, P.O. Box 1
Campbell River, British Columbia V9W 4Z9
General Information   Fishing resort serving 120 guests. Established in 1945. Owned by Peterson family. Affiliated with Special Places, Unique Northwestern Country Inns. 180-acre facility located 100 miles north of Vancouver. Features: all rooms have ocean view; 180 acres of forest for walking; extensive ocean frontage; world-class diving adventures.
Profile of Summer Employees   Total number: 120; average age: 25; 50% male, 50% female, 2% minorities, 20% high school students, 20% college students, 58% local residents.
Employment Information   Openings are from April 1 to September 31. Jobs available: *kitchen workers* at $6.50–$8 per hour; *grounds workers* at $6.50–$8 per hour; *fishing guides (contractors)* at $13.25–$21.25 per hour; *dock workers* with experience dealing with the public at $6.50–$8 per hour.
Benefits   Laundry facilities.
Contact   Neal Rolfe, Operations Manager, April Point Lodge and Fishing Resort, Department SJ, P.O. Box 1, Campbell River, British Columbia, Canada V9W 4Z9; 604-285-2222, Fax 604-285-2411.

CAMP CHAWUTHEN
Seventh-day Adventist Church, Box 369
Hope, British Columbia V0X 1L0
General Information   Coeducational residential camp serving 100 campers ages 8–18, in respective age groups, weekly. Established in 1939. Owned by Seventh-day Adventist Church, British Columbia Conference. Affiliated with Christian Camping International-British Columbia region, British Columbia Camping Association, Camp Horsemanship and Safety Association. 120-acre facility located 60 miles east of Vancouver. Features: mountain trails; full-size gym; riding trails; lake for skiing and canoeing; natural country setting; swimming pool.
Profile of Summer Employees   Total number: 38; average age: 19; 45% male, 55% female, 5% minorities, 20% high school students, 70% college students, 1% retirees, 1% international, 60% local residents, 1% teachers. Nonsmokers only.
Employment Information   Openings are from June 6 to August 24. Jobs available: 6 *counselors* at $315–$342 per week; 2 *wranglers* with CHA certification at $315–$342 per week. International students encouraged to apply (position must be on a volunteer basis).
Benefits   Preemployment training, on-site room and board at $120 per week, laundry facilities.
Contact   Jim Gaull, Director, Camp Chawuthen, Department SJ, Box 1000, Abbotsford,

British Columbia, Canada V2S 4P5; 604-853-5451, Fax 604-853-8681. Application deadline: February 1.

From the Employer *Employees have the opportunity to counsel, instruct, and participate in programming and group fellowship. Employees may be able to work with blind campers. Room and board are automatically deducted from wages.*

CAMP TULAHEAD
12642 100 Avenue
Surrey, British Columbia V3V 2X7
General Information Residential camp serving 70 coed campers weekly. Established in 1978. Operated by Camp Tulahead Society. Affiliated with Christian Camping International, British Columbia Camping. 100-acre facility located south of Kelowna. Features: freshwater lake shared with only two other homes; extensive nature area with beaver ponds, lodges, and dams; bird sanctuary; mini golf course; sand volleyball courts; small-scale Western town; petting farm.
Profile of Summer Employees Total number: 23; average age: 20; 40% male, 60% female, 90% college students. Nonsmokers only.
Employment Information Openings are from July 1 to August 31. Jobs available: 1 *program director;* 1 *activities coordinator;* 1 *head lifeguard* with NLS, WSI 1 and 2, and 2 years lifeguarding experience; 2 *assistant lifeguards* with NLS and WSI 1 and 2 certification; 10 *counselors;* 4 *activity instructors;* 1 *cook.* All positions offered at $1000–$1500 per season. International students encouraged to apply.
Benefits Preemployment training, on-site room and board at no charge, laundry facilities, pay scale increases for return workers ($1000-first year, $1200-2nd year, $1500-3rd year).
Contact Camp Tulahead, Department SJ, 12642 100 Avenue, Surrey, British Columbia, Canada V3V 2X7; 604-581-5488. Application deadline: June 15.

From the Employer *A summer at Camp Tulahead provides staff members with the opportunity to fine-tune their strengths and develop competence in areas of weakness. Working at Camp Tulahead gives you a bird's eye view of future careers and helps you determine specific areas to focus on. We offer a seven-day precamp orientation for all areas of camping. There are weekly evaluations. The staff-camper ratio is 1:7.*

1ST TOURS DIVISION OF HARBOUR FERRIES LTD.
#1 North Foot of Denman Street
Vancouver, British Columbia V6G 2W9
General Information Tour operator running day trips up British Columbia's west coast using the Royal Hudson steam train in combination with the M.U. Britannia, as well as harbour tours and sunset dinner cruises using an authentic paddlewheeler. Established in 1982. Owned by Graham Clarke. Affiliated with Harbour Ferries Ltd. Features: waterfront offices.
Profile of Summer Employees Total number: 25; average age: 20; 10% male, 90% female, 100% college students. Nonsmokers preferred.
Employment Information Openings are from May 17 to September 17. Jobs available: *guest service representative (reservation agent)* at $7.50 per hour; *on-board services representative (catering/hosting staff)* at $6.50 per hour. International students encouraged to apply.
Benefits Contact with travelers from all over the world.
Contact Cindi Armstrong, Manager, Tour Operations, 1st Tours Division of Harbour

Ferries Ltd., #1 North Foot of Denman Street, Vancouver, British Columbia, Canada V6G 2W9; 604-688-7246, Fax 604-687-5868. Application deadline: March 15.

From the Employer *We provide an opportunity to learn the skills necessary to run the day-to-day operation of a dynamic tour company. Our employees learn how to be professional, organized team players with excellent customer service skills.*

THUNDERBIRD OUTDOOR CENTRE
880 Courtney Street
Victoria, British Columbia V8W 1C4
General Information   Residential facility serving up to 150 8–16 year old coed campers in six-, nine-, or twelve-day sessions. Established in 1935. Owned by Victoria YM-YWCA. Affiliated with Canadian Camping Association, British Columbia Camping Association, Institute for Earth Education. 1,200-acre facility located 22 miles southwest of Victoria. Features: 8-acre freshwater lake; rock climbing; ropes course; canoeing, sea kayaking, and swimming; over 100 miles of beautiful hikes with spectacular views; extensive out-tripping backpacking programs; strong, well-developed environmental awareness programs.
Profile of Summer Employees   Total number: 70; average age: 20; 50% male, 50% female, 15% high school students, 85% college students, 2% international, 60% local residents. Nonsmokers only.
Employment Information   Spring break, year-round positions offered. Jobs available: 3 *section coordinators* (minimum age 21) with supervisory and counseling experience and first aid training at $200–$210 per week; 20 *senior counselors* with extensive outdoor skills and leadership experience at $165–$235 per week; 2 *waterfront specialists* with NLS certification, swimming instructors certification, canoeing instructor's certification at $190–$220 per week; 2 *leadership coordinators* with counseling and trainer experience at $190–$220 per week; 1 *earth education resource* with experience in earth education at $185–$200 per week. International students encouraged to apply.
Benefits   Preemployment training, formal ongoing training, on-site room and board at no charge, laundry facilities, Y membership use of facility downtown while employed, local transportation available.
Contact   Jim Leggat, Director of Outdoor Education, Thunderbird Outdoor Centre, 880 Courtney Street, Victoria, British Columbia, Canada V8W 1C4; 604-386-7511, Fax 604-380-1933. Application deadline: March 1.

From the Employer   *Staff receive ten-day, unpaid training. Specialized training offered for out-tripping, kayaking, and rock climbing. Staff receive two days off every two weeks and three hours off per week. Camper-counselor ratio is 8:2.*

MANITOBA

GULL HARBOUR RESORT & CONFERENCE CENTRE
Winnipeg Sales Office Unit E 1771 Ness Avenue
Winnipeg, Manitoba R3J 0Y2
General Information   Established in 1975. Owned by Provincial Government. Affiliated with Manitoba Hotel Association. Situated on 160 acres. Features: fully equipped gymnasium;

swimming pool; sauna, and whirlpool; location on Hecla Island; 18-hole golf course; 240 campground sites; proximity to beach.

Profile of Summer Employees Total number: 100; 50% male, 50% female, 1% minorities, 10% high school students, 10% college students, 1% international, 75% local residents.

Employment Information Openings are from June 30 to September 30. Spring break, Christmas break positions also offered. Jobs available: 5 *serving personnel* at $6.50–$7.25 per hour; 4 *bartenders* at $6.50–$7.25 per hour; 3 *front desk clerks* at $7–$8 per hour; 3 *kitchen staff members* (cooks, dishwashers) at $6.50–$8 per hour; 5 *housekeeping staff members* at $6.50–$7.50 per hour. International students encouraged to apply.

Benefits Formal ongoing training, on-site room and board at $100 per month, laundry facilities, travel reimbursement.

Contact Steve Baram, Assistant General Manager, Gull Harbour Resort & Conference Centre, Department SJ, Gull Harbour Resort, Box 100, Riverton, Manitoba, Canada R0C 2R0; 204-279-2041, Fax 204-279-2000. Application deadline: June 30.

From the Employer *Generally there are 4 staff members per fully-equipped house.*

NOVA SCOTIA

CAMP HILLES
P.O. Box 12 West Paradise
Annapolis County, Nova Scotia B0S 1R0

General Information Seven-day residential camp for 66 children and adults with behavioral, developmental, or any one of a variety of special needs. Established in 1973. Owned by Department of Supply Services Province of Nova Scotia. Affiliated with Department of Community Services. 10-acre facility located 100 miles west of Halifax. Features: location on the Annapolis River; 10 acres of playing fields; basketball, volleyball, and soccer; swimming pool; wonderful hiking trails; high ropes adventure course; good out-tripping facilities.

Profile of Summer Employees Total number: 18; average age: 19; 50% male, 50% female, 5% minorities, 30% high school students, 70% college students. Nonsmokers preferred.

Employment Information Openings are from June 18 to September 2. Jobs available: *experienced director* at $275 per week; *experienced assistant director* at $240 per week; *certified first aid personnel* at $200 per week; *canoe instructor* with Lind III Canoe certification (Nova Scotia) at $220; *ropes instructor* with adventure training at $220 per week; *lifeguard* with national lifeguard certification at $220 per week; *counselor* with experience in the Department of Community Services nine-week counselor-in-training program at $200 per week.

Benefits On-site room and board at no charge, laundry facilities, excellent training experience in a fun setting.

Contact Norma Lloyd, Coordinator of Special Projects, Camp Hilles, Department of Community Services, P.O. Box 696, Halifax, Nova Scotia, Canada B3J 2T7; 902-424-4371, Fax 902-424-0708.

From the Employer *We provide excellent precamp training in the following areas: counseling, directing, adventure, training, driving, canoeing, first aid, and Project Adventure.*

CAMP PAGWEAK
Pugwash
Cumberland County, Nova Scotia B0K 1L0
General Information General residential camp serving 80 campers weekly. Established in 1946. Owned by Churches in Cumb, Gol, and Pictou Counties. Affiliated with Northern Association of Baptists. 6-acre facility located 70 miles northeast of Halifax, Nova Scotia. Features: volleyball; sports field; sandy beach and ocean swimming; outside campfire and chapel area; nature trails and tours; 10 cabins; main lodge for eating; male and female washrooms with flush toilets; game area and craft lodge; enclosed outside showers.
Profile of Summer Employees Total number: 5; average age: 25; 40% male, 60% female, 50% high school students, 40% college students, 10% retirees, 85% local residents. Nonsmokers preferred.
Employment Information Openings are from June 28 to August 2. Jobs available: *camp director* at $225 per week; *cook* at $200 per week; *swimming instructor* at $200 per week; *mission leaders* at $200 per week. International students encouraged to apply.
Benefits Formal ongoing training, on-site room and board at no charge, health insurance.
Contact W. O. Christensen, Manager-Treasurer, Camp Pagweak, 7 Allison Avenue, Amherst, Nova Scotia, Canada B4H 3U3; 902-667-3435. Application deadline: April 1.

From the Employer *All employees and leaders attend workshops and can participate in swimming sessions, sports programs, tours, and nature walks. Staff members are expected to help clean up and maintain buildings and property. Generally, 1 leader and 7 campers share a cabin.*

ONTARIO

BLUE MOUNTAIN CAMP
RR 3
Collingwood, Ontario L9Y 3Z2
General Information Residential camp serving 72 campers biweekly. Established in 1937. Owned by The Easter Seal Society of Ontario. Affiliated with Ontario Camping Association, Canadian Rehabilitation Council for the Disabled. Situated on 40 acres. Features: heated swimming pool; creative, adaptive playground; waterfront; large sports fields; recreation hall with gym; nature trail.
Profile of Summer Employees 22% male, 78% female, 9% minorities, 46% high school students, 46% college students, 2% teachers. Nonsmokers preferred.
Employment Information Openings are from June 20 to August 30. Jobs available: *camp director* at $450–$500 per week; *head counselor* at $325–$350 per week; *head program specialist* at $325–$350 per week; *cabin counselors* at $170–$260 per week; *registered nurses* at $280–$485 per week; *driver* at $230–$260 per week; *program specialists* at $230–$305 per week.
Benefits Preemployment training, on-site room and board at no charge, laundry facilities.
Contact Bev Unger, Director of Camping and Recreation, Blue Mountain Camp, 250

Ferrand Drive, Suite #200, Don Mills, Ontario, Canada M3C 3P2; 416-421-8377, Fax 416-696-1035.

From the Employer *We offer a one-week precamp training for staff members. Our senior staff and nursing staff have an additional three-day workshop. The camper-staff ratio ranges from 1:1 to 4:1.*

BOLTON CAMP
P.O. Box 151
Bolton, Ontario L7E 5T2
General Information Residential camp for children ages 7–14, mothers with children under six years old, and families with leadership training for teenagers ages 15–16. Serves 450 campers per session. Established in 1922. Owned by Family Service Association of Metropolitan Toronto. Affiliated with Ontario Camping Association, International Camping Fellowship, Project Adventure, Association of Conference Centers International, Canadian Camping Association. 353-acre facility located 30 miles northwest of Toronto. Features: high ropes course; 2 swimming pools and a winding creek; many large open fields with rolling wooded surroundings; rustic cabins for children and families; hotel and dormitory-style housing for mothers and small children; comprehensive programming, including life skills, dance, crafts, outdoor skills, environmental education, swimming, co-op games, archery, sports, and adventure.
Profile of Summer Employees Total number: 150; 40% male, 60% female, 40% minorities, 47% high school students, 46% college students, 2% retirees, 85% local residents, 5% teachers.
Employment Information Openings are from June 1 to August 30. Jobs available: *counselor* with child supervisory experience at $100–$150 per week; *mothers'counselor* with background in women's issues and life skill training at $175 per week; *program instructors* with certification in specific area such as swimming, outdoor skills, or archery at $175 per week; *head counselor* with supervisory and camp experience at $175 per week.
Benefits Preemployment training, formal ongoing training, on-site room and board at $45 per week, instruction on techniques to manage individuals with difficult behavior.
Contact Barb Huatiak or Karen Gorden, Program Supervisors, Bolton Camp, Box 151, Bolton, Ontario, Canada L7E 5T2; 905-857-3993, Fax 905-857-9106. Application deadline: July 1.

From the Employer *At a five-day precamp session all staff members (paid and volunteer) learn how to implement an effective program for individuals experiencing difficult life situations. All staff members are trained in areas of anti-racism, issues of equity, and behavior management and are held accountable in the implementation of these issues and appropriate social behaviors. Knowing a second language is an asset. Working at Bolton Camp provides an opportunity for personal development and for making long-term friendships. A few positions include May and June.*

CAMP AROWHON
72 Lyndhurst Avenue
Toronto, Ontario M5R 2Z7
General Information Residential camp for 220 girls and boys ages 7–16. Established in 1934. Owned by Camp Arowhon Limited. Operated by Camp Arowhon. Affiliated with American Camping Association, Ontario Camping Association, Association for Experiential Education. Situated on 100 acres. Features: large private lake in the heart of the beautiful

Algonquin Park wilderness; 22 sailboats; 25 sailboards; 65 canoes; 14 horses, 2 large teaching rings, and many woodland trails; 4 tennis courts.

Profile of Summer Employees Total number: 85; average age: 19; 40% male, 60% female, 20% minorities, 20% high school students, 70% college students, 10% international, 90% local residents, 5% teachers. Nonsmokers preferred.

Employment Information Openings are from June 22 to August 23. Jobs available: 6 *waterfront instructors* (swimming) with WSI or Bronze Cross/NLS/St. John's/first aid/CPR certification at $1500–$2000 per season; 22 *waterfront instructors* (sailing, kayaking, canoeing, and windsurfing) with bronze medal or WSI certification at $1000–$1500 per season; *senior counselors; riding instructors* with St. John's/first aid/CPR certification at $1500–$2000 per season; *tennis instructor* with experience teaching children at $1500–$2000 per season; *drama instructor* with experience directing children's theater at $1500–$2000 per season. International students encouraged to apply only if they have camp experience.

Benefits Preemployment training, formal ongoing training, on-site room and board at no charge.

Contact Joanne Kates, Director, Camp Arowhon, 72 Lyndhurst Avenue, Toronto, Ontario, Canada M5R 2Z7; Fax 416-975-0130.

From the Employer *At precamp training, our staff learns communication, conflict mediation, and activity skills, as well as participates in a professional first aid course. We teach sailing, windsurfing, horseback riding, canoeing, tripping, kayaking, nature exploration, drama, crafts, tennis, archery, and land sports. Generally, 2 counselors and 8 campers share a cabin.*

CAMP CLOVER (DAY CAMP)
94 Frederick Street
Kitchener, Ontario N2H 2L7

General Information Day camp for boys and girls ages 5–14. Established in 1957. Owned by YWCA of Kitchener/Waterloo. Operated by Optimist Club. Affiliated with Ontario Camping Association. 39-acre facility located 14 miles northwest of Kitchener. Features: baseball diamond and volleyball court; large sports field; large wooded area for learning outdoor camp and survival skills; freshwater pond for swimming; walking trails in the forest; swamp for nature study.

Profile of Summer Employees Total number: 16; average age: 19; 35% male, 65% female, 20% minorities, 10% high school students, 90% college students, 80% local residents, 20% teachers. Nonsmokers preferred.

Employment Information Openings are from May 1 to August 1. Jobs available: *camp counselors* at $6.90–$7.25 per hour; *waterfront director* at $7.25–$7.50 per hour; *swimming instructor* (programming, not lessons) at $7–$7.25 per hour; *multicultural specialist* at $6.90–$7.25 per hour; *environmental specialist* at $6.90–$7.25 per hour; *on-site supervisor* at $9.50–$9.75 per hour. International students encouraged to apply.

Benefits Preemployment training, formal ongoing training.

Contact Anne Gloger, Program Coordinator, Camp Clover (Day Camp), Department SJ, 84

Frederick Street, Kitchener, Ontario, Canada N2H 2L7; 519-744-6507, Fax 519-744-7728. Application deadline: March 1.

From the Employer *In our precamp training session, all employees participate in workshops on emergency procedures, child development, behavior management, leadership, programming, cultural sensitivity, child abuse, daily duties and schedules, special needs, first aid and CPR, and staff relations. We provide safe, enjoyable day camp experiences for children while our well-trained, enthusiastic staff provide high-quality programming in the following areas: drama, swimming, arts and crafts, nature lore, camping skills, canoeing, orienteering, sleepovers, and cookouts.*

CAMP HURON
P.O. Box 509
Bayfield, Ontario N0M 1G0

General Information Coeducational residential camp serving 100 persons regardless of race, creed, economic status, and physical or mental abilities. Established in 1939. Operated by The Incorporated Synod of the Diocese of Huron. Affiliated with Ontario Camping Association, The Royal Lifesaving Society Ontario Division. 40-acre facility located 60 miles north of London, Ontario. Features: extensive freshwater lake frontage (Lake Huron); 2 large sports fields; 3 large program buildings; extensive off-site outdoor living; off-site canoe program.

Profile of Summer Employees Total number: 40; average age: 21; 51% male, 49% female, 1% minorities, 51% high school students, 49% college students, 1% international, 1% local residents, 1% teachers. Nonsmokers preferred.

Employment Information Openings are from June 1 to August 1. Jobs available: *experienced waterfront director* (minimum age 21) with NLS and CPR certification at $2200 per season; *experienced program director* at $2200 per season; *experienced outdoor living skills director* with Bronze Cross/Medallion, first aid, and CPR certification at $2200 per season; *L.I.T. counselors* with senior leadership experience, Bronze Cross/Medallion, first aid, and CPR certification at $1600–$1800; *cabin counselors* with Bronze Cross/Medallion, first aid, CPR certification, and L.I.T. graduate status or equivalent at $500–$1000. International students encouraged to apply.

Benefits College credit, preemployment training, on-site room and board at $74 per week, laundry facilities, travel reimbursement, health coverage is paid by Province for Canadian residents only, bonus of $147 per week for counselors working one-on-one with a disabled camper.

Contact Nick Wells, Director, Camp Huron, Department SJ, 472 Richmond Street, London, Ontario, Canada; 519-661-0536, Fax 519-434-8621. Application deadline: January 31.

From the Employer *Camp Huron offers in-service training on juvenile diabetes, Down's syndrome, spina bifada, cerebral palsy, developmental delay, behavior management, and small group dynamics. Typically, 2 staff members and up to 10 campers share a cabin. Room and board is a taxable gratuity.*

CAMP TRAILFINDER
Kawagama Lake
Dorset, Ontario P0A 1E0

General Information Residential camp serving up to 125 campers on a two-week minimum basis during July of each year. Resort serving schools, small corporate groups, seniors, and others for up to 100 persons in months other than July. Established in 1982. Owned by Paul

Rushton. Affiliated with Canadian Camping Association, Ontario Camping Association, Ontario Ministry of Tourism. 75-acre facility located 155 miles north of Toronto. Features: access to a big lake and sheltered lakefront bay; 5 adjacent lakes with easy access (portages); one of North America's finest canoe country areas; 50,000 acres of hardwood forest with many old logging trails; great water sports and fishing on Kawagama Lake; exceptionally clean water.

Profile of Summer Employees   Total number: 50; average age: 21; 40% male, 60% female, 20% high school students, 80% college students, 15% international, 5% local residents. Nonsmokers preferred.

Employment Information   Openings are from June 25 to August 31. Year-round positions also offered. Jobs available: *assistant program person* with competence, enthusiasm, and maturity at $1500 per season; *sailing person* with competence, enthusiasm, and maturity at $1000 per season; *kayak person* with competence, enthusiasm, and maturity at $1000 per season; *board sailing person* with competence, enthusiasm, and maturity at $1000 per season; *tripping/backpacking person* with competence, enthusiasm, and maturity at $1200 per season; *skiing person* with competence, enthusiasm, and maturity at $1200 per season; *low ropes-course person* with competence, enthusiasm, and maturity at $1200 per season; *swimming instructor* with WSI certification, Red Cross, Royal Life or equivalent instructor's rating at $1000 per season. International students encouraged to apply.

Benefits   College credit, preemployment training, formal ongoing training, on-site room and board at no charge, laundry facilities, health insurance.

Contact   Paul Rushton, Owner/Director, Camp Trailfinder, Department SJ, Box 250, Dorset, Ontario, Canada P0A 1E0; 705-766-2405, Fax 705-766-9320. Application deadline: April 1.

From the Employer   *Because of the great distances involved, orientation is done during precamp training only. Also, a nucleus of staff members come from our resort entity, which nicely supplements our camp staff. Higher income opportunities are available at our resort, particularly for those qualified in various aspects of degreed outdoor education.*   ·

HOCKEY OPPORTUNITY CAMP
P.O. Box 448
Sundridge, Ontario P0A 1Z0

General Information   Residential sports camp serving 200 boys—specializing in hockey, waterskiing, and mountain biking. Established in 1966. Owned by Lance and Kathy Barrs. Affiliated with Ontario Camping Association, Ontario Water Ski Association, South River and Area Chamber of Commerce. 85-acre facility located 45 miles south of North Bay. Features: 1,500 feet of shoreline; modern cabin units; weight-training facility (universal gym); two recreation halls with basketball courts; outdoor street hockey court.

Profile of Summer Employees   Total number: 85; average age: 18; 80% male, 20% female, 5% minorities, 80% high school students, 20% college students, 5% international, 20% local residents, 3% teachers. Nonsmokers preferred.

Employment Information   Openings are from July 1 to August 1. Jobs available: 5 *section heads* with college student status and experience working with children at $175–$225 per week; 20 *counselors* with high school senior status (minimum) and experience working with children at $125–$150 per week. International students encouraged to apply.

Benefits   Preemployment training, on-site room and board at no charge, laundry facilities.

Contact   Lance Barrs, Director, Hockey Opportunity Camp, Box 448, Sundridge, Ontario, Canada P0A 1Z0; 705-386-7702, Fax 705-386-7702.

THE HORSE PEOPLE
RR1
Wendover, Ontario K0A 3K0

General Information   Residential equestrian training center serving 60 coed students biweekly. Keen competition with long-term goals remain for the eight-week duration. Established in 1976. Owned by Bev and Wolfgang Schinke. Affiliated with American Camping Association, Canadian Camping Association, Ontario Equestrian Federation. 200-acre facility located 25 miles east of Ottawa. Features: indoor riding arena, 60' x 150', attached to a barn with viewing lounge on upper level; cross-country championship site for training and preliminary level evenring including steeplechase; 2 dressage rings, 20' x 40' and 20' x 60'; permanent hunt course, beautifully built and framed; professional jump course; all cabins have showers and bathrooms; location bordered by 11-acre reserve with unlimited access to trails.

Profile of Summer Employees   Total number: 20; average age: 23; 25% male, 75% female, 1% minorities, 1% high school students, 95% college students, 1% retirees, 1% international, 1% local residents. Nonsmokers only.

Employment Information   Openings are from June 19 to August 13. Jobs available: *child counselors; swimming staff; extracurricular activities staff; riding instructors.* All positions offered at $75–$375 per week. International students encouraged to apply.

Benefits   Preemployment training, formal ongoing training, on-site room and board at no charge, health insurance, riding lessons for interested staff at no charge, laundry service.

Contact   Bev Schinke, The Horse People, Department SJ, RR 1, Wendover, Ontario, Canada K0A 3K0; 613-673-5905, Fax 613-673-4787. Application deadline: April 15.

From the Employer   *We have a very high success rate and a high return rate. Staff-camper ratio is 1:3.*

LAKEWOOD CAMP
RR#2
Wainfleet, Ontario L0S 1V0

General Information   Residential camp serving 60 campers biweekly. Established in 1954. Owned by The Easter Seal Society of Ontario. Affiliated with Ontario Camping Association, Canadian Rehabilitation Council for the Disabled. Situated on 50 acres. Features: heated swimming pool; creative, adaptive playground; waterfront; large sports fields; nature trail; recreation hall with gym.

Profile of Summer Employees   22% male, 78% female, 9% minorities, 46% high school students, 46% college students, 2% teachers. Nonsmokers preferred.

Employment Information   Openings are from June 20 to August 30. Jobs available: *camp director* at $450–$500 per week; *head counselor* at $325–$350 per week; *head program specialist* at $325–$350 per week; *cabin counselors* at $170–$260 per week; *registered nurses* at $280–$485 per week; *driver* at $230–$260 per week; *program specialists* with experience in one or more of the following areas: swimming, arts and crafts, sailing, canoeing, music, drama, computers, sports, and games at $230–$305 per week.

Benefits   Preemployment training, on-site room and board at no charge, laundry facilities.

Contact   Bev Unger, Director of Camping and Recreation, Lakewood Camp, 250 Ferrand Drive, Suite #200, Don Mills, Ontario, Canada M3C 3P2; 416-421-8377, Fax 416-696-1035.

From the Employer   *We offer a one-week precamp training for staff members. Our senior staff and nursing staff have an additional three-day workshop. The camper-staff ratio ranges from 1:1 to 4:1.*

MERRYWOOD CAMP
Perth, Ontario K7H 3C7
General Information   Residential camp serving 60 campers biweekly. Established in 1948. Owned by The Easter Seal Society of Ontario. Affiliated with Ontario Camping Association, Canadian Rehabilitation Council for the Disabled. Situated on 30 acres. Features: heated swimming pool; creative, adaptive playground; waterfront; large sports fields; nature trail; recreation hall with gym; pontoon boats.
Profile of Summer Employees   22% male, 78% female, 9% minorities, 46% high school students, 46% college students, 2% teachers. Nonsmokers preferred.
Employment Information   Openings are from June 20 to August 30. Jobs available: *camp director* at $450–$500 per week; *head counselor* at $325–$350 per week; *head program specialist* at $325–$350 per week; *cabin counselors* at $170–$260 per week; *registered nurses* at $280–$485 per week; *driver* at $230–$260 per week; *program specialists* with experience in one or more of the following areas: swimming, arts and crafts, sailing, canoeing, music, drama, computers, sports, and games at $230–$305.
Benefits   Preemployment training, on-site room and board at no charge, laundry facilities.
Contact   Bev Unger, Director of Camping and Recreation, Merrywood Camp, 250 Ferrand Drive, Suite #200, Don Mills, Ontario, Canada M3C 3P2; 416-421-8377, Fax 416-696-1035.

From the Employer   *We offer a one-week precamp training for staff members. Our senior staff and nursing staff have an additional three-day workshop. The camper-staff ratio ranges from 1:1 to 4:1.*

NORTHWOOD CAMP
Site 3, Box B-8
Sesekinika, Ontario P0K 1S0
General Information   Residential camp serving up to 48 physically disabled children in two-week sessions. Established in 1954. Owned by The Easter Seal Society. Affiliated with Ontario Camping Association. Situated on 43 acres. Features: indoor heated swimming pool; freshwater lakefront with sand beach; riding stables with trails; fish pond stocked with trout; accessible new playground; volleyball and basketball courts.
Profile of Summer Employees   20% male, 80% female, 10% minorities, 25% high school students, 75% college students, 10% international, 75% local residents. Nonsmokers preferred.
Employment Information   Openings are from June 30 to August 31. Jobs available: *senior counselors* at $250–$350 per week; *junior counselor* at $200–$250 per week; *program counselors* at $275–$350 per week; *swimming and waterfront personnel* at $375–$400 per week. International students encouraged to apply.
Benefits   On-site room and board at no charge, laundry facilities.
Contact   Bev Unger, Director, Camping and Recreation, Northwood Camp, 250 Ferrand Drive, Suite 200, Don Mills, Ontario, Canada M3C 3P2; 416-421-8377, Fax 416-698-1035.

PROJECT C.A.N.O.E.
P.O. Box 720, Station P
Toronto, Ontario M5S 2Y4
General Information   Canoe out-tripping organization for youth at risk, conducting trips eight to twenty-five days in duration for 120 campers per summer. Established in 1976. Affiliated with Ontario Camping Association, Ontario Recreational Canoeing Association. Closest major city is Toronto.
Profile of Summer Employees   Total number: 13; average age: 22; 50% male, 50% female,

25% minorities, 10% high school students, 90% college students, 25% local residents.
Employment Information   Openings are from May 1 to September 1. Jobs available: 10
trip leaders with ORCA II canoe tripping or equivalent, bronze medallion, and CPR/first aid
certification at $6.70 per hour; 1 *referral coordinator* with experience working with social
service agencies at $6.70 per hour.
Benefits   On-site room and board at $150 per month.
Contact   Cameron Wong, Coordinator, Project C.A.N.O.E., Department SJ, P.O. Box 720,
Station P, Toronto, Ontario, Canada M5S 2Y4; 416-222-2203, Fax 416-222-4405. Application deadline: March 1.

From the Employer   *Project C.A.N.O.E. offers training in conflict resolution, cooperative
decision making, and other areas facilitating work with youth-at-risk. In addition, wilderness
first aid training and ORCA canoe tripping certification can be achieved.*

SCOTT MISSION FRESH AIR CAMP
RR 3
Caledon, Ontario L0N 1C0
General Information   Residential camp serving 120 disadvantaged children and youth in
four 10-day sessions. Also included is a program for mothers and toddlers. Established in
1941. Owned by The Scott Mission. Affiliated with Ontario Camping Association, Christian
Camping Association. 100-acre facility located 40 miles north of Toronto. Features: 2
outdoor tennis courts; large swimming pool; pond for canoeing; 100 acres of rolling
countryside, including 15 acres of hardwood forest; Red Cross swimming instruction;
accommodations include lodge and cedar cabins.
Profile of Summer Employees   Total number: 40; average age: 20; 50% male, 50% female,
25% high school students, 75% college students, 100% local residents.
Employment Information   Openings are from July 1 to August 31. Jobs available: *counselor/
lifeguard* with Red Cross bronze medallion/bronze cross or National Lifesaving certification
at $250 per week; *counselor* at $200.
Benefits   On-site room and board at no charge.
Contact   Monica Lauber, Camp Director, Scott Mission Fresh Air Camp, The Scott Mission, 502 Spadina Avenue, Toronto, Ontario, Canada M5S 2H1; 416-923-8872, Fax 416-
923-1067. Application deadline: March 1.

From the Employer   *We offer a five-day intensive precamp training session. Staff members
work in a Christian community while developing child/youth worker skills in a challenging
summer job.*

WOODEDEN CAMP
RR 3
London, Ontario N6A 4B7
General Information   Residential camp serving 64 campers biweekly and a three-week day
camp for both able-bodied and disabled children. Established in 1946. Owned by The Easter
Seal Society of Ontario. Affiliated with Ontario Camping Association, Canadian Rehabilitation Council for the Disabled. Situated on 106 acres. Features: heated swimming pool;
creative adaptive playground; large sports fields; nature trail; recreation hall with gym;
accessible treehouse.
Profile of Summer Employees   22% male, 78% female, 9% minorities, 46% high school
students, 46% college students, 2% teachers. Nonsmokers preferred.
Employment Information   Openings are from June 20 to August 30. Jobs available: *camp*

director at $450–$500 per week; *head counselor* at $325–$350 per week; *head program specialist* at $325–$350 per week; *cabin counselors* at $170–$260 per week; *registered nurses* at $280–$485 per week; *driver* at $230–$260 per week; *program specialists* with experience in one or more of the following areas: swimming, arts and crafts, sailing, canoeing, music, drama, computers, sports, and games at $230–$305 per week.

Benefits Preemployment training, on-site room and board at no charge, laundry facilities.

Contact Bev Unger, Director of Camping and Recreation, Woodeden Camp, 250 Ferrand Drive, Suite #200, Don Mills, Ontario, Canada M3C 3P2; 416-421-8377, Fax 416-696-1035.

From the Employer *We offer a one-week precamp training for staff members. Our senior staff and nursing staff have an additional three-day workshop. The camper-staff ratio ranges from 1:1 to 4:1.*

QUEBEC

CAMP NOMININGUE
Lac Nominingue, Quebec J0W 1R0

General Information Residential camp for 220 boys ages 7–15 providing a place to cultivate friendships, self-confidence, and a sense of achievement. Established in 1925. Owned by Peter F. Van Wagner. Affiliated with Ontario Camping Association, Quebec Camping Association, Canadian Camping Association. 400-acre facility located 120 miles north of Montreal. Features: 1 mile of extensive freshwater lake frontage; proximity to excellent wilderness canoe-tripping country; 4 outdoor tennis courts; many sports fields and mixed woods for games; extensive and varied equipment for all sports, including a fleet of 100 canoes, kayaks, rowboats, sail boats, and sail boards; fully equipped wood-working shop.

Profile of Summer Employees Total number: 100; average age: 21; 99% male, 1% female, 15% minorities, 10% high school students, 70% college students, 1% retirees, 80% local residents, 5% teachers. Nonsmokers preferred.

Employment Information Openings are from November 1 to April 1. Jobs available: *windsurfing instructors; sailing instructors; woodworking instructors; nature awareness instructors.*

Benefits Preemployment training, formal ongoing training, on-site room and board at $135 per week, opportunity to learn new skills, use of camp equipment, opportunity to lead wilderness canoe trips.

Contact Shannon Van Wagner, Executive Director, Camp Nominingue, 119 Guy, Vaudreuil, Quebec, Canada J7V 8B1; 514-455-4447, Fax 514-455-7062.

From the Employer *At a five-day presummer staff training program, all employees participate in programming, canoe trip skills, first aid, and group dynamics workshops. Campers stay a minimum of twenty-three days.*

CAMP OUAREAU
29 Summer Street
Lennoxville, Quebec J1M 1G4

General Information Traditional girls' camp with bilingual program serving 106 campers. Established in 1922. Owned by Madelene Allen. Affiliated with Ontario Camping Association, Quebec Camping Association, Canadian Camping Association. 15-acre facility located

90 miles north of Montreal. Features: 2,000 feet of waterfront on large lake; 22 canoes; 8 sailboats; 10 Windsurfers; beautiful setting.

Profile of Summer Employees Total number: 45; average age: 21; 1% male, 99% female, 100% college students.

Employment Information Openings are from January 1 to June 1. Jobs available: 2 *sailing instructors* at $1550–$1700 per season.

Benefits On-site room and board at no charge, health insurance.

Contact Mrs. J. Raill, Camp Ouareau, 2494 Route 125 South, Saint Donat, Quebec, Canada JOT 2CO; 819-424-2662. Application deadline: June 1.

From the Employer *As a bilingual camp, all staff members must have a strong working knowledge of French. This is a wonderful opportunity for those in a French language studies program, since half of our campers don't speak English. Camp Ouareau runs alternately every two days in English and French.*

WESTCOAST CONNECTION TRAVEL CAMP
217 Wolseley Road North
Montreal, Quebec H4X 1W1

General Information Exciting travel programs for students ages 13–17 and 18–22, including active teen tours, beginner level cycling tours, and outdoor adventure trips. Established in 1982. Affiliated with Canadian Camping Association.

Profile of Summer Employees 50% male, 50% female, 50% college students, 100% local residents, 10% teachers. Nonsmokers only.

Employment Information Openings are from June 29 to August 20. Jobs available: *tour staff* with experience working with teens at $50–$300 per week. International students encouraged to apply (personal interview is required).

Benefits Preemployment training, on-site room and board at no charge, laundry facilities, chance to tour Washington, Canada, or Europe, all group activities included.

Contact Mr. Mark Segal, Director, Westcoast Connection Travel Camp, Department SJ, 217 Wolseley Road North, Montreal West, Quebec, Canada H4X 1W1; 514-488-8920, Fax 514-482-5425. Application deadline: February 1.

From the Employer *There is a four-day camping training retreat for all staff. Tour staff have a great opportunity to work with teens while traveling. These positions are very demanding—responsibilities are all day, seven days a week. Activities include rafting, rock climbing, hiking, skiing, kayaking, mountain biking, and road biking.*

Category Index

Camps–Horsemanship

Camps–Learning Disabilities

Camps–Outdoor Adventure and Travel

Camps–Performing and Fine Arts

Camps–Physical Disabilities

Camps–Visual Impairments

Conference Centers

Conservation and Environmental Programs

Expeditions, Guide Trips, and Tours *(Includes guided tours, hiking, canoe trips, white water rafting, and outdoor adventure.)*

Ranches *(Includes working dude ranches and resort ranches.)*

Resorts *(Also see* **State and National Parks** *and* **Ranches.***)*

Theaters/Summer Theaters
*(Includes acting and technical/
auxiliary staff opportunities.)*

State and National Parks
*(Commercially operated visitor
services in State and National
Parks, including resorts,
restaurants, concessions,
transportation, etc.)*

Theme and Amusement Parks/
Attractions *(Includes local
historic sites and attractions.)*

Volunteer Programs

Employer Index

Job Titles Index

$$
\begin{array}{r}
24 \\
3 \\
\hline
27 \\
18 \\
\hline
45 \\
7.50 \\
\hline
52.50
\end{array}
$$

$$
\begin{array}{r}
12 \\
30 \\
42 \\
33.56 \\
\hline
75.56
\end{array}
$$

$$
\begin{array}{r}
12 \\
6 \\
\hline
18 \\
12 \\
\hline
30
\end{array}
$$

$$
\begin{array}{r}
128 \\
300 \\
\hline
428
\end{array}
$$

Great Events

The

FIRST MOON
LANDING

*Written and Illustrated
by Gillian Clements*

W
FRANKLIN WATTS
LONDON•SYDNEY

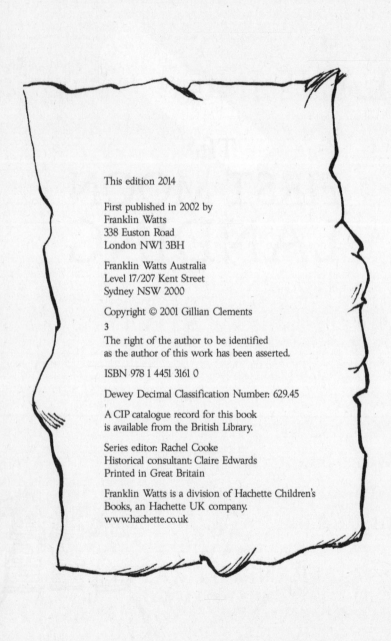

This edition 2014

First published in 2002 by
Franklin Watts
338 Euston Road
London NW1 3BH

Franklin Watts Australia
Level 17/207 Kent Street
Sydney NSW 2000

Copyright © 2001 Gillian Clements
3
The right of the author to be identified
as the author of this work has been asserted.

ISBN 978 1 4451 3161 0

Dewey Decimal Classification Number: 629.45

A CIP catalogue record for this book
is available from the British Library.

Series editor: Rachel Cooke
Historical consultant: Claire Edwards
Printed in Great Britain

Franklin Watts is a division of Hachette Children's
Books, an Hachette UK company.
www.hachette.co.uk

The
FIRST MOON
LANDING

RROOOAAARRR!
"Lift-off! We have
lift-off!"

It is 16th July 1969,
and America's
historic *Apollo 11*
is soaring into clear
blue Florida skies.
Its destination – the
Moon. Soon men will
walk on another
world for the very
first time.

3

People have always been fascinated by the Moon. Long ago, they worshipped it as a god or goddess. Many noticed how the Moon changed shape, from a tiny slither to a full circle and back again. They named the time this took a "month".

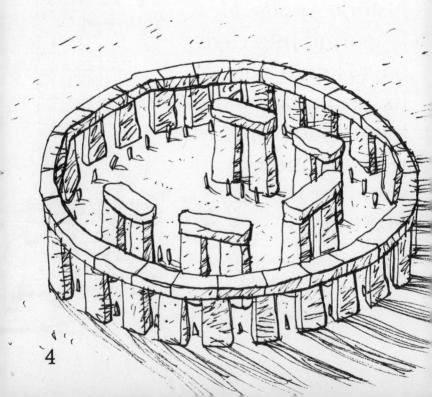

Later astronomers found a new way to study the Moon. In 1610, Galileo used a telescope to look at it – and he saw mountains and craters! Before this, everyone had thought the Moon was perfectly smooth. Galileo made fine drawings of his discoveries.

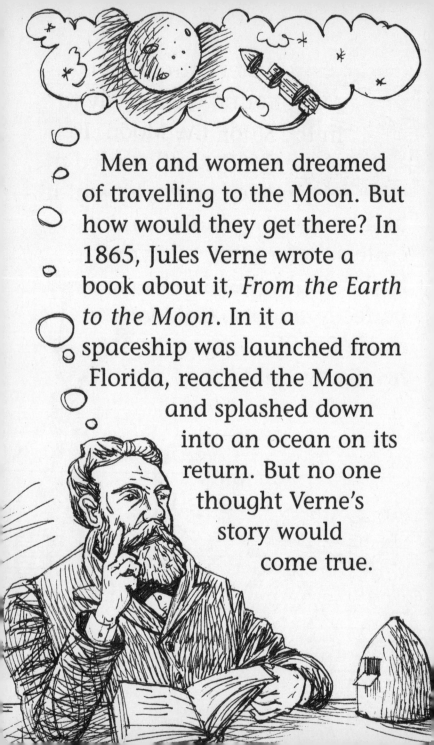

Men and women dreamed of travelling to the Moon. But how would they get there? In 1865, Jules Verne wrote a book about it, *From the Earth to the Moon*. In it a spaceship was launched from Florida, reached the Moon and splashed down into an ocean on its return. But no one thought Verne's story would come true.

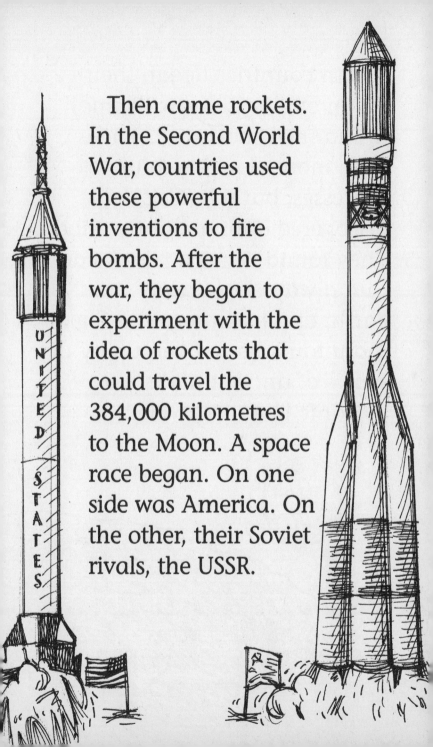

Then came rockets. In the Second World War, countries used these powerful inventions to fire bombs. After the war, they began to experiment with the idea of rockets that could travel the 384,000 kilometres to the Moon. A space race began. On one side was America. On the other, their Soviet rivals, the USSR.

Both countries began their Moon explorations with small unmanned spacecraft. There were more disasters than successes, but scientists discovered a lot about the Moon. They found it has a "dark side" that always faces away from Earth; and its craters and mountains are broken up by dry seas – of ancient and solid volcanic lava, not water.

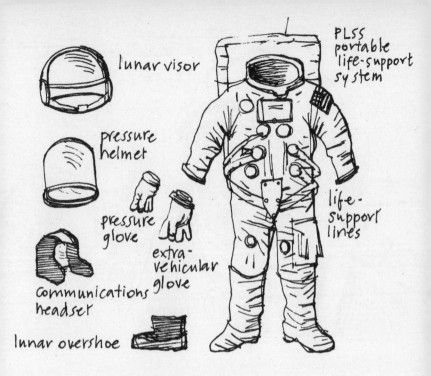

lunar visor

PLSS portable life-support system

pressure helmet

pressure glove

extra-vehicular glove

communications headset

life-support lines

lunar overshoe

Gravity, the force which pulls us to the ground, is much less on the Moon, and there is no air to breathe. And the temperatures can be so hot people will fry, or so cold that they will freeze! So scientists had to design spacesuits to help astronauts stay alive on the Moon.

9

In August 1961, a man soared
into space at last! After many
practice missions by the USSR and
America, a 27-year-old Soviet
cosmonaut, Yuri Gagarin, reached
orbit. In less than two hours he
had circled the world once, and
returned to Earth. The USSR had
pulled ahead in the space race.

America reacted by giving 25 billion dollars to its space agency, NASA. Surely its new "Project Apollo" would succeed!

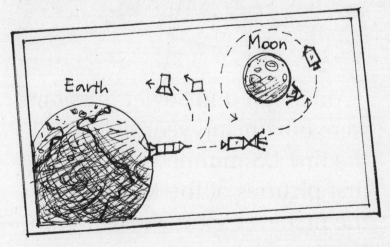

But there were so many problems, and mistakes could be deadly. US scientists decided they would need two spacecraft: one to circle above the Moon while another landed on it. Everything would need to be tested in Earth orbit first.

John Glenn First American to orbit Earth

First Moon -close-up

American and Soviet missions were advancing year by year... the first US-manned orbit, the first pictures of the Moon, then the first ever spacewalk – by the Russian Alexei Leonov.

Alexei Leonov

12

Gemini 3

In March 1965, millions of Americans saw their own astronauts orbit Earth and do practice moves in the *Gemini 3* spacecraft. These were important preparations for future Moon missions.

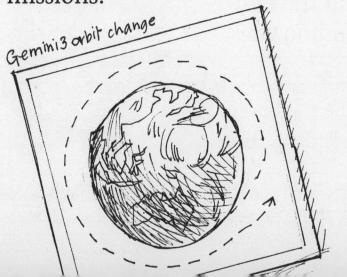

Gemini 3 orbit change

The US scientists were pleased. The *Gemini* and *Apollo* practice missions – in Earth and Moon orbits – had been declared safe and successful. Now the scientists studied pictures of the Moon to find the best landing sites.

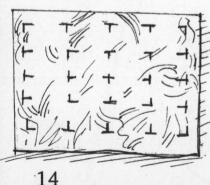

By 14th July 1969, a three day countdown began. At the end of it the *Apollo 11* mission would be launched into space, its destination – the Moon. America hoped it was finally going to beat the Soviets!

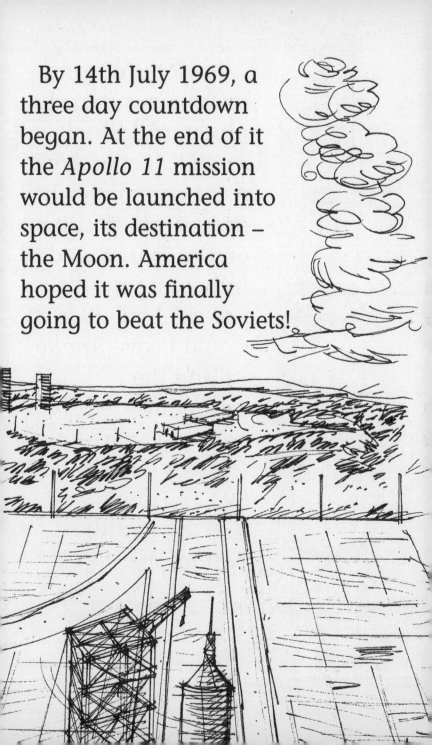

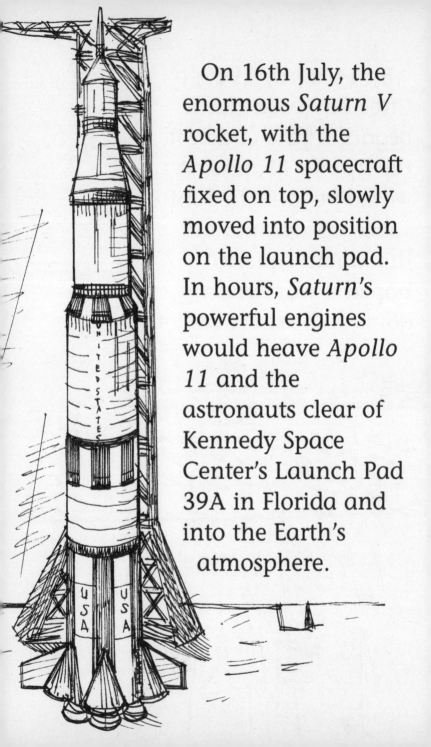

On 16th July, the enormous *Saturn V* rocket, with the *Apollo 11* spacecraft fixed on top, slowly moved into position on the launch pad. In hours, *Saturn's* powerful engines would heave *Apollo 11* and the astronauts clear of Kennedy Space Center's Launch Pad 39A in Florida and into the Earth's atmosphere.

The three astronauts – *Apollo 11*'s Flight Crew – awoke before dawn. Neil Armstrong, Edwin "Buzz" Aldrin and Michael Collins were trained and ready for their historic mission.

Every minute was carefully planned: breakfast, a doctor's examination, getting into spacesuits. At 6.30 a.m. the three men began the drive to the launch pad.

Excitement grew as the minutes passed. On Florida's beaches close by, a million Americans held their breath. Onlookers at Kennedy Space Center stood in awe. As the Sun rose, the three nervous astronauts stepped into the launch pad lift.

At last the three astronauts strapped themselves into *Apollo 11*'s Command Module, on top of the towering *Saturn V* rocket. At 7.30 a.m. the checks began.

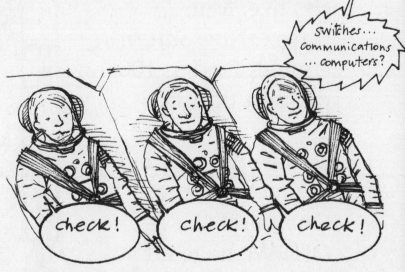

At 7.52 a.m. NASA technicians closed the hatch. Five minutes to go. "Happy journey!" radioed Mission Control in Houston, Texas. *Saturn V*'s computer took control of the launch.

Ten seconds. Nine, the start up began. A spray of water cooled the launch pad... Eight, seven, six, five, four, three... Now *Saturn's* engines fired at 100 per cent thrust... Two... flames, and clouds spurted from the rocket's base... One, zero! "LIFT-OFF! We have lift off!" The Moon voyagers roared away at 9.32 a.m.

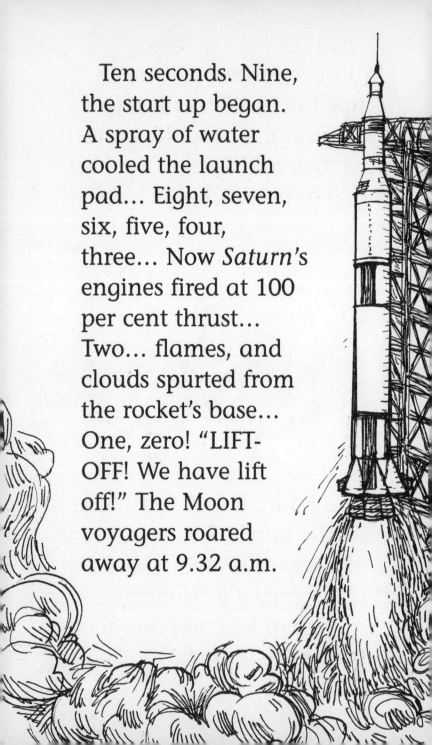

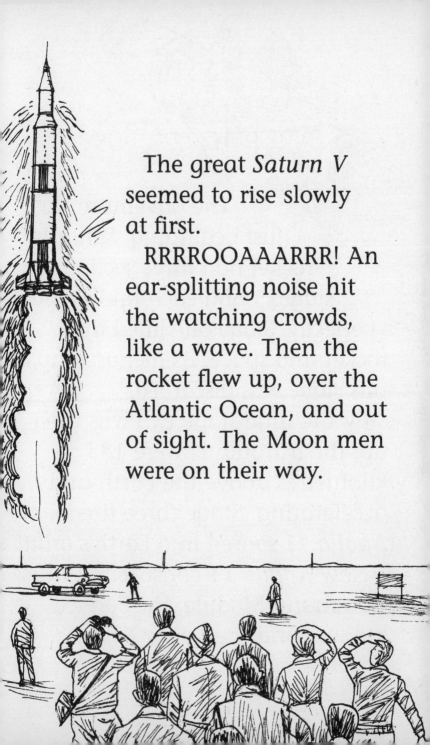

The great *Saturn V* seemed to rise slowly at first.

RRRROOAAARRR! An ear-splitting noise hit the watching crowds, like a wave. Then the rocket flew up, over the Atlantic Ocean, and out of sight. The Moon men were on their way.

The adventure was just beginning. *Saturn's* rocket had three sections or "stages", and each had to fire perfectly. Stage one lifted the rocket into space. Its fuel used up, this stage was discarded.

By the time stage two was used up, the astronauts were 183 kilometres above the Earth and accelerating. Stage three fired. *Apollo 11* soared into Earth's orbit!

Now *Apollo 11* consisted of the Command Module, the Service Module and the Lunar Module.

With the rocket fuel used up, Michael Collins carefully flew the Command Module away from the rocket.

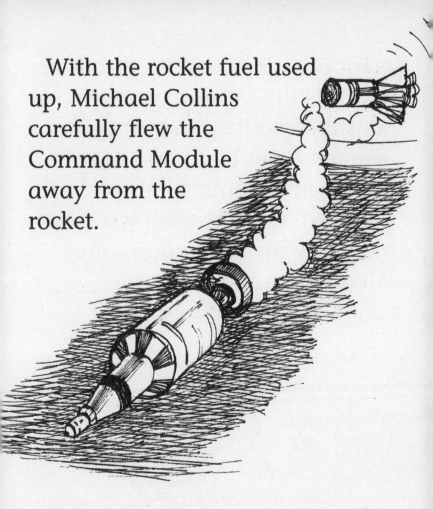

Then he turned his Module back towards the rocket in order to dock with the Lunar Module, the *Eagle*, stored inside it.

23

For four days, *Apollo 11* hurtled towards the Moon. It was a journey into the unknown. TV cameras kept Earth and the crewmen in contact.

At last, through their windows, they saw the magnificent grey Moon loom into view.

In less than an hour, *Apollo 11* swung round behind the Moon – to the dark side never seen from Earth.

Engines fired into life, and slowed the spacecraft down to slot into a Moon, or lunar orbit.

It was 20th July, 1969, an historic date. "The Moon looks like the pictures," said Armstrong. "But there's no substitute for actually being here."

Now it was time
for Armstrong and
Aldrin to move into
the Lunar Module
Eagle.

Again, *Apollo 11*
swung round to the dark side of
the Moon, out of contact with
Mission Control. The *Eagle* began
to separate from the Command
Module. "The Eagle has
wings... looking good!"
said Armstrong.

The two spacecraft
swung back, to
the visible,
front side, of
the Moon.

26

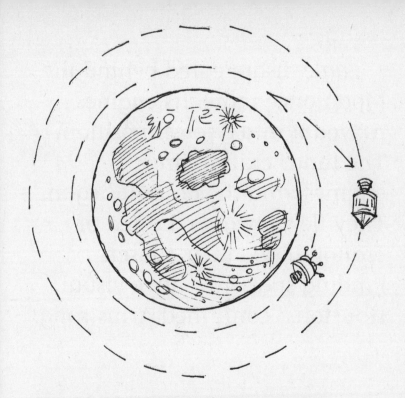

Michael Collins steered the Command Module into a higher orbit, where he would wait for his companions to rejoin him in a day or so – after the Moon landing.

Armstrong and Aldrin checked the *Eagle*'s engines. If anything went wrong now, the whole mission would fail.

Eagle disappeared behind the Moon once more. Its engines moved it into a lower position. The lunar craft re-fired its engines, and the descent began. They flew towards the Sea of Tranquillity – their chosen landing spot. "We have visual, Houston," confirmed Armstrong.

Just a few minutes to go to a
Moon landing. This was the final
phase. *Eagle* was vertical now.
Armstrong could see the Moon
below, rushing towards him.
"THERE'S A CRATER RIGHT
BELOW!" he cried. He snatched
the landing controls from the
computers.

The fuel was low. *Eagle* had to land in 60 seconds or the mission would fail! It hovered 23 metres above the Moon. Clouds of Moon dust, disturbed by the engines, blocked Armstrong's view. "Picking up some dust!" he said. Time was running out...

Armstrong made sure *Eagle* was vertical. "Contact light," said Aldrin, nervous but excited. "OK… engine stop… descent engine command override, off… engine arm, off. 413 is in." Then silence. Finally Armstrong spoke four historic words to Houston Control:

"THE *EAGLE* HAS LANDED!"

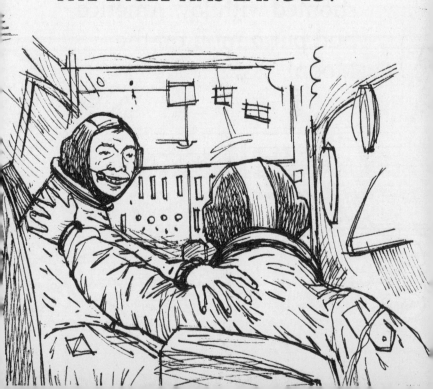

On Earth, millions sat by their TVs and radios, hardly daring to move. The impossible had happened... men had landed on the Moon! At Mission Control, scientists shouted with joy. America had put a man on the Moon!

Armstrong and Aldrin stepped into their Moon spacesuits.

Carefully crawling on his hands and knees, Armstrong backed out of *Eagle*'s tiny hatch. Slowly he began his climb down the ladder. Spacecraft cameras broadcast his progress to the world.

Now Armstrong stood on the pad at the base of one of *Eagle*'s legs. He took a step, his right boot disturbing the Moon dust.

At last he spoke: "That's one small step for man, one giant leap for mankind!"

Then he took a sample of Moon dust from his boot.

Aldrin climbed down too.
"Magnificent desolation," he
exclaimed. Then the astronauts
set to work. They had just two
hours to complete their tasks.
Moving in hops, Armstrong and
Aldrin fixed a TV camera and
tripod near their spacecraft, and
began their scientific experiments.

They set up equipment, including a Laser Ranging Retro Reflector. It was pointed towards Earth, and it picked up laser beams projected from Earth ground stations. Scientists could tell how far the Moon was from Earth to the nearest 15 centimetres!

Armstrong and Aldrin completed their experiments.

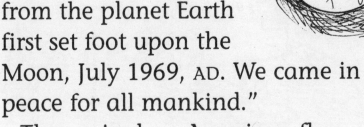

Then they unveiled a plaque: "Here men from the planet Earth first set foot upon the Moon, July 1969, AD. We came in peace for all mankind."

They raised an American flag too, and spoke to President Richard Nixon down on Earth.

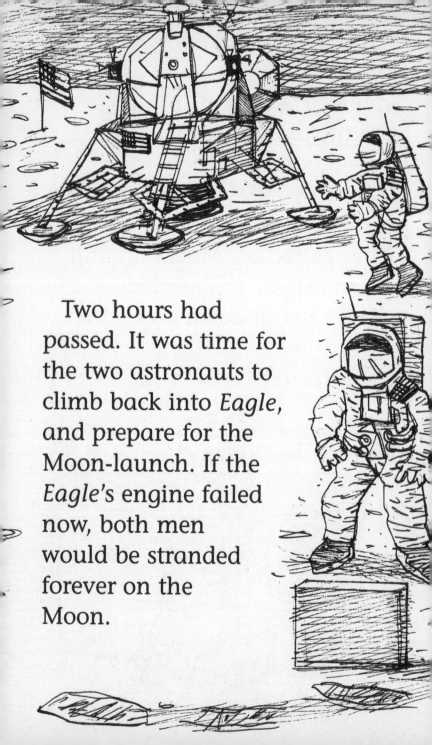

Two hours had passed. It was time for the two astronauts to climb back into *Eagle*, and prepare for the Moon-launch. If the *Eagle*'s engine failed now, both men would be stranded forever on the Moon.

Aldrin and Armstrong did a check. Then Mission Control announced, "You're clear for take-off." "Roger," replied Aldrin.

Eagle's engine burst into life, sending the ascent stage into the blackness above. Behind them on the Moon, they left the flag and plaque, *Eagle*'s landing engine – and their footprints.

Way overhead, Collins was orbiting in the Command Module. Aldrin steered the lunar craft up to dock with it. He had practised this many times before. Then two relieved moonwalkers quickly moved themselves and their Moon souvenirs from the *Eagle* and it was discarded.

VROOSH! The Command Module fired its engines and sent the astronauts out of lunar orbit – and, at 38,616 kmph, hurtling home to Earth.

Most of the Command Module could be cast off now. Only the tiny protective capsule would be needed, when the astronauts hit Earth's atmosphere.

The engines fired, and the capsule turned. Its vital heatshield withstood the fiery temperatures of re-entry, caused by friction from Earth's atmosphere. Communications blacked out in the heat. The silence was terrible. Then huge parachutes unfurled, to check the capsule's fall.

SPLASSSHH! 195 hours after their lift-off in Florida, the three heroes were home at last, bobbing in the choppy Pacific Ocean! Navy frogmen opened the capsule's hatch, and threw in biological isolation suits. In minutes the astronauts, freshly dressed, were winched into a helicopter and set down safely on a Navy ship.

43

On land in Houston,
the *Apollo* crew settled
into the Lunar Receiving
Laboratory – their home
for the next three weeks.
If astronauts had
brought back deadly
Moon microbes, they
needed to be found!
President Nixon greeted
Armstrong, Aldrin and
Collins through the
laboratory window.

Millions of people saw Aldrin and Armstrong step on the Moon. Fewer noticed the other ten men who landed later.
   Space scientists began to look elsewhere and dream of flying further out in space. Perhaps in our lifetime astronauts will fly from Earth's new orbiting space station to land on the red planet, Mars!

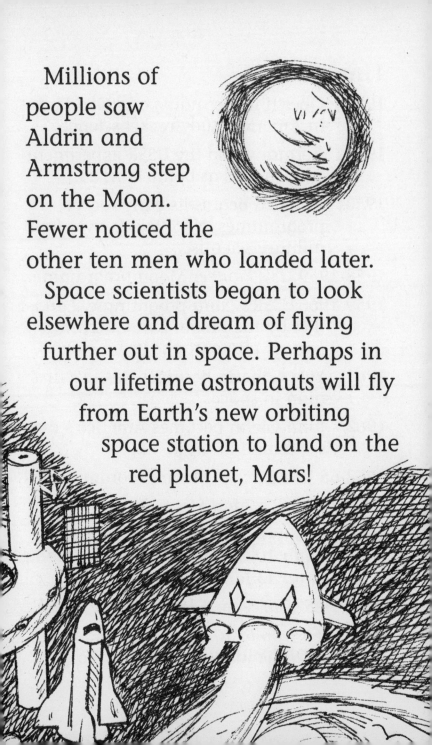

Timeline

1920s Oberth in Germany, and Goddard in America study rocket science.

1930s Germany and the USSR experiment with rockets as bomb carriers.

1950s America begins its early rocket programmes. NASA takes over from military scientists.

1958-1959 US's *Pioneer* Moon programme.

1959-1966 USSR's *Luna* programme. *Luna 1* flies by the Moon, *Luna 2* crashes, *Luna 3* photographs its far side.

1961 Yuri Gagarin becomes Russia's first man in space.

1962 John Glenn becomes America's first spaceman in orbit.

1962-65 US's *Ranger* Moon programme.

1965-70 USSR's *Zond* Moon programme.

1966 USSR's *Luna 9* lands on the Moon, *Luna 10, 11,* and *12* orbit the Moon, *Luna 13* lands on the Moon.

1967 US's *Surveyor 6* lands on the Moon.

May 1969 *Apollo 10* flies by the Moon, and tests the lunar lander module.

July 1969 *Apollo 11* lands the first astronauts on the Moon.

1969 *Apollo 12* lands on the Moon.

1970 An explosion prevents *Apollo 13* from landing on the Moon but it returns safely to Earth.

1970 The USSR send the *Lunakhod* to the Moon. In 1971 this Moon rover explores the Moon.

1971 *Apollo 14* lands on the Moon. *Apollo 15* astronauts explore the Moon's surface in the lunar rover.

1972 *Apollo 16* and *17* land the last men on the Moon.

1986-95 Construction in space of *Mir* space station.

1995 International Space Agencies (US, Canada, Japan, the European Space Agency and Russia) decide to build a space station.

1996 NASA sends missions to Mars.

2000 The first crew go aboard the International Space Station.

2003 European Space Agency's *Beagle 2* lander looks for life on Mars.

Glossary

Apollo 11 The whole spacecraft: the Command, Service and Lunar Modules.

biological isolation suit Germ-proof rubber body suit.

crater Huge hole on the Moon's surface.

desolation A lifeless, deserted place.

dock To link spacecraft together.

friction The rubbing together of one surface against another.

gravity The force which pulls everything to the ground.

laboratory A room or building where scientific experiments take place.

lunar Anything relating to the Moon.

module Word to describe one complete part of the spacecraft.

NASA National Aeronautical Space Administration based in Houston, Texas.

orbit The circling path around the Moon, the Earth or the Sun.

stage A section of a rocket.

vertical Upright.

USSR Union of Soviet Socialist Republics.